VERSUS FIGHTING STORY

Round 1

IZU KALON MADD

NG LINGO? WORRY NOT!
ID OF THIS VOLUME!

TRANSLATED AND LETTERED BY FAIRSQUARE COMICS
(FABRICE SAPOLSKY, LILLIAH CAMPAGNA)

FOR ABLAZE

RICH YOUNG
MANAGING EDITOR

KEVIN KETNER
EDITOR

RODOLFO MURAGUCHI
DESIGNER

ABLAZE

PUBLISHER'S CATALOGING-IN-PUBLICATION DATA

Names: Izu, author. | Kalon, illustrator. | Madd, illustrator.
Title: Versus Fighting Story, Vol. 1 / [written by] Izu; [illustrated by] Kalon, Madd.
Description: Portland, OR: Ablaze Publishing, 2021.
Identifiers: ISBN: 978-1-950912-37-7
Subjects: LCSH Video games—Fiction. | Video games—Comic books, strips, etc. |
Sports—Fiction. | Sports—Computer network resources—Fiction. |
Internet games—Fiction. | Graphic novels. | BISAC
Classification: LCC PN6747.I98 V47 2021 | DDC 741.5—dc23

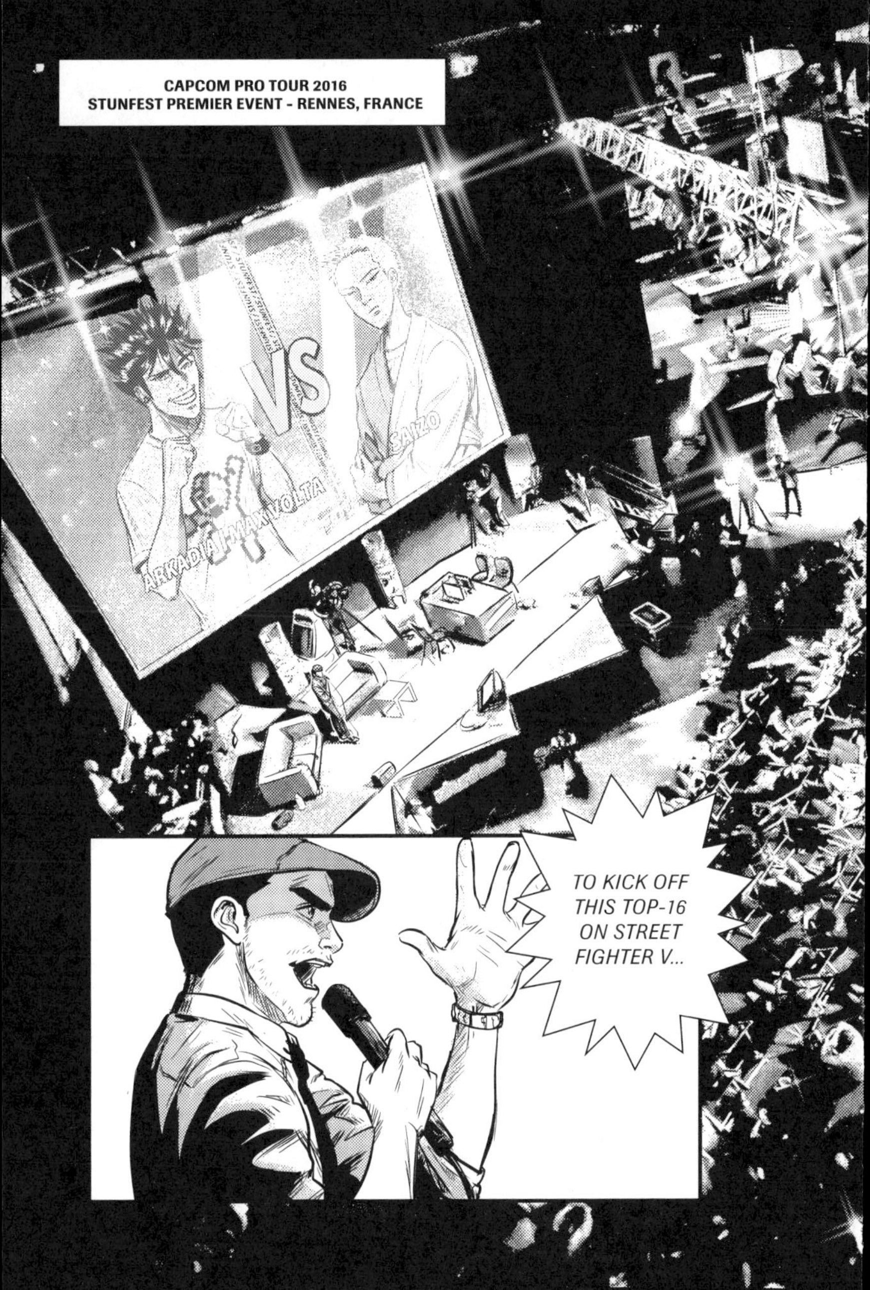
CAPCOM PRO TOUR 2016
STUNFEST PREMIER EVENT - RENNES, FRANCE
ARKADIA1 MAXVOLTA
VS
SAIZO
TO KICK OFF THIS TOP-16 ON STREET FIGHTER V...

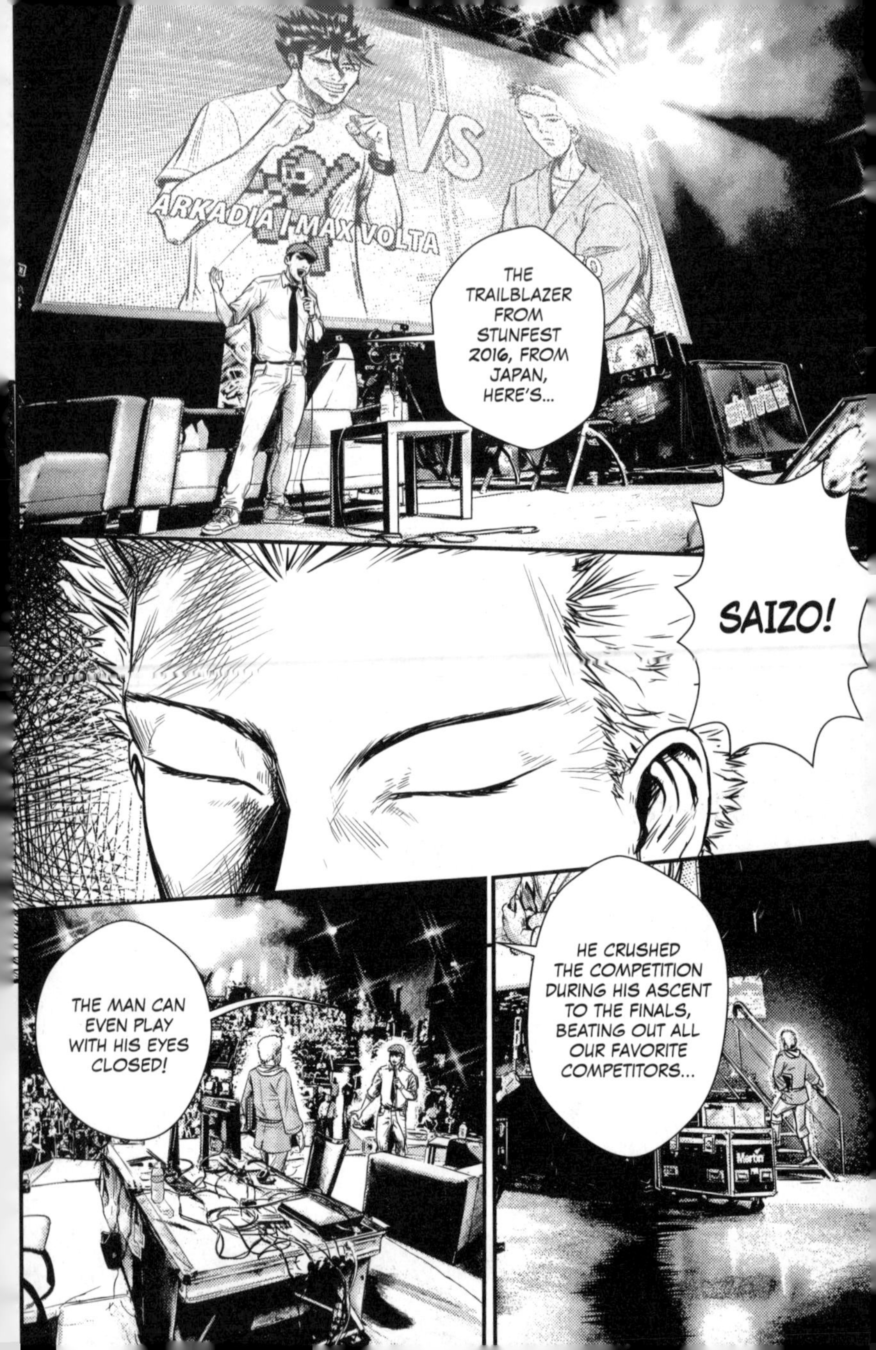
VS
ARKADIA I MAX VOLTA
THE TRAILBLAZER FROM STUNFEST 2016, FROM JAPAN, HERE'S...
SAIZO!
HE CRUSHED THE COMPETITION DURING HIS ASCENT TO THE FINALS, BEATING OUT ALL OUR FAVORITE COMPETITORS...
THE MAN CAN EVEN PLAY WITH HIS EYES CLOSED!

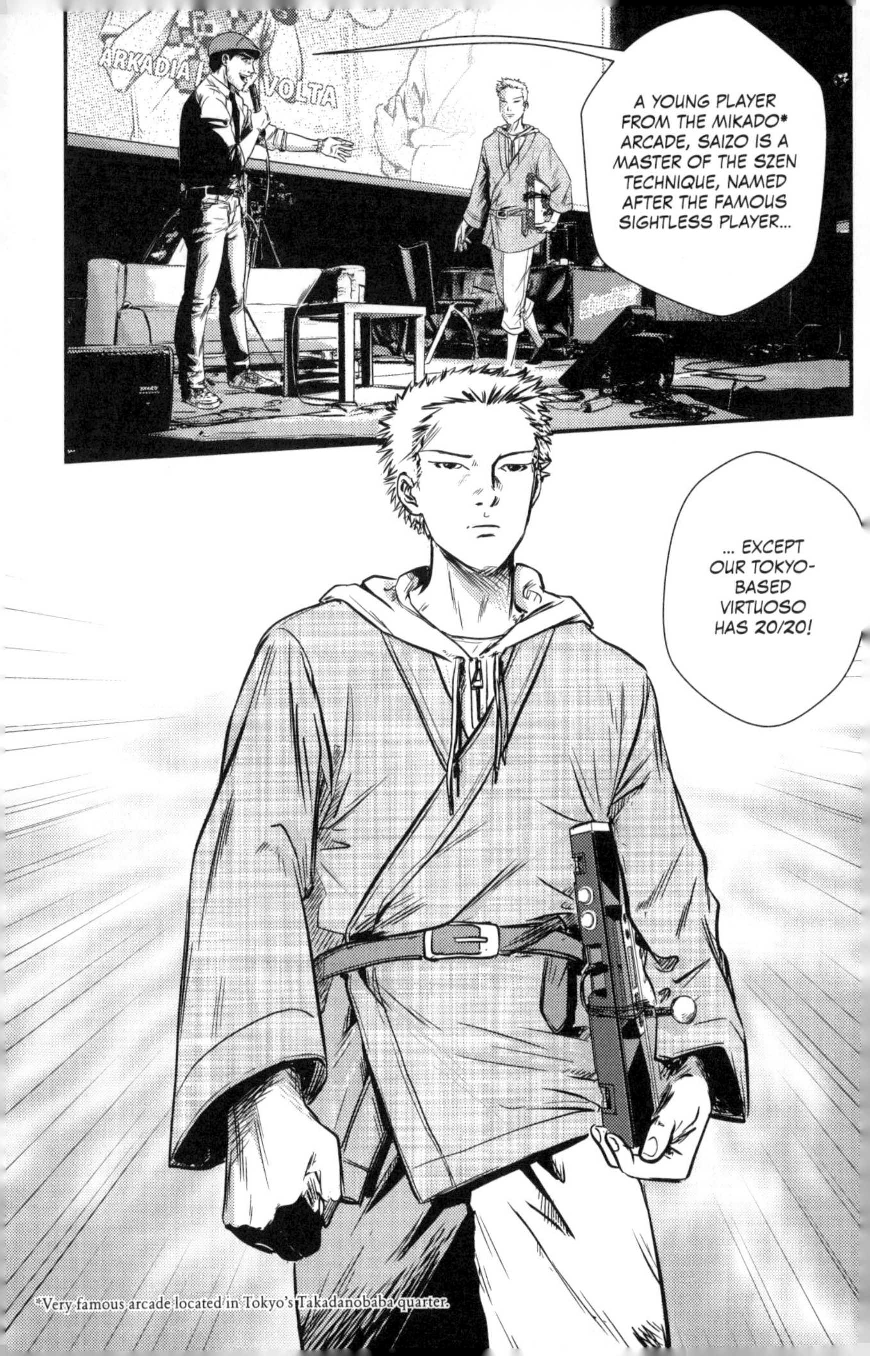
A YOUNG PLAYER FROM THE MIKADO* ARCADE, SAIZO IS A MASTER OF THE SZEN TECHNIQUE, NAMED AFTER THE FAMOUS SIGHTLESS PLAYER...
... EXCEPT OUR TOKYO-BASED VIRTUOSO HAS 20/20!

*Very famous arcade located in Tokyo's Takadanobaba quarter.

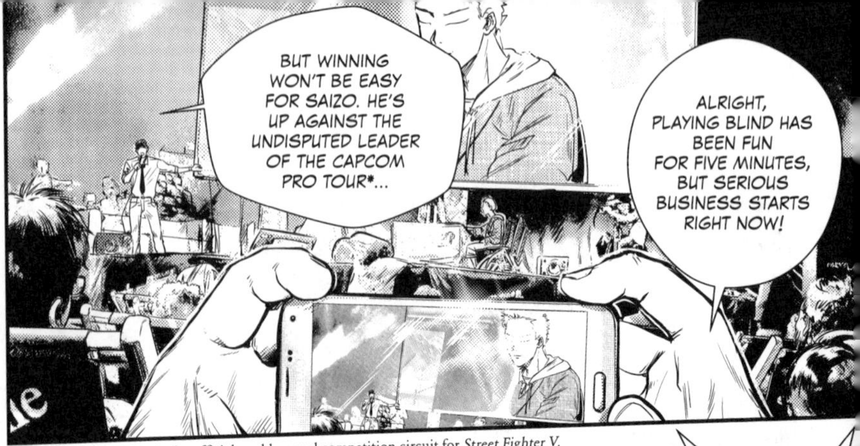
ALRIGHT, PLAYING BLIND HAS BEEN FUN FOR FIVE MINUTES, BUT SERIOUS BUSINESS STARTS RIGHT NOW!
BUT WINNING WON'T BE EASY FOR SAIZO. HE'S UP AGAINST THE UNDISPUTED LEADER OF THE CAPCOM PRO TOUR*...

*The Capcom Pro Tour is the official world annual competition circuit for *Street Fighter V.*

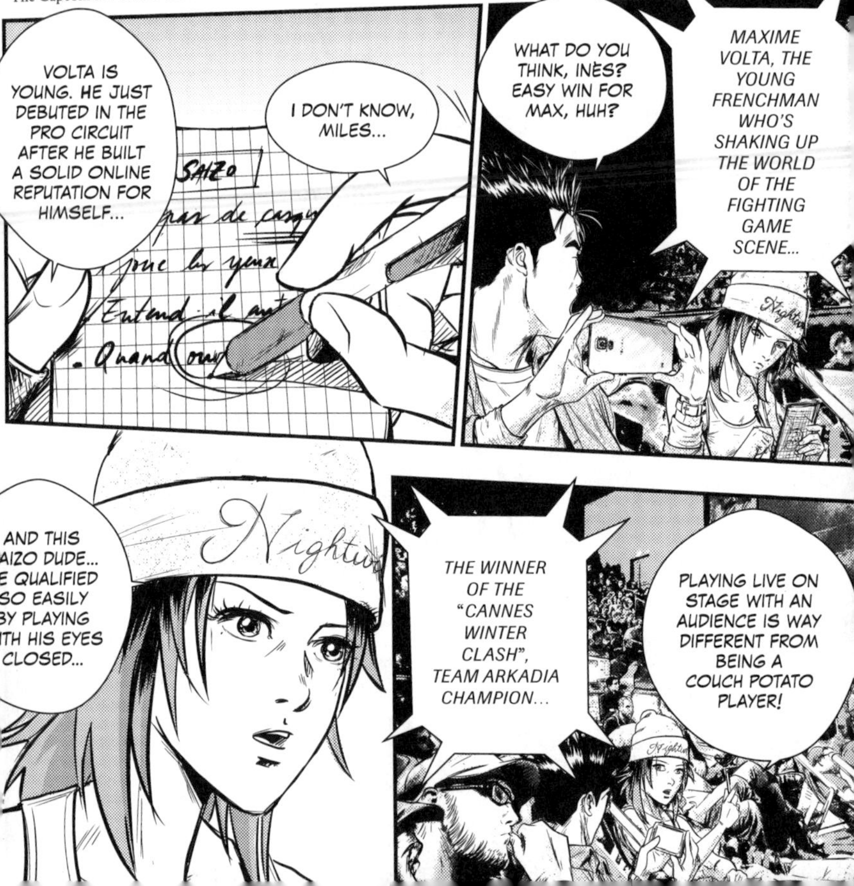
MAXIME VOLTA, THE YOUNG FRENCHMAN WHO'S SHAKING UP THE WORLD OF THE FIGHTING GAME SCENE...
WHAT DO YOU THINK, INES? EASY WIN FOR MAX, HUH?
I DON'T KNOW, MILES...
VOLTA IS YOUNG. HE JUST DEBUTED IN THE PRO CIRCUIT AFTER HE BUILT A SOLID ONLINE REPUTATION FOR HIMSELF...
SAIZO
PLAYING LIVE ON STAGE WITH AN AUDIENCE IS WAY DIFFERENT FROM BEING A COUCH POTATO PLAYER!
THE WINNER OF THE "CANNES WINTER CLASH", TEAM ARKADIA CHAMPION...
AND THIS AIZO DUDE... E QUALIFIED SO EASILY BY PLAYING ITH HIS EYES CLOSED...

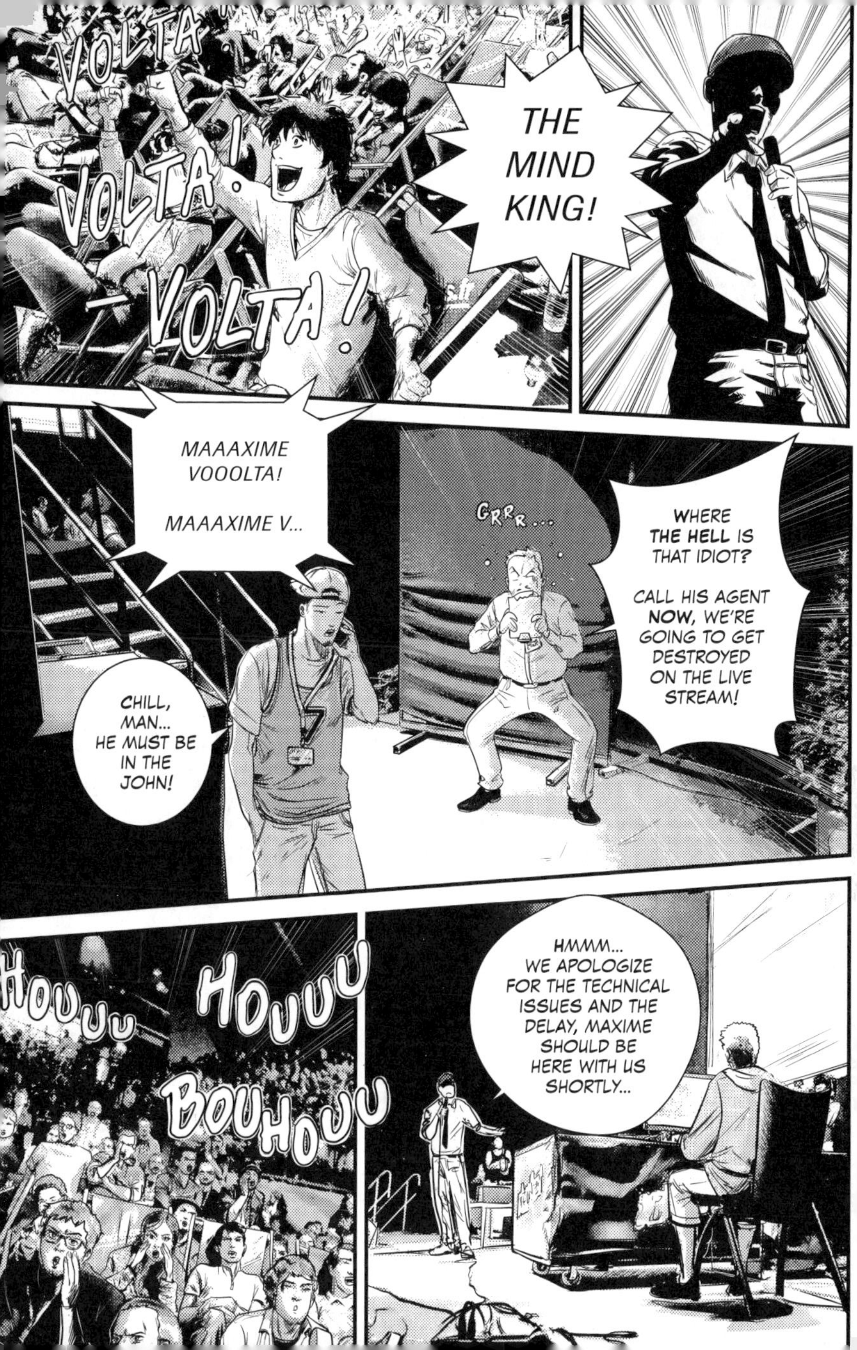
THE MIND KING!
VOLTA!
VOLTA!
VOLTA!
WHERE THE HELL IS THAT IDIOT?
CALL HIS AGENT NOW, WE'RE GOING TO GET DESTROYED ON THE LIVE STREAM!
GRRR...
MAAAXIME VOOOLTA!
MAAAXIME V...
CHILL, MAN... HE MUST BE IN THE JOHN!
HMMM... WE APOLOGIZE FOR THE TECHNICAL ISSUES AND THE DELAY, MAXIME SHOULD BE HERE WITH US SHORTLY...
HOUUU
HOUUU
BOUHOUU

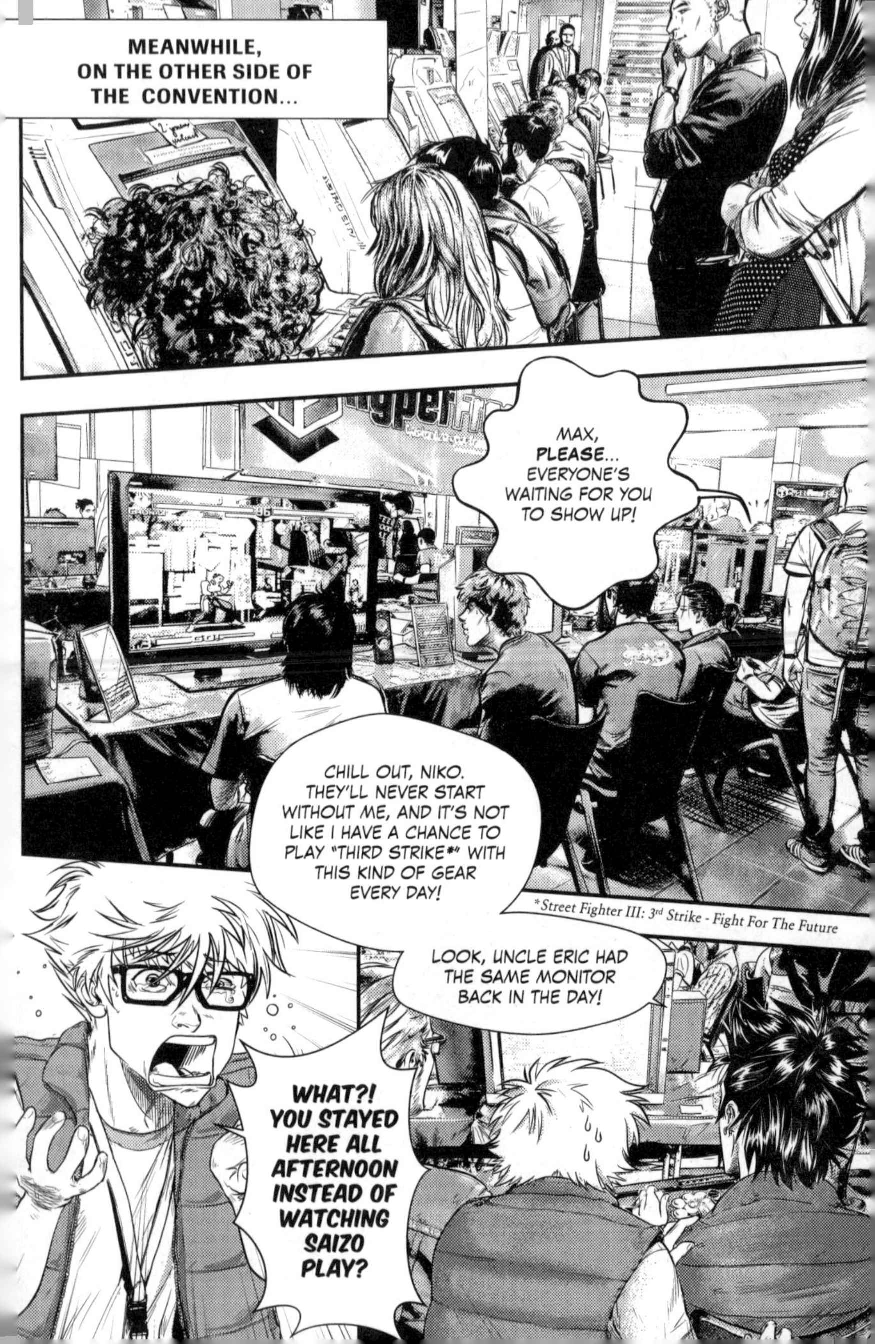
MEANWHILE, ON THE OTHER SIDE OF THE CONVENTION...
MAX, PLEASE... EVERYONE'S WAITING FOR YOU TO SHOW UP!
CHILL OUT, NIKO. THEY'LL NEVER START WITHOUT ME, AND IT'S NOT LIKE I HAVE A CHANCE TO PLAY "THIRD STRIKE*" WITH THIS KIND OF GEAR EVERY DAY!
*Street Fighter III: 3rd Strike - Fight For The Future
LOOK, UNCLE ERIC HAD THE SAME MONITOR BACK IN THE DAY!
WHAT?! YOU STAYED HERE ALL AFTERNOON INSTEAD OF WATCHING SAIZO PLAY?

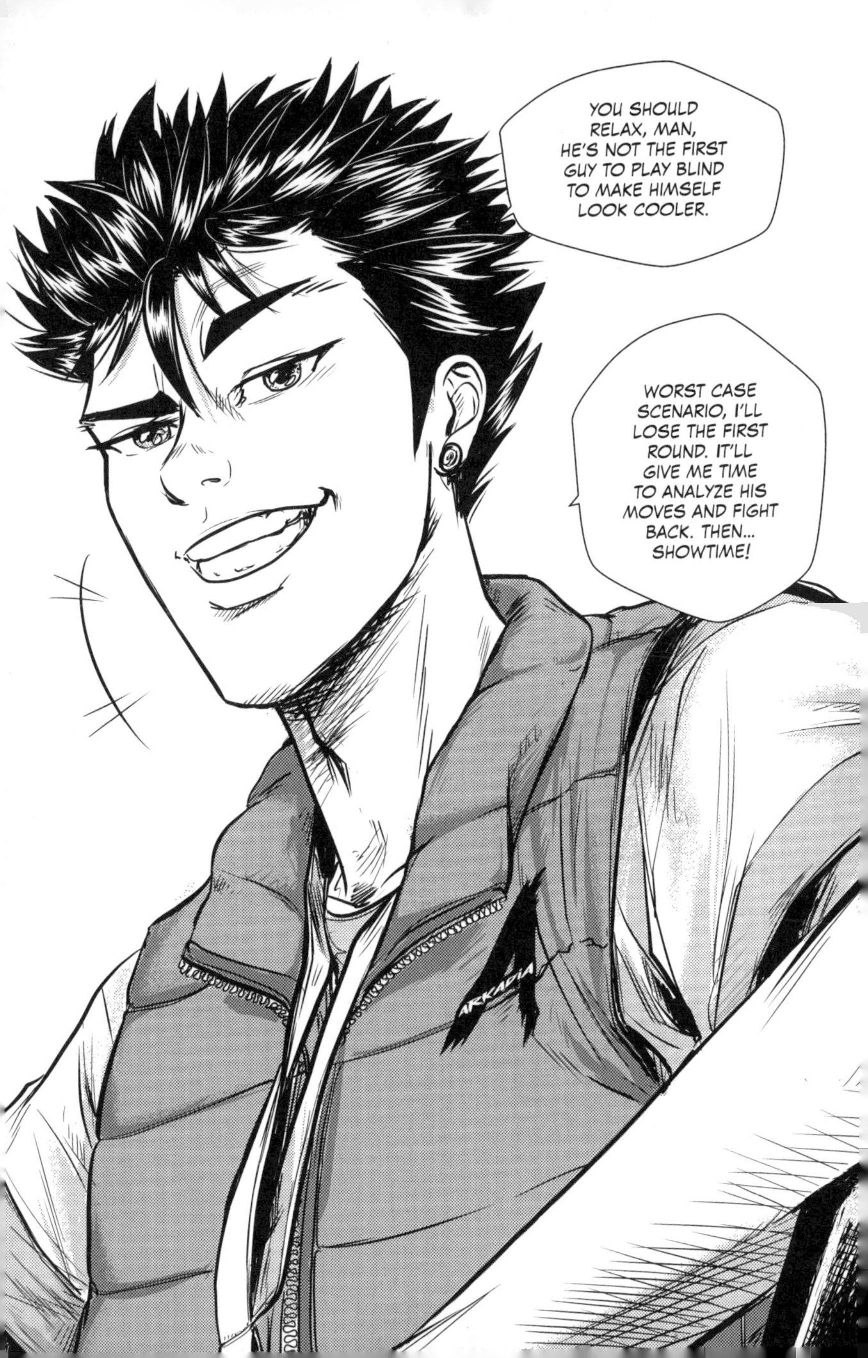
YOU SHOULD RELAX, MAN, HE'S NOT THE FIRST GUY TO PLAY BLIND TO MAKE HIMSELF LOOK COOLER.
WORST CASE SCENARIO, I'LL LOSE THE FIRST ROUND. IT'LL GIVE ME TIME TO ANALYZE HIS MOVES AND FIGHT BACK. THEN... SHOWTIME!
ARKADIA

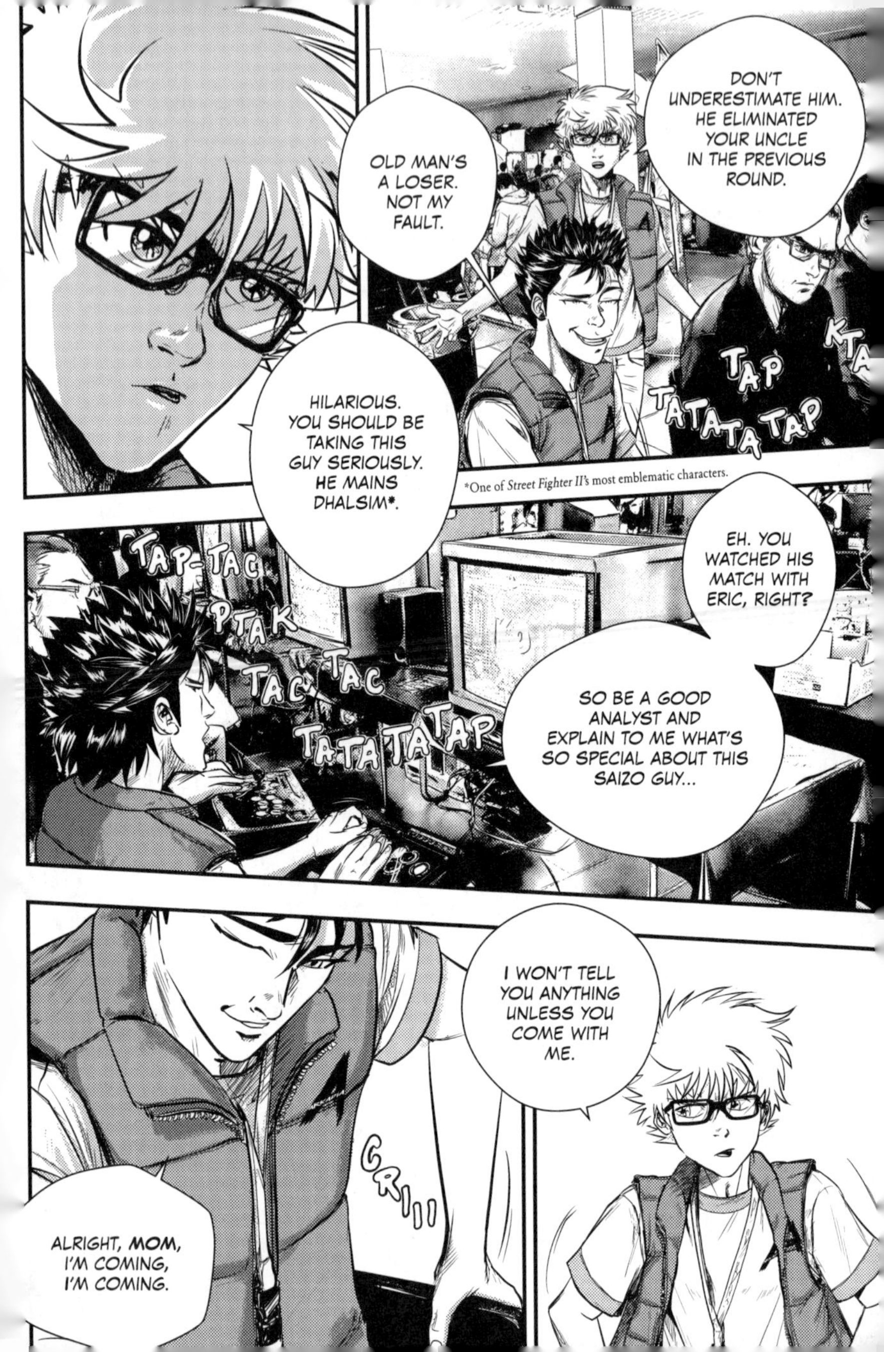
DON'T UNDERESTIMATE HIM. HE ELIMINATED YOUR UNCLE IN THE PREVIOUS ROUND.
OLD MAN'S A LOSER. NOT MY FAULT.
KTA
TAP
TATATA TAP
HILARIOUS. YOU SHOULD BE TAKING THIS GUY SERIOUSLY. HE MAINS DHALSIM*.
EH. YOU WATCHED HIS MATCH WITH ERIC, RIGHT?
SO BE A GOOD ANALYST AND EXPLAIN TO ME WHAT'S SO SPECIAL ABOUT THIS SAIZO GUY...
TAP-TAC
PTAK
TAC TAC
TATATATAP
I WON'T TELL YOU ANYTHING UNLESS YOU COME WITH ME.
CRIII
ALRIGHT, **MOM**, I'M COMING, I'M COMING.
*One of *Street Fighter II*'s most emblematic characters.

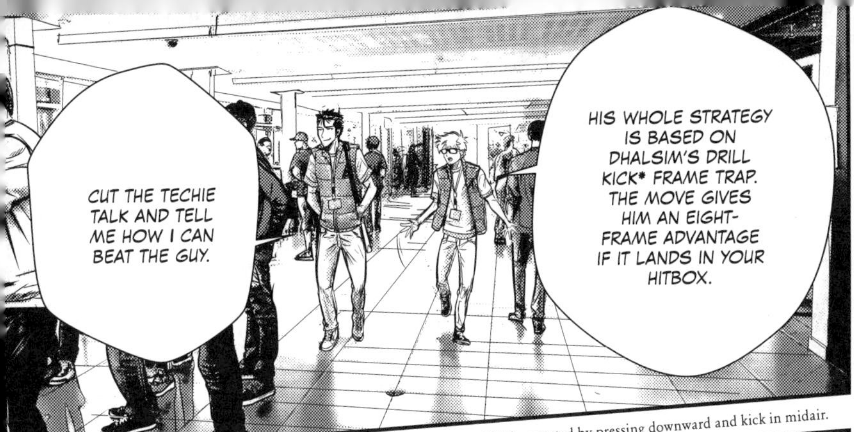
HIS WHOLE STRATEGY IS BASED ON DHALSIM'S DRILL KICK* FRAME TRAP. THE MOVE GIVES HIM AN EIGHT-FRAME ADVANTAGE IF IT LANDS IN YOUR HITBOX.
CUT THE TECHIE TALK AND TELL ME HOW I CAN BEAT THE GUY.

*A downward special kick executed by pressing downward and kick in midair.

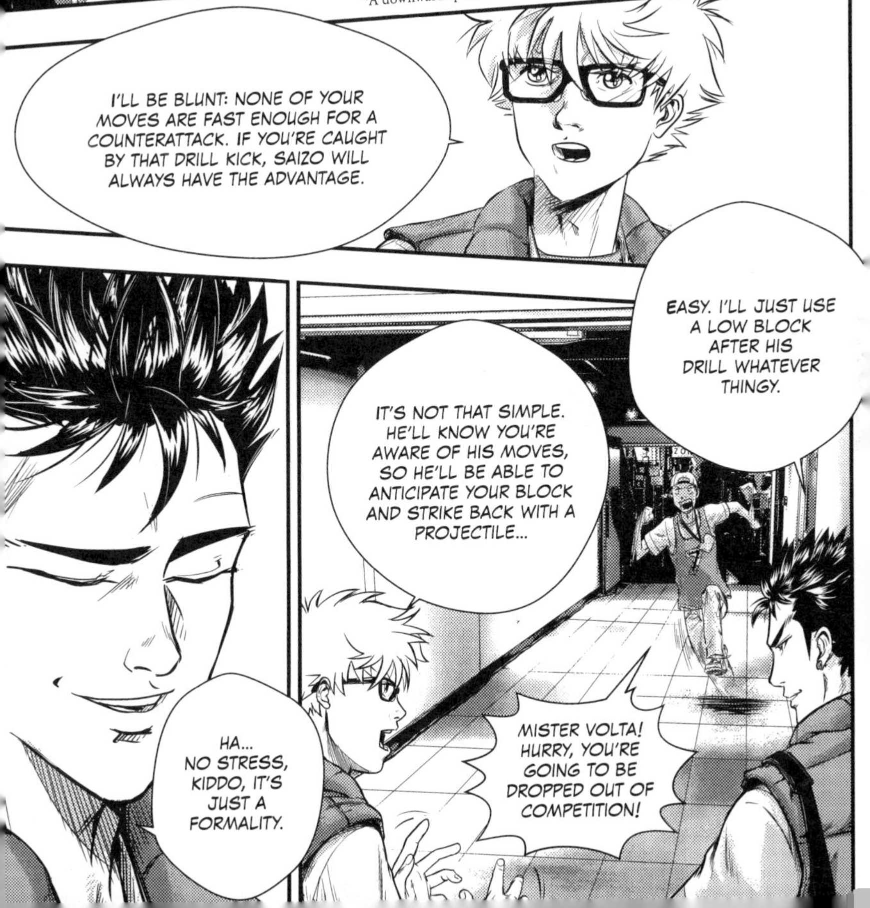
I'LL BE BLUNT: NONE OF YOUR MOVES ARE FAST ENOUGH FOR A COUNTERATTACK. IF YOU'RE CAUGHT BY THAT DRILL KICK, SAIZO WILL ALWAYS HAVE THE ADVANTAGE.
EASY. I'LL JUST USE A LOW BLOCK AFTER HIS DRILL WHATEVER THINGY.
IT'S NOT THAT SIMPLE. HE'LL KNOW YOU'RE AWARE OF HIS MOVES, SO HE'LL BE ABLE TO ANTICIPATE YOUR BLOCK AND STRIKE BACK WITH A PROJECTILE...
MISTER VOLTA! HURRY, YOU'RE GOING TO BE DROPPED OUT OF COMPETITION!
HA... NO STRESS, KIDDO, IT'S JUST A FORMALITY.

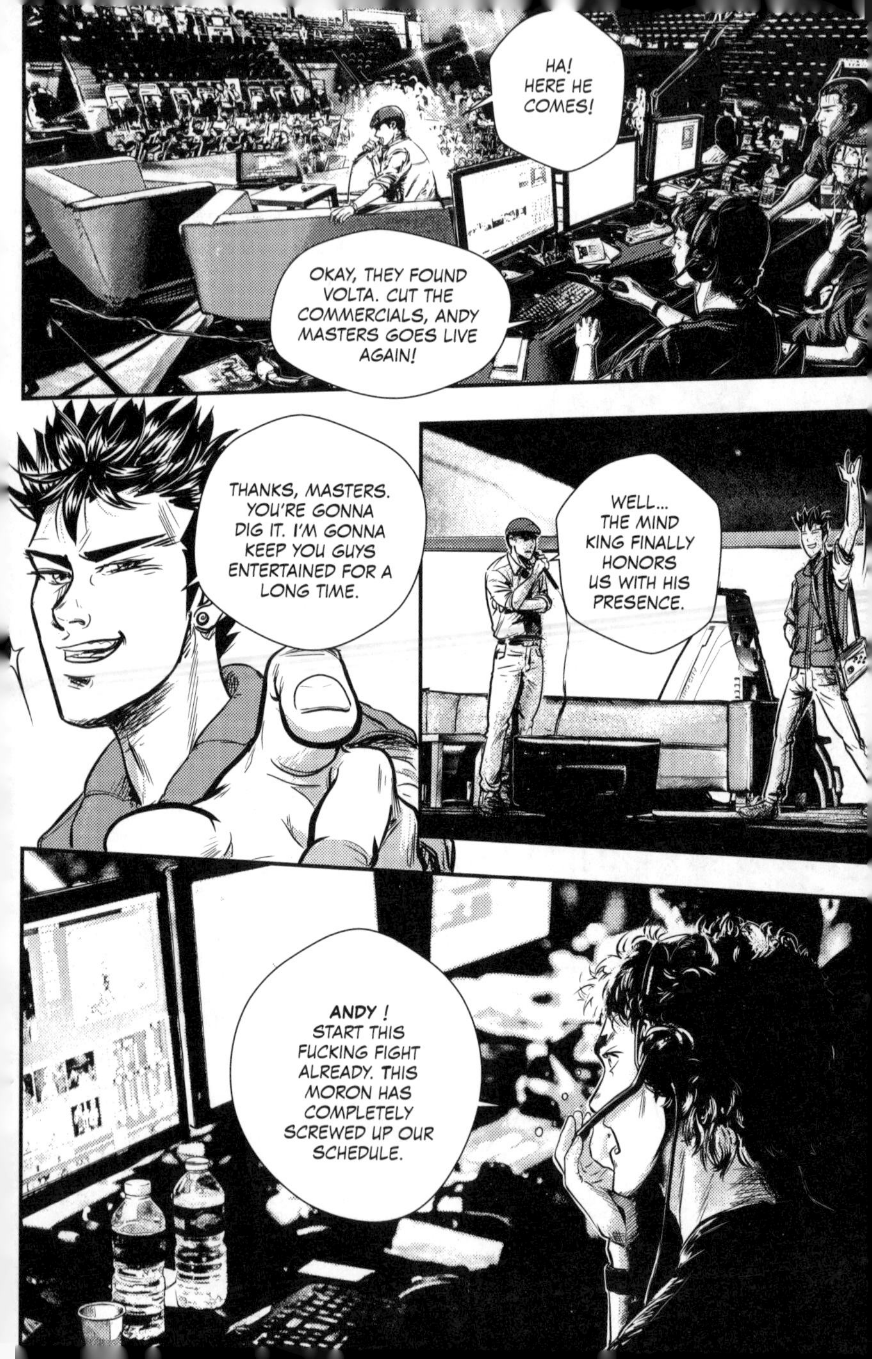
HA! HERE HE COMES!
OKAY, THEY FOUND VOLTA. CUT THE COMMERCIALS, ANDY MASTERS GOES LIVE AGAIN!
WELL... THE MIND KING FINALLY HONORS US WITH HIS PRESENCE.
THANKS, MASTERS. YOU'RE GONNA DIG IT. I'M GONNA KEEP YOU GUYS ENTERTAINED FOR A LONG TIME.
ANDY ! START THIS FUCKING FIGHT ALREADY. THIS MORON HAS COMPLETELY SCREWED UP OUR SCHEDULE.

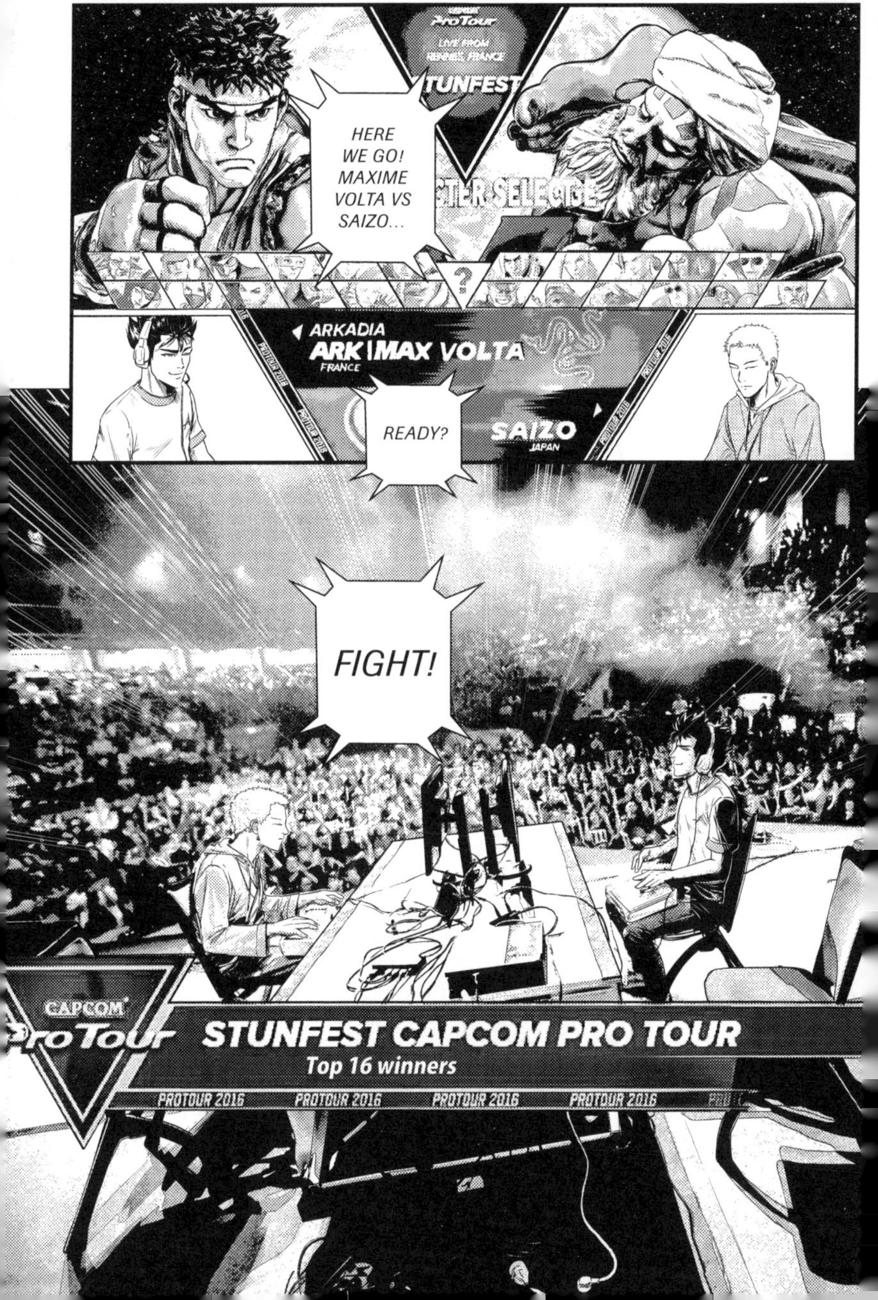
Pro Tour
LIVE FROM RENNES, FRANCE
STUNFEST
HERE WE GO! MAXIME VOLTA VS SAIZO…
ARKADIA
ARK|MAX VOLTA
FRANCE
READY?
SAIZO
JAPAN
FIGHT!
CAPCOM Pro Tour
STUNFEST CAPCOM PRO TOUR
Top 16 winners
PROTOUR 2016 PROTOUR 2016 PROTOUR 2016 PROTOUR 2016

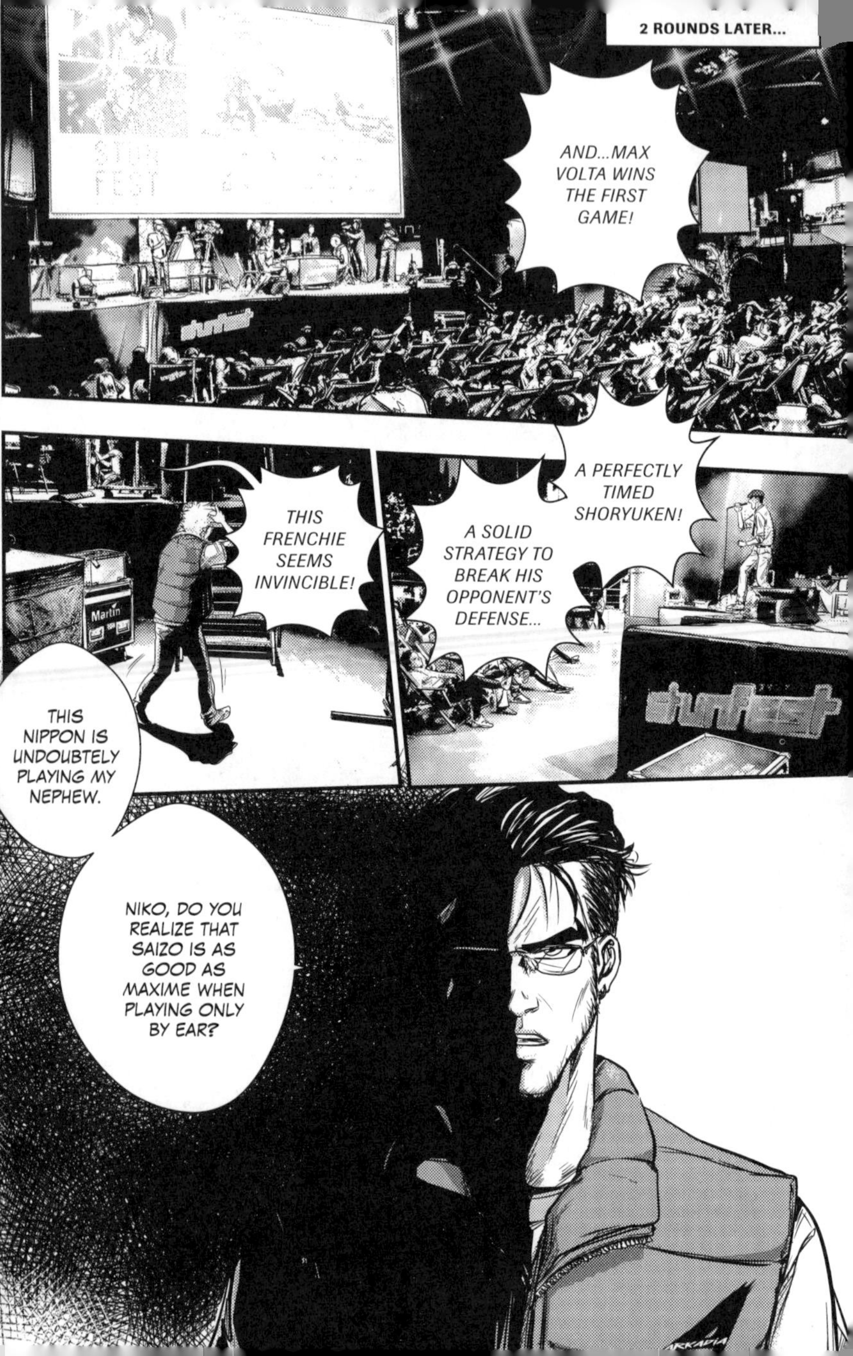
2 ROUNDS LATER...
AND...MAX VOLTA WINS THE FIRST GAME!
A PERFECTLY TIMED SHORYUKEN!
A SOLID STRATEGY TO BREAK HIS OPPONENT'S DEFENSE...
THIS FRENCHIE SEEMS INVINCIBLE!
THIS NIPPON IS UNDOUBTELY PLAYING MY NEPHEW.
NIKO, DO YOU REALIZE THAT SAIZO IS AS GOOD AS MAXIME WHEN PLAYING ONLY BY EAR?

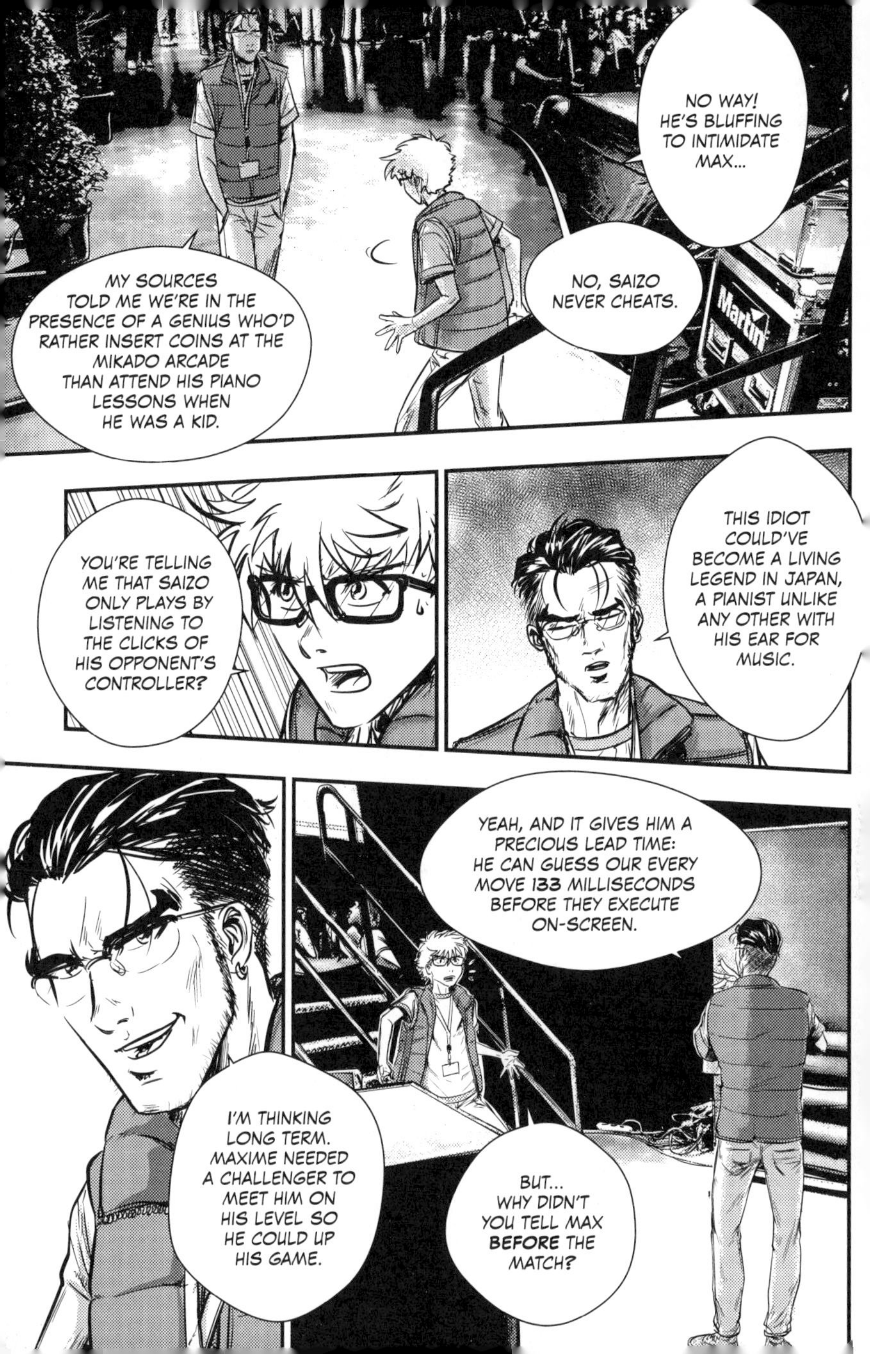
NO WAY! HE'S BLUFFING TO INTIMIDATE MAX...
NO, SAIZO NEVER CHEATS.
MY SOURCES TOLD ME WE'RE IN THE PRESENCE OF A GENIUS WHO'D RATHER INSERT COINS AT THE MIKADO ARCADE THAN ATTEND HIS PIANO LESSONS WHEN HE WAS A KID.
Martin
THIS IDIOT COULD'VE BECOME A LIVING LEGEND IN JAPAN, A PIANIST UNLIKE ANY OTHER WITH HIS EAR FOR MUSIC.
YOU'RE TELLING ME THAT SAIZO ONLY PLAYS BY LISTENING TO THE CLICKS OF HIS OPPONENT'S CONTROLLER?
YEAH, AND IT GIVES HIM A PRECIOUS LEAD TIME: HE CAN GUESS OUR EVERY MOVE 133 MILLISECONDS BEFORE THEY EXECUTE ON-SCREEN.
BUT... WHY DIDN'T YOU TELL MAX **BEFORE** THE MATCH?
I'M THINKING LONG TERM. MAXIME NEEDED A CHALLENGER TO MEET HIM ON HIS LEVEL SO HE COULD UP HIS GAME.

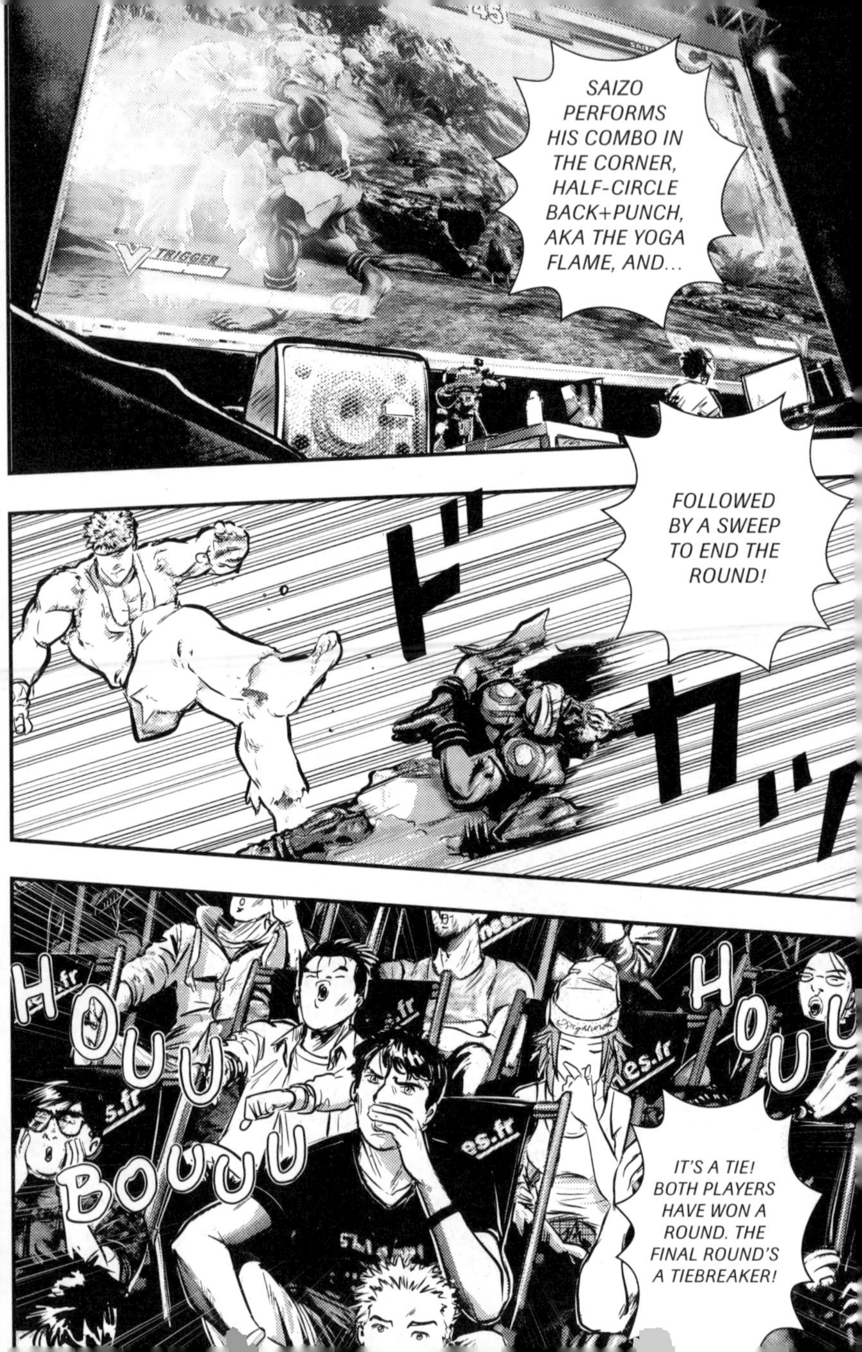
SAIZO PERFORMS HIS COMBO IN THE CORNER, HALF-CIRCLE BACK+PUNCH, AKA THE YOGA FLAME, AND...
FOLLOWED BY A SWEEP TO END THE ROUND!
ドカッ
HOUUU
HOUU
BOUUU
IT'S A TIE! BOTH PLAYERS HAVE WON A ROUND. THE FINAL ROUND'S A TIEBREAKER!

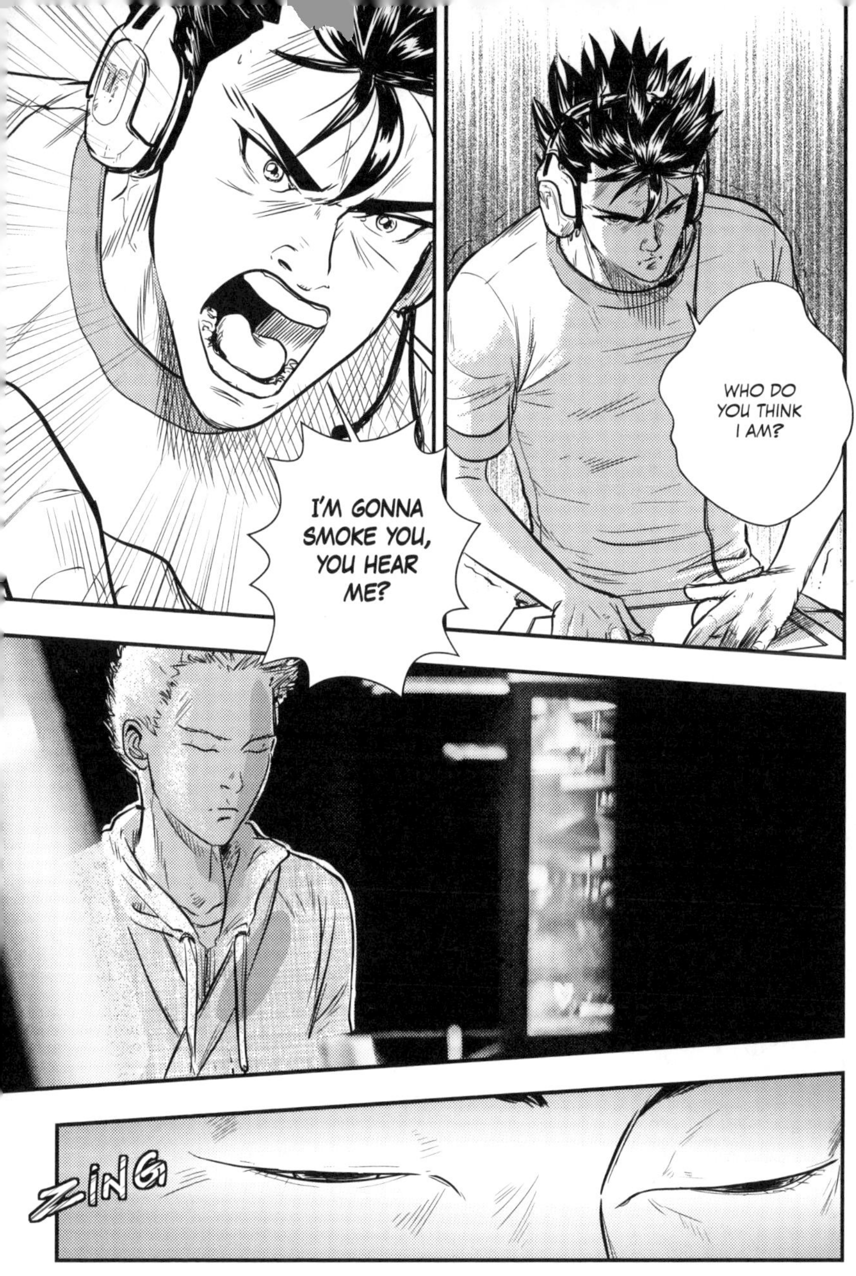
WHO DO YOU THINK I AM?
I'M GONNA SMOKE YOU, YOU HEAR ME?
ZING

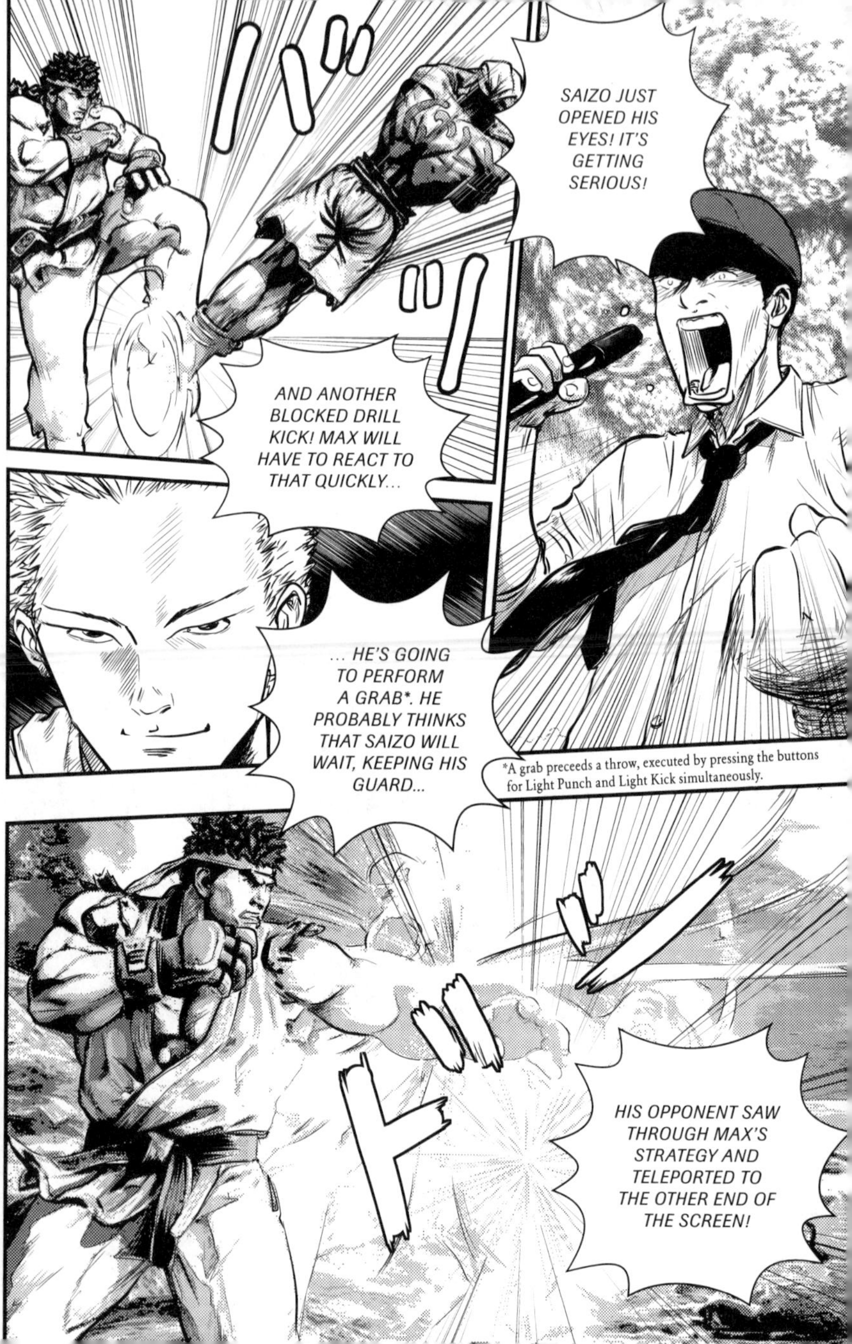
SAIZO JUST OPENED HIS EYES! IT'S GETTING SERIOUS!
AND ANOTHER BLOCKED DRILL KICK! MAX WILL HAVE TO REACT TO THAT QUICKLY...
... HE'S GOING TO PERFORM A GRAB*. HE PROBABLY THINKS THAT SAIZO WILL WAIT, KEEPING HIS GUARD...
HIS OPPONENT SAW THROUGH MAX'S STRATEGY AND TELEPORTED TO THE OTHER END OF THE SCREEN!

*A grab preceeds a throw, executed by pressing the buttons for Light Punch and Light Kick simultaneously.

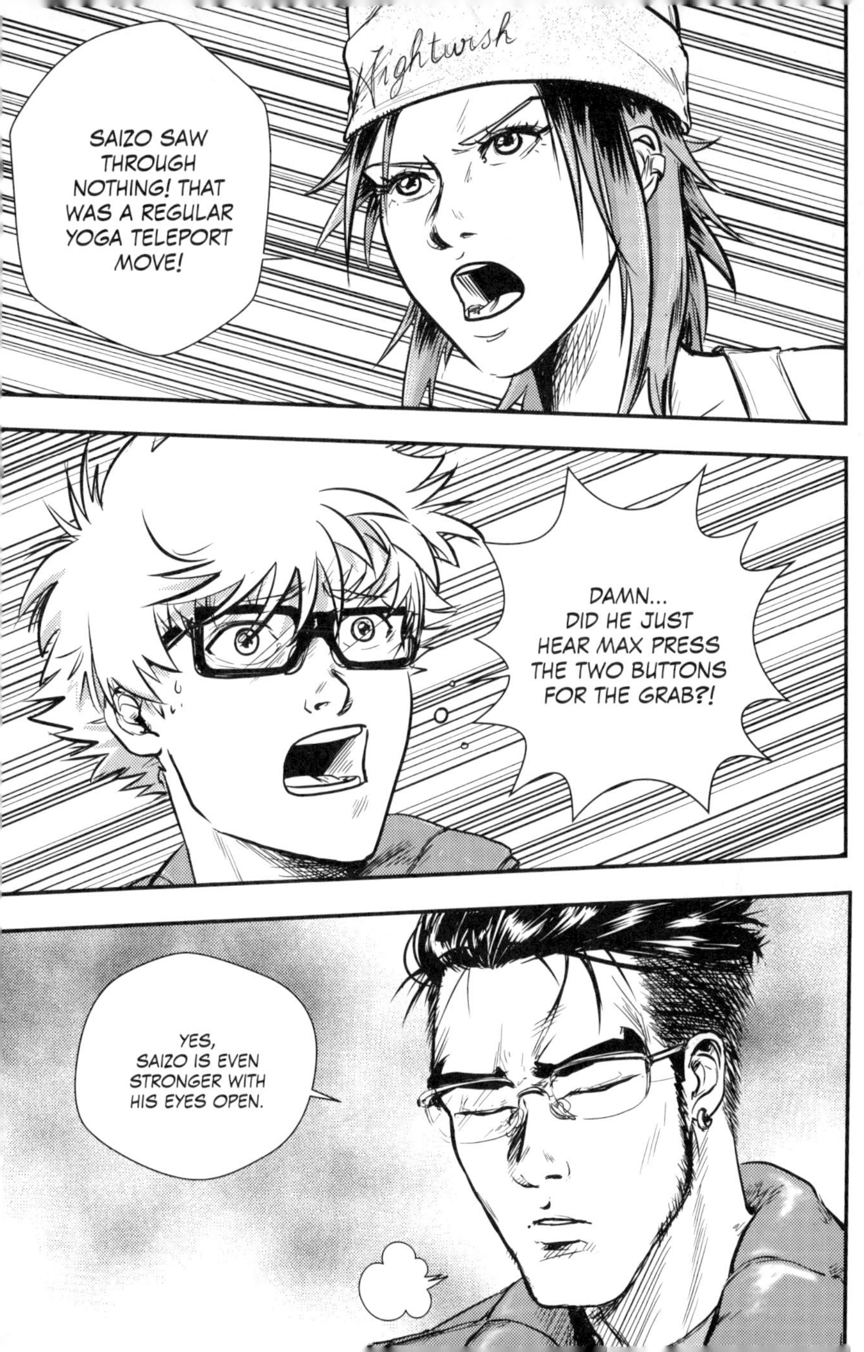
Nightwish
SAIZO SAW THROUGH NOTHING! THAT WAS A REGULAR YOGA TELEPORT MOVE!
DAMN... DID HE JUST HEAR MAX PRESS THE TWO BUTTONS FOR THE GRAB?!
YES, SAIZO IS EVEN STRONGER WITH HIS EYES OPEN.

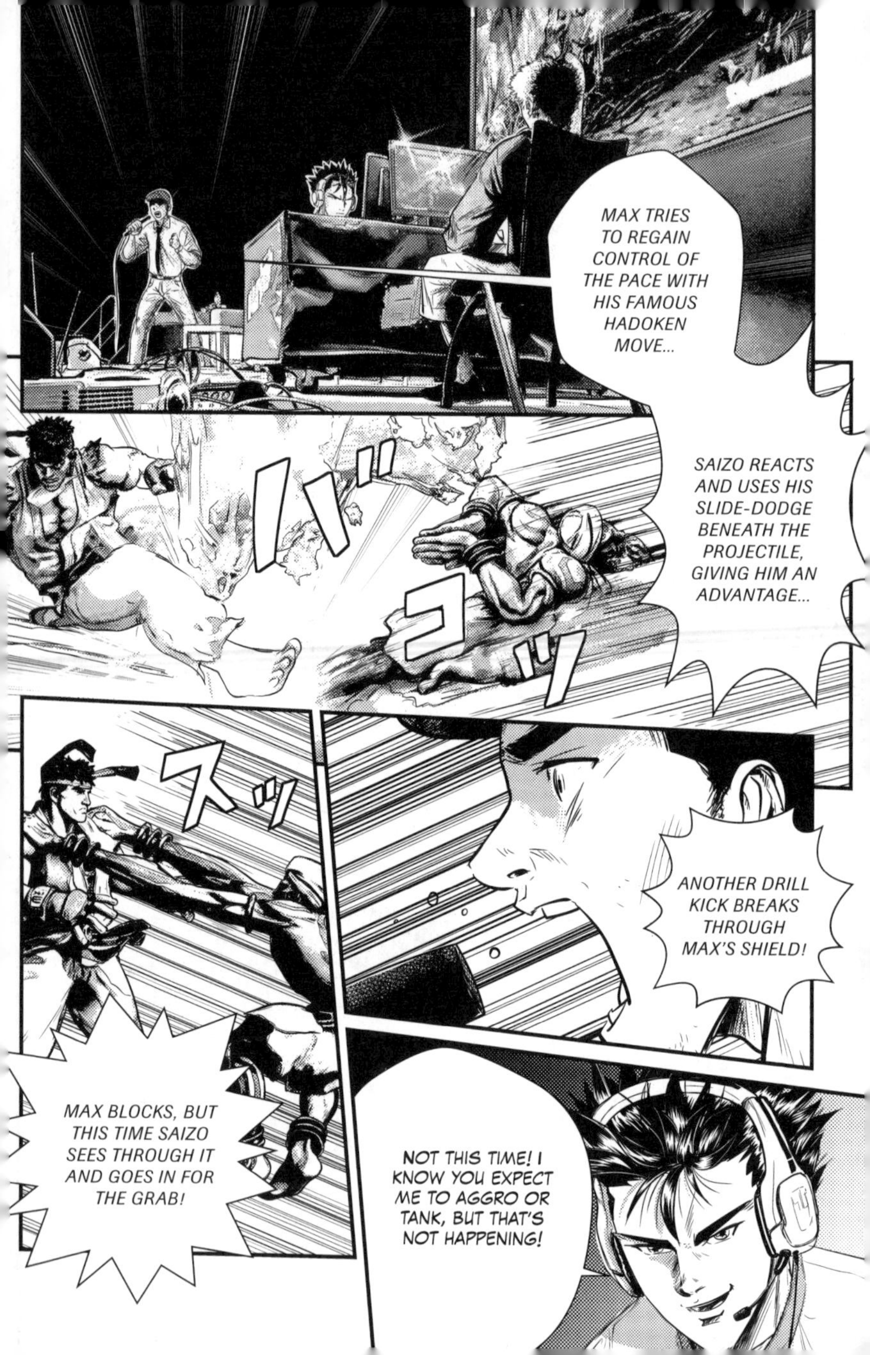
MAX TRIES TO REGAIN CONTROL OF THE PACE WITH HIS FAMOUS HADOKEN MOVE...
SAIZO REACTS AND USES HIS SLIDE-DODGE BENEATH THE PROJECTILE, GIVING HIM AN ADVANTAGE...
バ
ゴッ
ANOTHER DRILL KICK BREAKS THROUGH MAX'S SHIELD!
NOT THIS TIME! I KNOW YOU EXPECT ME TO AGGRO OR TANK, BUT THAT'S NOT HAPPENING!
スッ
MAX BLOCKS, BUT THIS TIME SAIZO SEES THROUGH IT AND GOES IN FOR THE GRAB!

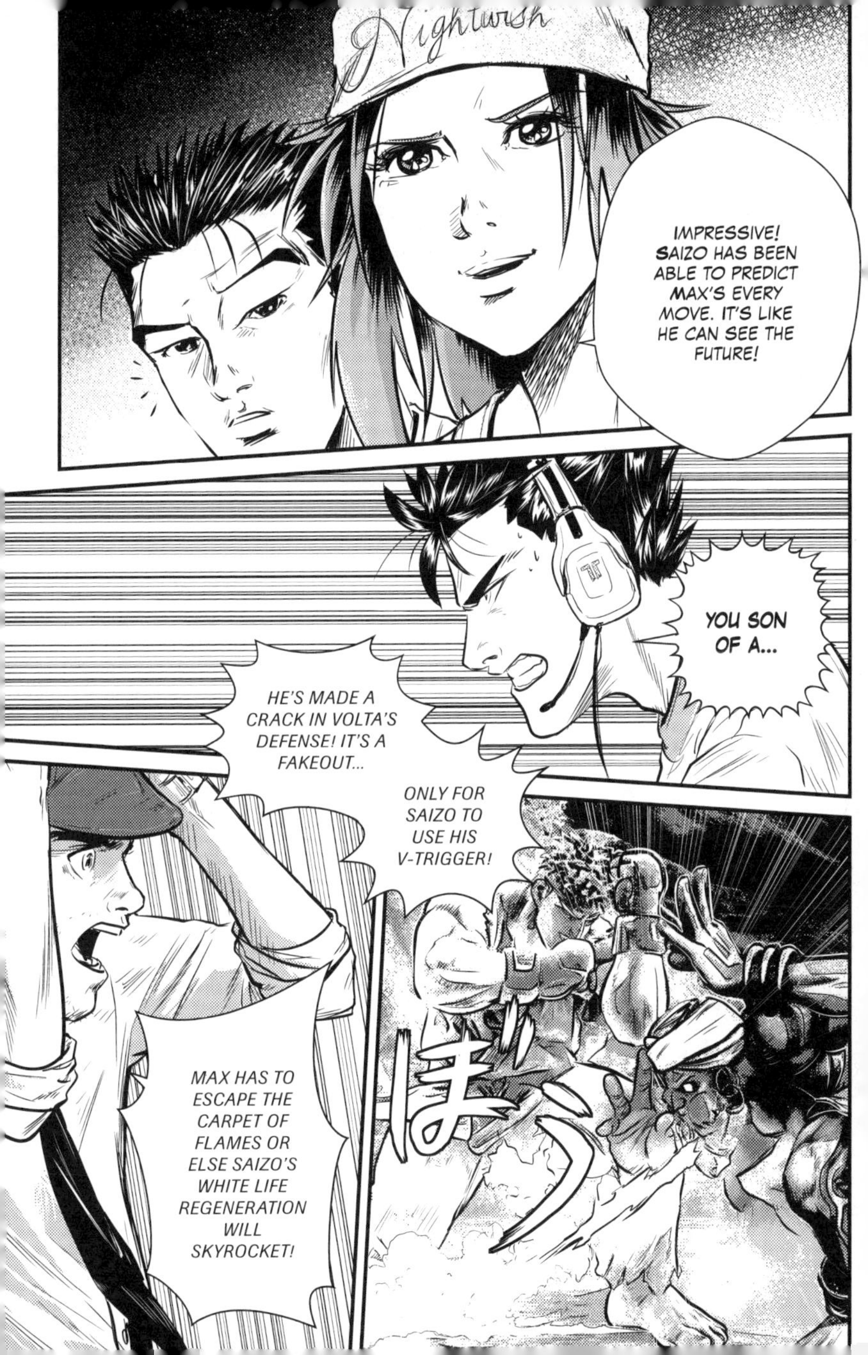

Nightwish
IMPRESSIVE! SAIZO HAS BEEN ABLE TO PREDICT MAX'S EVERY MOVE. IT'S LIKE HE CAN SEE THE FUTURE!
YOU SON OF A...
HE'S MADE A CRACK IN VOLTA'S DEFENSE! IT'S A FAKEOUT...
ONLY FOR SAIZO TO USE HIS V-TRIGGER!
ぼっ
MAX HAS TO ESCAPE THE CARPET OF FLAMES OR ELSE SAIZO'S WHITE LIFE REGENERATION WILL SKYROCKET!

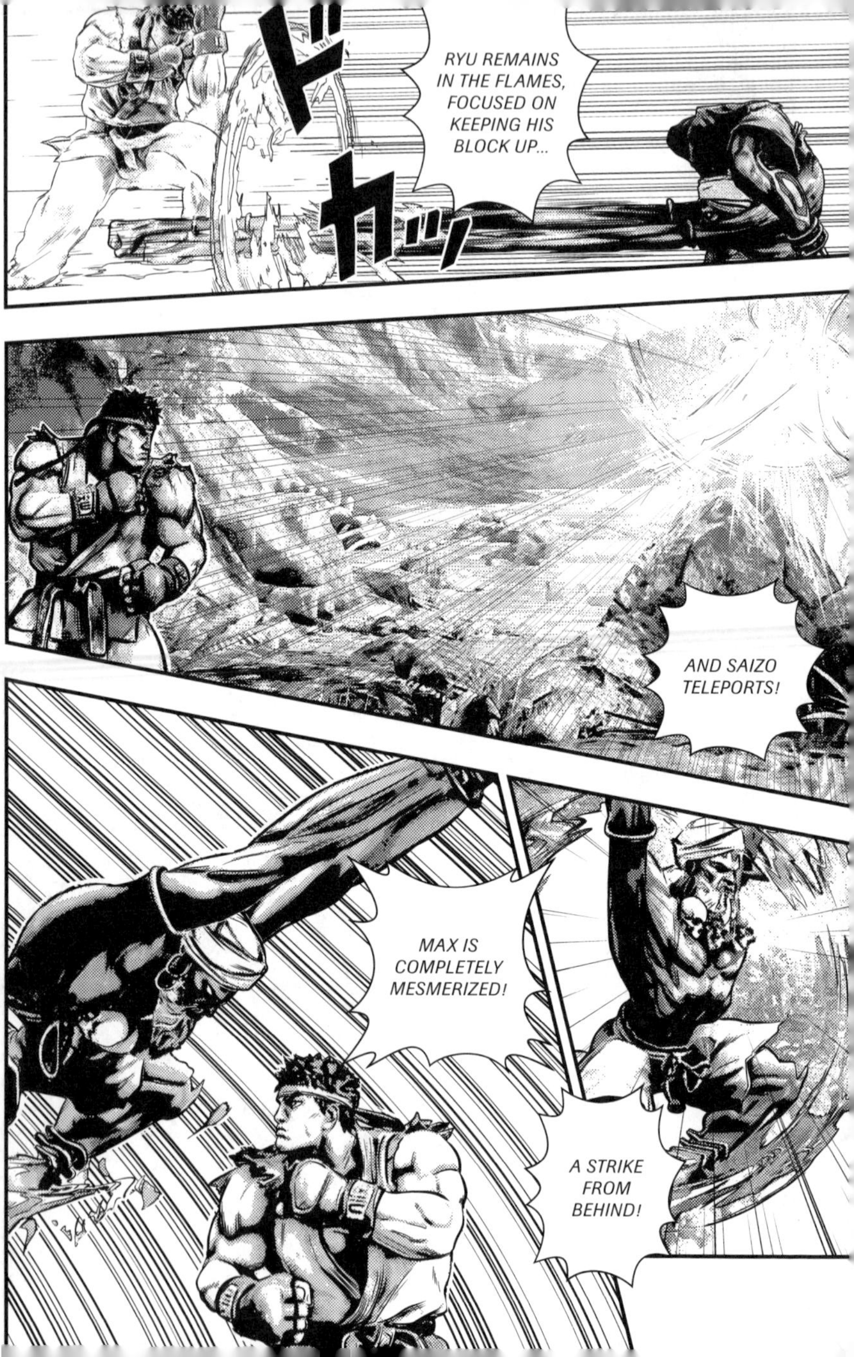
ドカッ
RYU REMAINS IN THE FLAMES, FOCUSED ON KEEPING HIS BLOCK UP...
AND SAIZO TELEPORTS!
A STRIKE FROM BEHIND!
MAX IS COMPLETELY MESMERIZED!

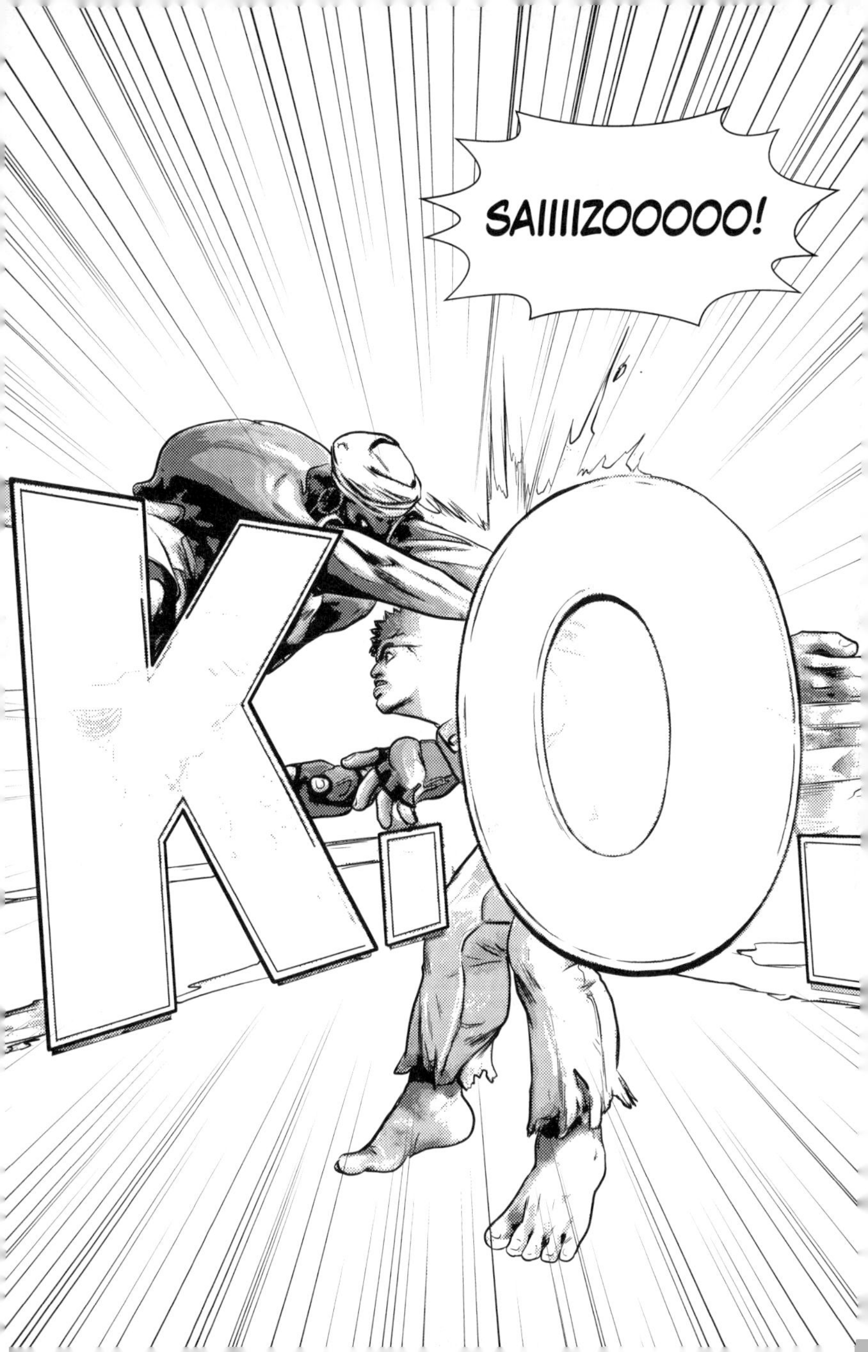
SAIIIIZOOOOO!
K.O.

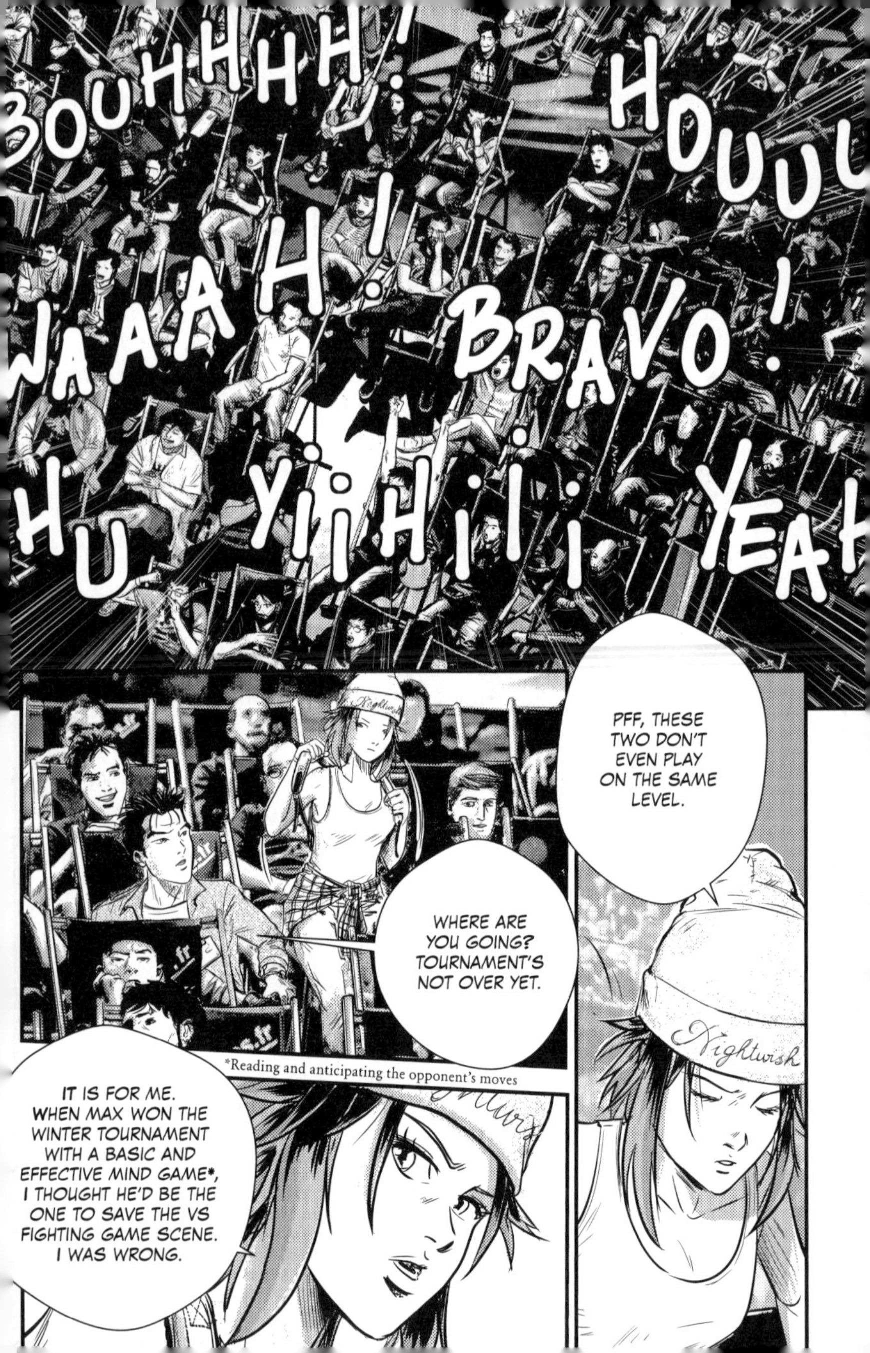
HOUUU
BOUHHHH!
BRAVO!
WAAAH!
YEAH
YIIIHIII
HUU
PFF, THESE TWO DON'T EVEN PLAY ON THE SAME LEVEL.
WHERE ARE YOU GOING? TOURNAMENT'S NOT OVER YET.
IT IS FOR ME. WHEN MAX WON THE WINTER TOURNAMENT WITH A BASIC AND EFFECTIVE MIND GAME*, I THOUGHT HE'D BE THE ONE TO SAVE THE VS FIGHTING GAME SCENE. I WAS WRONG.
Nightwish

*Reading and anticipating the opponent's moves

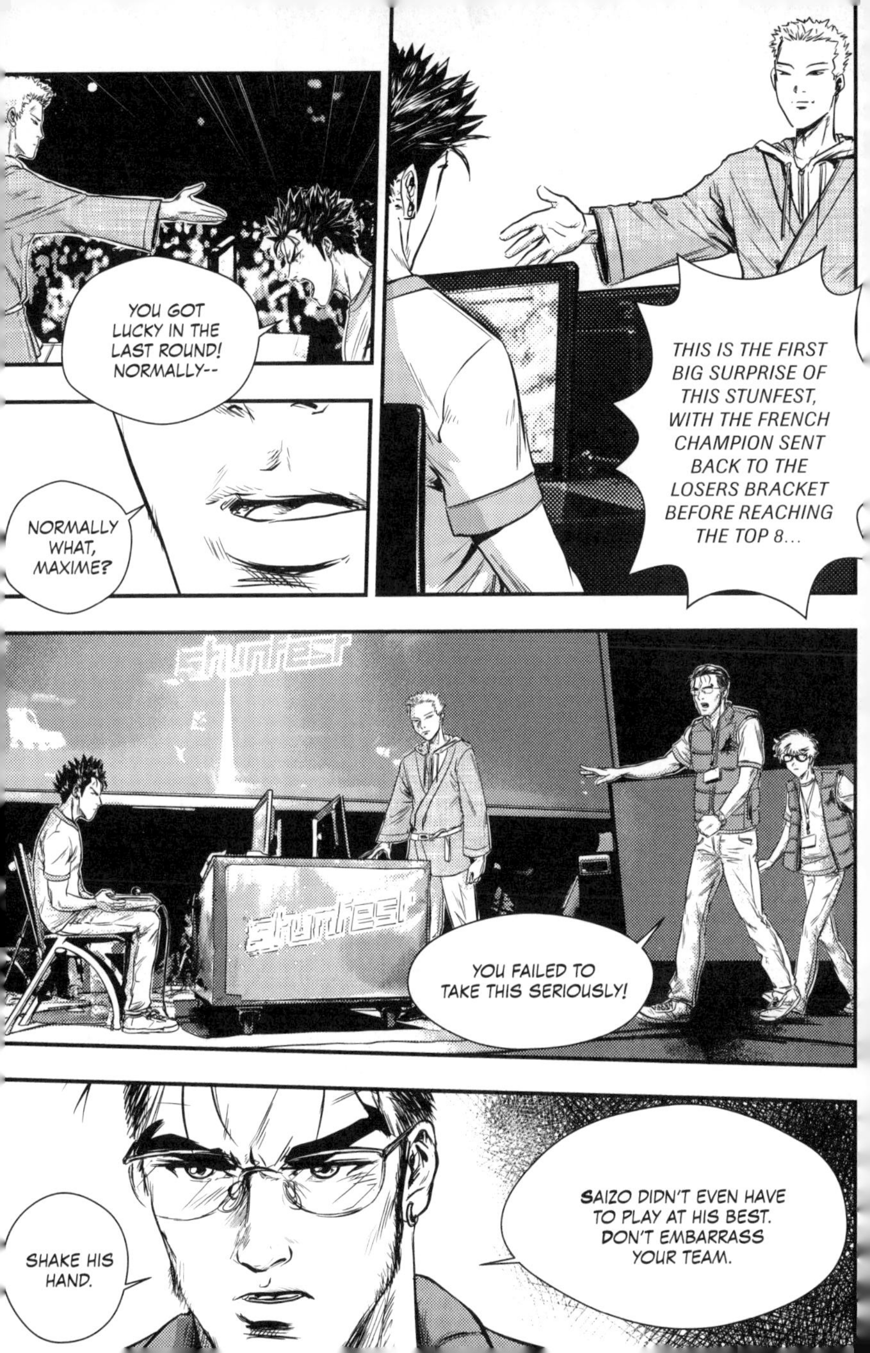
YOU GOT LUCKY IN THE LAST ROUND! NORMALLY--
NORMALLY WHAT, MAXIME?
THIS IS THE FIRST BIG SURPRISE OF THIS STUNFEST, WITH THE FRENCH CHAMPION SENT BACK TO THE LOSERS BRACKET BEFORE REACHING THE TOP 8...
YOU FAILED TO TAKE THIS SERIOUSLY!
SAIZO DIDN'T EVEN HAVE TO PLAY AT HIS BEST. DON'T EMBARRASS YOUR TEAM.
SHAKE HIS HAND.

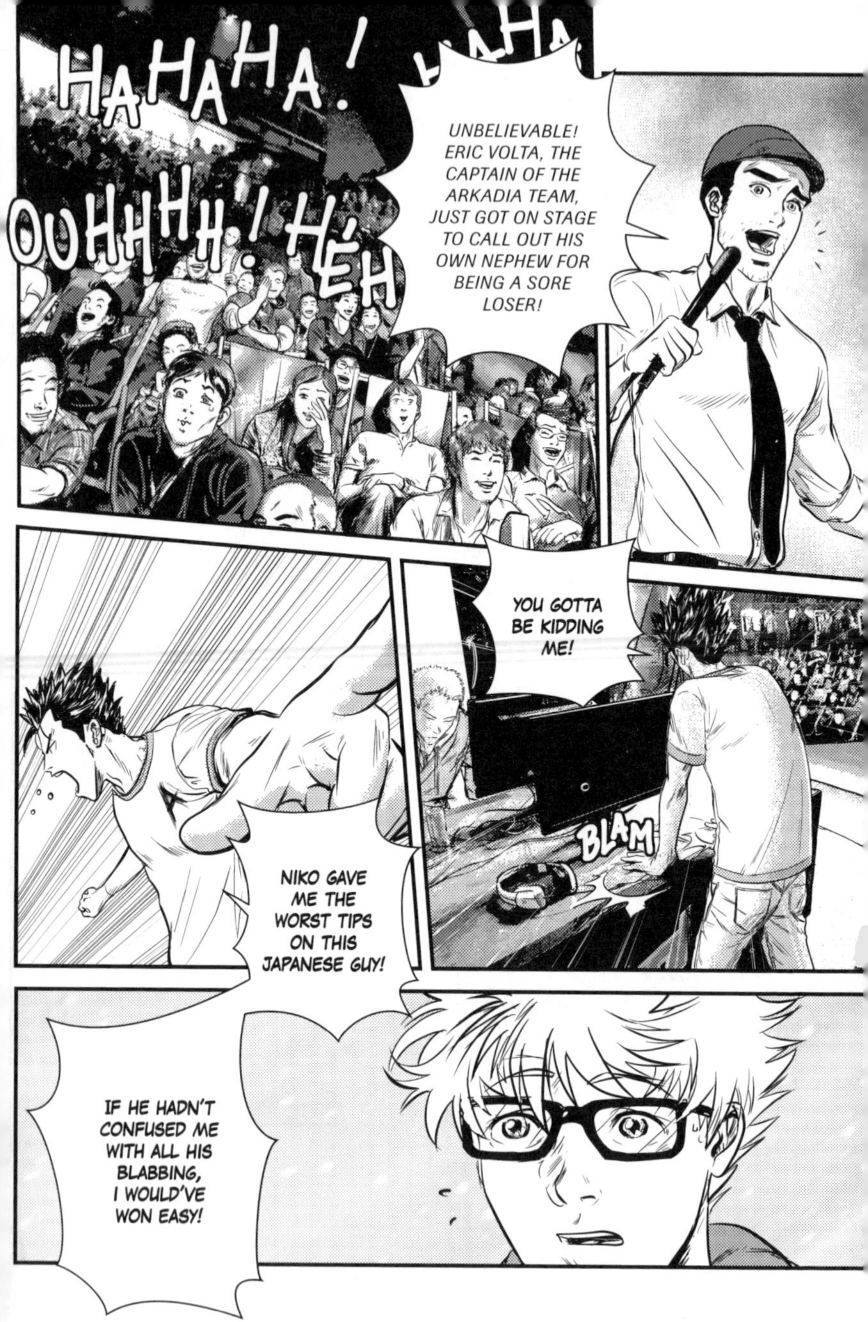
UNBELIEVABLE! ERIC VOLTA, THE CAPTAIN OF THE ARKADIA TEAM, JUST GOT ON STAGE TO CALL OUT HIS OWN NEPHEW FOR BEING A SORE LOSER!
HAHA
HAHAHA!
OUHHHH!
HÉH
HÉH
YOU GOTTA BE KIDDING ME!
BLAM
NIKO GAVE ME THE WORST TIPS ON THIS JAPANESE GUY!
IF HE HADN'T CONFUSED ME WITH ALL HIS BLABBING, I WOULD'VE WON EASY!

BLAM

TAK

SCREW THIS!

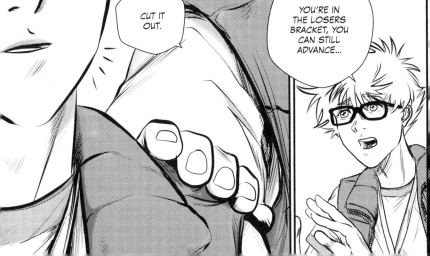

CUT IT OUT.

YOU'RE IN THE LOSERS BRACKET, YOU CAN STILL ADVANCE...

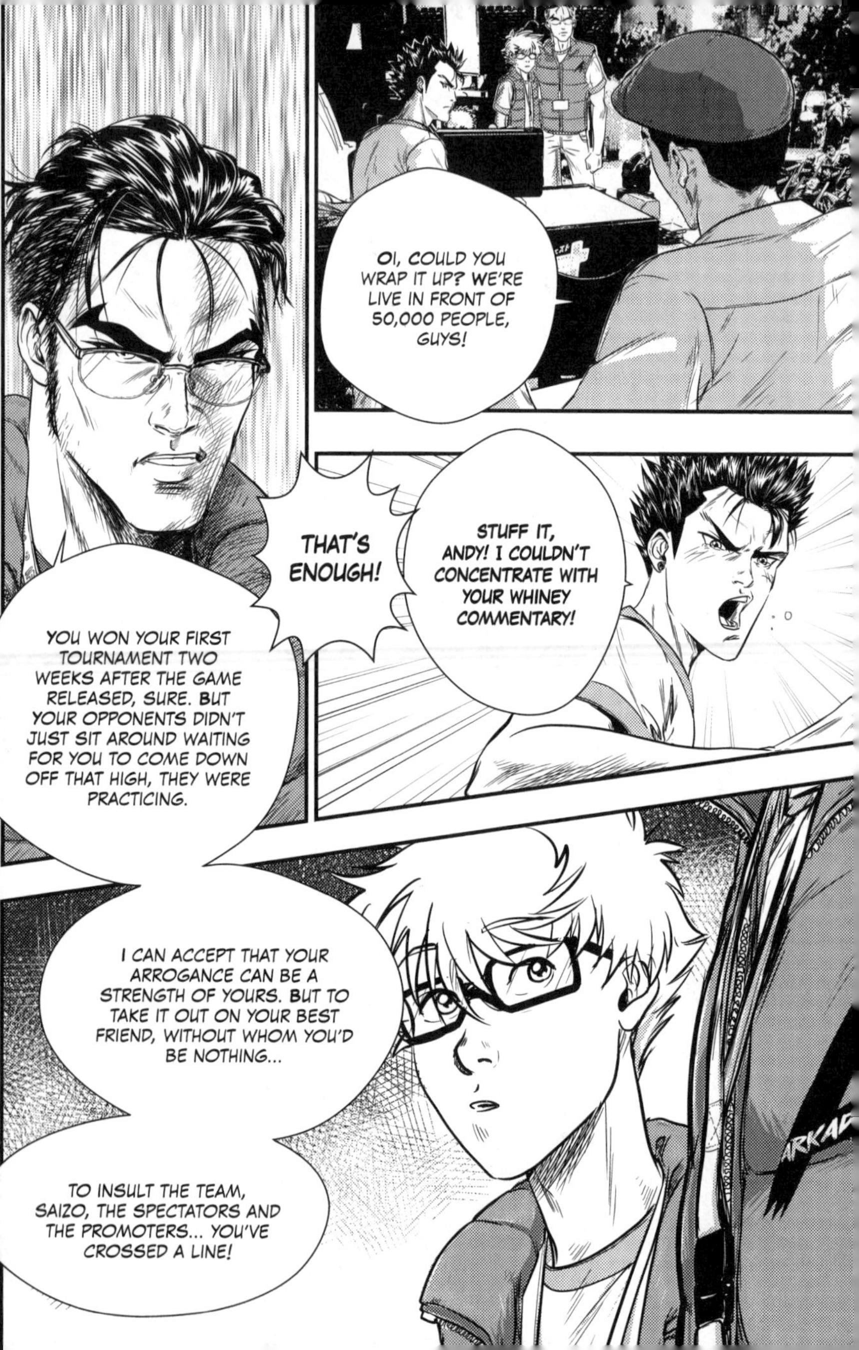
OI, COULD YOU WRAP IT UP? WE'RE LIVE IN FRONT OF 50,000 PEOPLE, GUYS!
STUFF IT, ANDY! I COULDN'T CONCENTRATE WITH YOUR WHINEY COMMENTARY!
THAT'S ENOUGH!
YOU WON YOUR FIRST TOURNAMENT TWO WEEKS AFTER THE GAME RELEASED, SURE. BUT YOUR OPPONENTS DIDN'T JUST SIT AROUND WAITING FOR YOU TO COME DOWN OFF THAT HIGH, THEY WERE PRACTICING.
I CAN ACCEPT THAT YOUR ARROGANCE CAN BE A STRENGTH OF YOURS. BUT TO TAKE IT OUT ON YOUR BEST FRIEND, WITHOUT WHOM YOU'D BE NOTHING...
TO INSULT THE TEAM, SAIZO, THE SPECTATORS AND THE PROMOTERS... YOU'VE CROSSED A LINE!

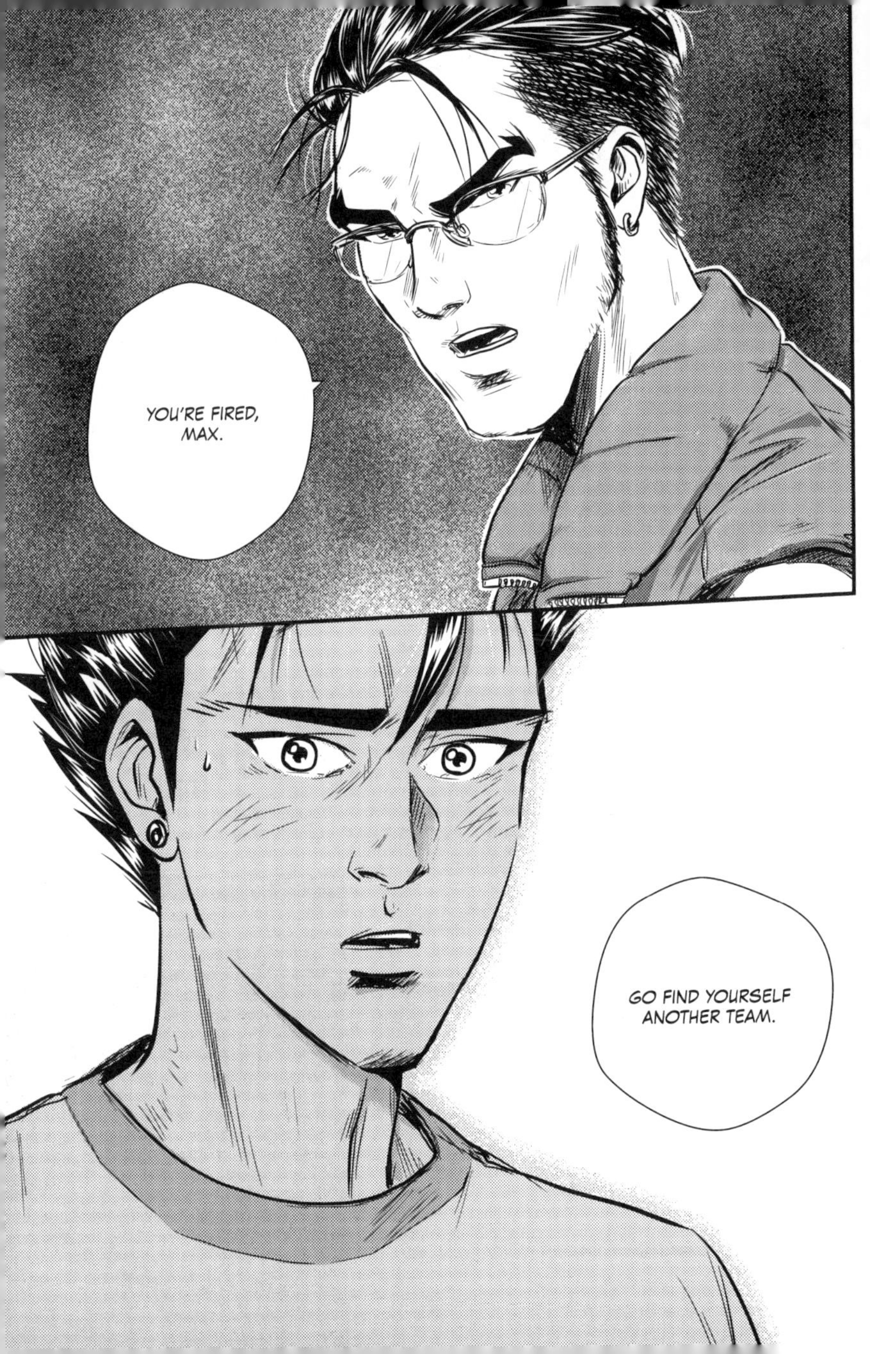
YOU'RE FIRED, MAX.
GO FIND YOURSELF ANOTHER TEAM.

CHARACTER SELECT !

MAXIME VOLTA

THE MIND KING

BACKGROUND

In March 2016, Maxime Volta made a sensational entry into the Capcom Pro Tour by winning the first tournament of the season, the Cannes Winter Clash. He ended the season as the frontrunner of the championship and an official member of the E-Sports team headed by his uncle, Eric Volta: Team Arkadia.

Max's innate talent for predicting an opponent's strategy has earned him the nickname "The Mind King". Combined with his instincts, it makes him a formidable weapon.

His strength is also his weakness: his entire strategy rests on his ability to read the game. What happens when he stumbles across a player one step ahead of him?

That player is Japan's Saizo, who Max faces at Stunfest 2016. Arrogant and callous, Max underestimates his opponent and suffers a crushing defeat...

CHARACTER DESIGN

The 1st design for Max was much more of a bad boy, but he lacked the charisma a protagonist needs. I then decided on giving him an intentionally-messy "relaxed" look. Max is always picky about his appearance... except when he's depressed.

BY KALON

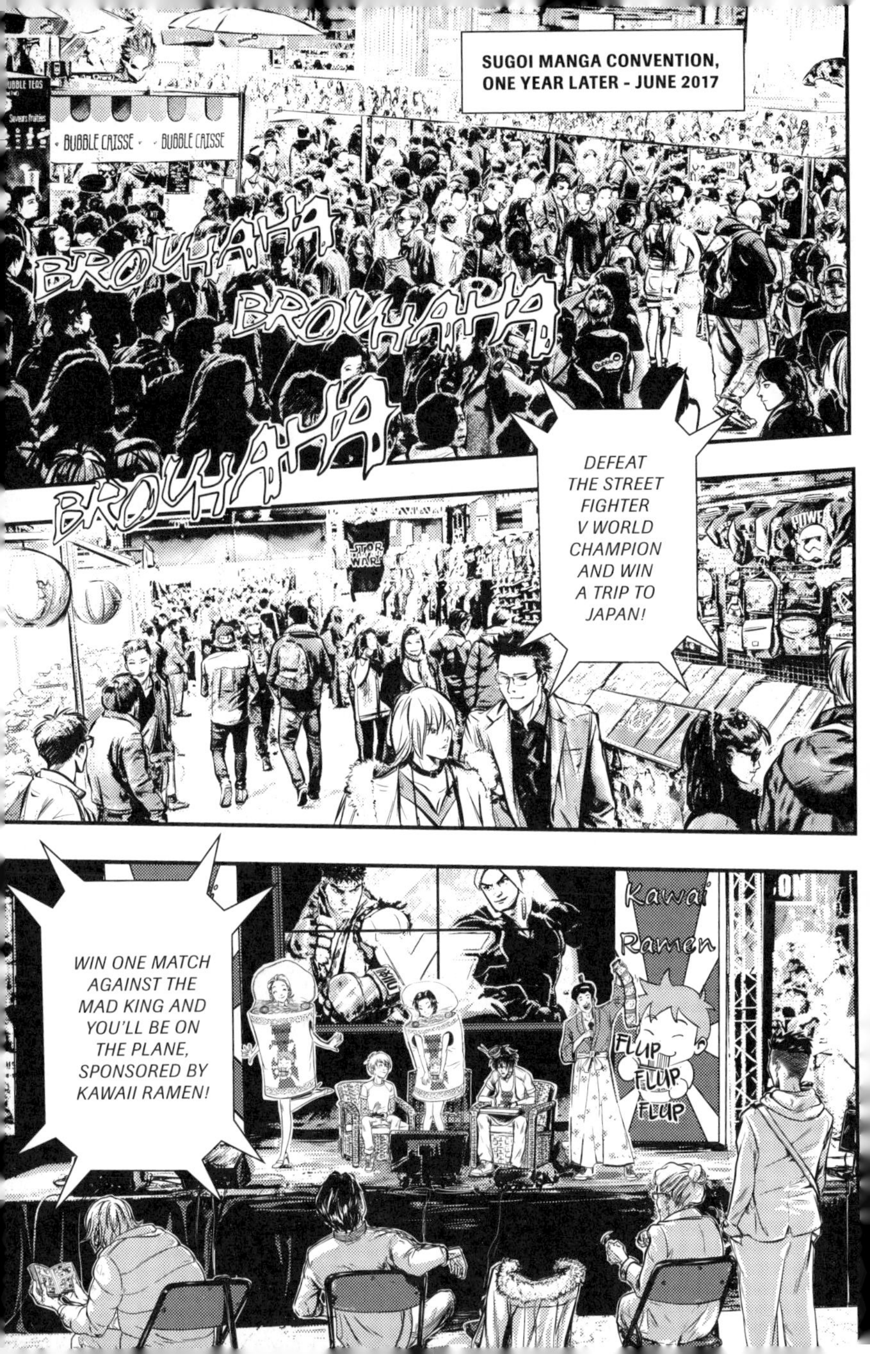
SUGOI MANGA CONVENTION, ONE YEAR LATER - JUNE 2017
BUBBLE CAISSE
BUBBLE CAISSE
BROUHAHA
BROUHAHA
BROUHAHA
DEFEAT THE STREET FIGHTER V WORLD CHAMPION AND WIN A TRIP TO JAPAN!
WIN ONE MATCH AGAINST THE MAD KING AND YOU'LL BE ON THE PLANE, SPONSORED BY KAWAII RAMEN!
Kawai Ramen
FLUP
FLUP
FLUP

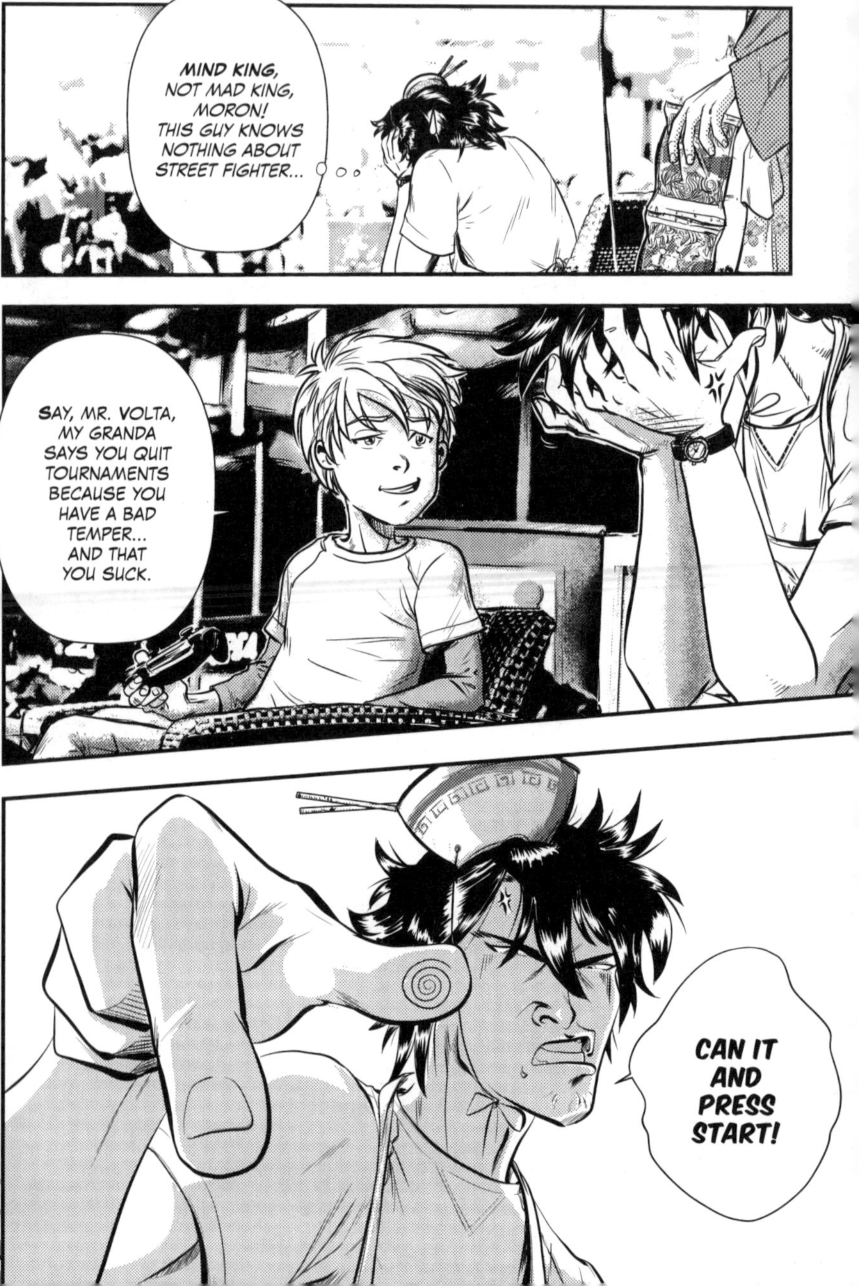
MIND KING, NOT MAD KING, MORON! THIS GUY KNOWS NOTHING ABOUT STREET FIGHTER...
SAY, MR. VOLTA, MY GRANDA SAYS YOU QUIT TOURNAMENTS BECAUSE YOU HAVE A BAD TEMPER... AND THAT YOU SUCK.
CAN IT AND PRESS START!

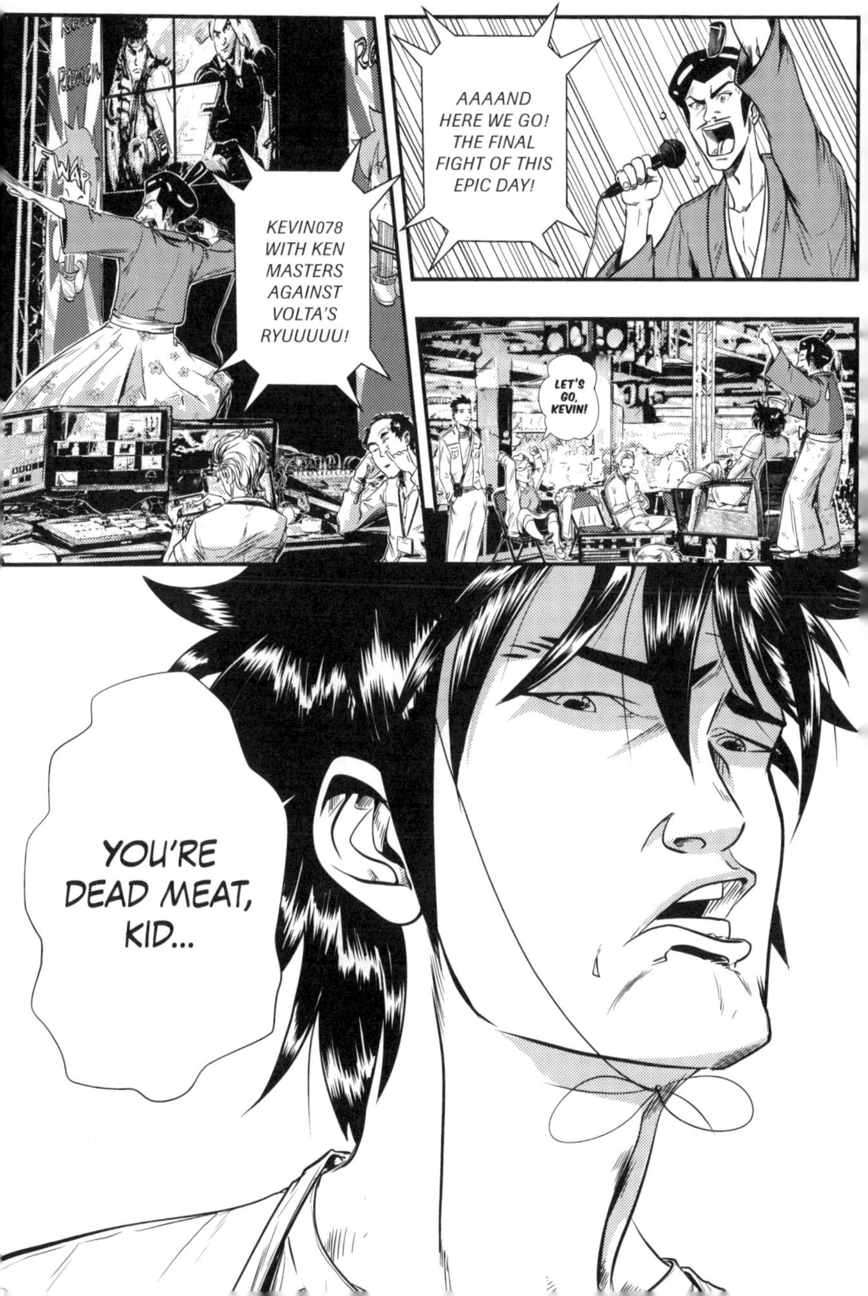
AAAAND HERE WE GO! THE FINAL FIGHT OF THIS EPIC DAY!
KEVIN078 WITH KEN MASTERS AGAINST VOLTA'S RYUUUUU!
LET'S GO, KEVIN!
YOU'RE DEAD MEAT, KID...

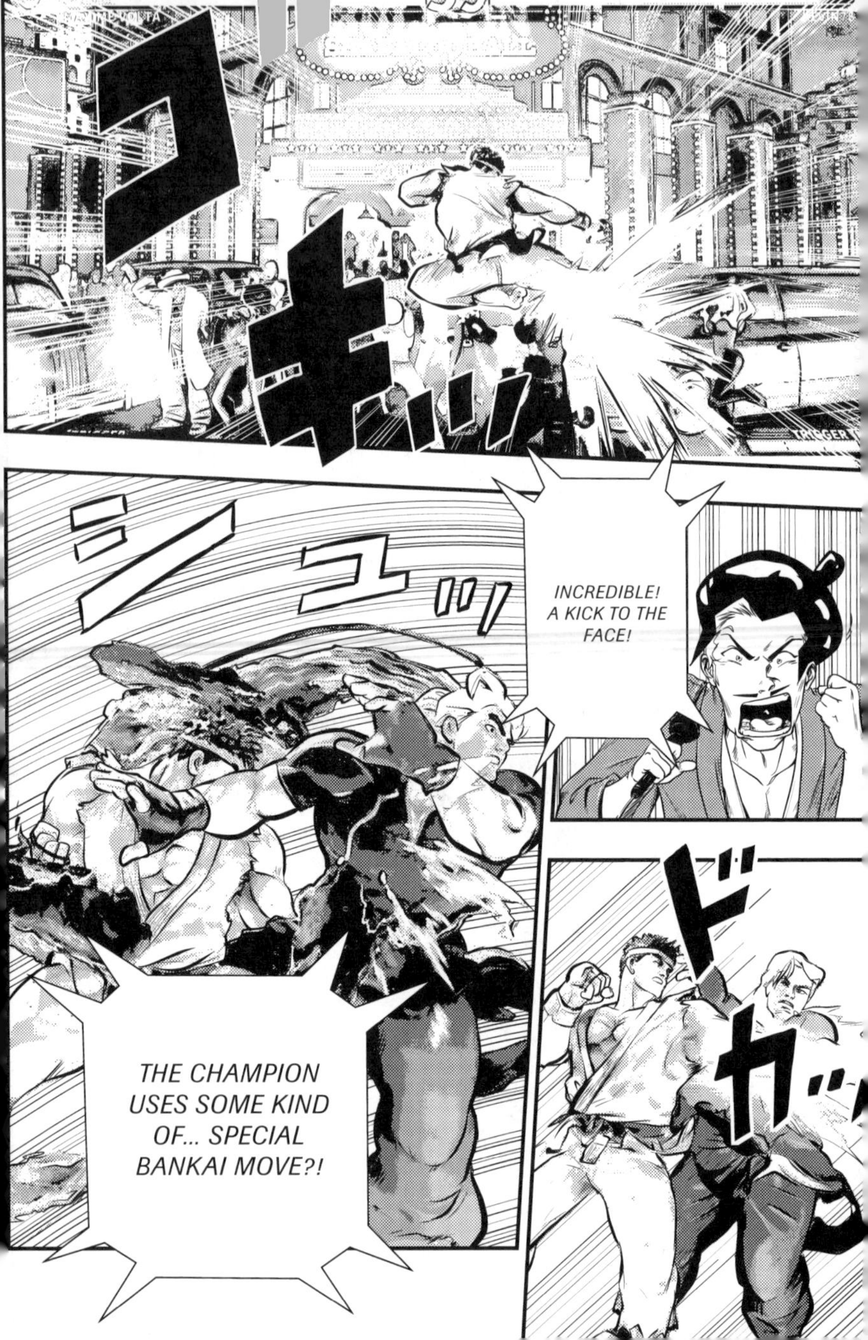

INCREDIBLE! A KICK TO THE FACE!
THE CHAMPION USES SOME KIND OF... SPECIAL BANKAI MOVE?!

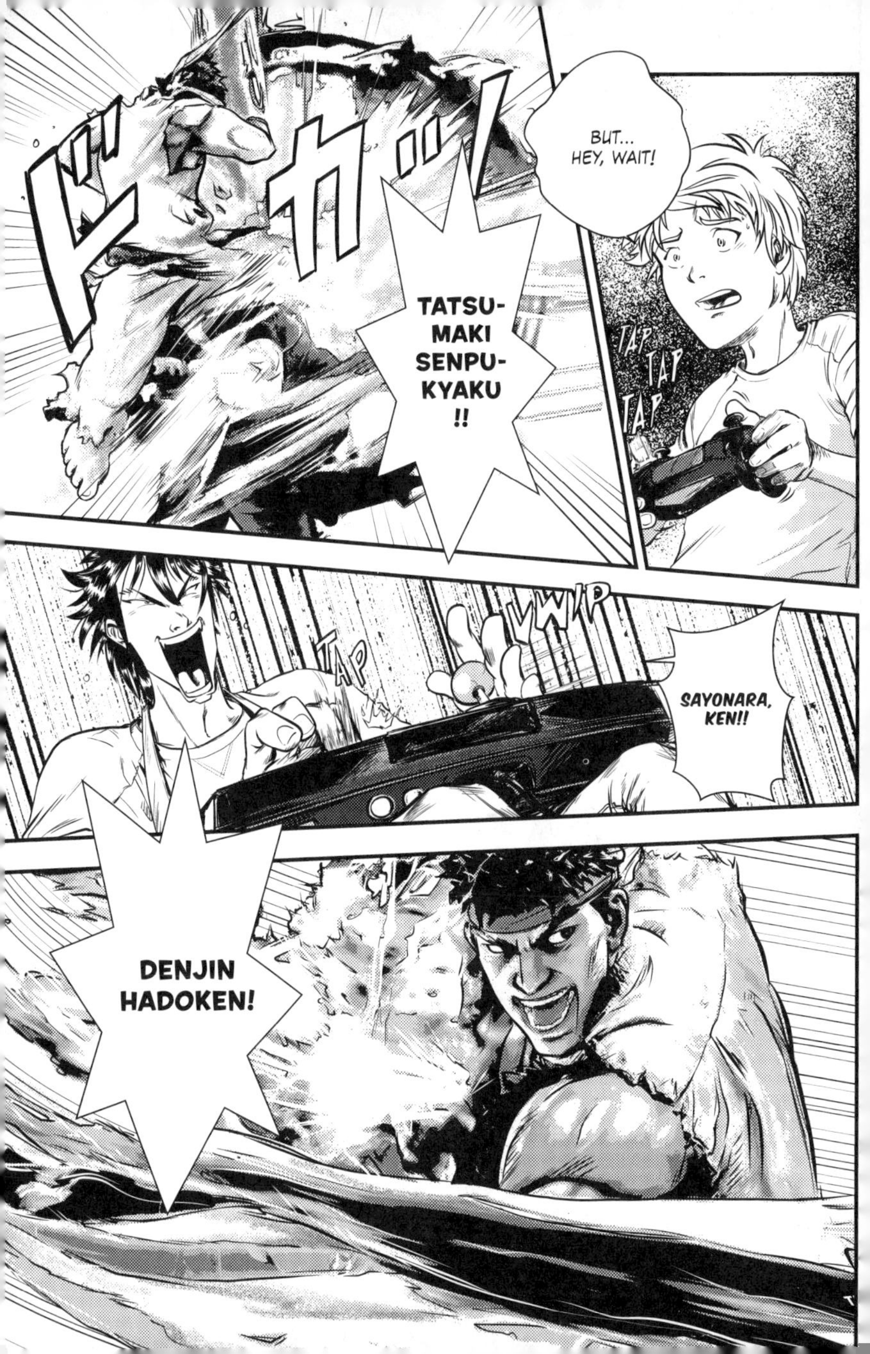

BUT... HEY, WAIT!
TAP TAP TAP
TATSU-MAKI SENPU-KYAKU!!
SAYONARA, KEN!!
VWIP
TAP
DENJIN HADOKEN!

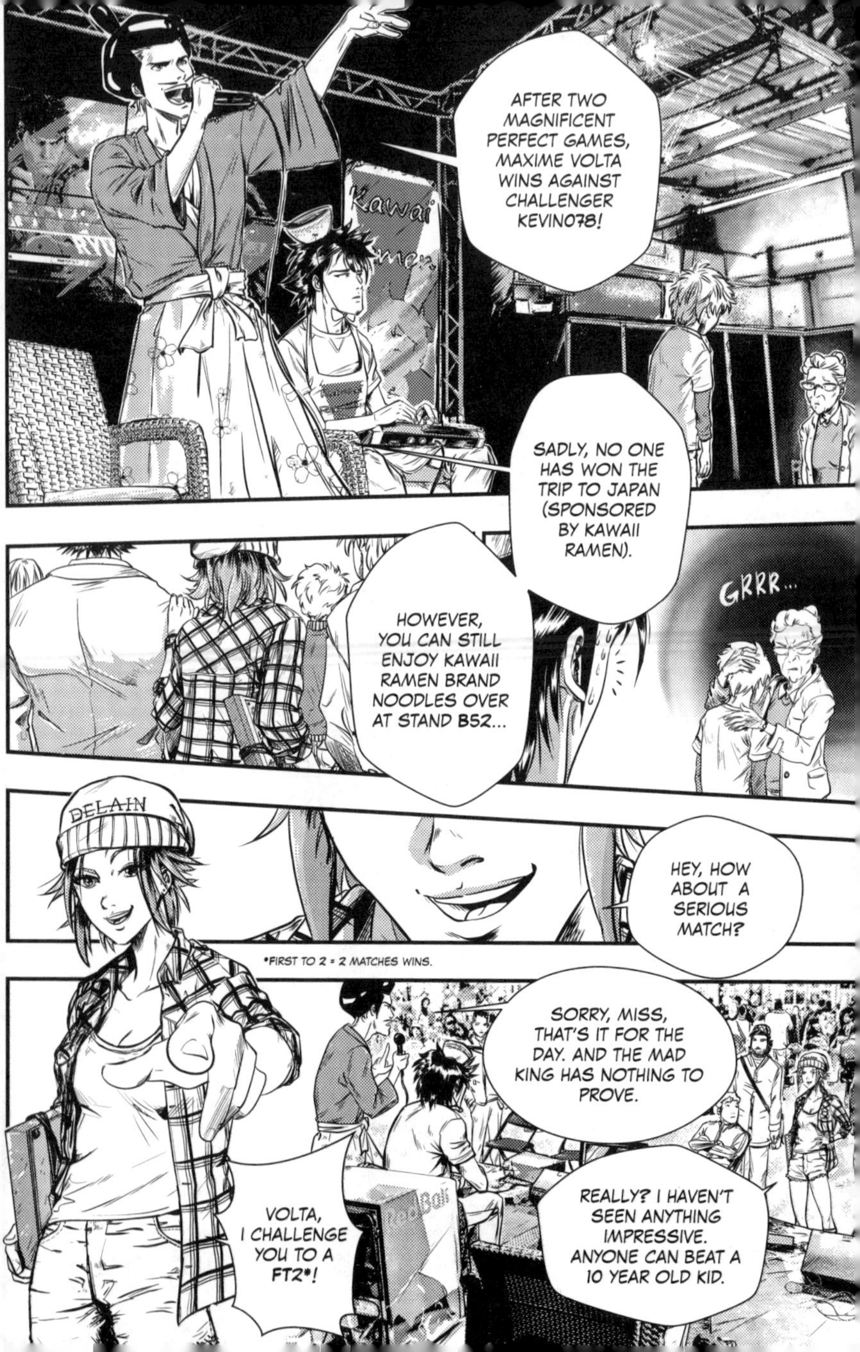
AFTER TWO MAGNIFICENT PERFECT GAMES, MAXIME VOLTA WINS AGAINST CHALLENGER KEVIN078!
Kawaii Ramen
SADLY, NO ONE HAS WON THE TRIP TO JAPAN (SPONSORED BY KAWAII RAMEN).
HOWEVER, YOU CAN STILL ENJOY KAWAII RAMEN BRAND NOODLES OVER AT STAND B52...
GRRR...
DELAIN
HEY, HOW ABOUT A SERIOUS MATCH?
*FIRST TO 2 = 2 MATCHES WINS.
VOLTA, I CHALLENGE YOU TO A FT2*!
SORRY, MISS, THAT'S IT FOR THE DAY. AND THE MAD KING HAS NOTHING TO PROVE.
REALLY? I HAVEN'T SEEN ANYTHING IMPRESSIVE. ANYONE CAN BEAT A 10 YEAR OLD KID.

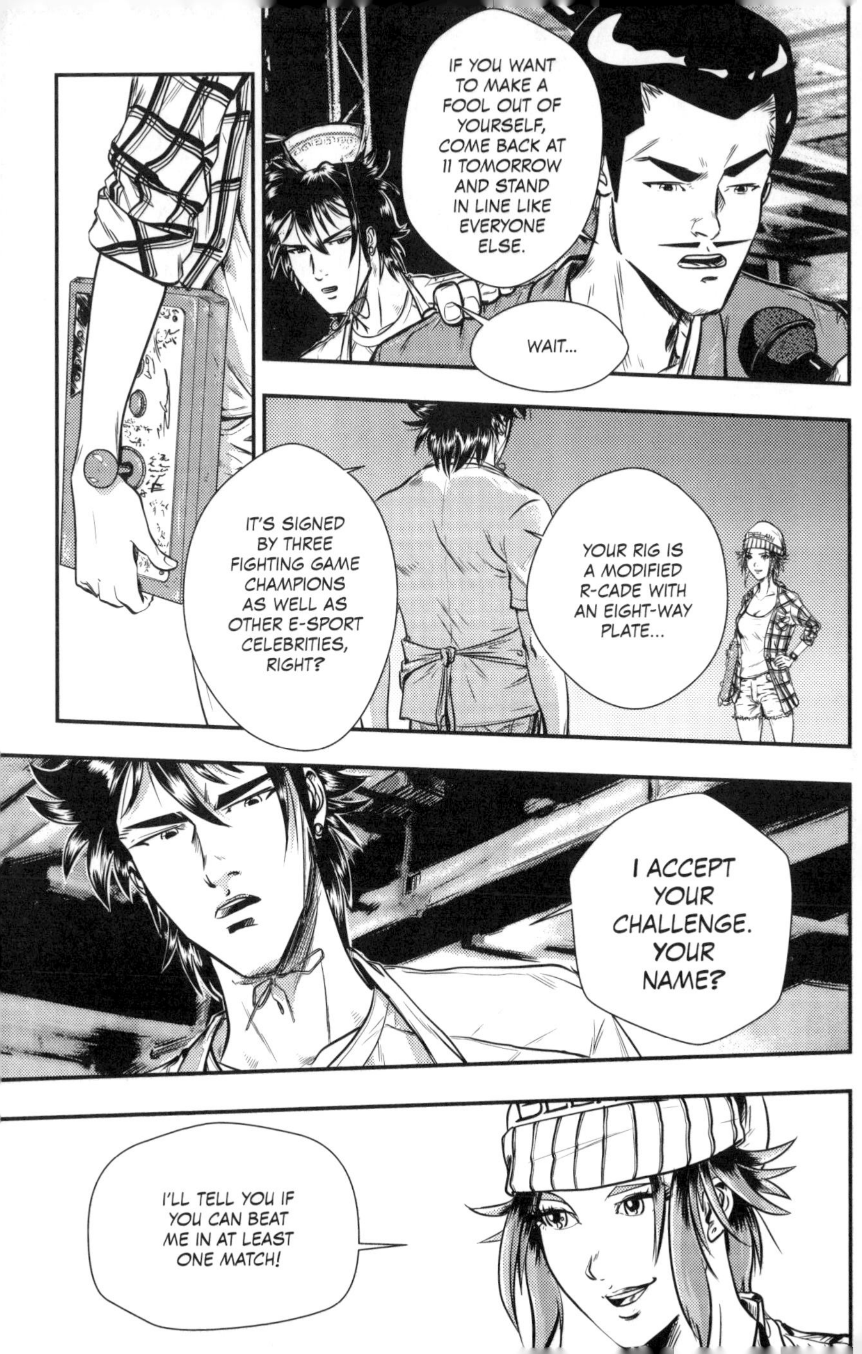
IF YOU WANT TO MAKE A FOOL OUT OF YOURSELF, COME BACK AT 11 TOMORROW AND STAND IN LINE LIKE EVERYONE ELSE.
WAIT...
YOUR RIG IS A MODIFIED R-CADE WITH AN EIGHT-WAY PLATE...
IT'S SIGNED BY THREE FIGHTING GAME CHAMPIONS AS WELL AS OTHER E-SPORT CELEBRITIES, RIGHT?
I ACCEPT YOUR CHALLENGE. YOUR NAME?
I'LL TELL YOU IF YOU CAN BEAT ME IN AT LEAST ONE MATCH!

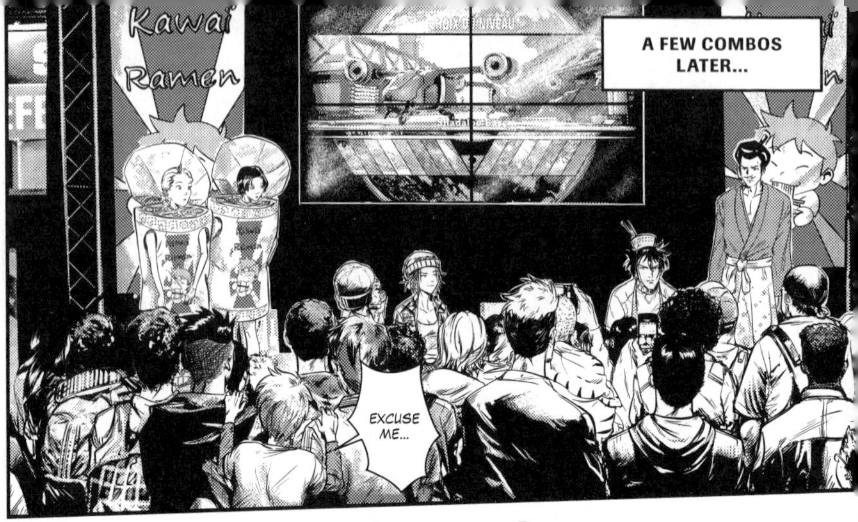
A FEW COMBOS LATER...
Kawai Ramen
EXCUSE ME...
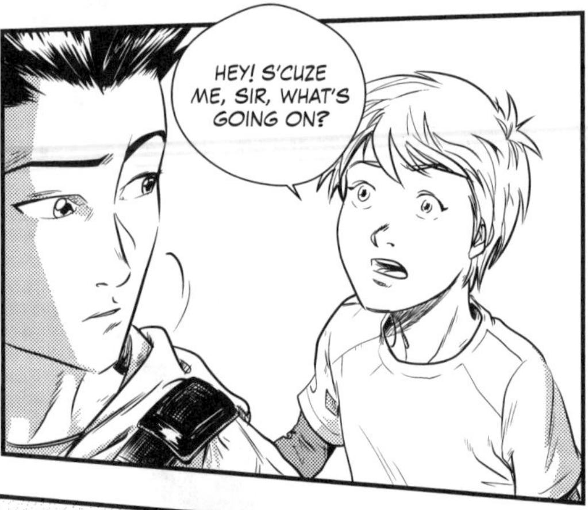
HEY! S'CUZE ME, SIR, WHAT'S GOING ON?
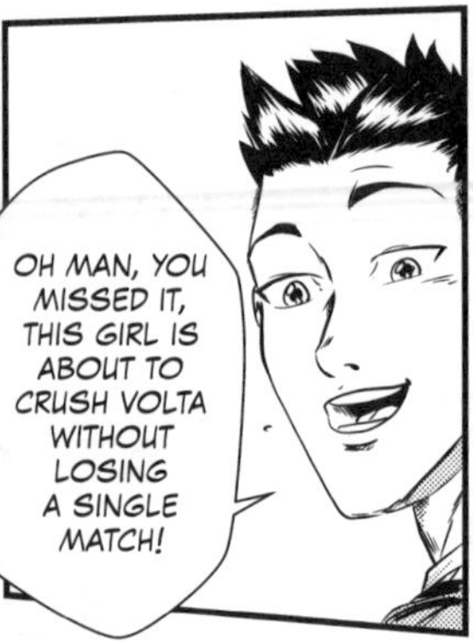
OH MAN, YOU MISSED IT, THIS GIRL IS ABOUT TO CRUSH VOLTA WITHOUT LOSING A SINGLE MATCH!
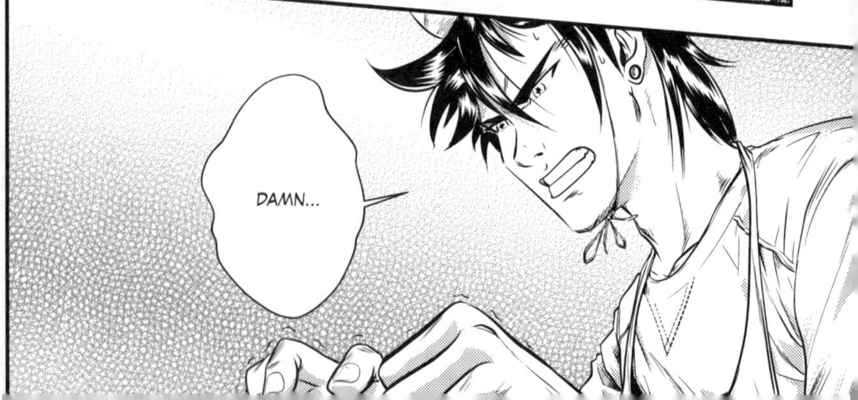
DAMN...

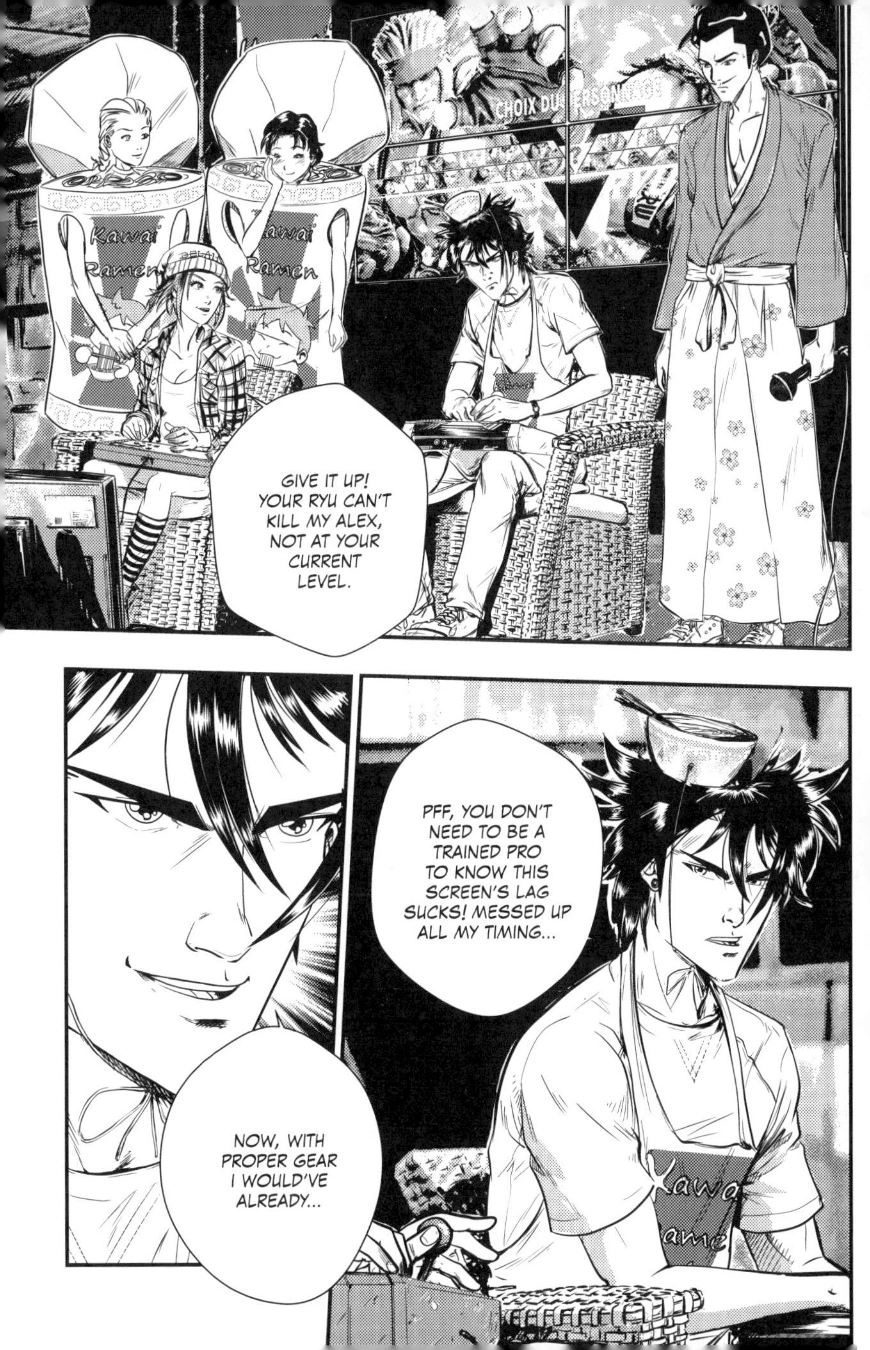
Kawai Ramen
Kawai Ramen
GIVE IT UP! YOUR RYU CAN'T KILL MY ALEX, NOT AT YOUR CURRENT LEVEL.
PFF, YOU DON'T NEED TO BE A TRAINED PRO TO KNOW THIS SCREEN'S LAG SUCKS! MESSED UP ALL MY TIMING...
NOW, WITH PROPER GEAR I WOULD'VE ALREADY...

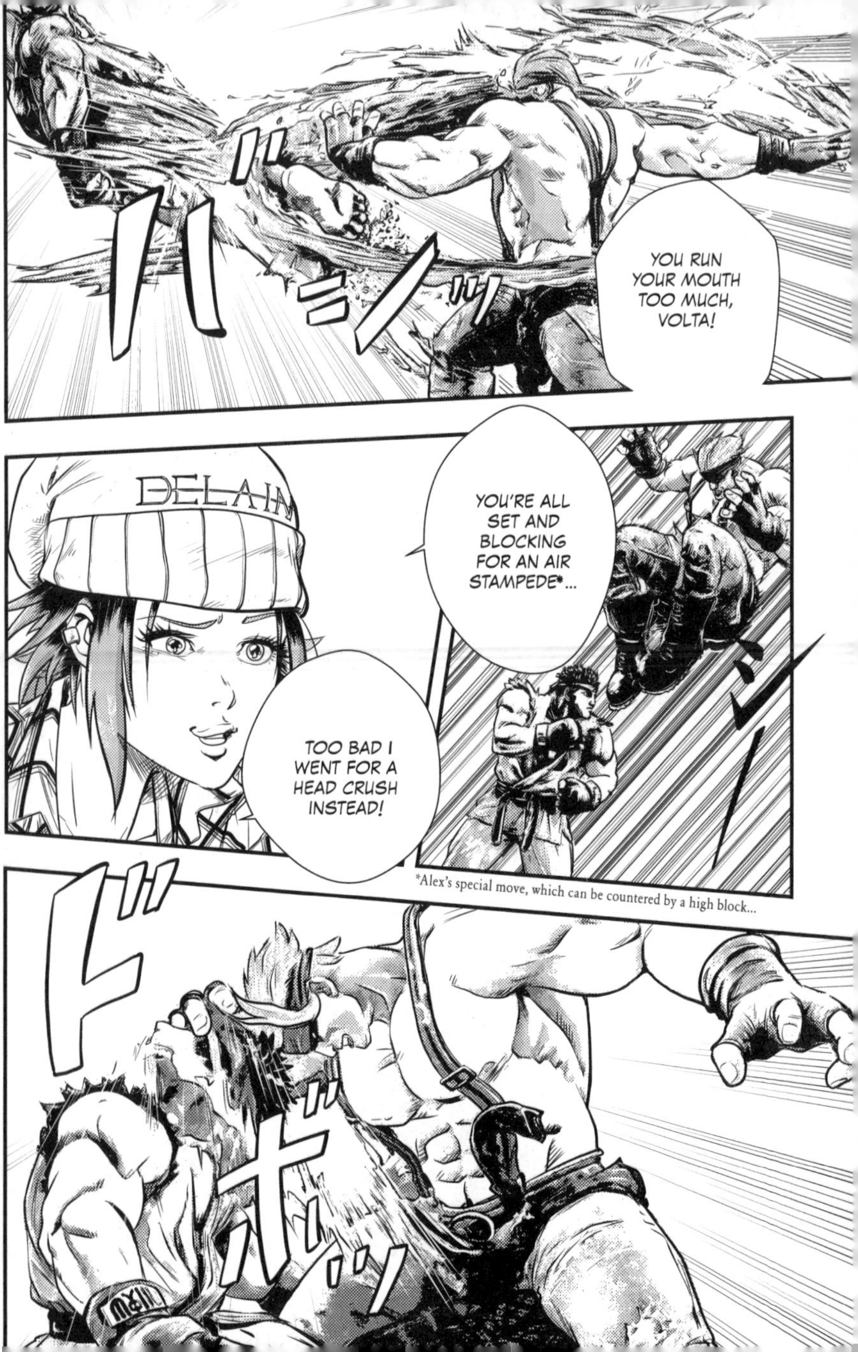
YOU RUN YOUR MOUTH TOO MUCH, VOLTA!
YOU'RE ALL SET AND BLOCKING FOR AN AIR STAMPEDE*...
TOO BAD I WENT FOR A HEAD CRUSH INSTEAD!

*Alex's special move, which can be countered by a high block...

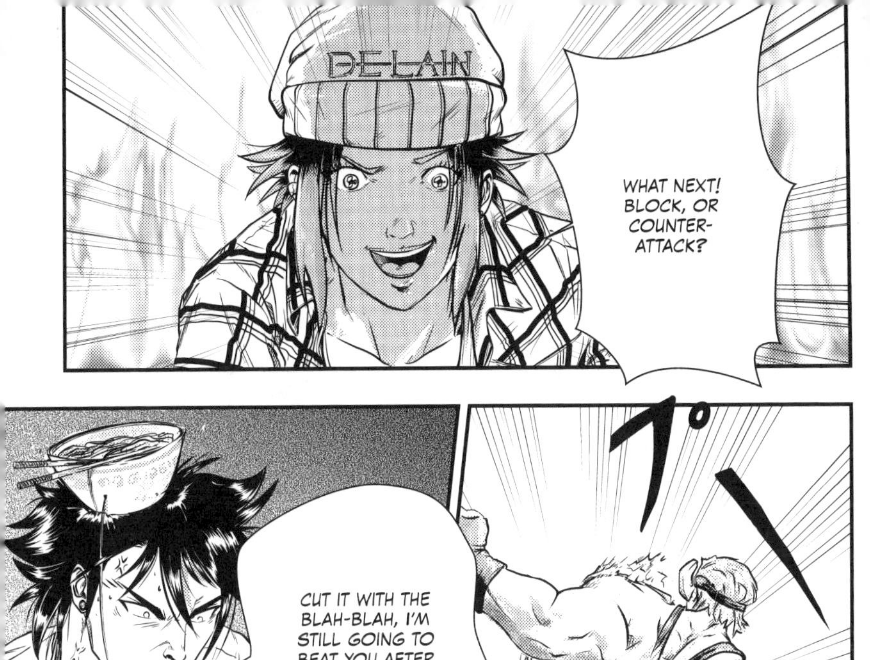
DE-LAIN
WHAT NEXT! BLOCK, OR COUNTER-ATTACK?
CUT IT WITH THE BLAH-BLAH, I'M STILL GOING TO BEAT YOU AFTER YOUR STUPID FRAME TRAP*!
PAK

*Move that retains priority on the next step, even if it is blocked.

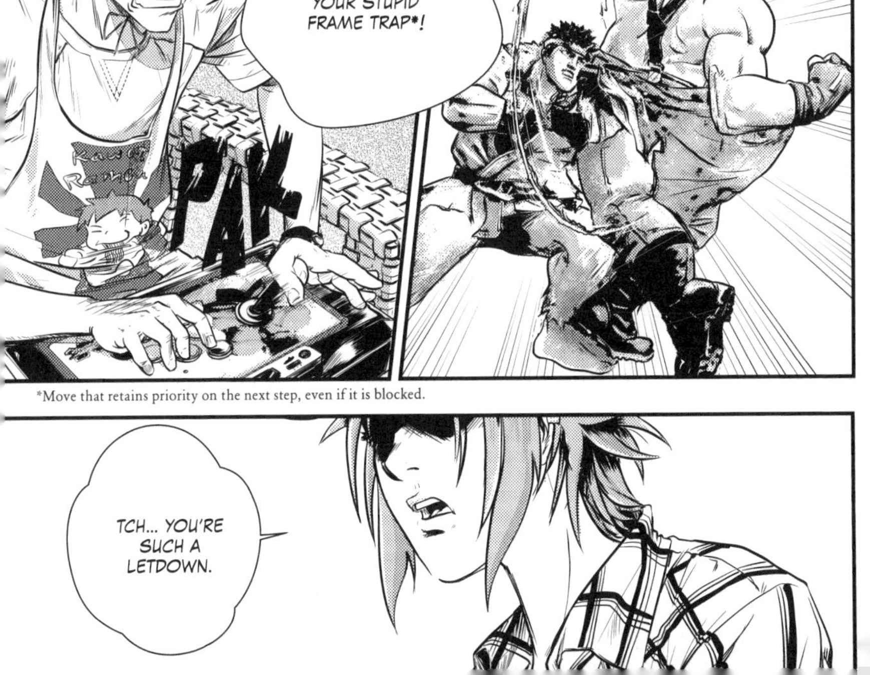
TCH... YOU'RE SUCH A LETDOWN.

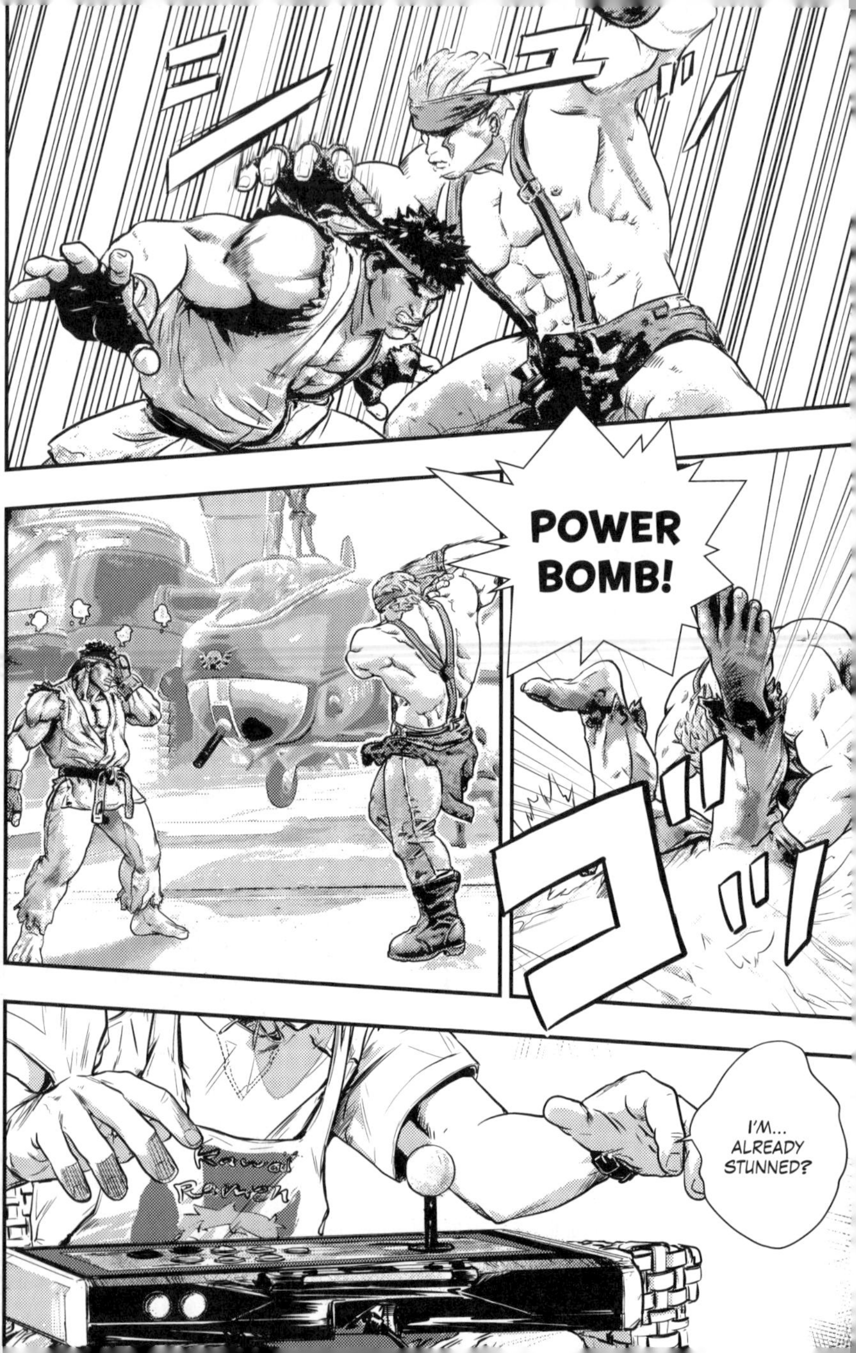
POWER BOMB!
I'M... ALREADY STUNNED?

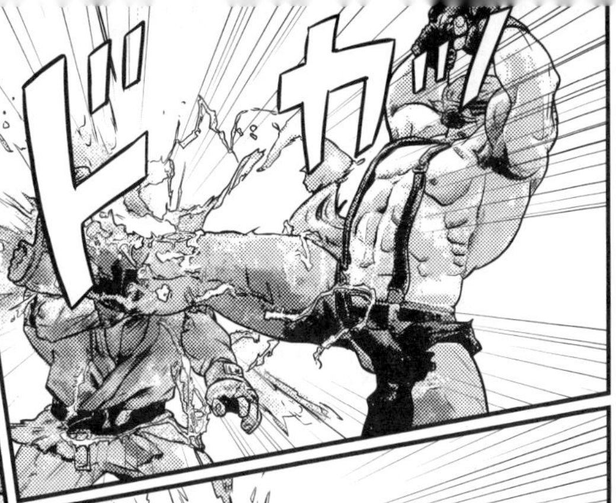
ドカッ!!
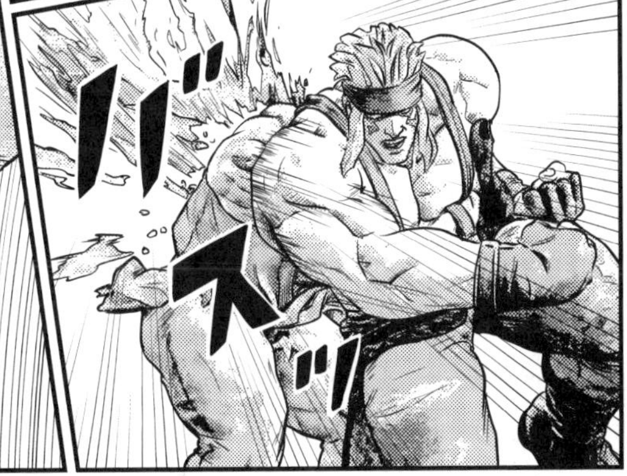
バズッ
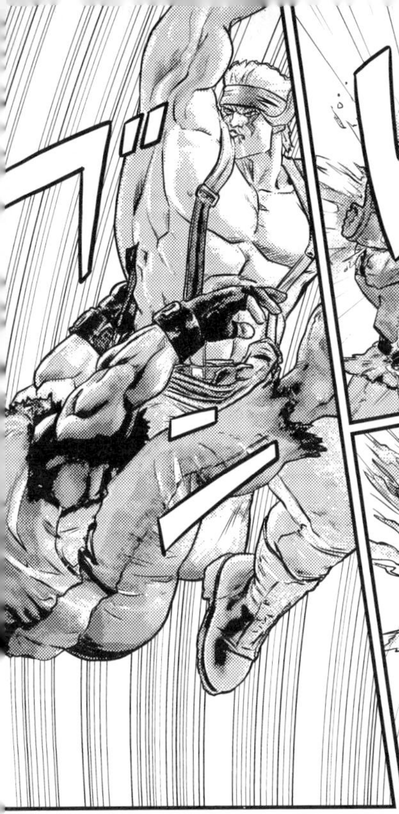
ブーー
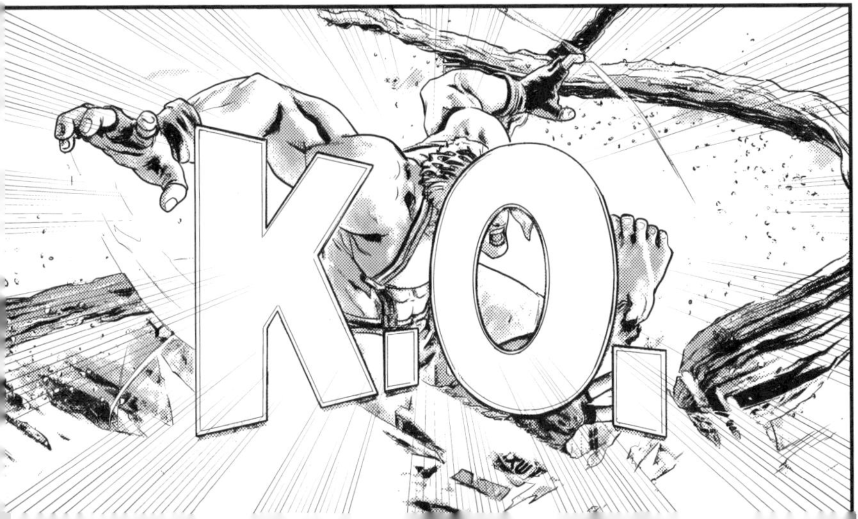
K.O.

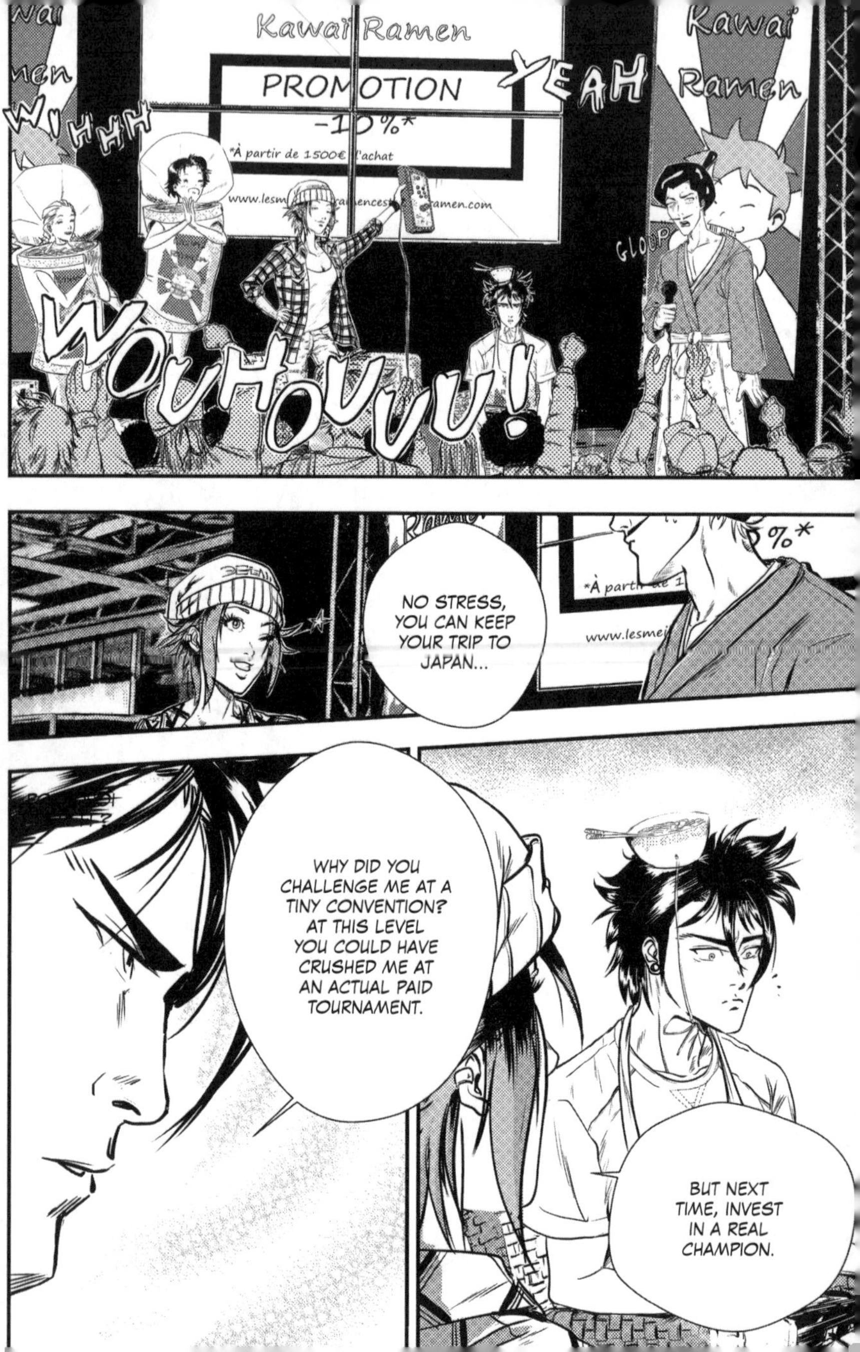
Kawai Ramen
YEAH
Kawai Ramen
PROMOTION
-10%*
WIHHH
GLOUP
WOUHOUUUU!
NO STRESS, YOU CAN KEEP YOUR TRIP TO JAPAN...
BUT NEXT TIME, INVEST IN A REAL CHAMPION.
WHY DID YOU CHALLENGE ME AT A TINY CONVENTION? AT THIS LEVEL YOU COULD HAVE CRUSHED ME AT AN ACTUAL PAID TOURNAMENT.

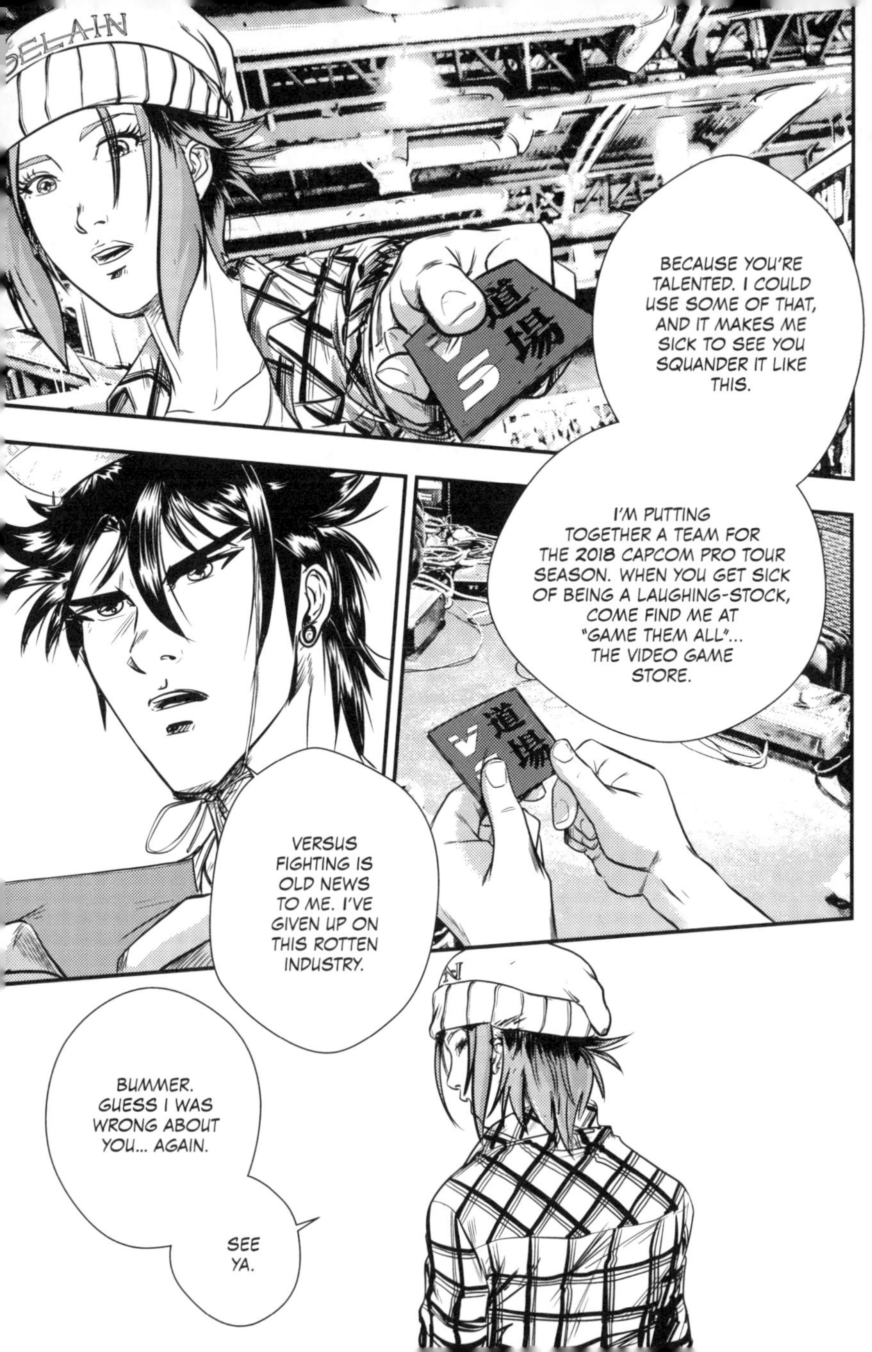
BECAUSE YOU'RE TALENTED. I COULD USE SOME OF THAT, AND IT MAKES ME SICK TO SEE YOU SQUANDER IT LIKE THIS.
I'M PUTTING TOGETHER A TEAM FOR THE 2018 CAPCOM PRO TOUR SEASON. WHEN YOU GET SICK OF BEING A LAUGHING-STOCK, COME FIND ME AT "GAME THEM ALL"... THE VIDEO GAME STORE.
道場
VERSUS FIGHTING IS OLD NEWS TO ME. I'VE GIVEN UP ON THIS ROTTEN INDUSTRY.
BUMMER. GUESS I WAS WRONG ABOUT YOU... AGAIN.
SEE YA.

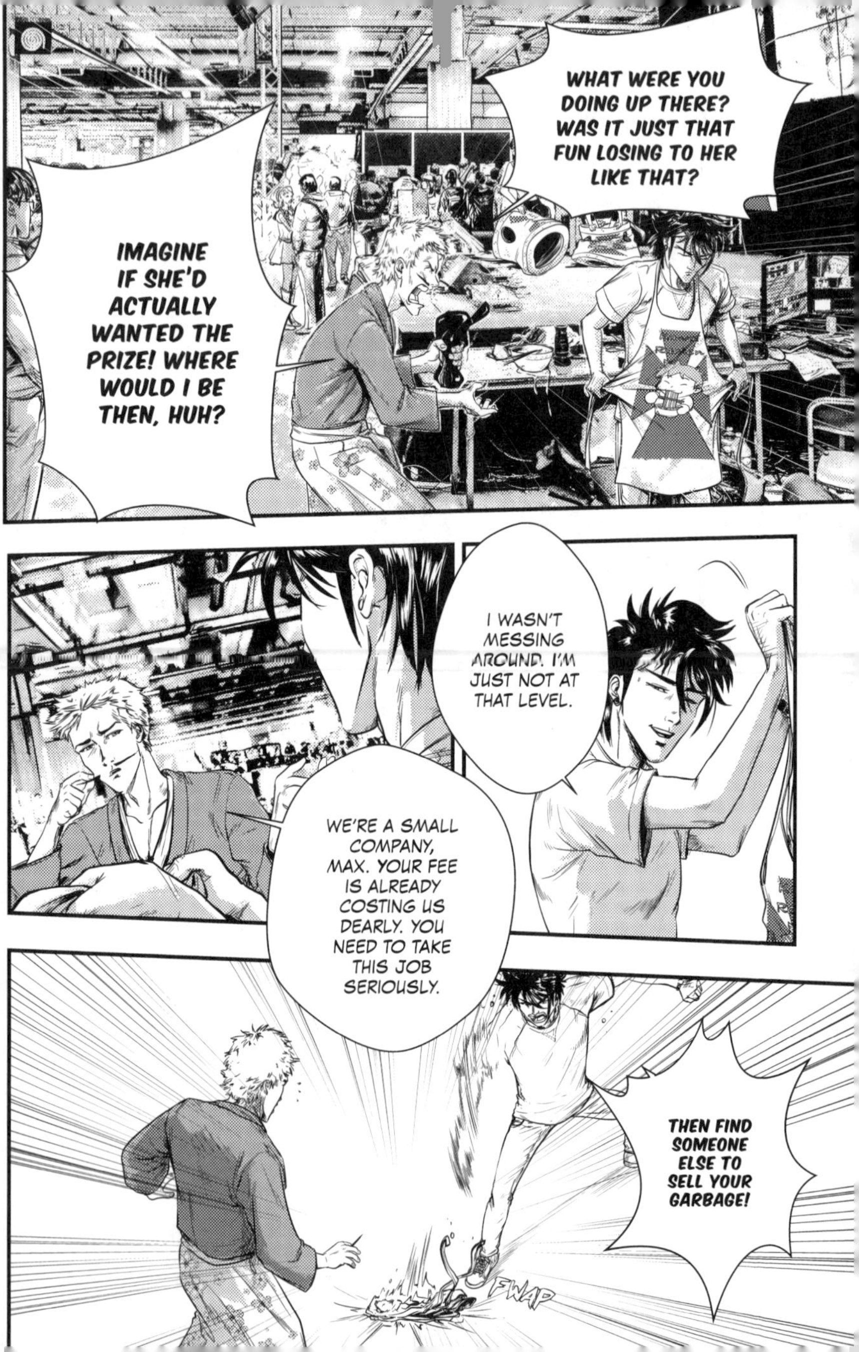
WHAT WERE YOU DOING UP THERE? WAS IT JUST THAT FUN LOSING TO HER LIKE THAT?
IMAGINE IF SHE'D ACTUALLY WANTED THE PRIZE! WHERE WOULD I BE THEN, HUH?
I WASN'T MESSING AROUND. I'M JUST NOT AT THAT LEVEL.
WE'RE A SMALL COMPANY, MAX. YOUR FEE IS ALREADY COSTING US DEARLY. YOU NEED TO TAKE THIS JOB SERIOUSLY.
THEN FIND SOMEONE ELSE TO SELL YOUR GARBAGE!
FWAP

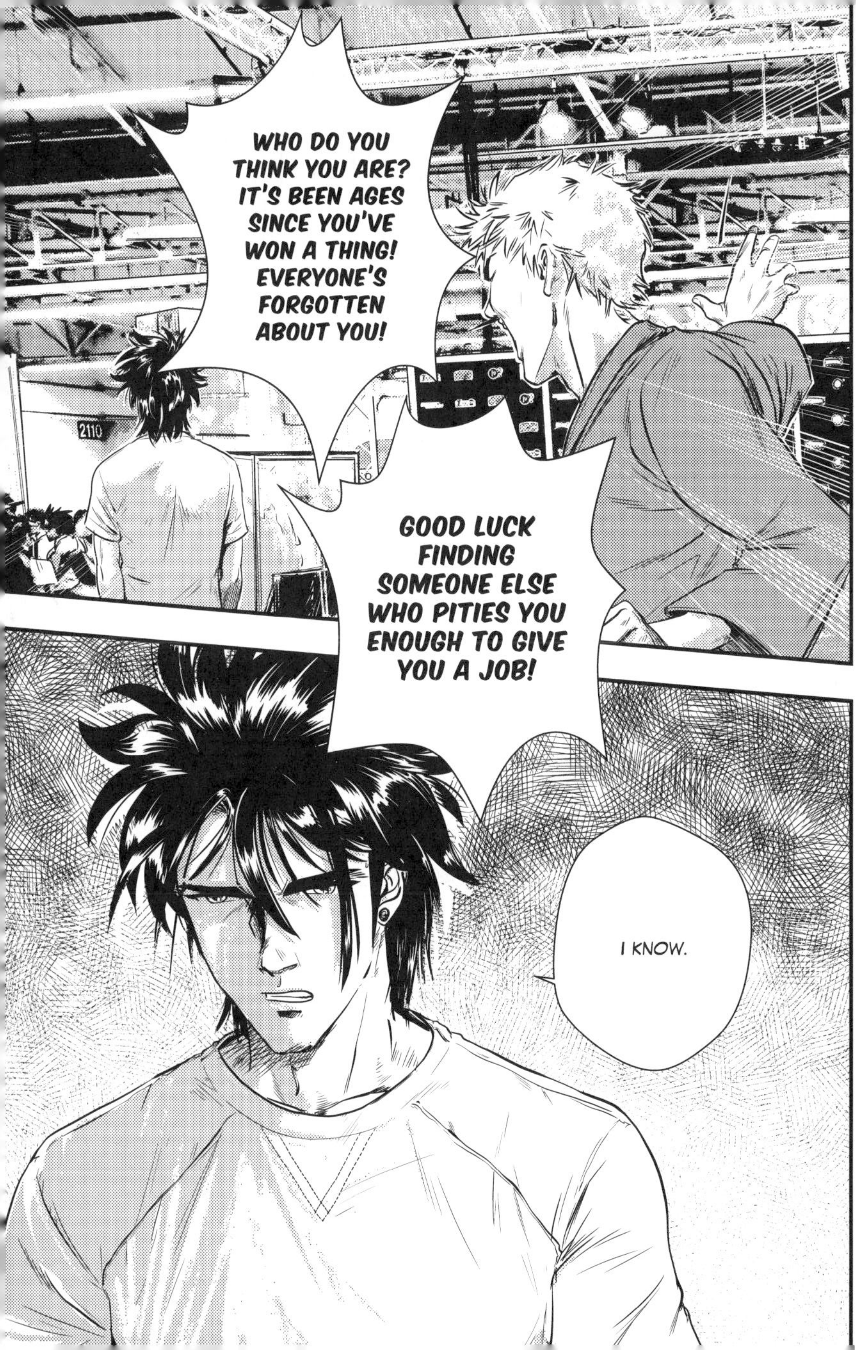
WHO DO YOU THINK YOU ARE? IT'S BEEN AGES SINCE YOU'VE WON A THING! EVERYONE'S FORGOTTEN ABOUT YOU!
2110
GOOD LUCK FINDING SOMEONE ELSE WHO PITIES YOU ENOUGH TO GIVE YOU A JOB!
I KNOW.

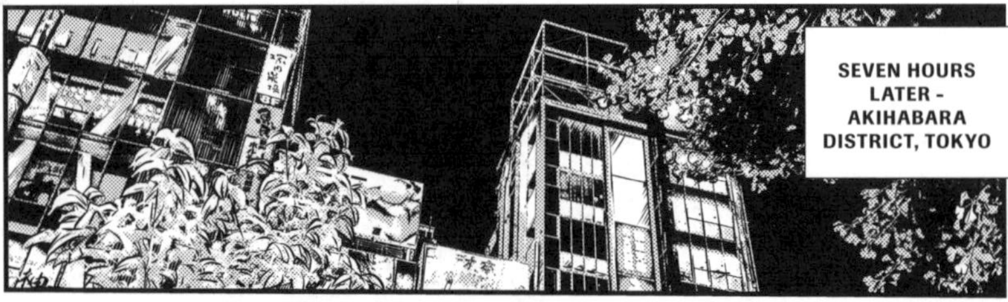
SEVEN HOURS LATER - AKIHABARA DISTRICT, TOKYO
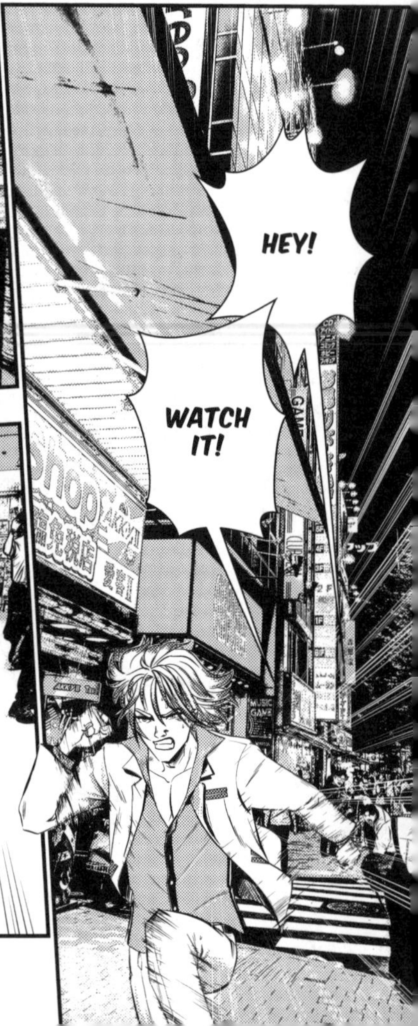
HEY!
WATCH IT!
Shop
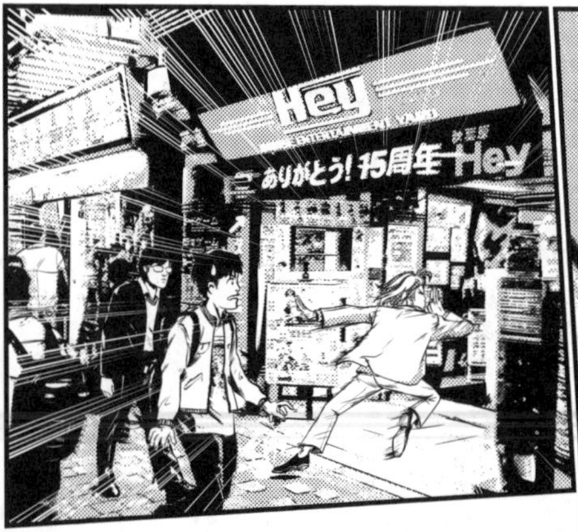
Hey
ありがとう! 15周年 Hey
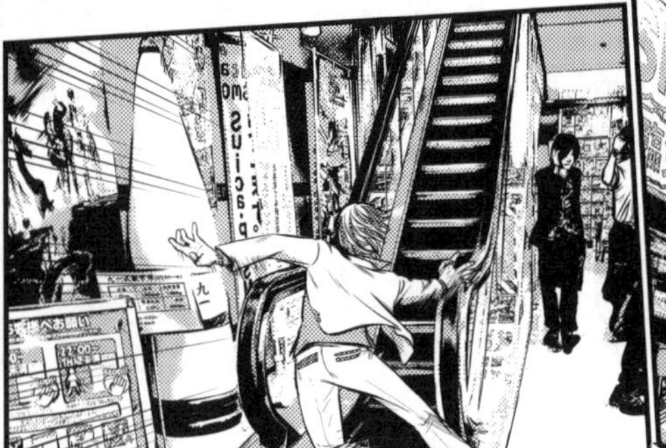

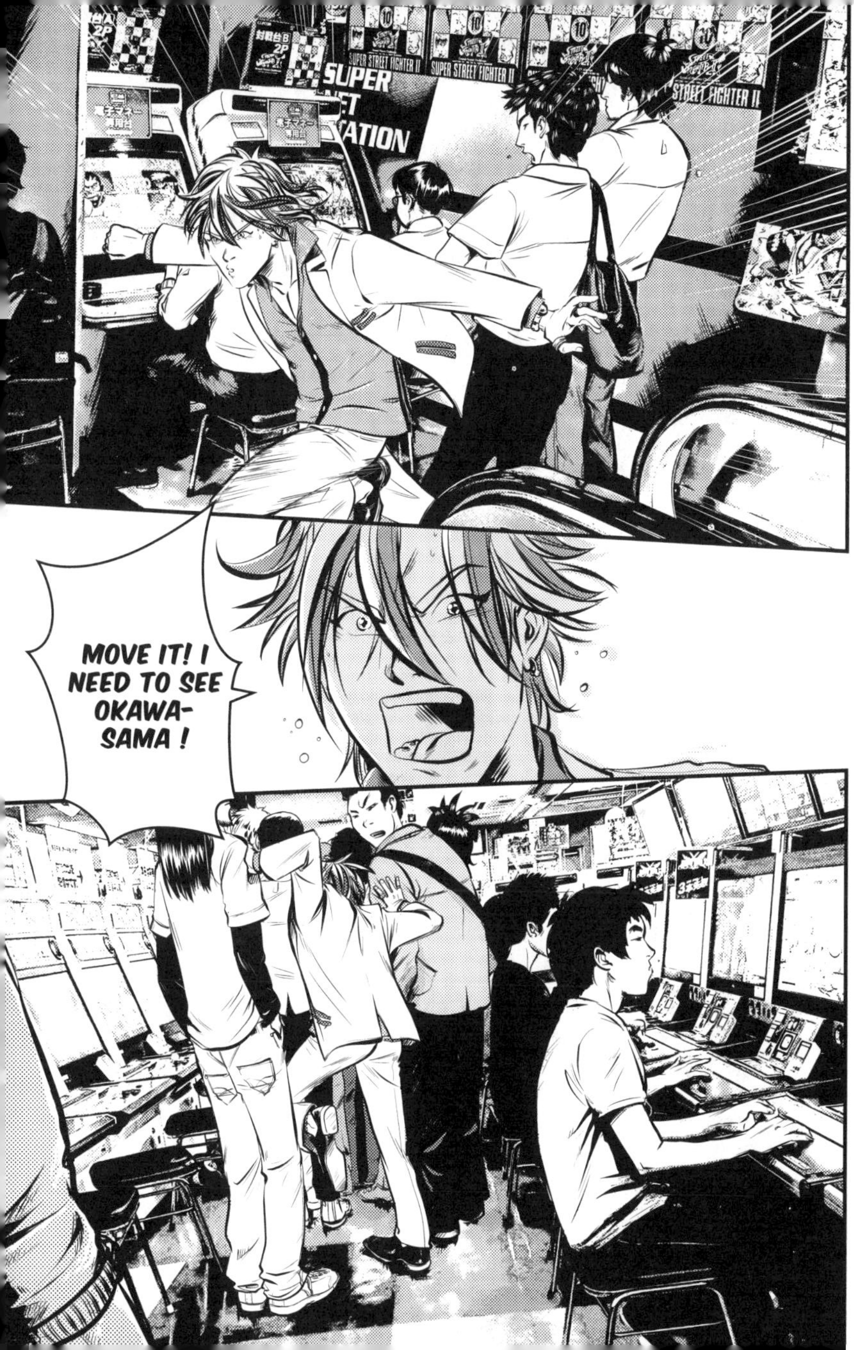
SUPER STREET FIGHTER II
SUPER STREET FIGHTER II
STREET FIGHTER II
MOVE IT! I NEED TO SEE OKAWA-SAMA !

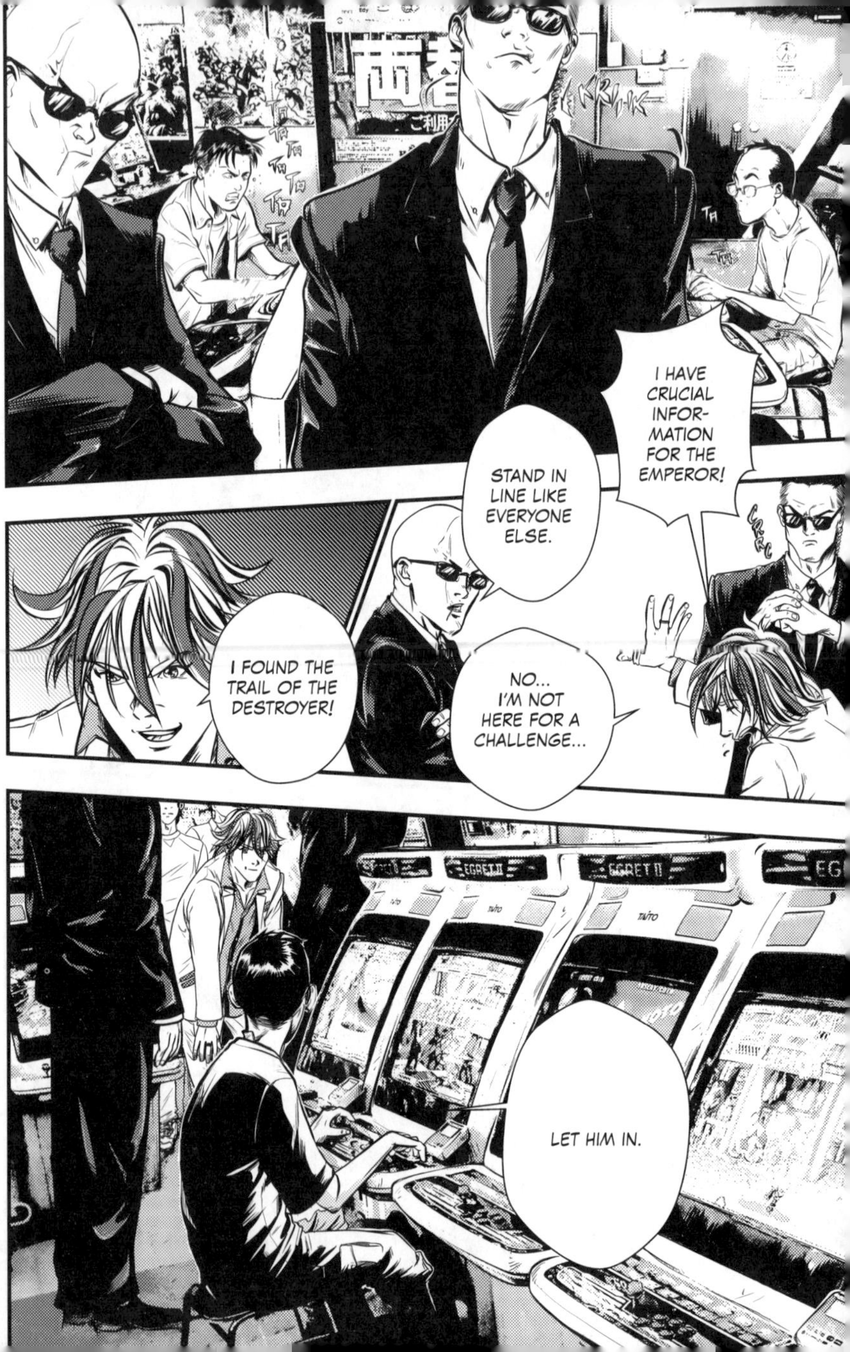
KRIIK
TA TA TA TA TA TA TA
TA
I HAVE CRUCIAL INFOR-MATION FOR THE EMPEROR!
CRRC
STAND IN LINE LIKE EVERYONE ELSE.
NO... I'M NOT HERE FOR A CHALLENGE...
I FOUND THE TRAIL OF THE DESTROYER!
EGRET II
EGRET II
LET HIM IN.

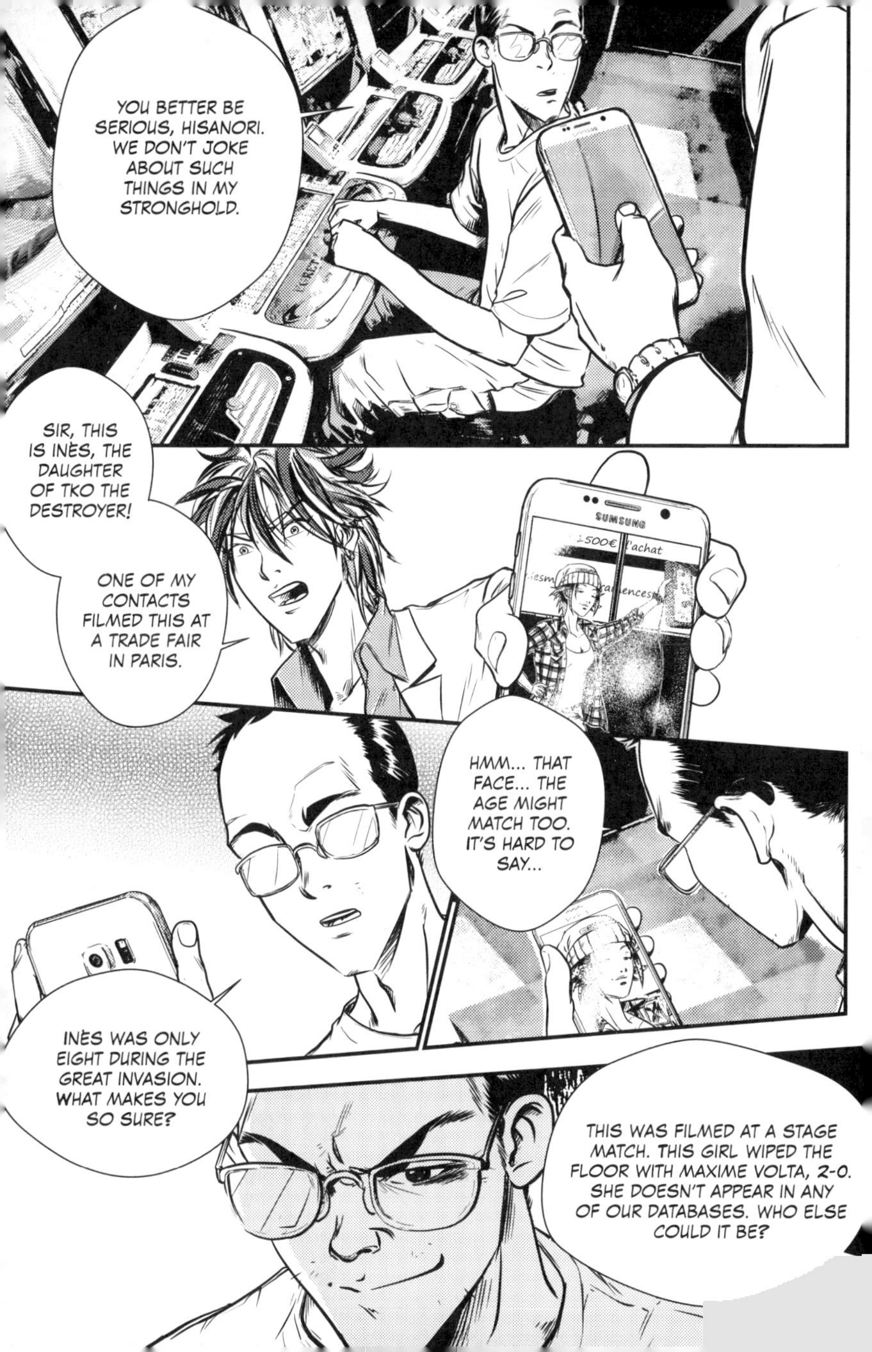
YOU BETTER BE SERIOUS, HISANORI. WE DON'T JOKE ABOUT SUCH THINGS IN MY STRONGHOLD.
SIR, THIS IS INÈS, THE DAUGHTER OF TKO THE DESTROYER!
ONE OF MY CONTACTS FILMED THIS AT A TRADE FAIR IN PARIS.
SUMSUNG
HMM... THAT FACE... THE AGE MIGHT MATCH TOO. IT'S HARD TO SAY...
INÈS WAS ONLY EIGHT DURING THE GREAT INVASION. WHAT MAKES YOU SO SURE?
THIS WAS FILMED AT A STAGE MATCH. THIS GIRL WIPED THE FLOOR WITH MAXIME VOLTA, 2-0. SHE DOESN'T APPEAR IN ANY OF OUR DATABASES. WHO ELSE COULD IT BE?

CHARACTER SELECT!

OKAWA TAKASHIMA

THE SECOND EMPEROR

BACKGROUND

Okawa is the Second Emperor of Fighting Games, a title given only to the greatest players of all time. Born in Tokyo, he cut his teeth on Arcade Street Fighter II in 1991. Legend has it that he already looked like a 45-year-old salaryman at the time,

From 2000 to 2003, Okawa reigned supreme over the Tougeki Super Battle Opera (the region's premiere arcade tournament) at Street Fighter III: Third Strike. He did not lose a single round in three years, which caught the attention of the First Emperor, who then offered him to be his successor,,,

For reasons unknown, Okawa has pursued a single goal for a decade: to challenge the legendary player TKO the Destroyer... but no one knows where he is hiding!

VERSUS FIGHTING STORY

CHARACTER DESIGN

Okawa has a completely unremarkable, mundane appearance. He could be any random guy, or a badly dressed salaryman, small and unassuming. Having been in comics for a while, I admit I still have a hard time making him as skinny as he should be...

BY KALON

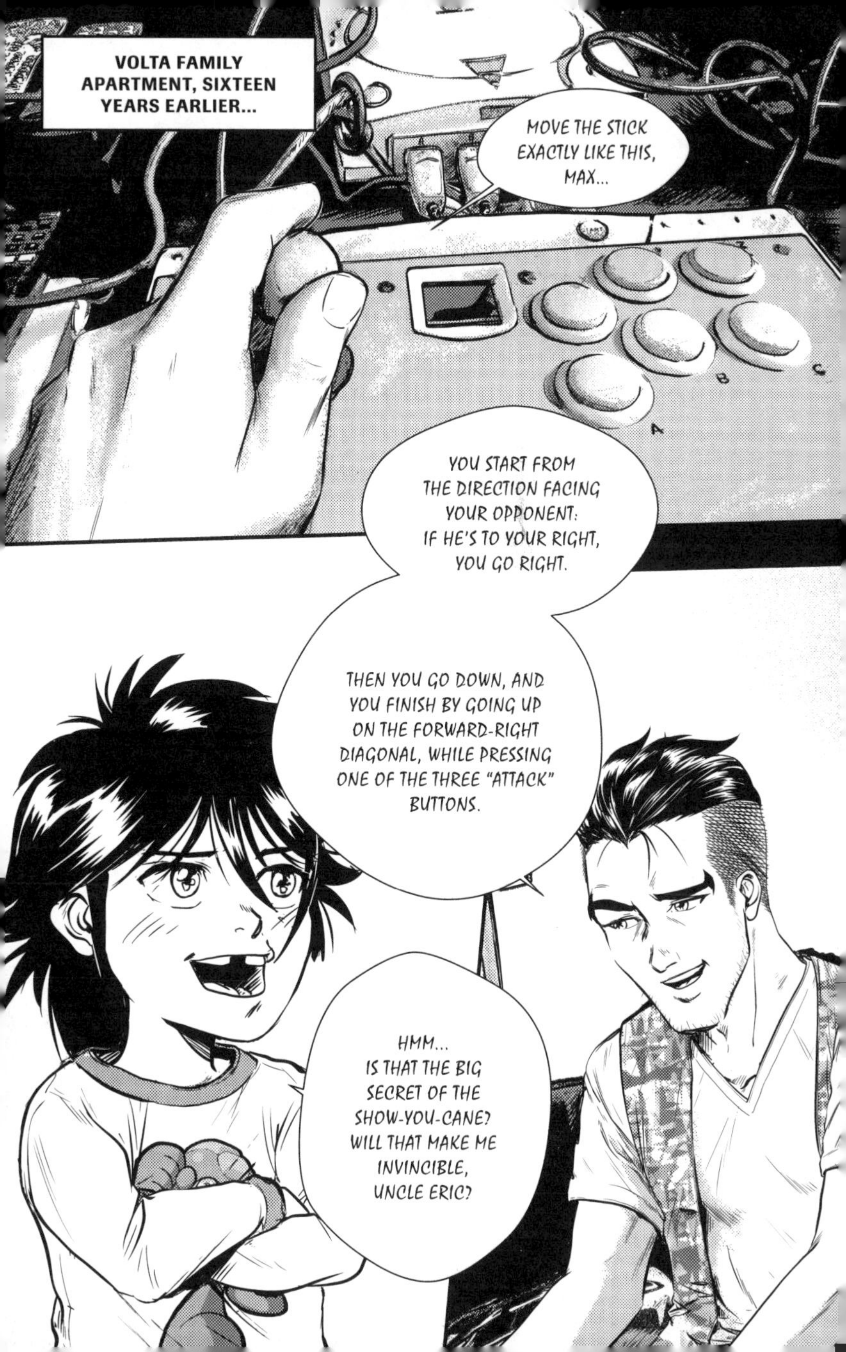
VOLTA FAMILY APARTMENT, SIXTEEN YEARS EARLIER...
MOVE THE STICK EXACTLY LIKE THIS, MAX...
YOU START FROM THE DIRECTION FACING YOUR OPPONENT: IF HE'S TO YOUR RIGHT, YOU GO RIGHT.
THEN YOU GO DOWN, AND YOU FINISH BY GOING UP ON THE FORWARD-RIGHT DIAGONAL, WHILE PRESSING ONE OF THE THREE "ATTACK" BUTTONS.
HMM... IS THAT THE BIG SECRET OF THE SHOW-YOU-CANE? WILL THAT MAKE ME INVINCIBLE, UNCLE ERIC?

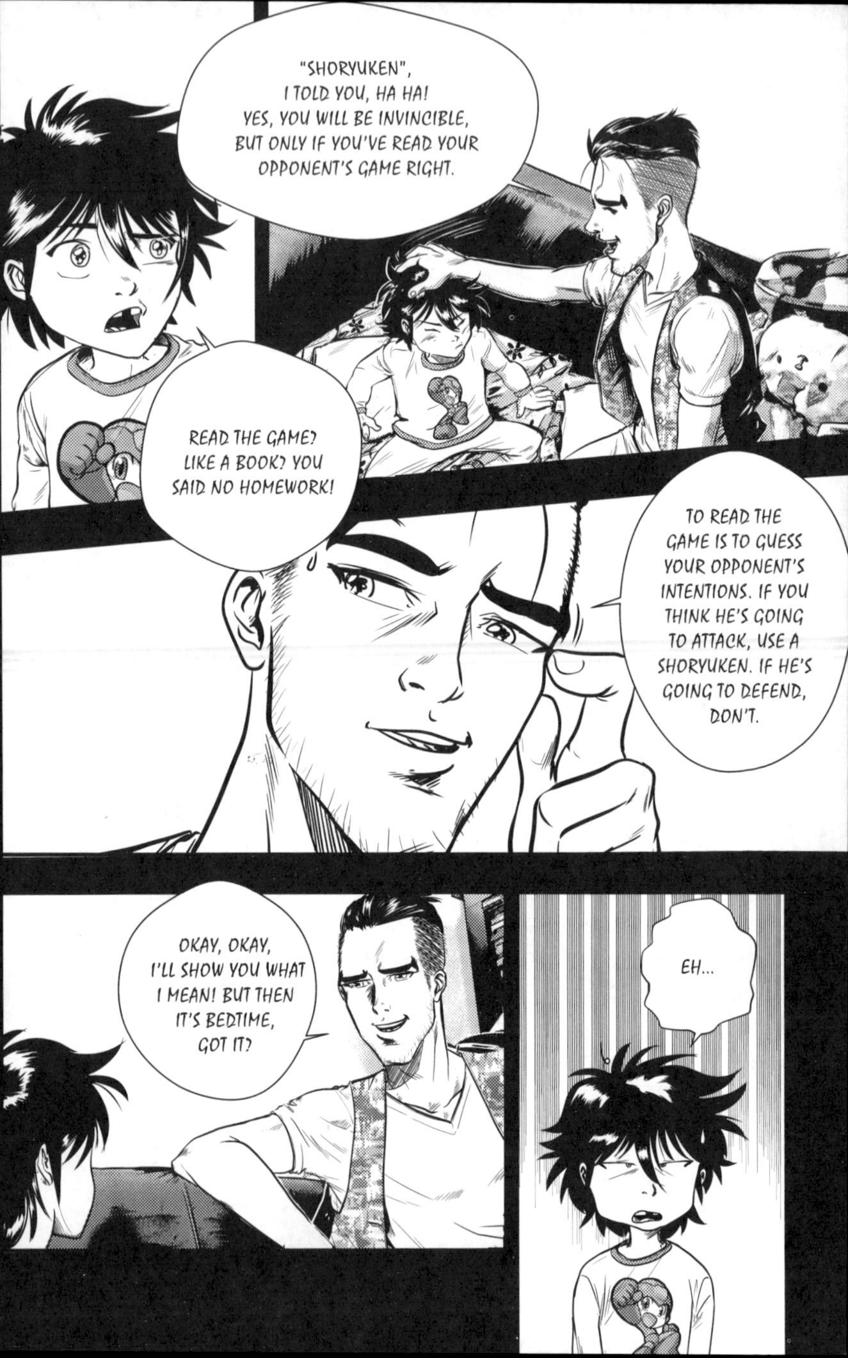
"SHORYUKEN", I TOLD YOU, HA HA! YES, YOU WILL BE INVINCIBLE, BUT ONLY IF YOU'VE READ YOUR OPPONENT'S GAME RIGHT.
READ THE GAME? LIKE A BOOK? YOU SAID NO HOMEWORK!
TO READ THE GAME IS TO GUESS YOUR OPPONENT'S INTENTIONS. IF YOU THINK HE'S GOING TO ATTACK, USE A SHORYUKEN. IF HE'S GOING TO DEFEND, DON'T.
OKAY, OKAY, I'LL SHOW YOU WHAT I MEAN! BUT THEN IT'S BEDTIME, GOT IT?
EH...

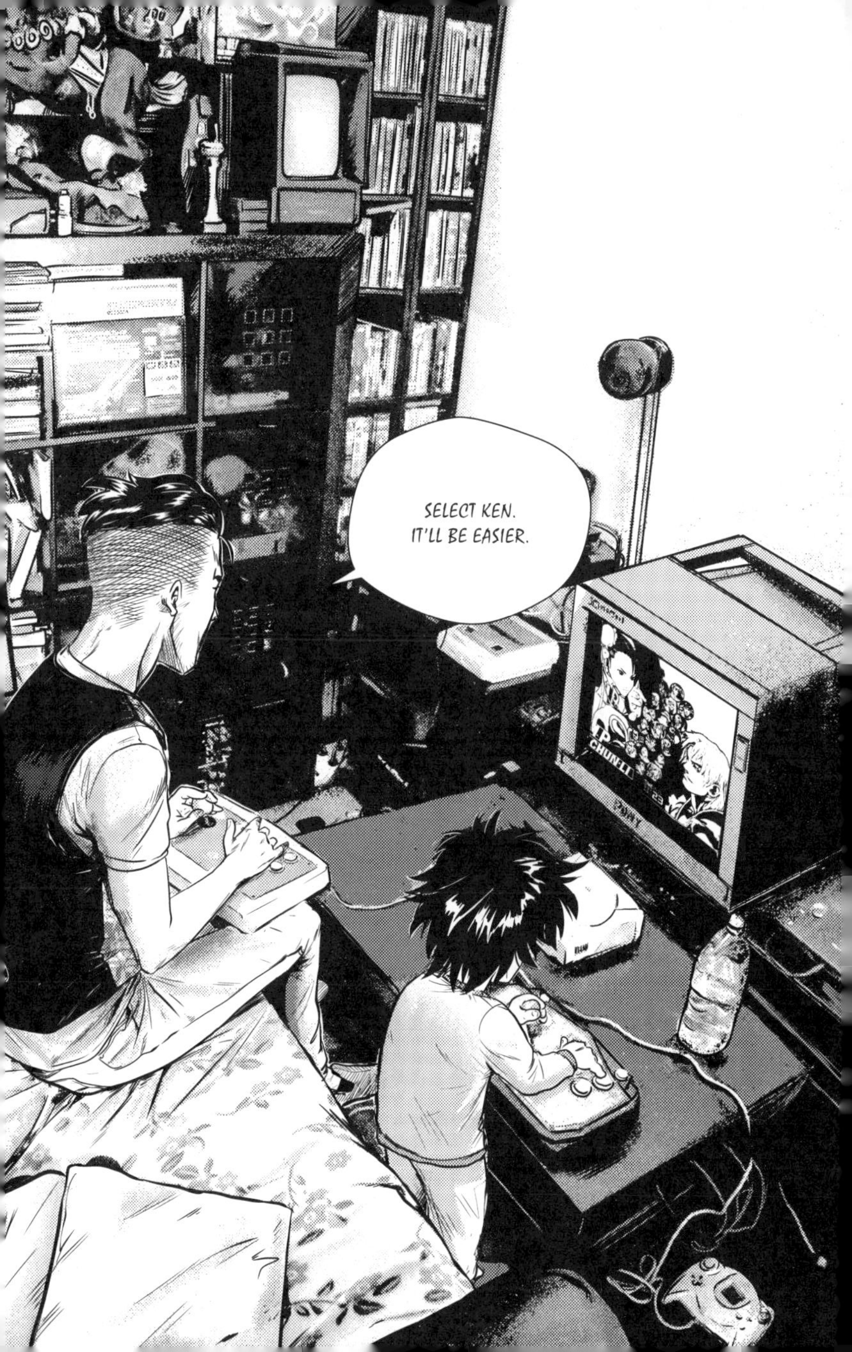
SELECT KEN.
IT'LL BE EASIER.

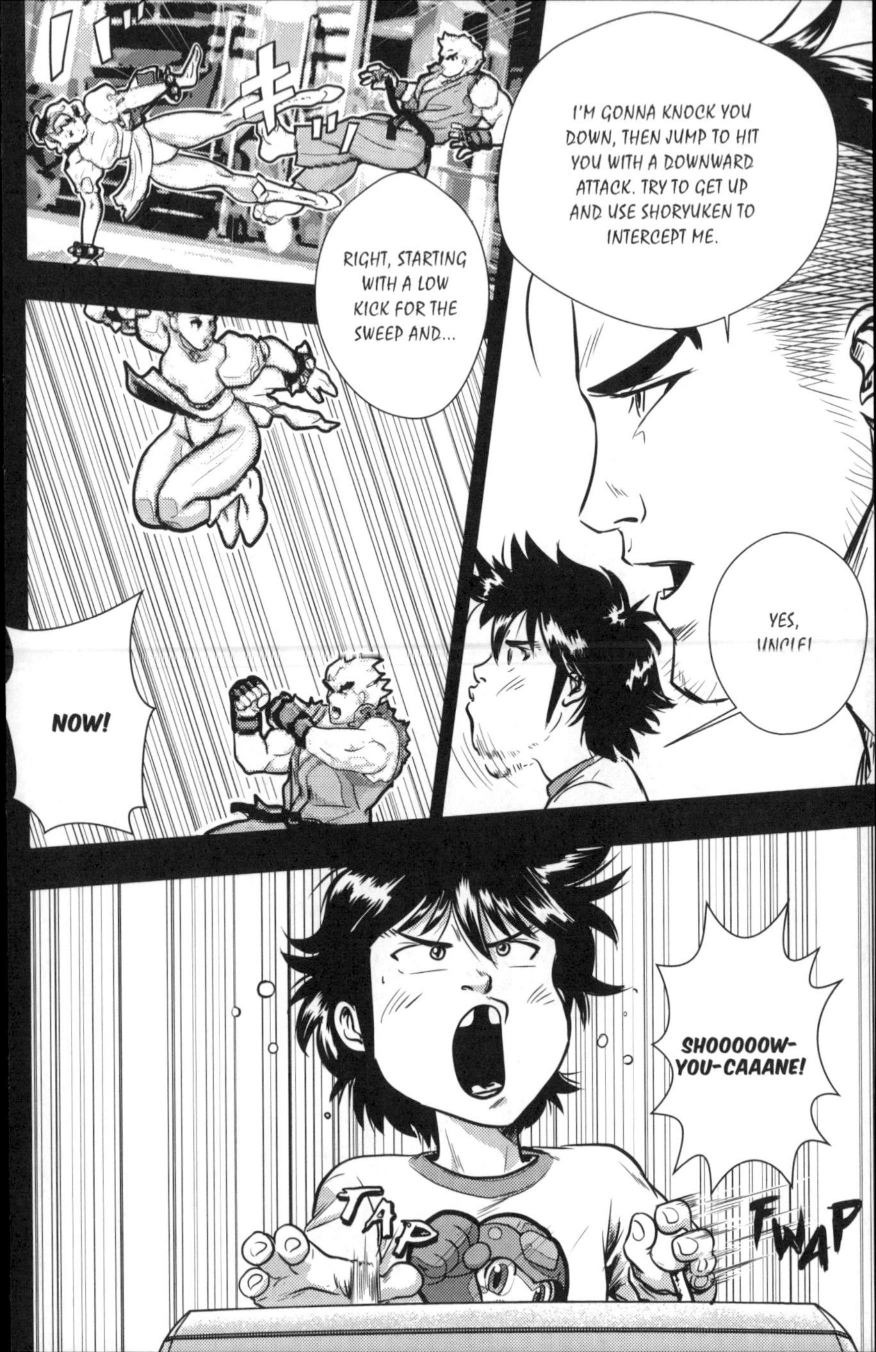
I'M GONNA KNOCK YOU DOWN, THEN JUMP TO HIT YOU WITH A DOWNWARD ATTACK. TRY TO GET UP AND USE SHORYUKEN TO INTERCEPT ME.
YES, UNCLE!
RIGHT, STARTING WITH A LOW KICK FOR THE SWEEP AND...
NOW!
SHOOOOOW-YOU-CAAANE!
FWAP
TAP

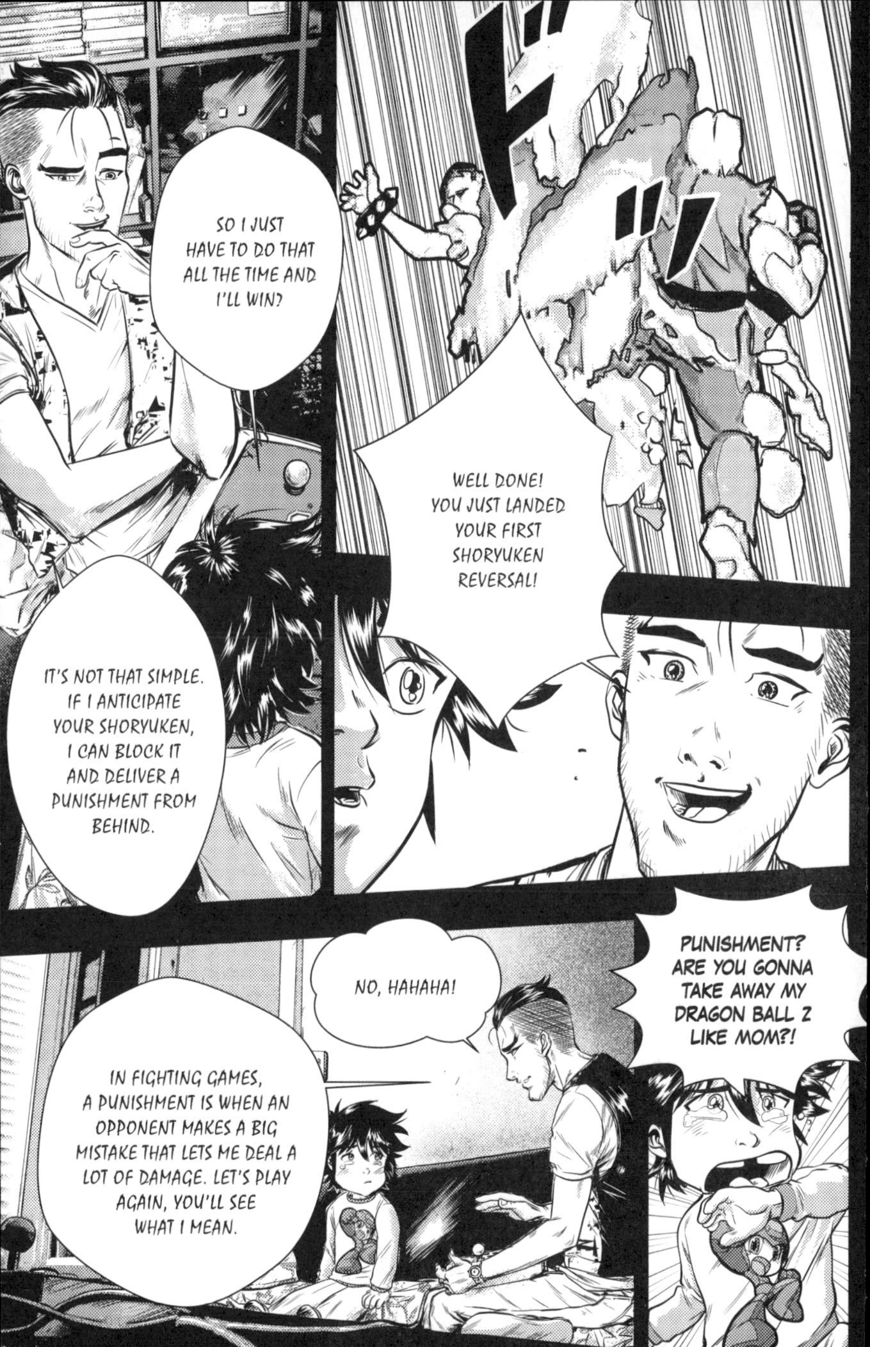
WELL DONE! YOU JUST LANDED YOUR FIRST SHORYUKEN REVERSAL!
SO I JUST HAVE TO DO THAT ALL THE TIME AND I'LL WIN?
IT'S NOT THAT SIMPLE. IF I ANTICIPATE YOUR SHORYUKEN, I CAN BLOCK IT AND DELIVER A PUNISHMENT FROM BEHIND.
PUNISHMENT? ARE YOU GONNA TAKE AWAY MY DRAGON BALL Z LIKE MOM?!
NO, HAHAHA!
IN FIGHTING GAMES, A PUNISHMENT IS WHEN AN OPPONENT MAKES A BIG MISTAKE THAT LETS ME DEAL A LOT OF DAMAGE. LET'S PLAY AGAIN, YOU'LL SEE WHAT I MEAN.

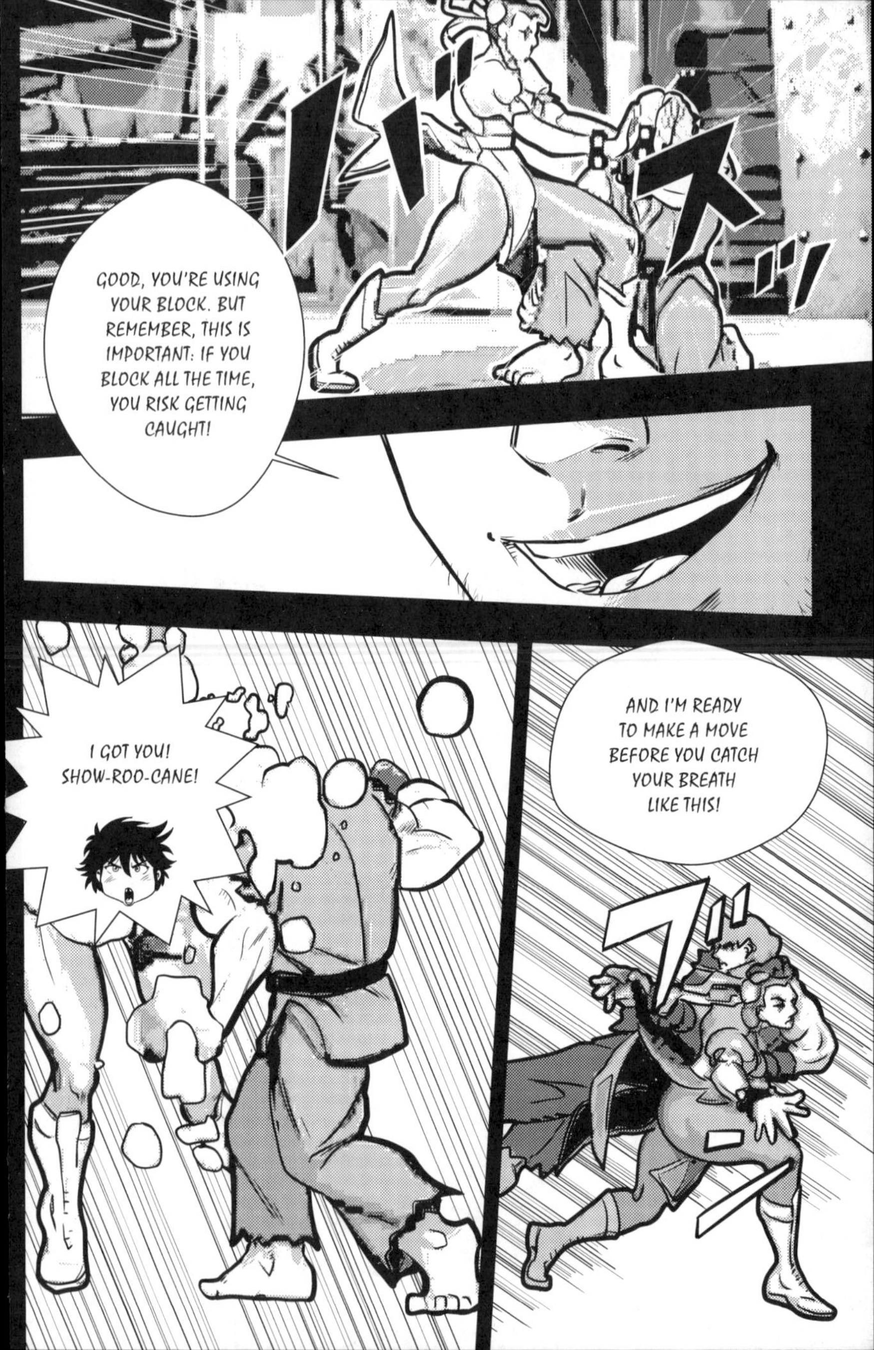
GOOD, YOU'RE USING YOUR BLOCK. BUT REMEMBER, THIS IS IMPORTANT: IF YOU BLOCK ALL THE TIME, YOU RISK GETTING CAUGHT!
AND I'M READY TO MAKE A MOVE BEFORE YOU CATCH YOUR BREATH LIKE THIS!
I GOT YOU! SHOW-ROO-CANE!

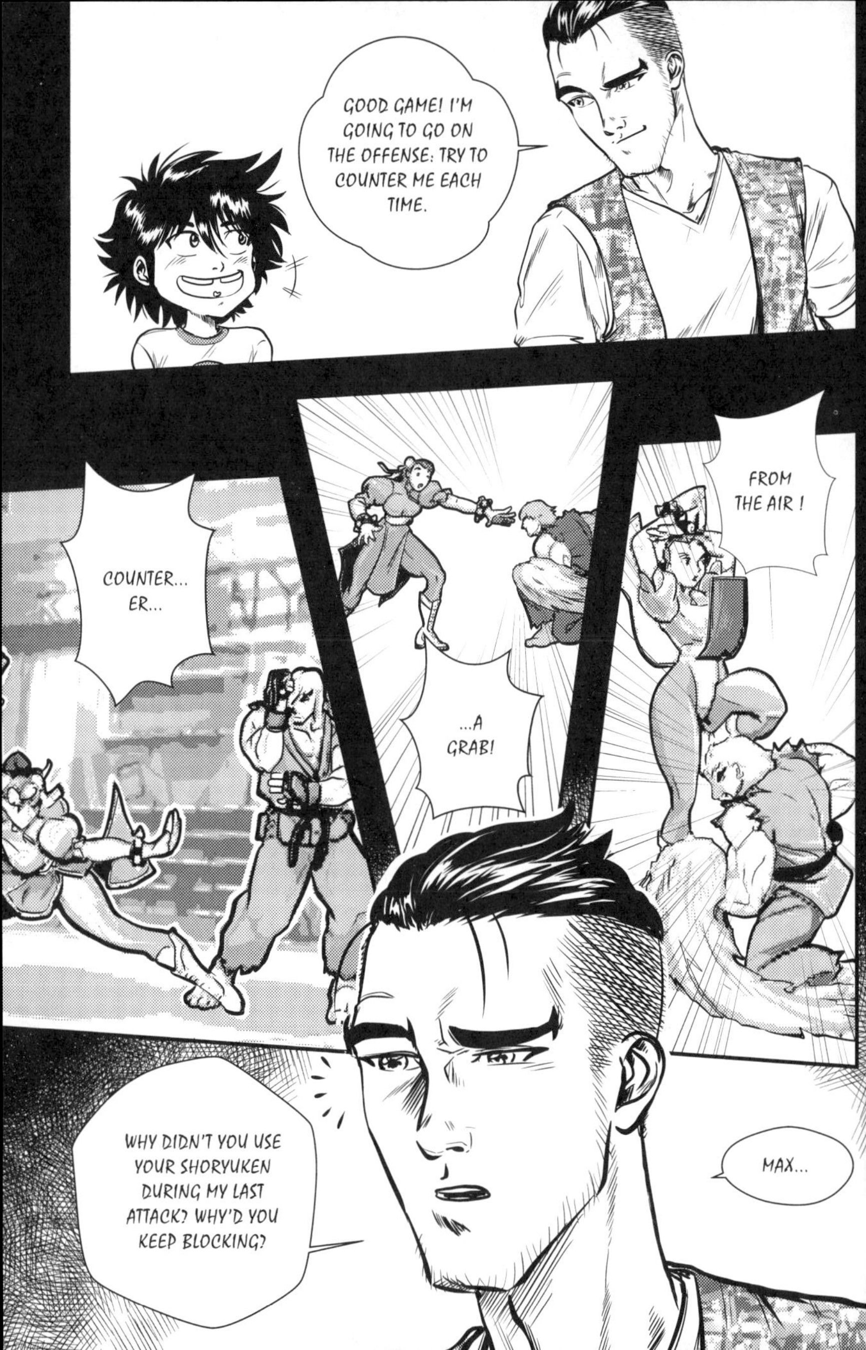
GOOD GAME! I'M GOING TO GO ON THE OFFENSE: TRY TO COUNTER ME EACH TIME.
COUNTER... ER...
...A GRAB!
FROM THE AIR !
WHY DIDN'T YOU USE YOUR SHORYUKEN DURING MY LAST ATTACK? WHY'D YOU KEEP BLOCKING?
MAX...

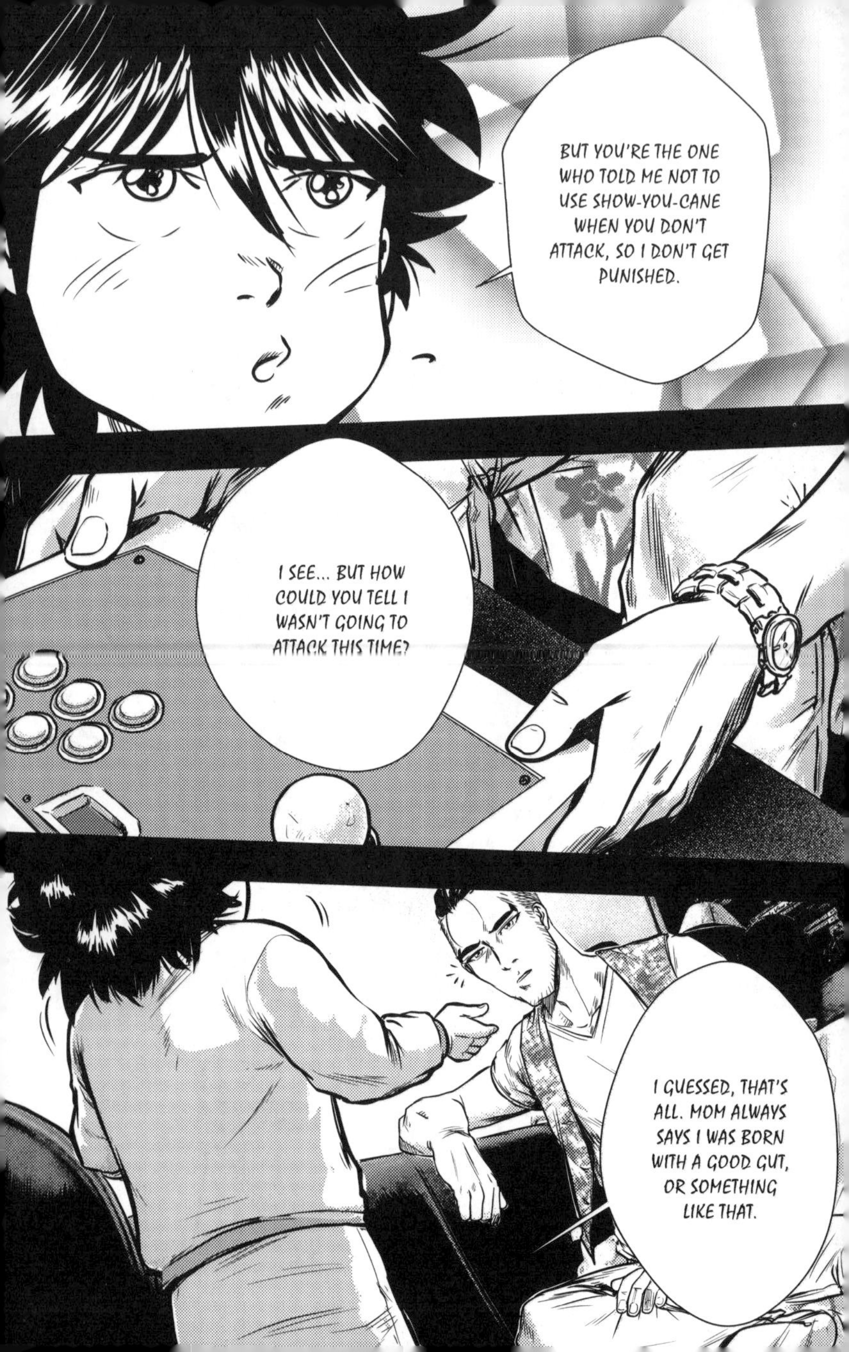
BUT YOU'RE THE ONE WHO TOLD ME NOT TO USE SHOW-YOU-CANE WHEN YOU DON'T ATTACK, SO I DON'T GET PUNISHED.
I SEE... BUT HOW COULD YOU TELL I WASN'T GOING TO ATTACK THIS TIME?
I GUESSED, THAT'S ALL. MOM ALWAYS SAYS I WAS BORN WITH A GOOD GUT, OR SOMETHING LIKE THAT.

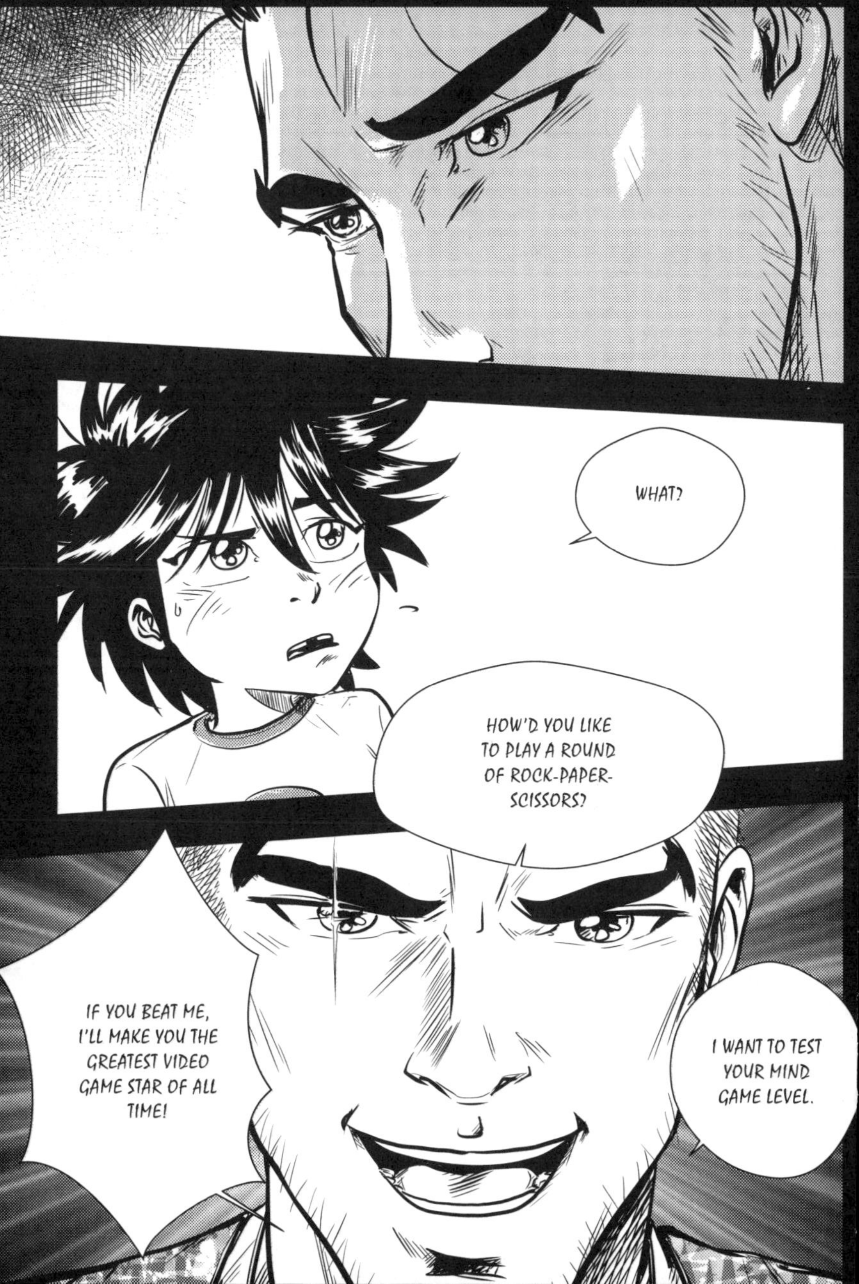
WHAT?
HOW'D YOU LIKE TO PLAY A ROUND OF ROCK-PAPER-SCISSORS?
I WANT TO TEST YOUR MIND GAME LEVEL.
IF YOU BEAT ME, I'LL MAKE YOU THE GREATEST VIDEO GAME STAR OF ALL TIME!

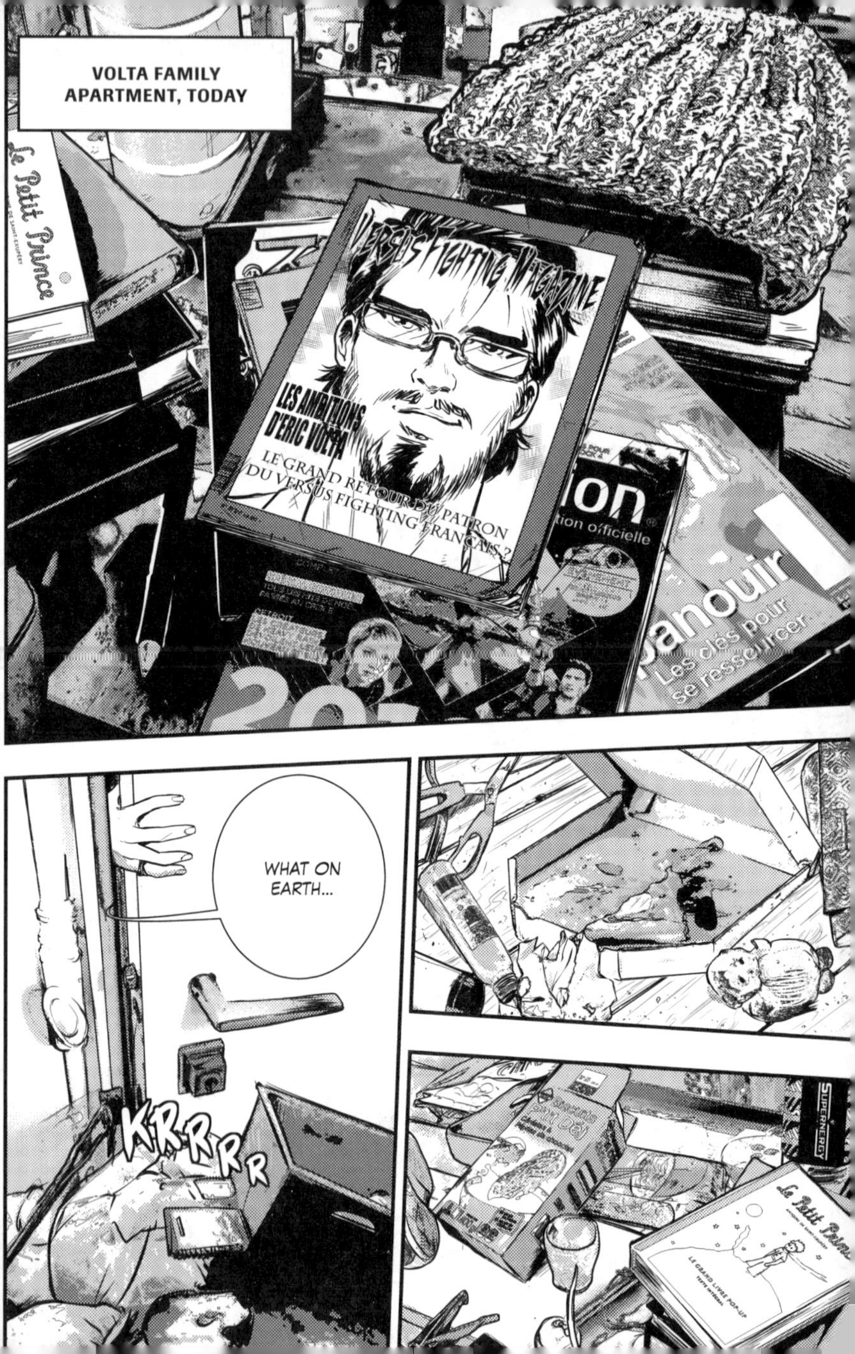
VOLTA FAMILY APARTMENT, TODAY
Le Petit Prince
VERSUS FIGHTING MAGAZINE
LES AMBITIONS D'ERIC VOLTA
LE GRAND RETOUR DU PATRON DU VERSUS FIGHTING FRANÇAIS ?
tion officielle
Les clés pour se ressourcer
Le Petit Prince
LE GRAND LIVRE POP-UP
WHAT ON EARTH...
KRRRRR

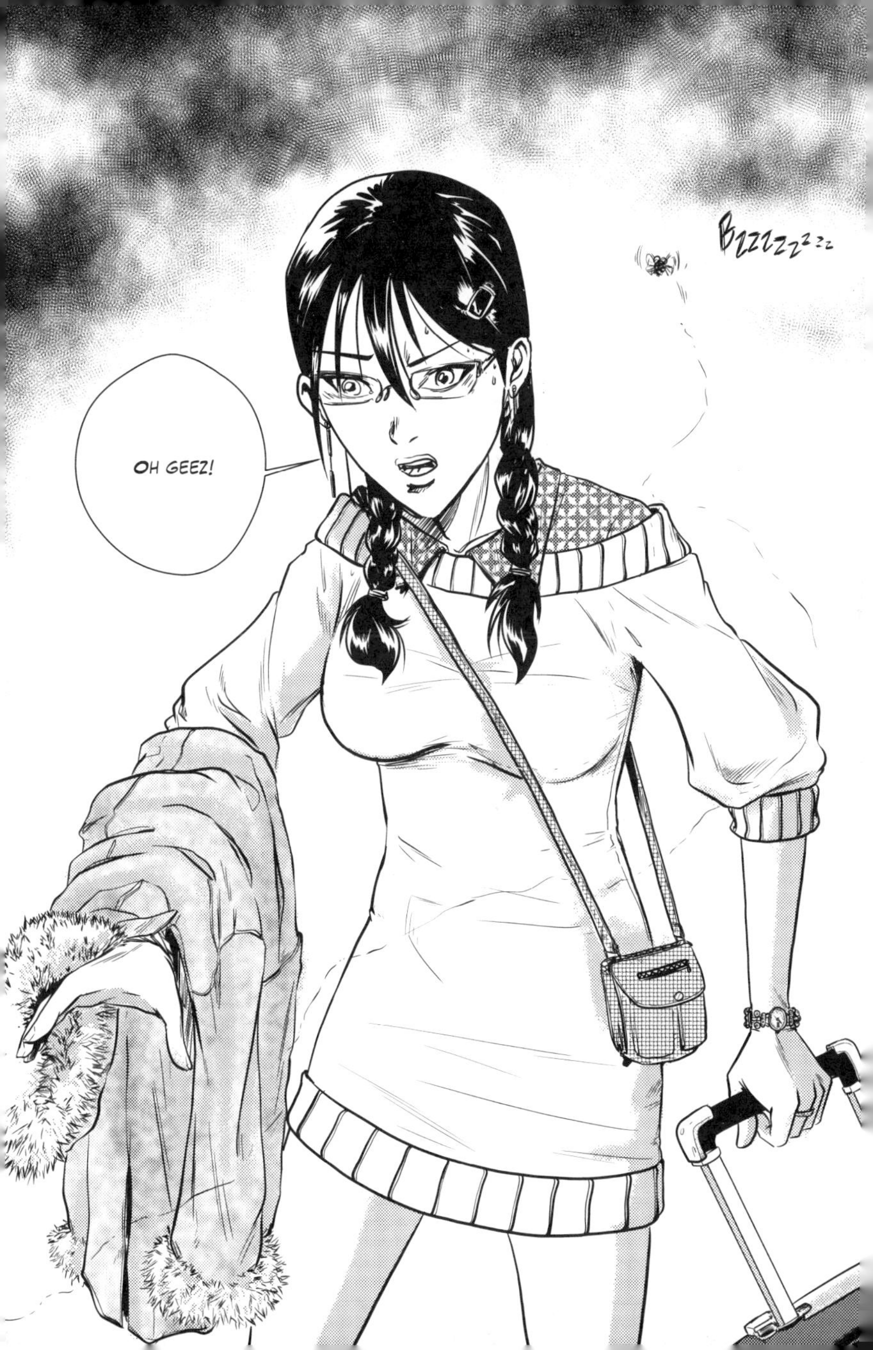
Bzzzzzzzzz
OH GEEZ!

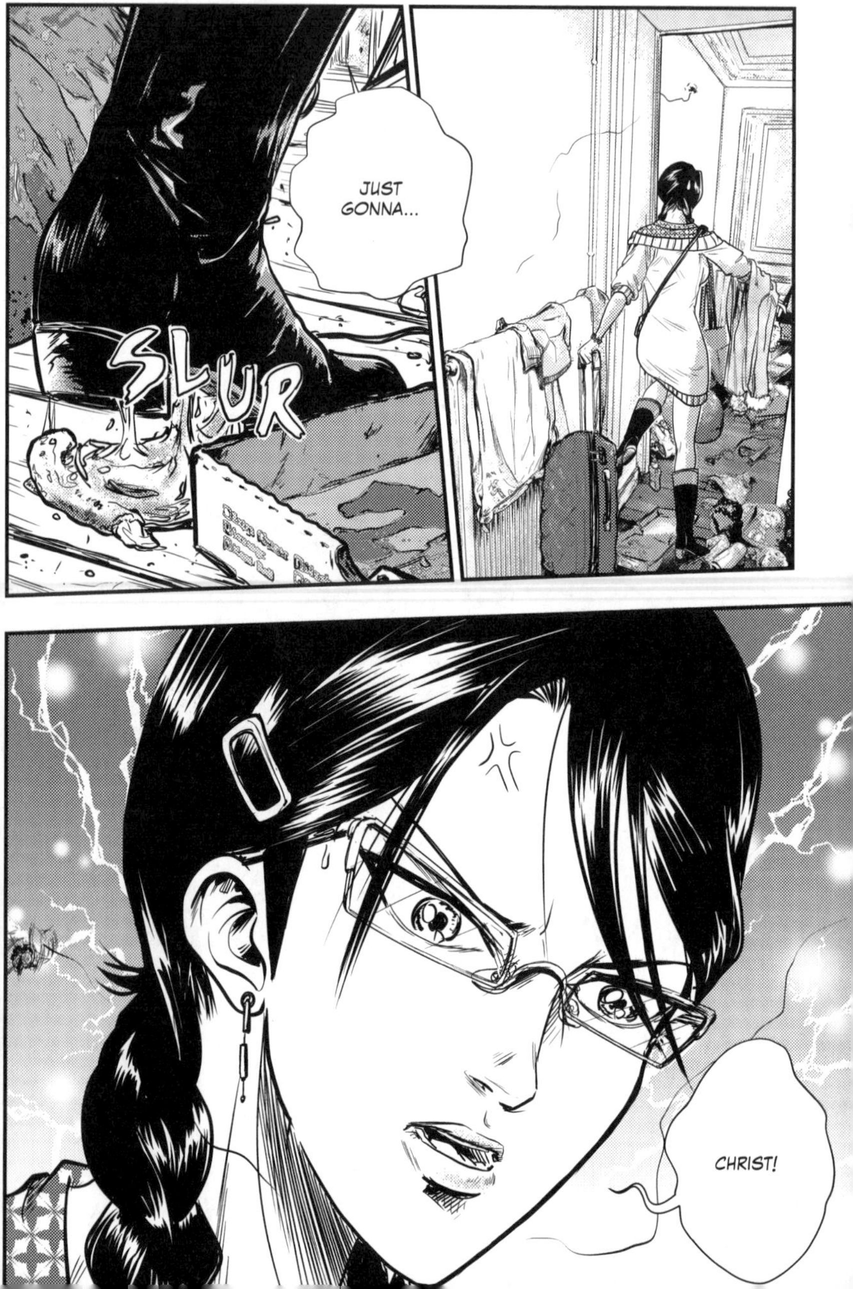
JUST GONNA...
SLUR
CHRIST!

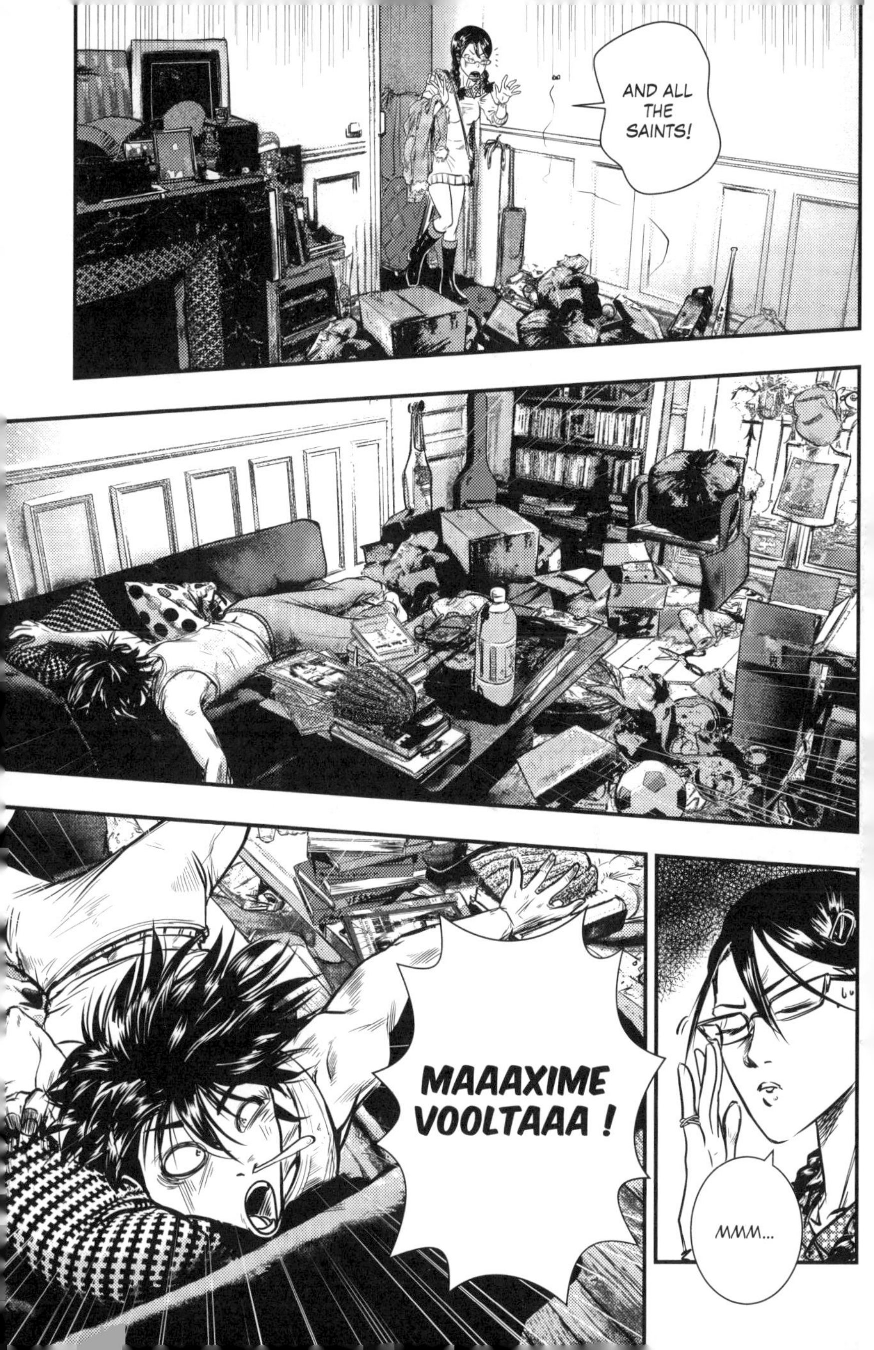
AND ALL THE SAINTS!
MAAAXIME VOOLTAAA !
MMM...

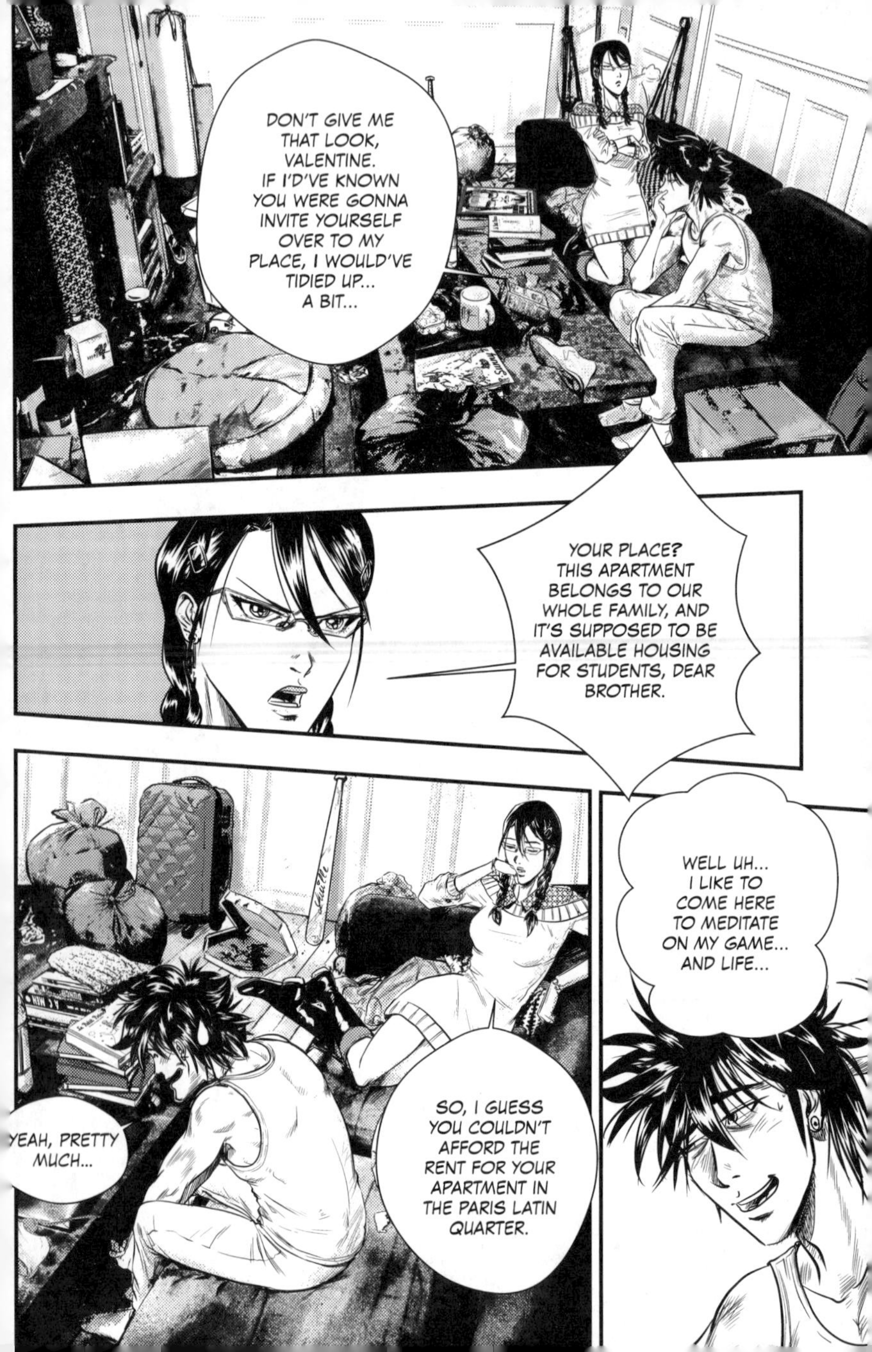

DON'T GIVE ME THAT LOOK, VALENTINE. IF I'D'VE KNOWN YOU WERE GONNA INVITE YOURSELF OVER TO MY PLACE, I WOULD'VE TIDIED UP... A BIT...
YOUR PLACE? THIS APARTMENT BELONGS TO OUR WHOLE FAMILY, AND IT'S SUPPOSED TO BE AVAILABLE HOUSING FOR STUDENTS, DEAR BROTHER.
WELL UH... I LIKE TO COME HERE TO MEDITATE ON MY GAME... AND LIFE...
SO, I GUESS YOU COULDN'T AFFORD THE RENT FOR YOUR APARTMENT IN THE PARIS LATIN QUARTER.
YEAH, PRETTY MUCH...

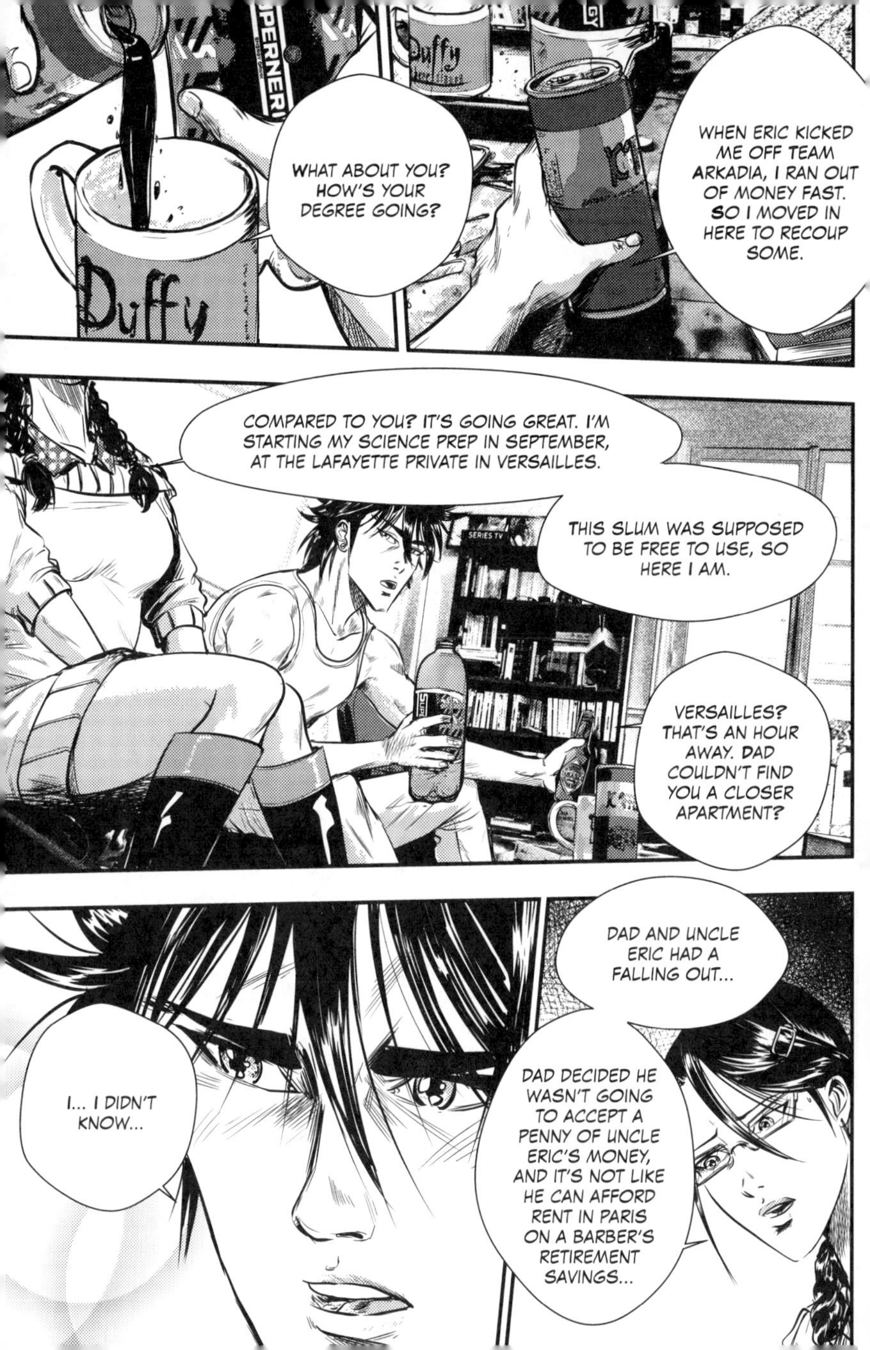
WHEN ERIC KICKED ME OFF TEAM ARKADIA, I RAN OUT OF MONEY FAST. SO I MOVED IN HERE TO RECOUP SOME.
WHAT ABOUT YOU? HOW'S YOUR DEGREE GOING?
COMPARED TO YOU? IT'S GOING GREAT. I'M STARTING MY SCIENCE PREP IN SEPTEMBER, AT THE LAFAYETTE PRIVATE IN VERSAILLES.
THIS SLUM WAS SUPPOSED TO BE FREE TO USE, SO HERE I AM.
VERSAILLES? THAT'S AN HOUR AWAY. DAD COULDN'T FIND YOU A CLOSER APARTMENT?
DAD AND UNCLE ERIC HAD A FALLING OUT...
DAD DECIDED HE WASN'T GOING TO ACCEPT A PENNY OF UNCLE ERIC'S MONEY, AND IT'S NOT LIKE HE CAN AFFORD RENT IN PARIS ON A BARBER'S RETIREMENT SAVINGS...
I... I DIDN'T KNOW...

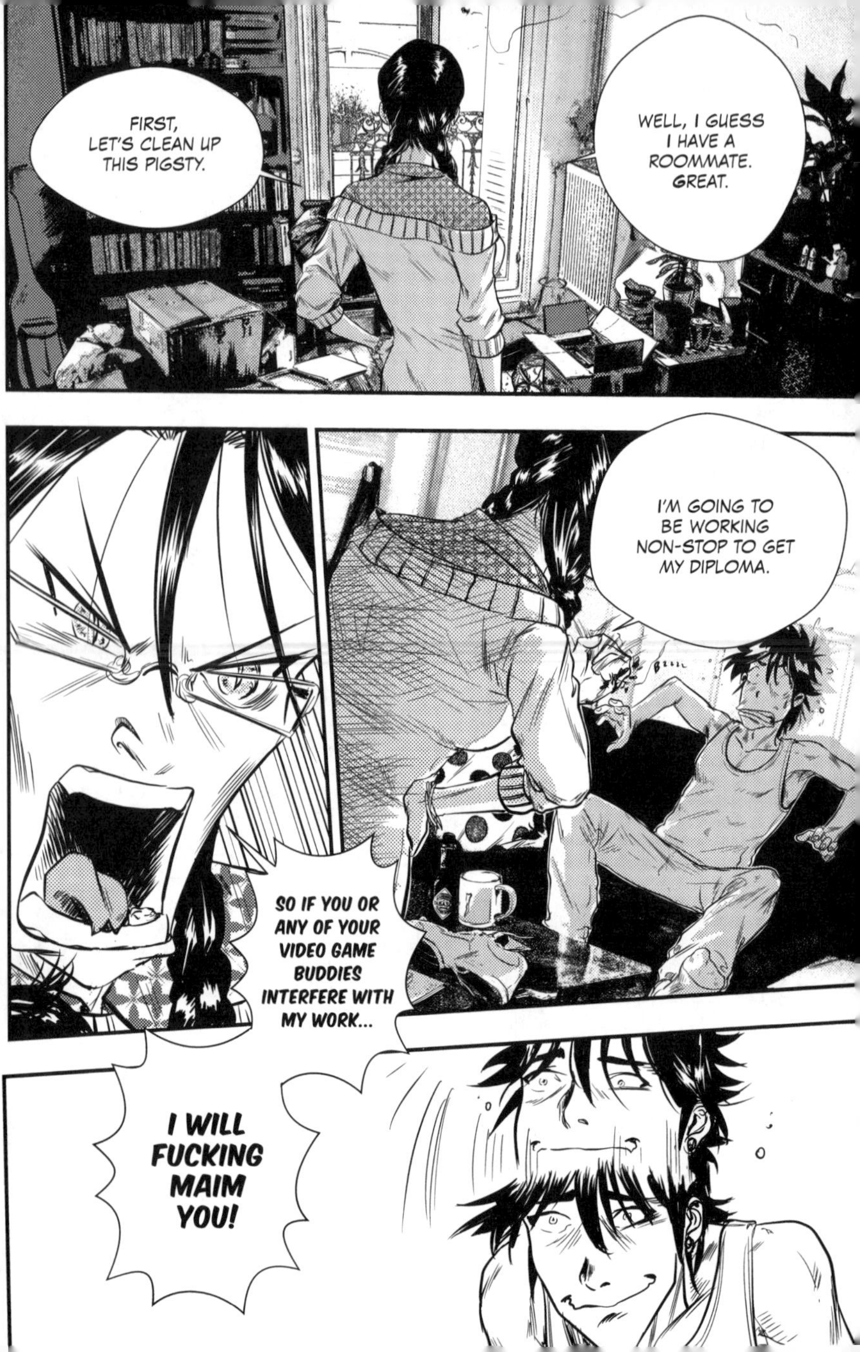
WELL, I GUESS I HAVE A ROOMMATE. GREAT.
FIRST, LET'S CLEAN UP THIS PIGSTY.
I'M GOING TO BE WORKING NON-STOP TO GET MY DIPLOMA.
SO IF YOU OR ANY OF YOUR VIDEO GAME BUDDIES INTERFERE WITH MY WORK...
I WILL FUCKING MAIM YOU!

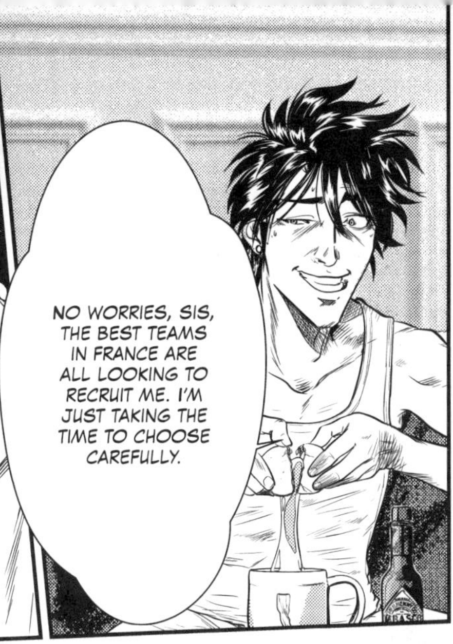
NO WORRIES, SIS, THE BEST TEAMS IN FRANCE ARE ALL LOOKING TO RECRUIT ME. I'M JUST TAKING THE TIME TO CHOOSE CAREFULLY.

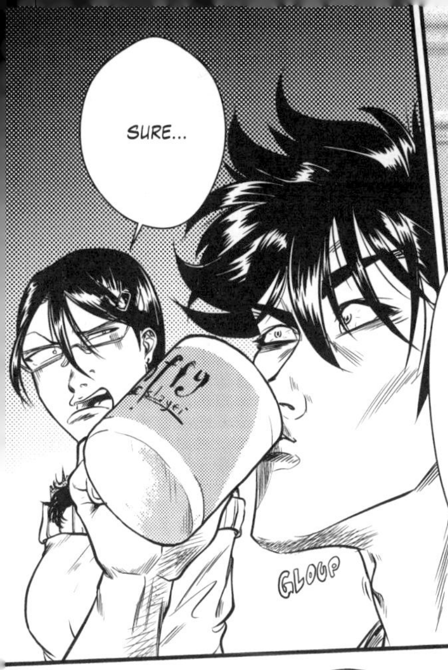
SURE...
GLOOP

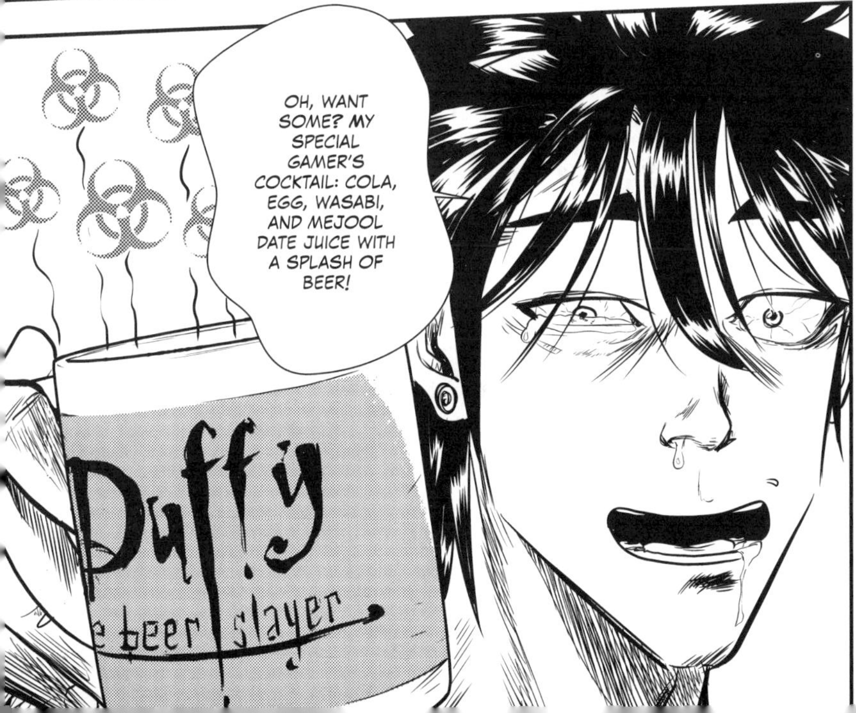
OH, WANT SOME? MY SPECIAL GAMER'S COCKTAIL: COLA, EGG, WASABI, AND MEJOOL DATE JUICE WITH A SPLASH OF BEER!

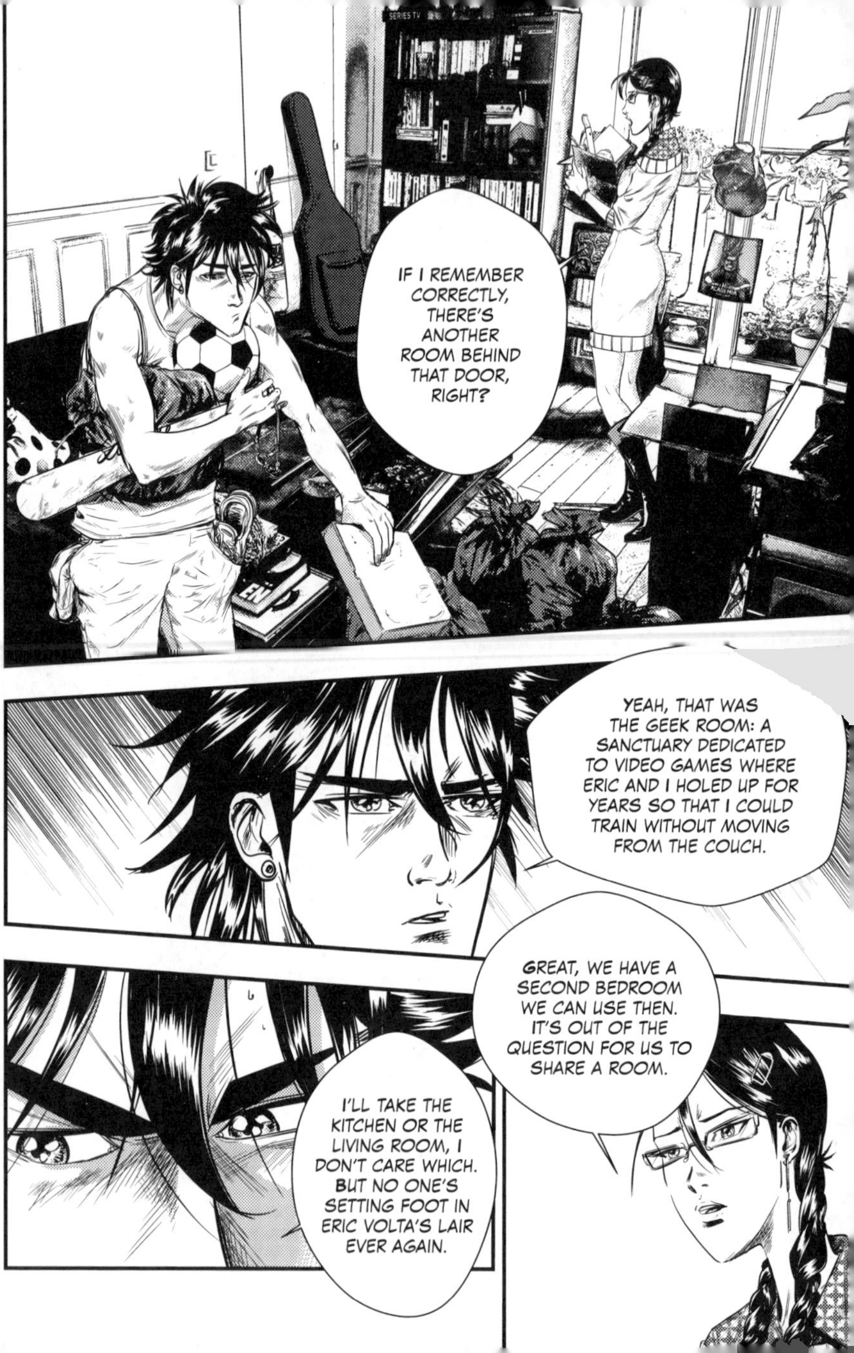
IF I REMEMBER CORRECTLY, THERE'S ANOTHER ROOM BEHIND THAT DOOR, RIGHT?
YEAH, THAT WAS THE GEEK ROOM: A SANCTUARY DEDICATED TO VIDEO GAMES WHERE ERIC AND I HOLED UP FOR YEARS SO THAT I COULD TRAIN WITHOUT MOVING FROM THE COUCH.
GREAT, WE HAVE A SECOND BEDROOM WE CAN USE THEN. IT'S OUT OF THE QUESTION FOR US TO SHARE A ROOM.
I'LL TAKE THE KITCHEN OR THE LIVING ROOM, I DON'T CARE WHICH. BUT NO ONE'S SETTING FOOT IN ERIC VOLTA'S LAIR EVER AGAIN.

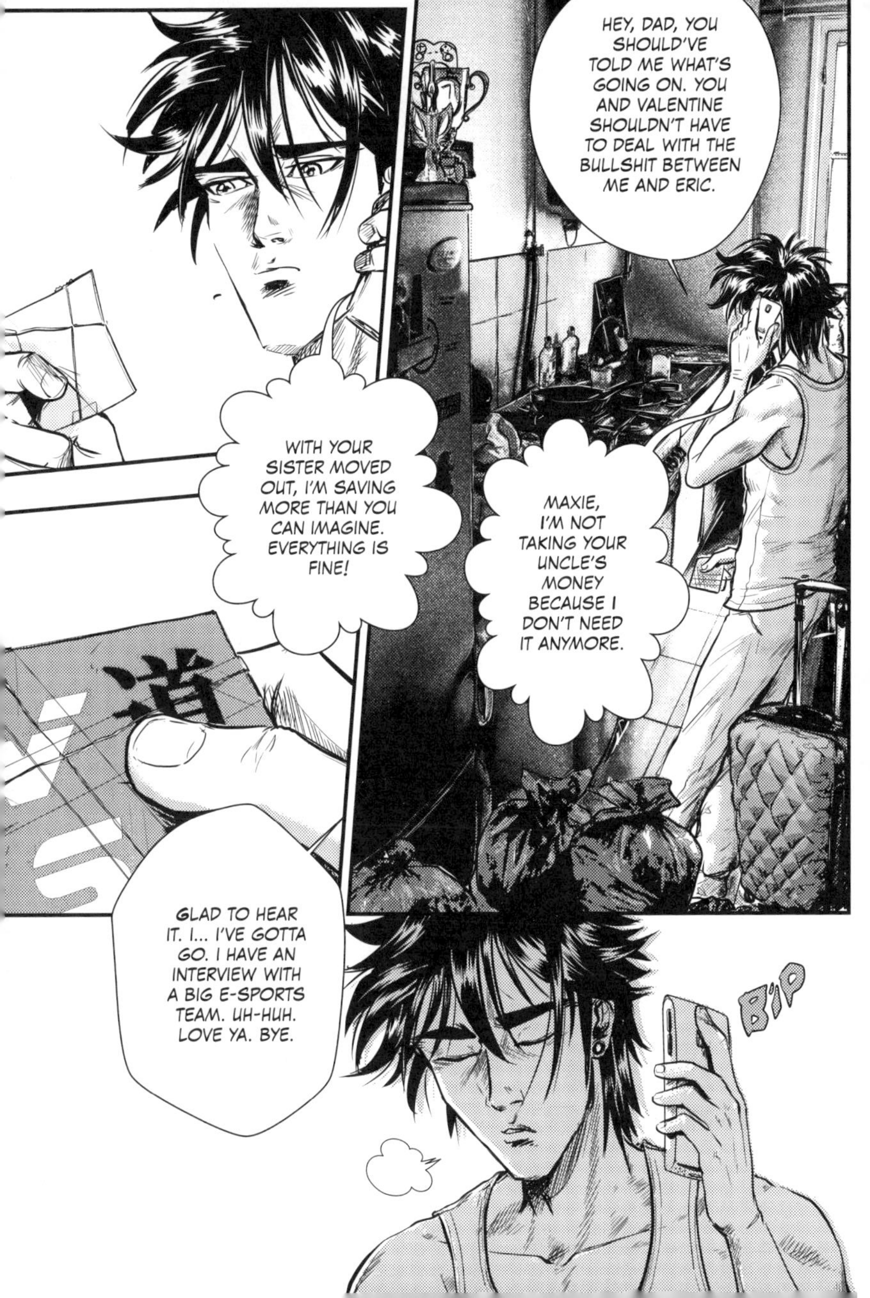
HEY, DAD, YOU SHOULD'VE TOLD ME WHAT'S GOING ON. YOU AND VALENTINE SHOULDN'T HAVE TO DEAL WITH THE BULLSHIT BETWEEN ME AND ERIC.
MAXIE, I'M NOT TAKING YOUR UNCLE'S MONEY BECAUSE I DON'T NEED IT ANYMORE.
WITH YOUR SISTER MOVED OUT, I'M SAVING MORE THAN YOU CAN IMAGINE. EVERYTHING IS FINE!
道
GLAD TO HEAR IT. I... I'VE GOTTA GO. I HAVE AN INTERVIEW WITH A BIG E-SPORTS TEAM. UH-HUH. LOVE YA. BYE.
BIP

CHARACTER SELECT!

MILES LUSIFAIR

THE REVOLUTIONARY

BACKGROUND

Miles is the famous editor-in-chief of Fight Game Magazine, the publication known as THE place for reporting the true facts of fighting game competitions.

The journalist is renowned for his radical views on the evolution of pro fighting games. Miles considers the community's roots to have been erased in order to make way for the E-sport scene where money is king. He defends a certain vision of Street Fighter V, which in his opinion should be regarded as a popular digital martial art. He's very close to Inès, who he feels represents the true retro-future of the game.

CHARACTER DESIGN

Miles is the character I had the least instruction on from Izu. When I designed him, I was reminded more and more of Sheldon from the Big Bang Theory. So I'm going to go fishing for geek t-shirts to draw him in! Besides, if you were looking for what to gift me when you come see me at a signing... I'll say no more!

BY KALON

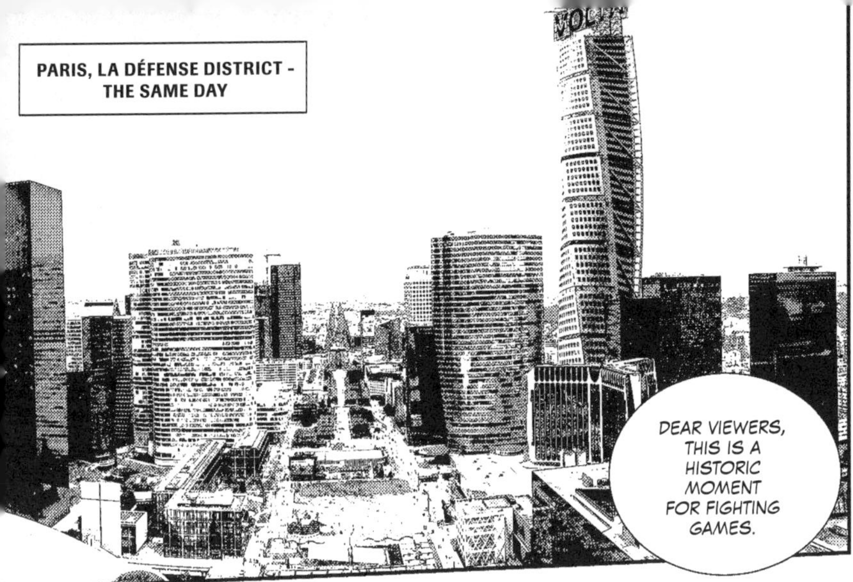
PARIS, LA DÉFENSE DISTRICT - THE SAME DAY
DEAR VIEWERS, THIS IS A HISTORIC MOMENT FOR FIGHTING GAMES.
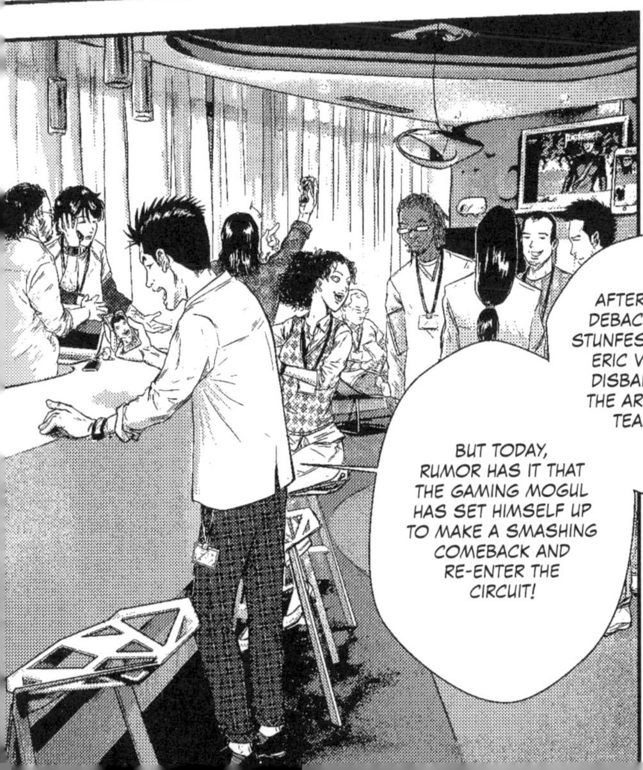
AFTER THE DEBACLE AT STUNFEST 2016, ERIC VOLTA DISBANDED THE ARKADIA TEAM.
BUT TODAY, RUMOR HAS IT THAT THE GAMING MOGUL HAS SET HIMSELF UP TO MAKE A SMASHING COMEBACK AND RE-ENTER THE CIRCUIT!
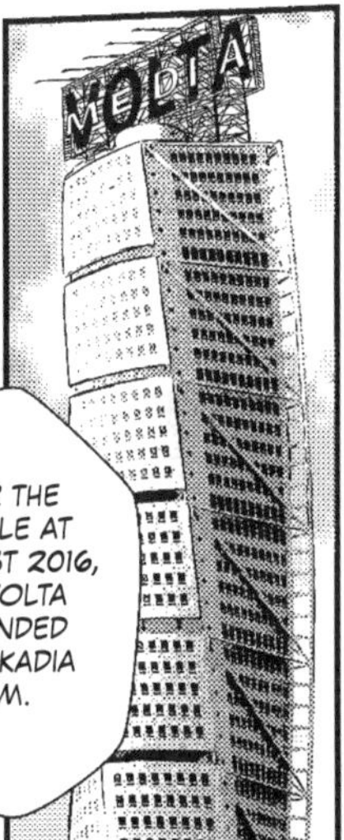
VOLTA

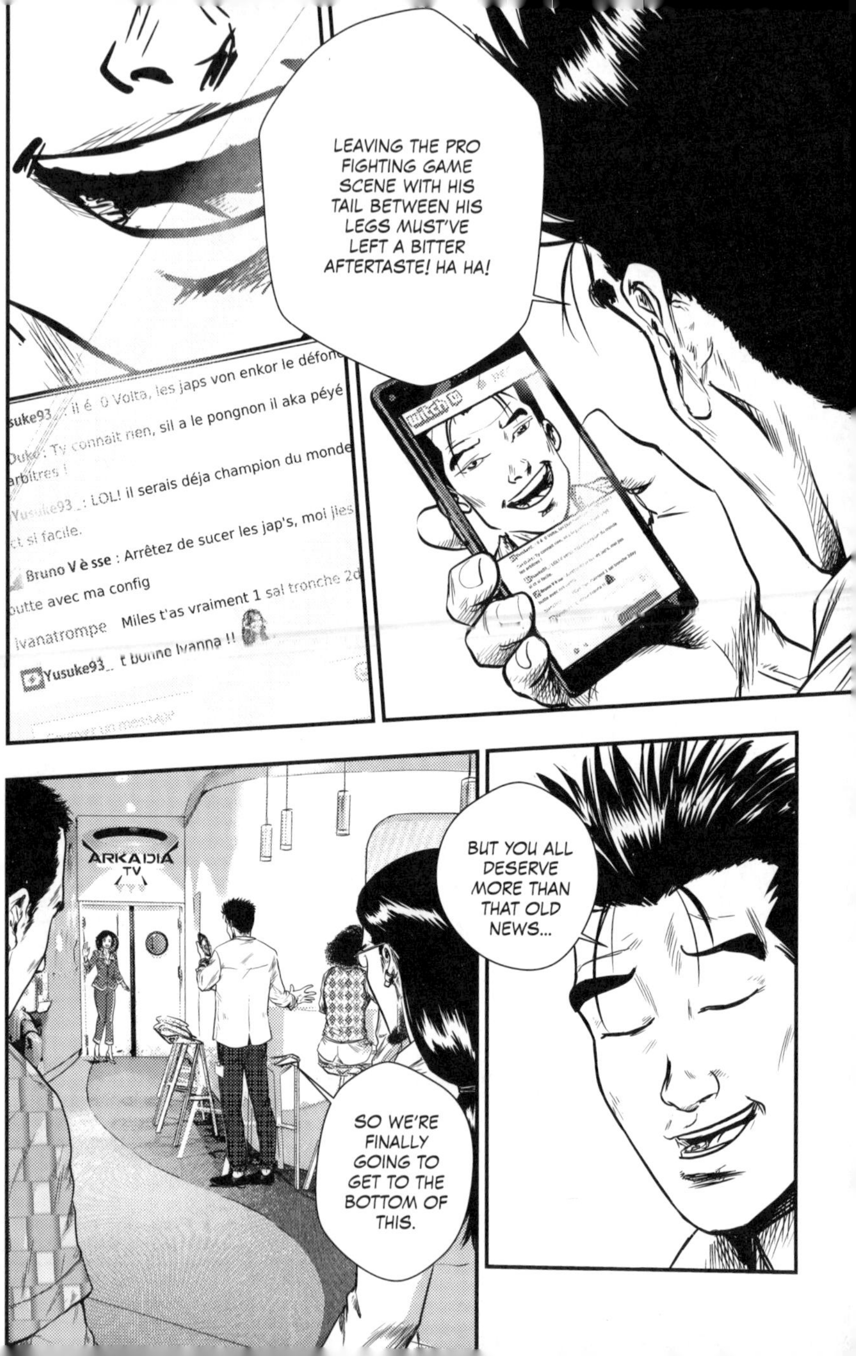
LEAVING THE PRO FIGHTING GAME SCENE WITH HIS TAIL BETWEEN HIS LEGS MUST'VE LEFT A BITTER AFTERTASTE! HA HA!
les japs von enkor le défon
il aka péyé
Ty connait rien, sil a le pongnon
arbitres !
LOL! il serais déja champion du monde
Arrêtez de sucer les jap's, moi jles
ct si facile.
Bruno V è sse
butte avec ma config
Miles t'as vraiment 1 sal tronche 2d
Ivanatrompe
t bonne Ivanna !!
Yusuke93_
ARKADIA TV
BUT YOU ALL DESERVE MORE THAN THAT OLD NEWS...
SO WE'RE FINALLY GOING TO GET TO THE BOTTOM OF THIS.

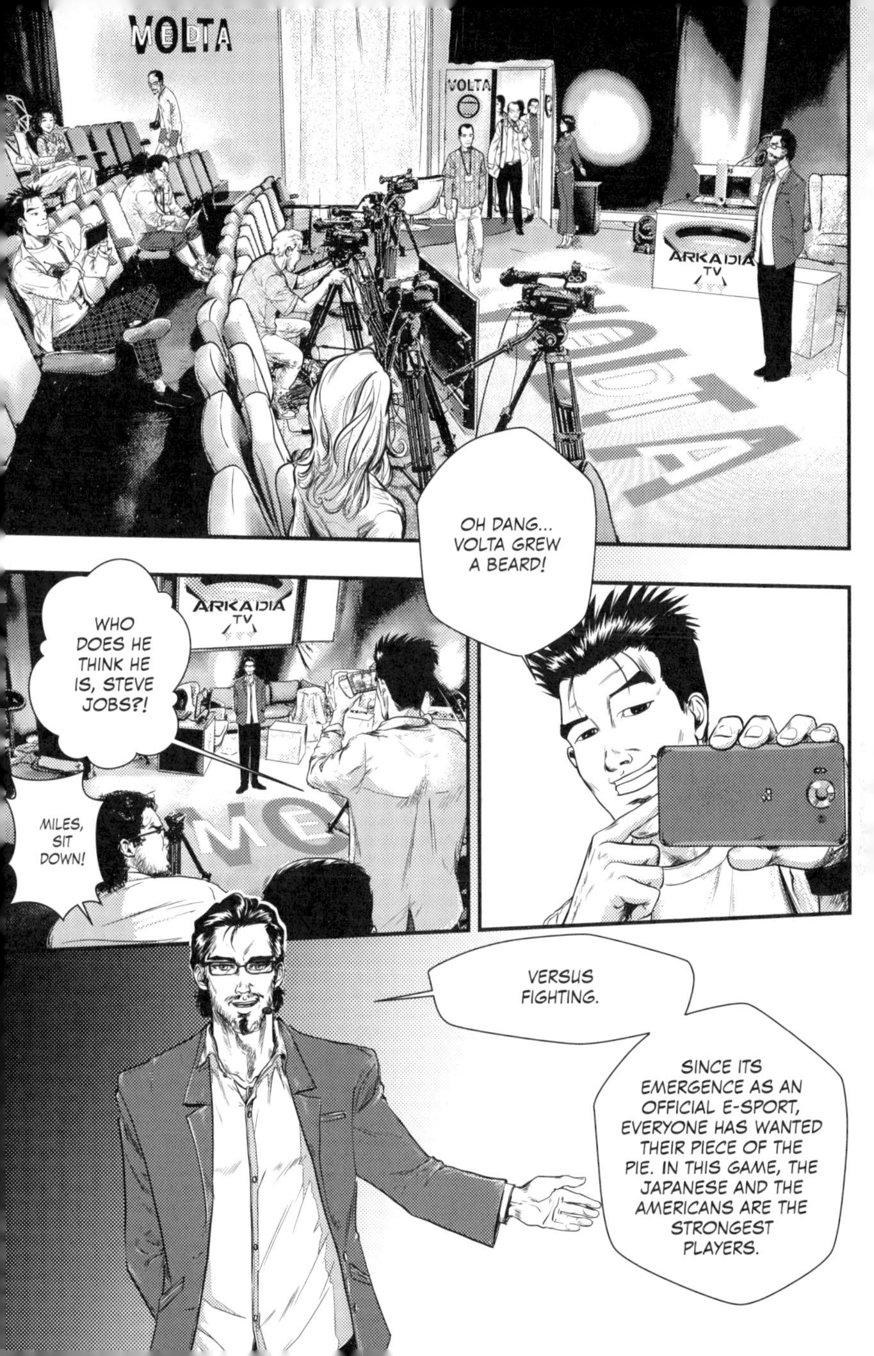
MOLTA
VOLTA
ARKADIA TV
OH DANG... VOLTA GREW A BEARD!
ARKADIA TV
WHO DOES HE THINK HE IS, STEVE JOBS?!
MILES, SIT DOWN!
VERSUS FIGHTING.
SINCE ITS EMERGENCE AS AN OFFICIAL E-SPORT, EVERYONE HAS WANTED THEIR PIECE OF THE PIE. IN THIS GAME, THE JAPANESE AND THE AMERICANS ARE THE STRONGEST PLAYERS.

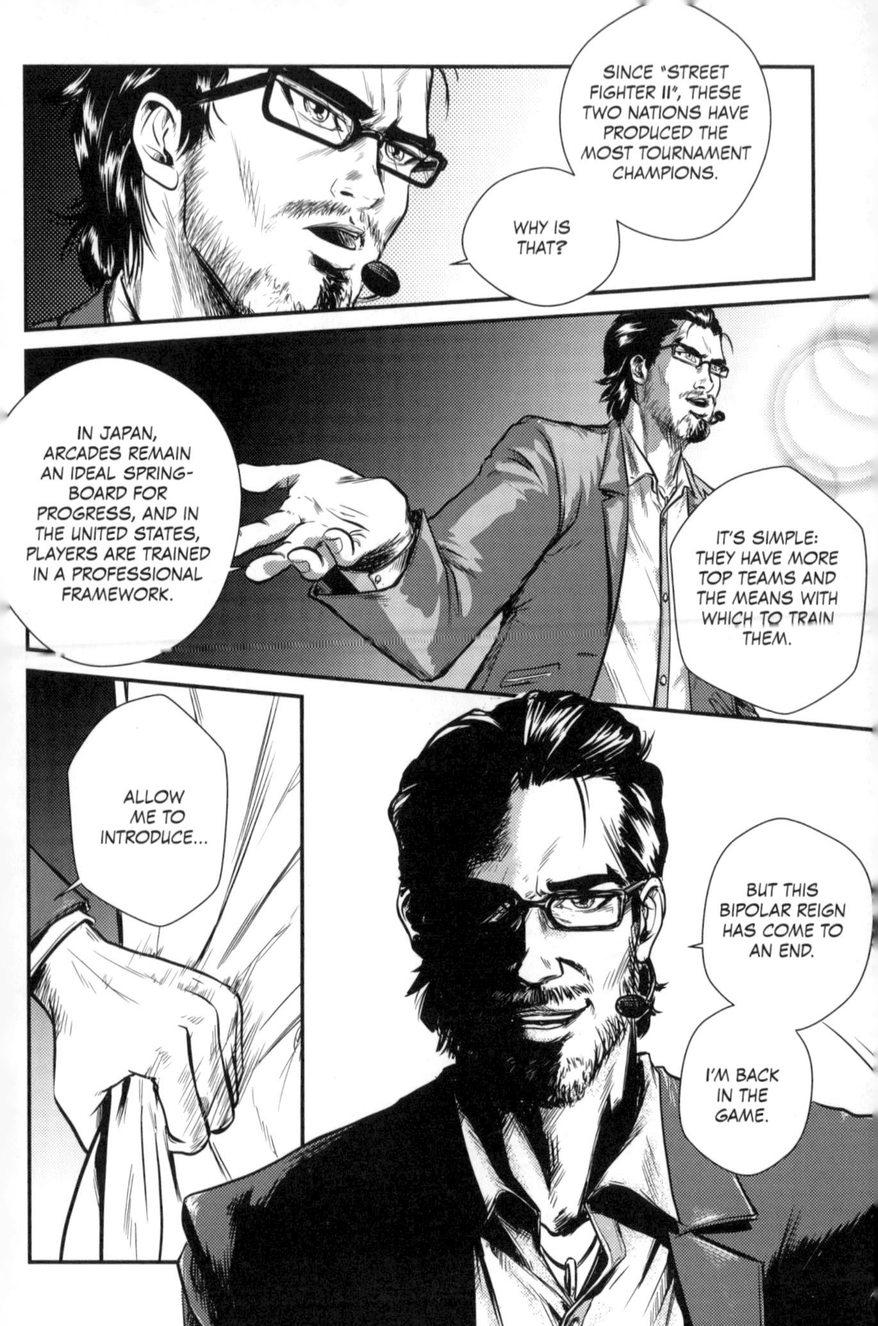
SINCE "STREET FIGHTER II", THESE TWO NATIONS HAVE PRODUCED THE MOST TOURNAMENT CHAMPIONS.
WHY IS THAT?
IT'S SIMPLE: THEY HAVE MORE TOP TEAMS AND THE MEANS WITH WHICH TO TRAIN THEM.
IN JAPAN, ARCADES REMAIN AN IDEAL SPRING-BOARD FOR PROGRESS, AND IN THE UNITED STATES, PLAYERS ARE TRAINED IN A PROFESSIONAL FRAMEWORK.
BUT THIS BIPOLAR REIGN HAS COME TO AN END.
I'M BACK IN THE GAME.
ALLOW ME TO INTRODUCE...

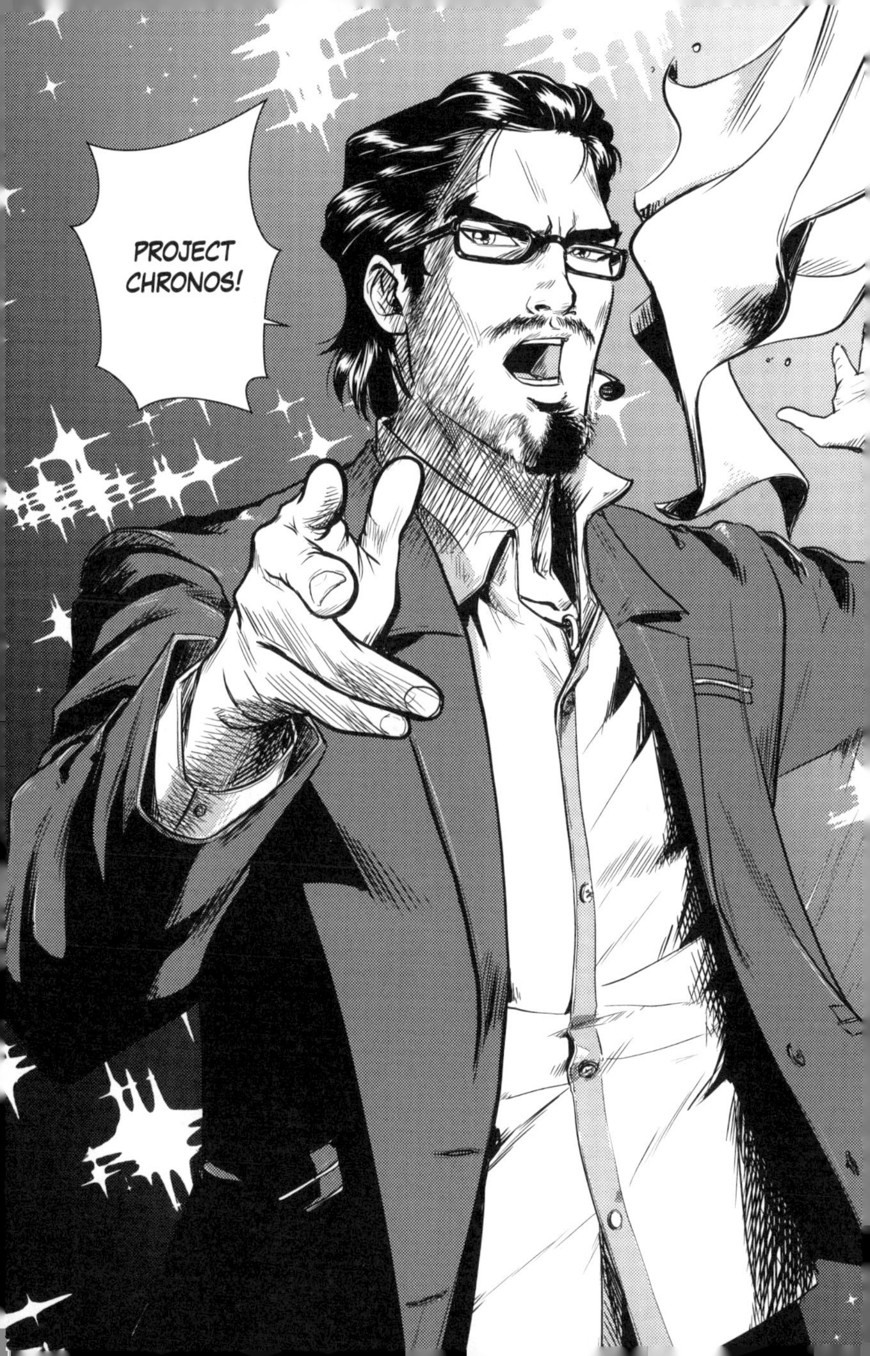
PROJECT CHRONOS!

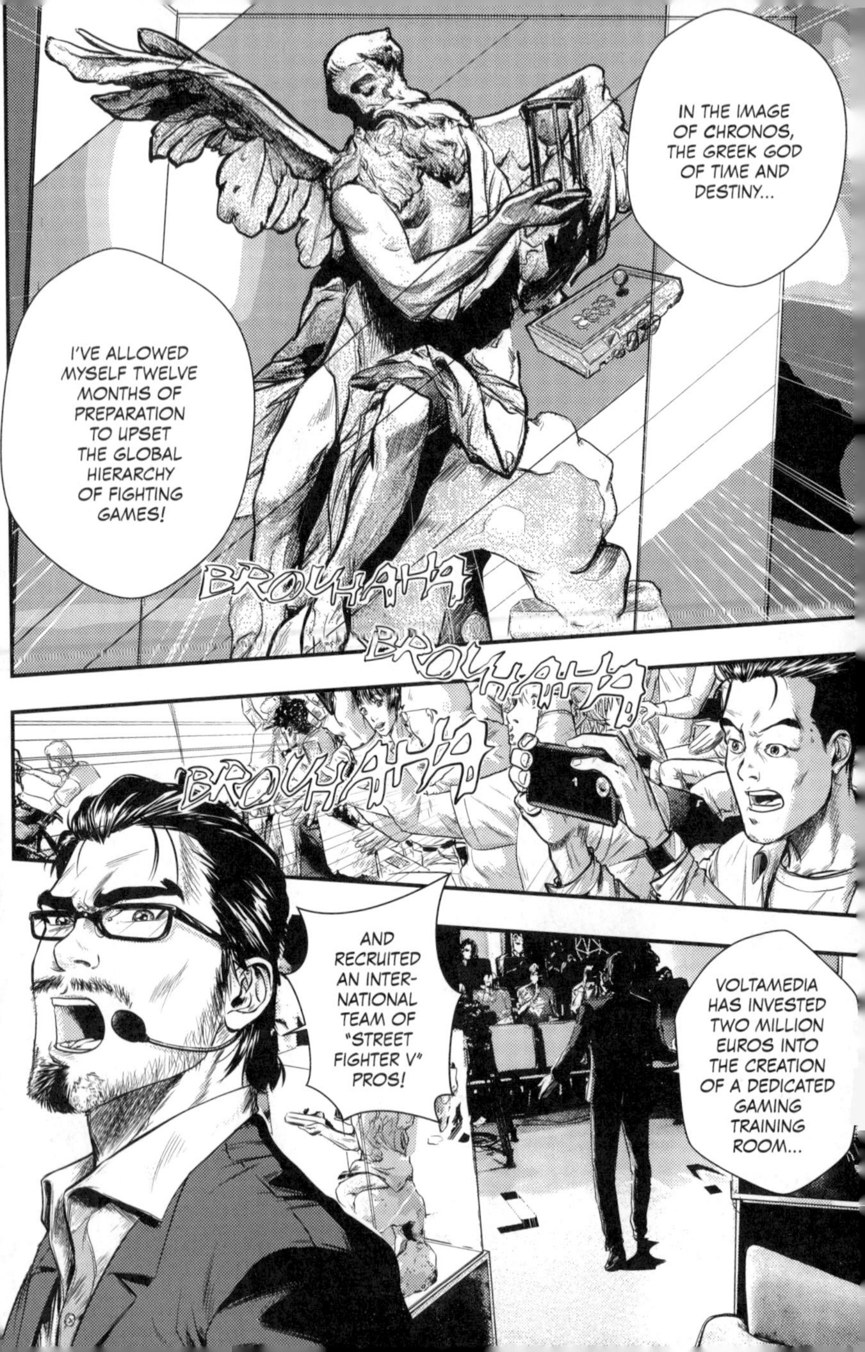
IN THE IMAGE OF CHRONOS, THE GREEK GOD OF TIME AND DESTINY...
I'VE ALLOWED MYSELF TWELVE MONTHS OF PREPARATION TO UPSET THE GLOBAL HIERARCHY OF FIGHTING GAMES!
BROUHAHA
BROUHAHA
BROUHAHA
VOLTAMEDIA HAS INVESTED TWO MILLION EUROS INTO THE CREATION OF A DEDICATED GAMING TRAINING ROOM...
AND RECRUITED AN INTER-NATIONAL TEAM OF "STREET FIGHTER V" PROS!

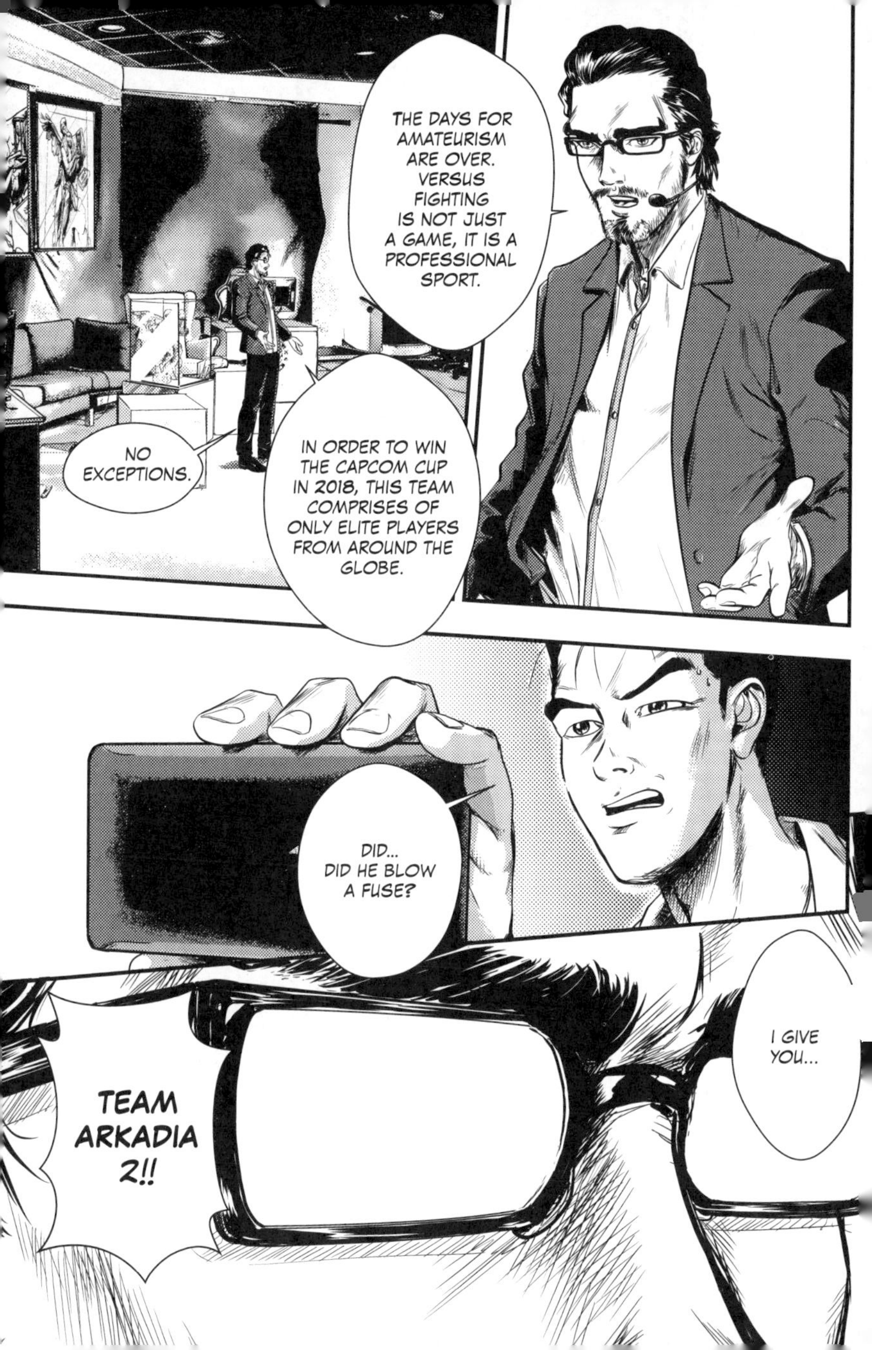
THE DAYS FOR AMATEURISM ARE OVER. VERSUS FIGHTING IS NOT JUST A GAME, IT IS A PROFESSIONAL SPORT.
IN ORDER TO WIN THE CAPCOM CUP IN 2018, THIS TEAM COMPRISES OF ONLY ELITE PLAYERS FROM AROUND THE GLOBE.
NO EXCEPTIONS.
DID... DID HE BLOW A FUSE?
I GIVE YOU...
TEAM ARKADIA 2!!

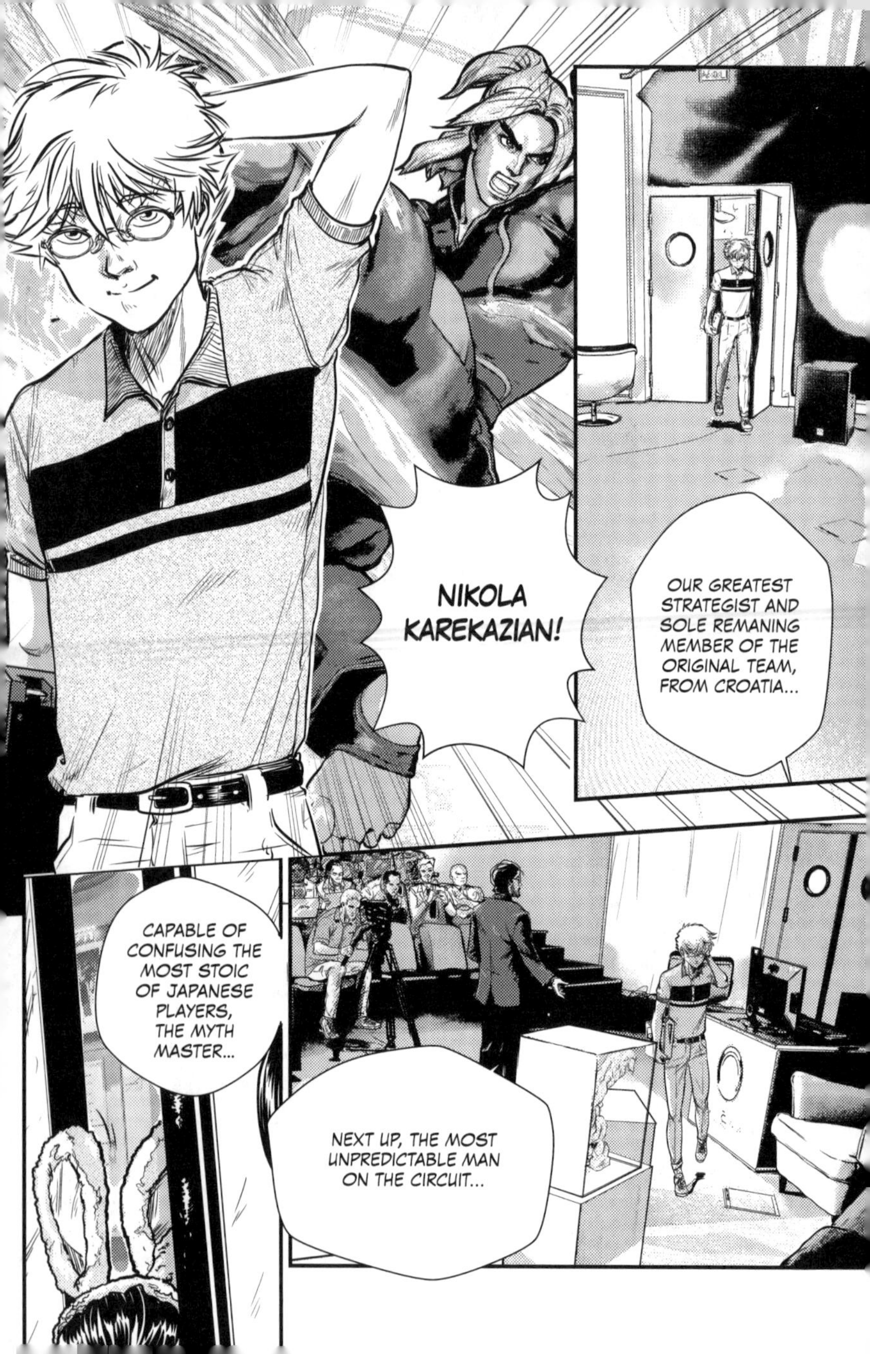
OUR GREATEST STRATEGIST AND SOLE REMANING MEMBER OF THE ORIGINAL TEAM, FROM CROATIA...
NIKOLA KAREKAZIAN!
NEXT UP, THE MOST UNPREDICTABLE MAN ON THE CIRCUIT...
CAPABLE OF CONFUSING THE MOST STOIC OF JAPANESE PLAYERS, THE MYTH MASTER...

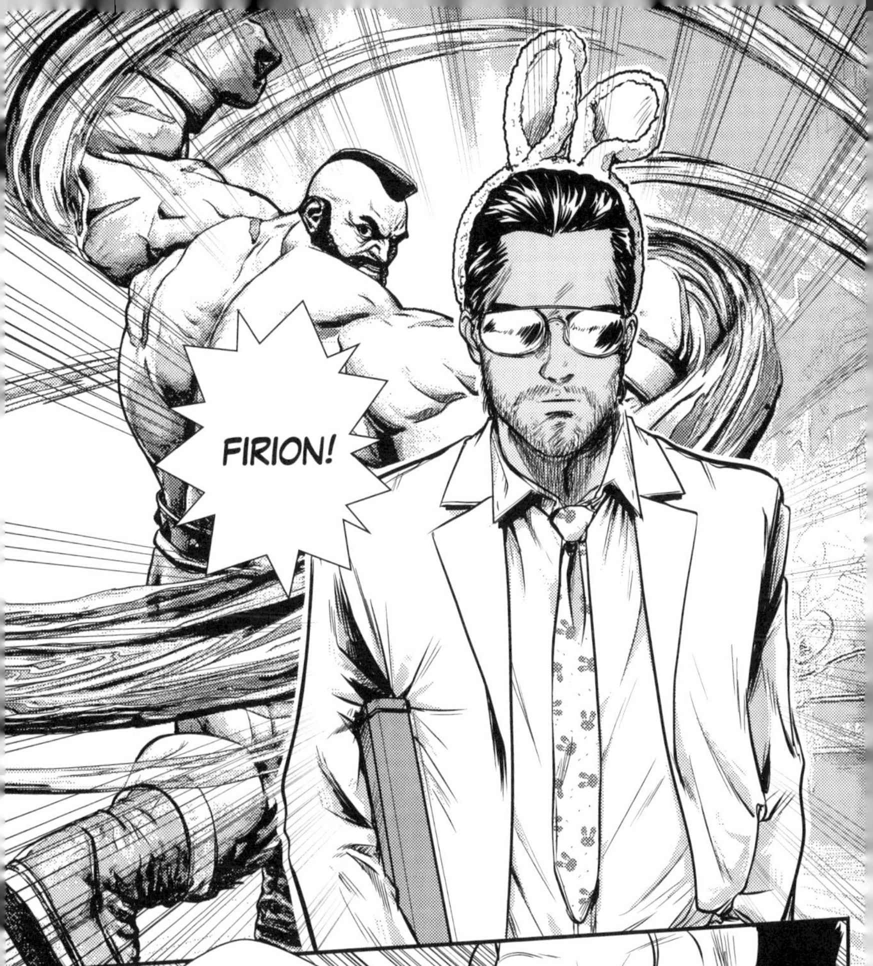
FIRION!
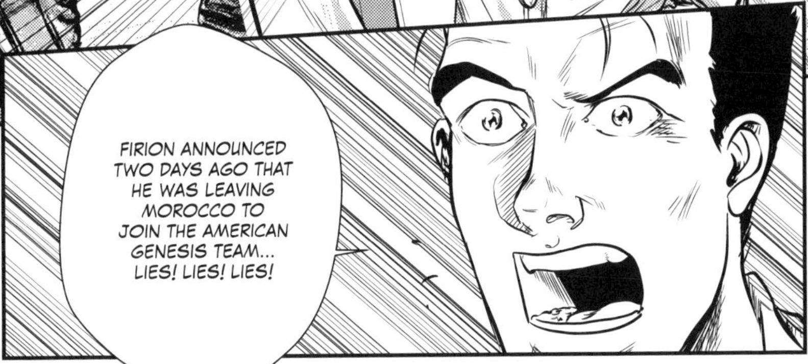
FIRION ANNOUNCED TWO DAYS AGO THAT HE WAS LEAVING MOROCCO TO JOIN THE AMERICAN GENESIS TEAM... LIES! LIES! LIES!

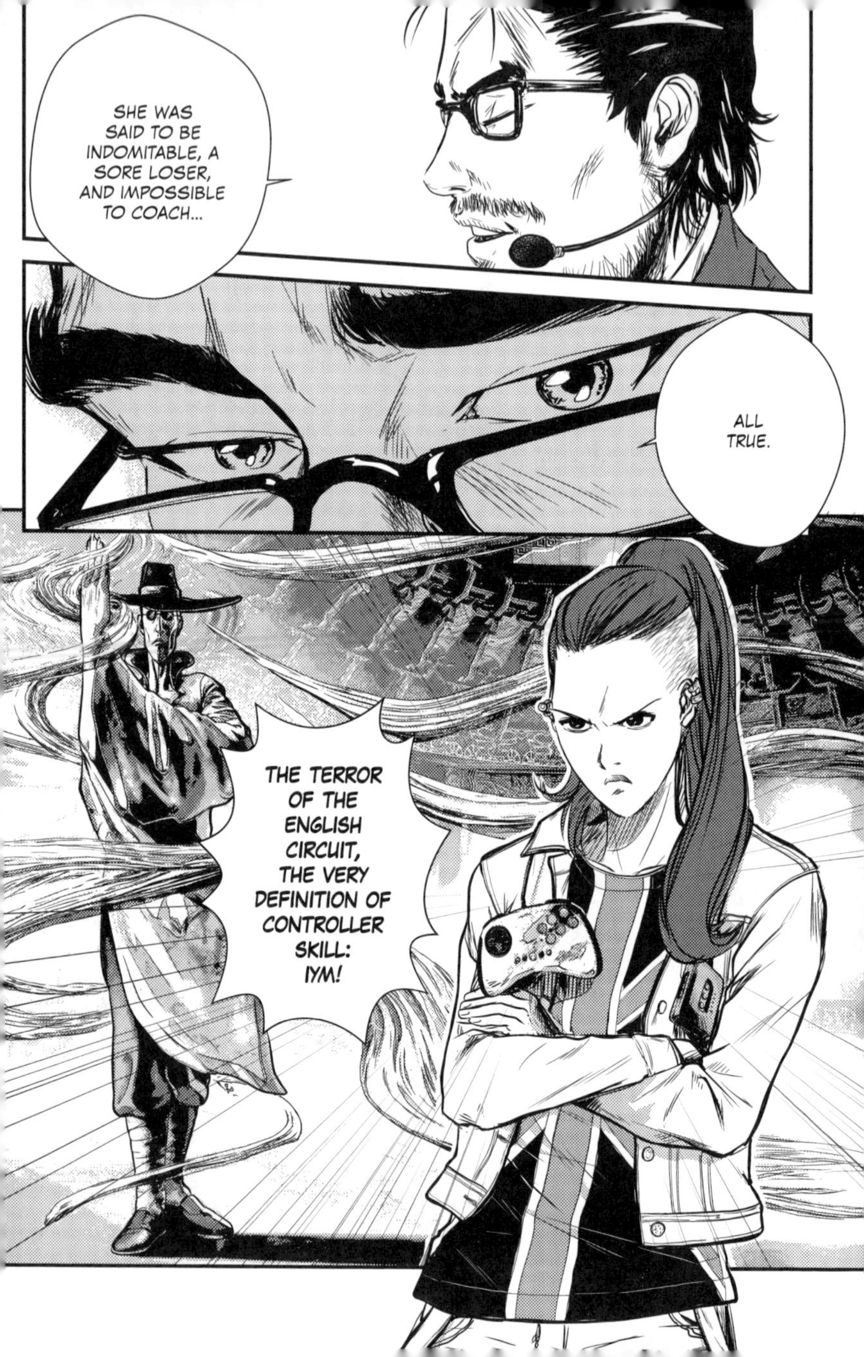
SHE WAS SAID TO BE INDOMITABLE, A SORE LOSER, AND IMPOSSIBLE TO COACH...
ALL TRUE.
THE TERROR OF THE ENGLISH CIRCUIT, THE VERY DEFINITION OF CONTROLLER SKILL: IYM!

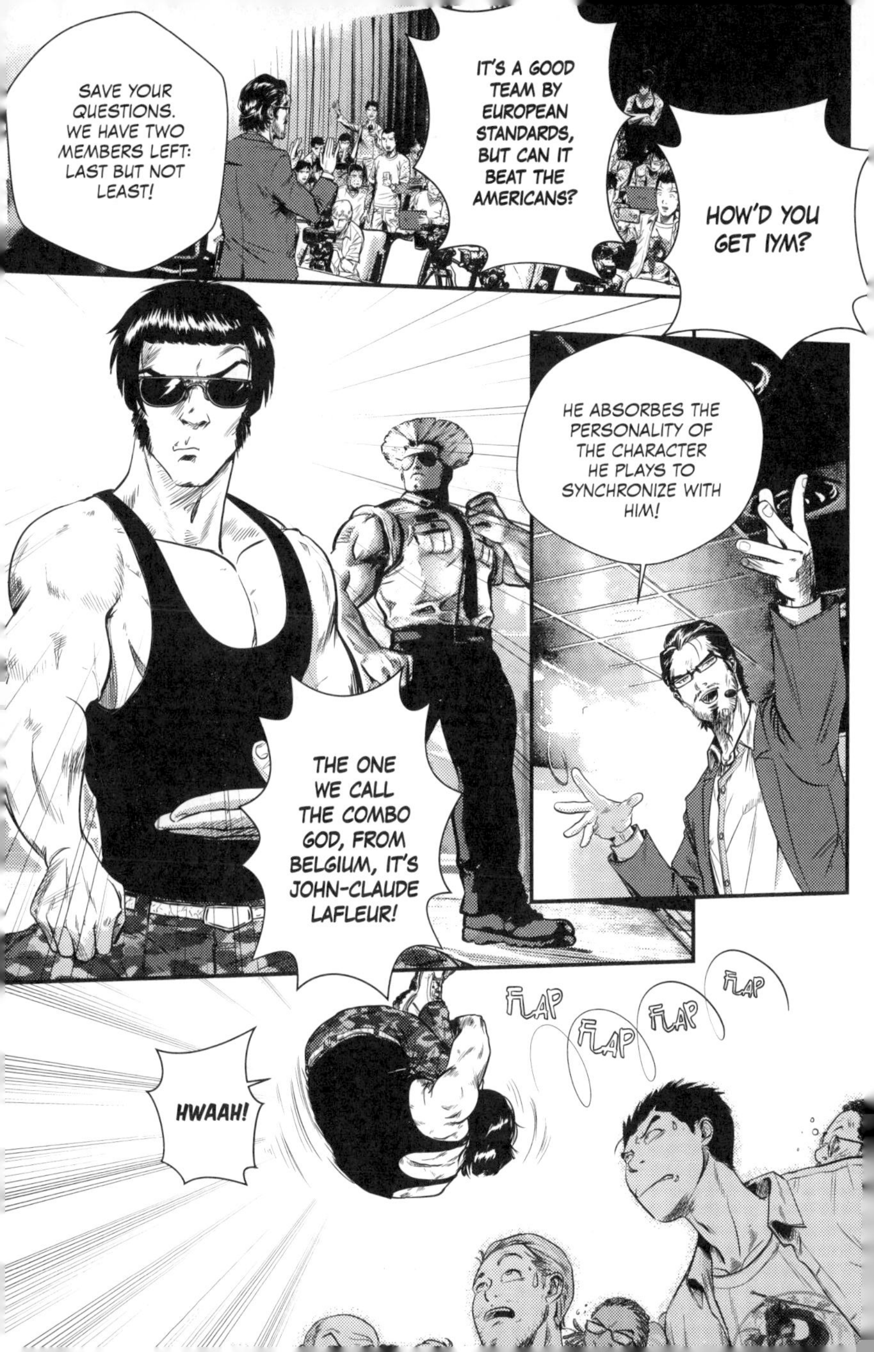

HOW'D YOU GET IYM?
IT'S A GOOD TEAM BY EUROPEAN STANDARDS, BUT CAN IT BEAT THE AMERICANS?
SAVE YOUR QUESTIONS. WE HAVE TWO MEMBERS LEFT: LAST BUT NOT LEAST!
HE ABSORBES THE PERSONALITY OF THE CHARACTER HE PLAYS TO SYNCHRONIZE WITH HIM!
THE ONE WE CALL THE COMBO GOD, FROM BELGIUM, IT'S JOHN-CLAUDE LAFLEUR!
FLAP
FLAP
FLAP
FLAP
HWAAH!

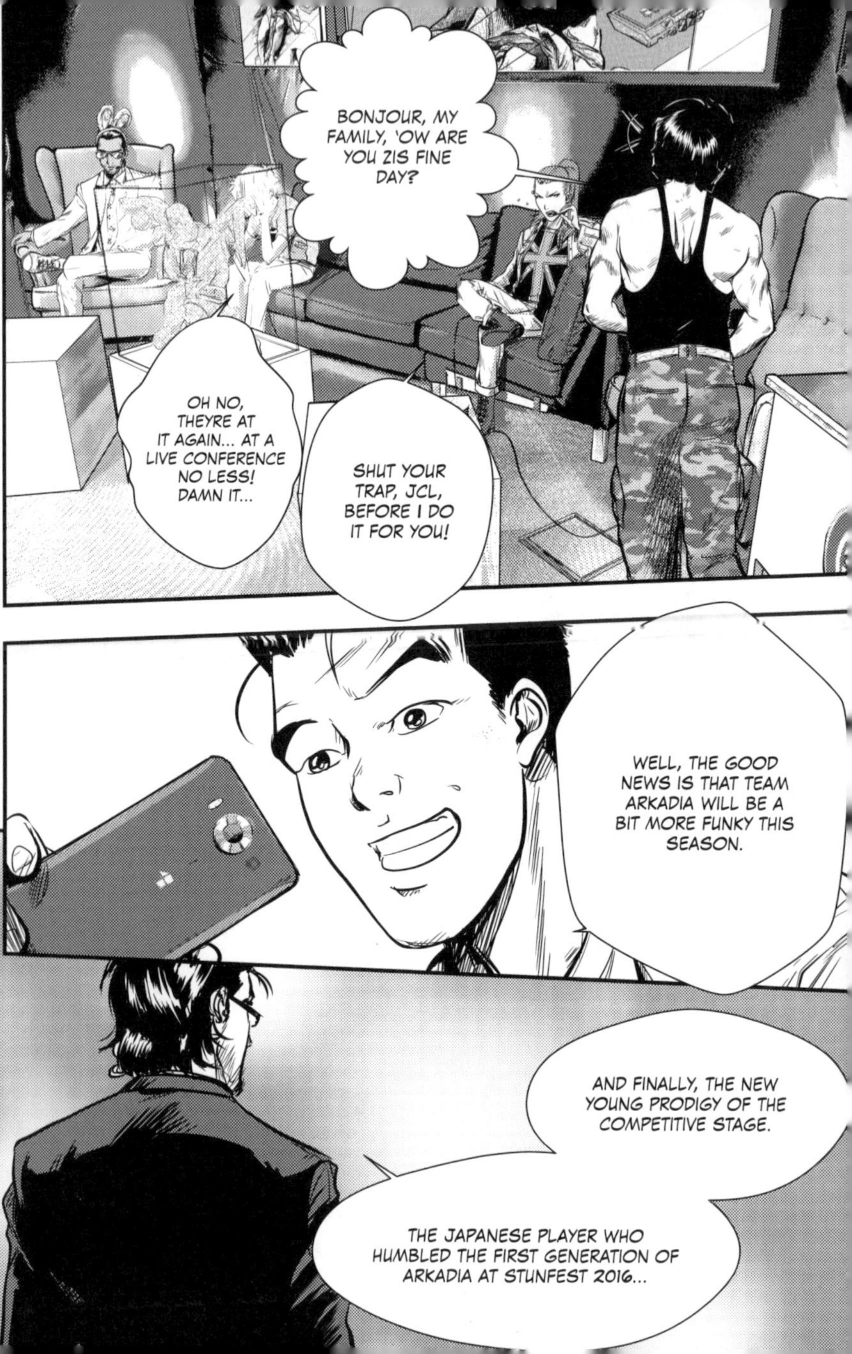
BONJOUR, MY FAMILY, 'OW ARE YOU ZIS FINE DAY?
OH NO, THEYRE AT IT AGAIN... AT A LIVE CONFERENCE NO LESS! DAMN IT...
SHUT YOUR TRAP, JCL, BEFORE I DO IT FOR YOU!
WELL, THE GOOD NEWS IS THAT TEAM ARKADIA WILL BE A BIT MORE FUNKY THIS SEASON.
AND FINALLY, THE NEW YOUNG PRODIGY OF THE COMPETITIVE STAGE.
THE JAPANESE PLAYER WHO HUMBLED THE FIRST GENERATION OF ARKADIA AT STUNFEST 2016...

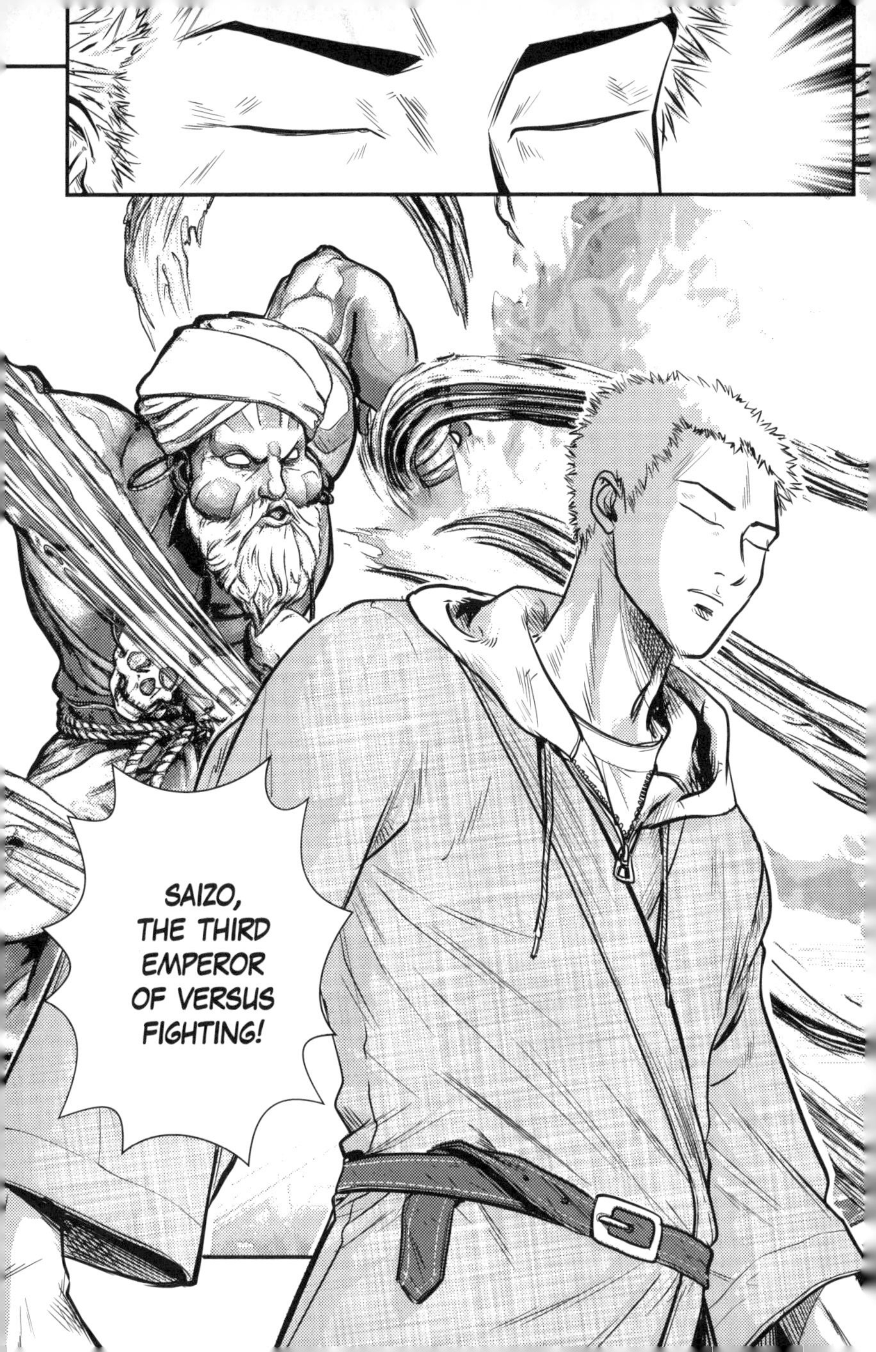
SAIZO, THE THIRD EMPEROR OF VERSUS FIGHTING!

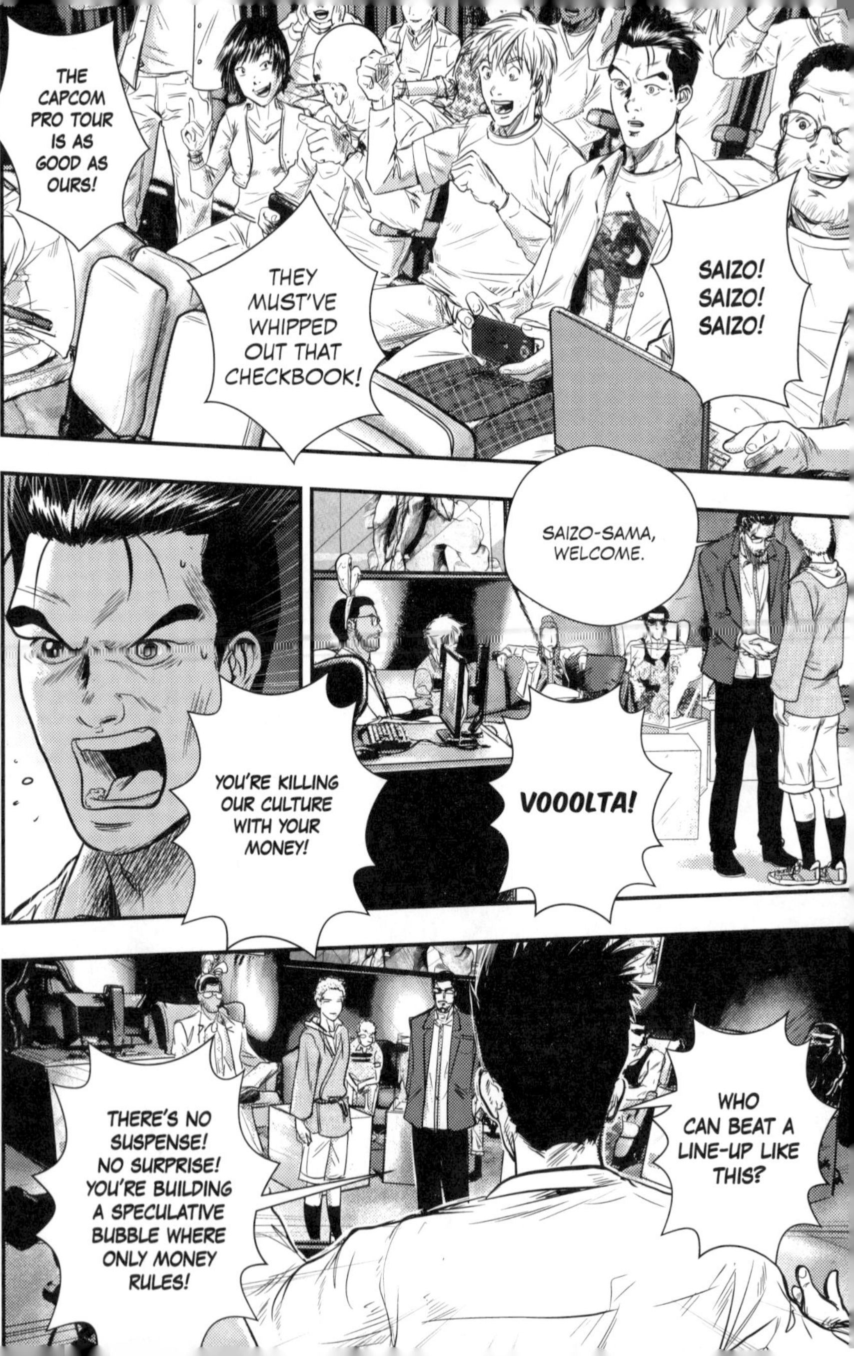
SAIZO! SAIZO! SAIZO!
THEY MUST'VE WHIPPED OUT THAT CHECKBOOK!
THE CAPCOM PRO TOUR IS AS GOOD AS OURS!
SAIZO-SAMA, WELCOME.
VOOOLTA!
YOU'RE KILLING OUR CULTURE WITH YOUR MONEY!
WHO CAN BEAT A LINE-UP LIKE THIS?
THERE'S NO SUSPENSE! NO SURPRISE! YOU'RE BUILDING A SPECULATIVE BUBBLE WHERE ONLY MONEY RULES!

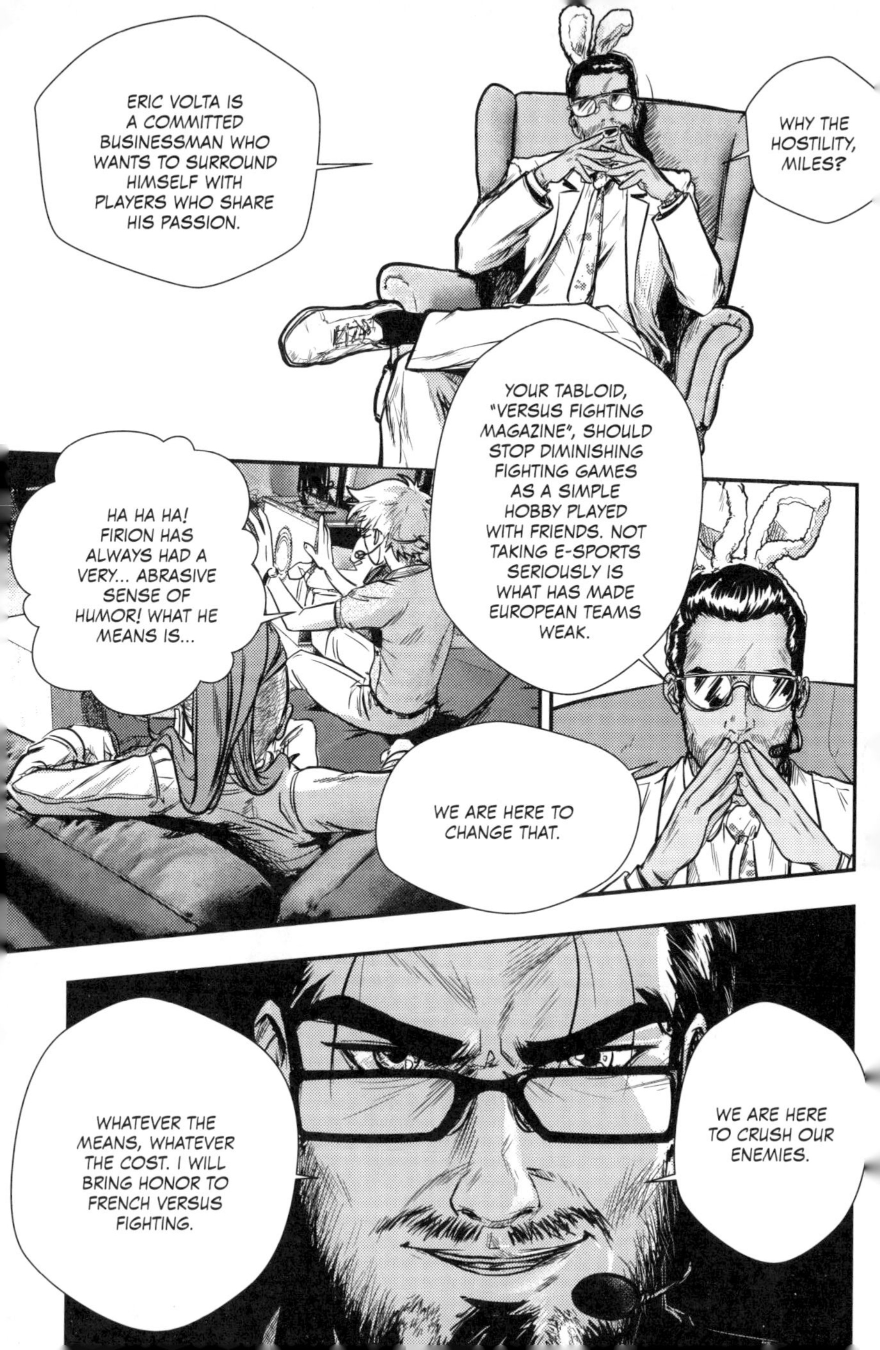
ERIC VOLTA IS A COMMITTED BUSINESSMAN WHO WANTS TO SURROUND HIMSELF WITH PLAYERS WHO SHARE HIS PASSION.
WHY THE HOSTILITY, MILES?
HA HA HA! FIRION HAS ALWAYS HAD A VERY... ABRASIVE SENSE OF HUMOR! WHAT HE MEANS IS...
YOUR TABLOID, "VERSUS FIGHTING MAGAZINE", SHOULD STOP DIMINISHING FIGHTING GAMES AS A SIMPLE HOBBY PLAYED WITH FRIENDS. NOT TAKING E-SPORTS SERIOUSLY IS WHAT HAS MADE EUROPEAN TEAMS WEAK.
WE ARE HERE TO CHANGE THAT.
WHATEVER THE MEANS, WHATEVER THE COST. I WILL BRING HONOR TO FRENCH VERSUS FIGHTING.
WE ARE HERE TO CRUSH OUR ENEMIES.

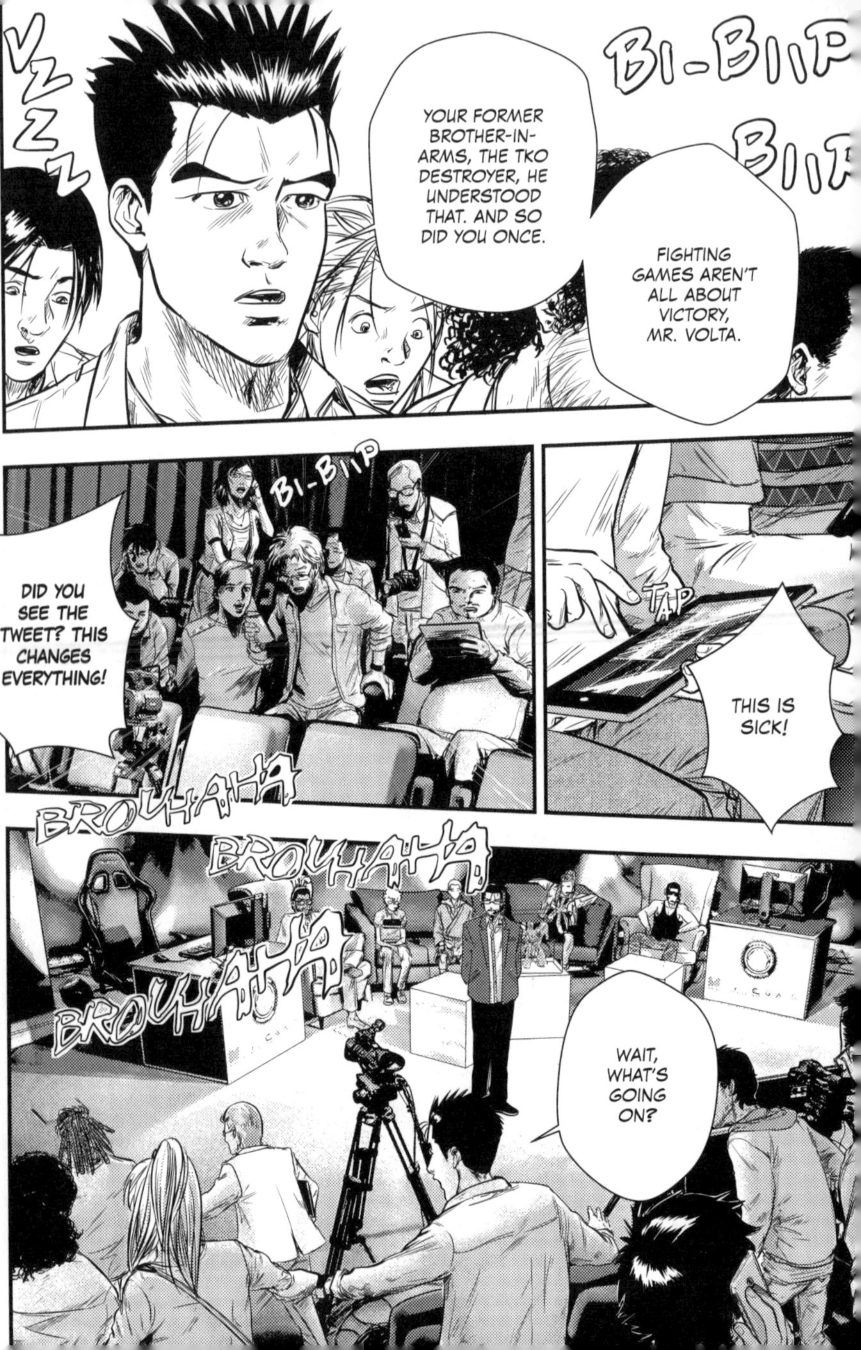
BI-BIIP
BIIP
FIGHTING GAMES AREN'T ALL ABOUT VICTORY, MR. VOLTA.
YOUR FORMER BROTHER-IN-ARMS, THE TKO DESTROYER, HE UNDERSTOOD THAT. AND SO DID YOU ONCE.
VZZZZ
TAP
THIS IS SICK!
BI-BIIP
DID YOU SEE THE TWEET? THIS CHANGES EVERYTHING!
BROUHAHA
BROUHAHA
WAIT, WHAT'S GOING ON?
BROUHAHA

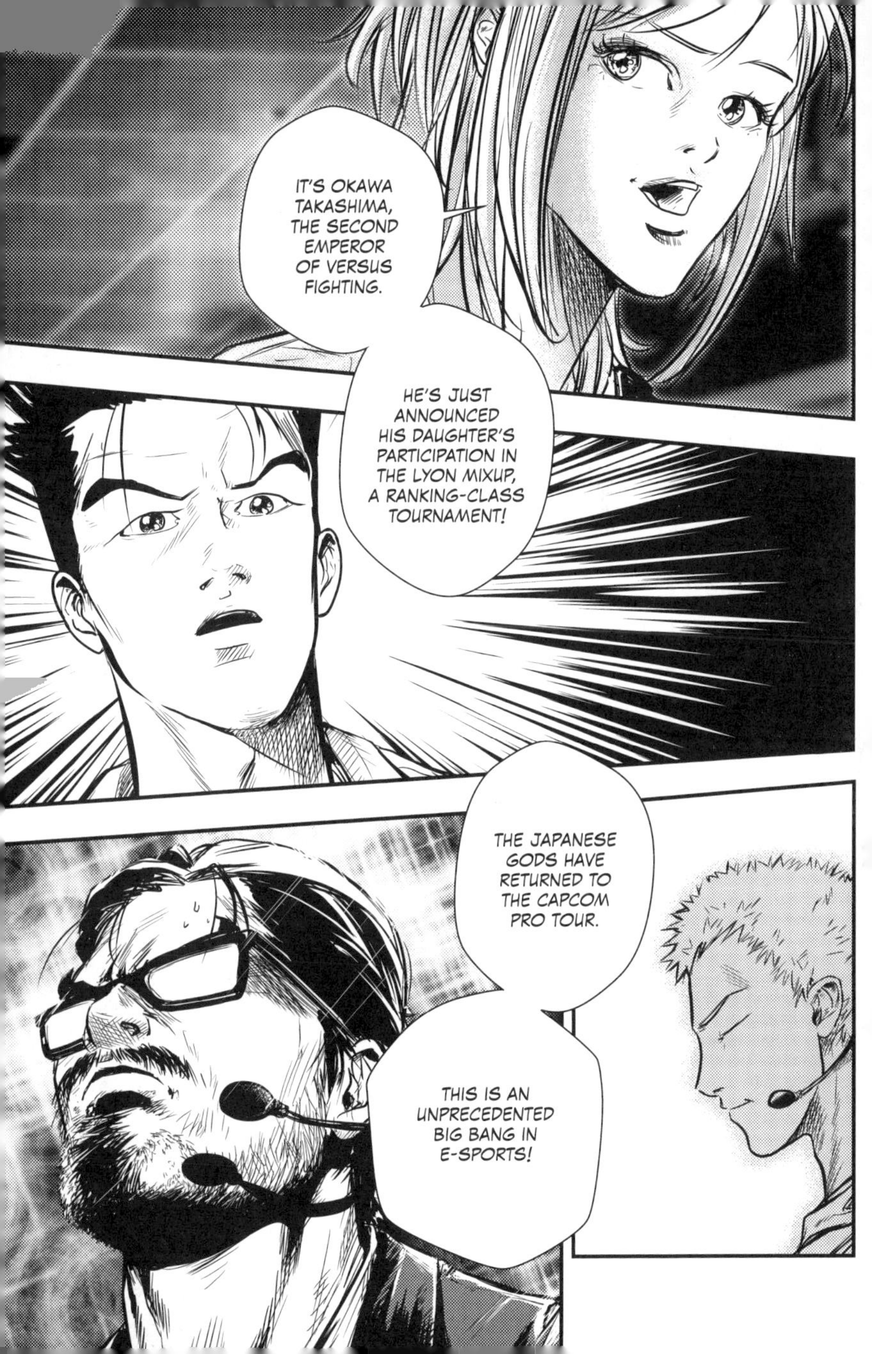
IT'S OKAWA TAKASHIMA, THE SECOND EMPEROR OF VERSUS FIGHTING.
HE'S JUST ANNOUNCED HIS DAUGHTER'S PARTICIPATION IN THE LYON MIXUP, A RANKING-CLASS TOURNAMENT!
THE JAPANESE GODS HAVE RETURNED TO THE CAPCOM PRO TOUR.
THIS IS AN UNPRECEDENTED BIG BANG IN E-SPORTS!

CHARACTER SELECT!

IYM

ANGRY PUNK-OH!

BACKGROUND

From England, IYM (I'M YOUR MUMMY, only to close friends) is a highly respected player in the circuit. All fighters know they must compliment her before, during, and after facing her (particularly if she loses).

But behind this fiery temperment lies a sweet young girl with a heart of gold... just kidding! IYM is a sore loser, and a hellish fear of losing usually keeps her from doing so, which is useful.

IYM plays with an XBOX 360 controller, with an adapter designed specifically to let it connect to the Playstation 4. Rumor has it, this set up could improve anyone's game...

CHARACTER DESIGN

A real badass, always respected and feared (but never vulgar... at least for the moment). I immediately designed her to look like a hooligan, with the Union Jack incorporated everywhere, from her T-shirt to her swimsuit!

BY KALON

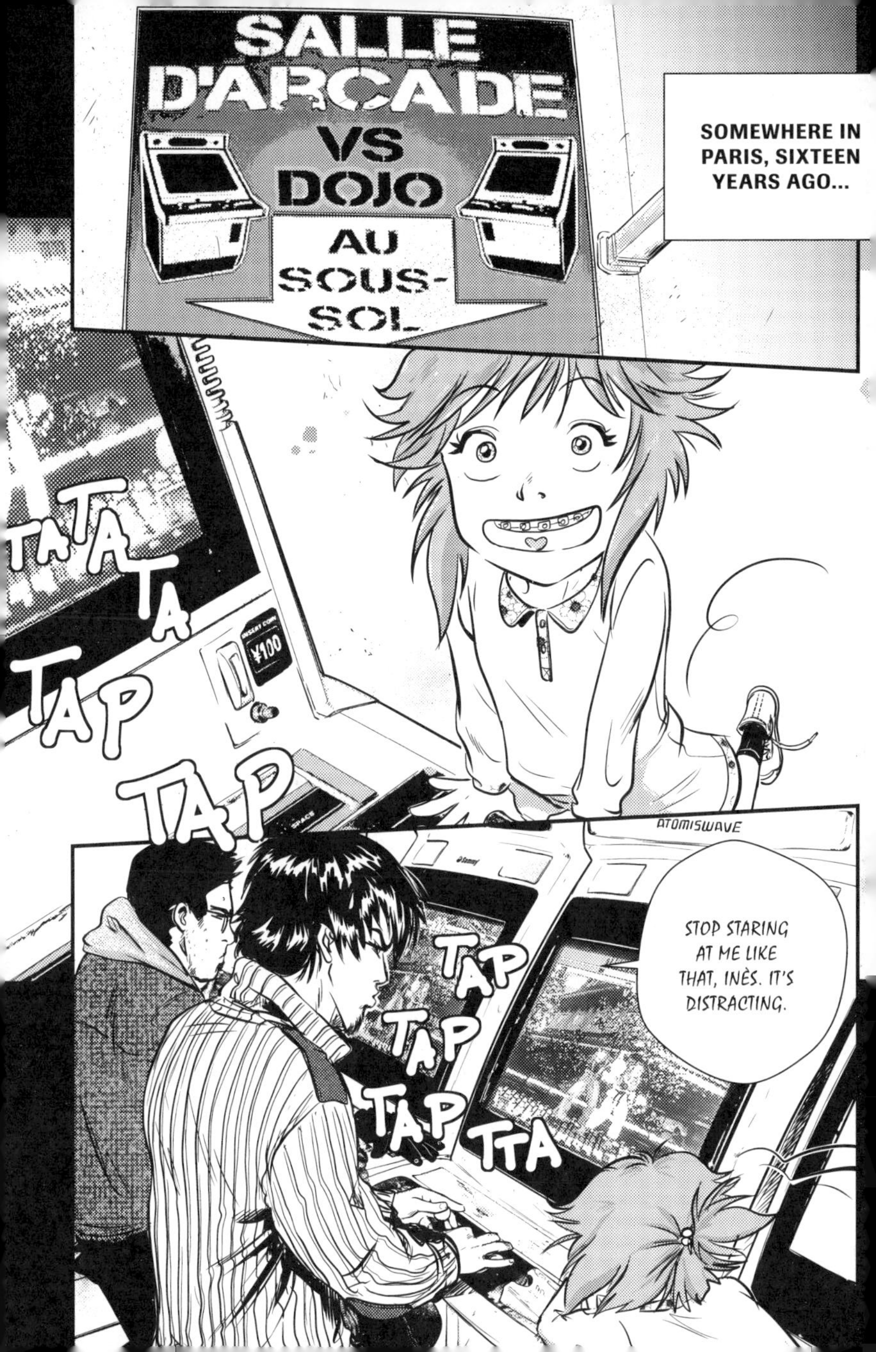
SALLE D'ARCADE
VS DOJO
AU SOUS-SOL
SOMEWHERE IN PARIS, SIXTEEN YEARS AGO...
TATATATA
TAP
TAP
ATOMISWAVE
STOP STARING AT ME LIKE THAT, INÈS. IT'S DISTRACTING.
TAP
TAP
TAP
TTA

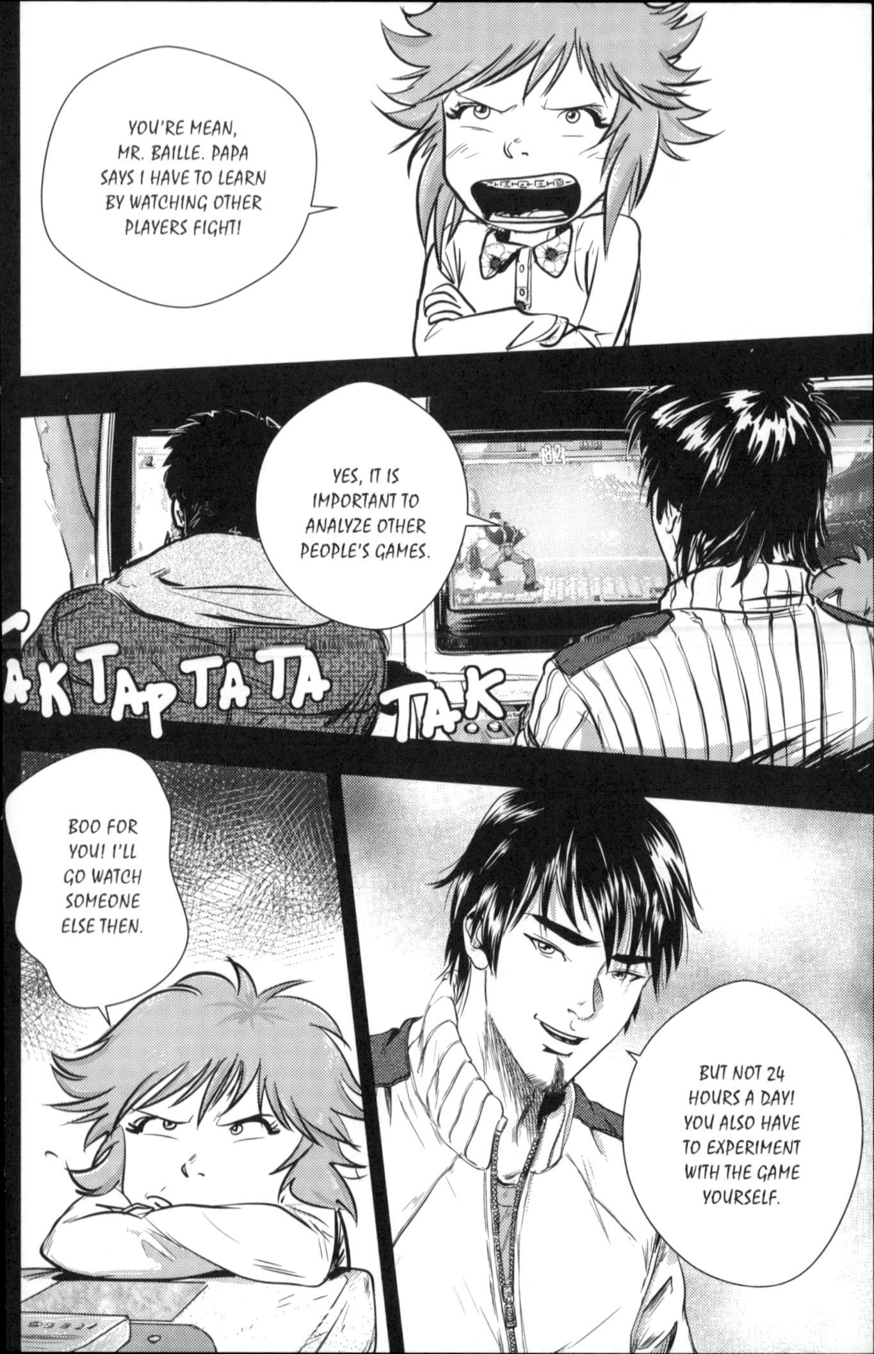
YOU'RE MEAN, MR. BAILLE. PAPA SAYS I HAVE TO LEARN BY WATCHING OTHER PLAYERS FIGHT!
YES, IT IS IMPORTANT TO ANALYZE OTHER PEOPLE'S GAMES.
AK TAP TA TA
TAK
BOO FOR YOU! I'LL GO WATCH SOMEONE ELSE THEN.
BUT NOT 24 HOURS A DAY! YOU ALSO HAVE TO EXPERIMENT WITH THE GAME YOURSELF.

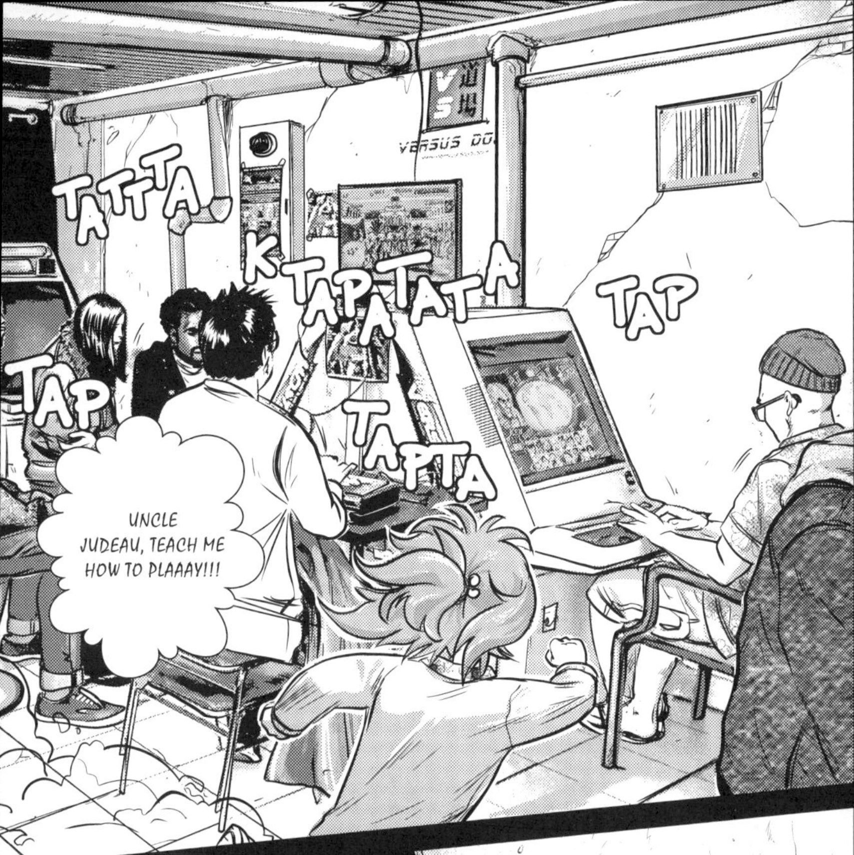
TAP
TAP
TAPTA
UNCLE JUDEAU, TEACH ME HOW TO PLAAAY!!!
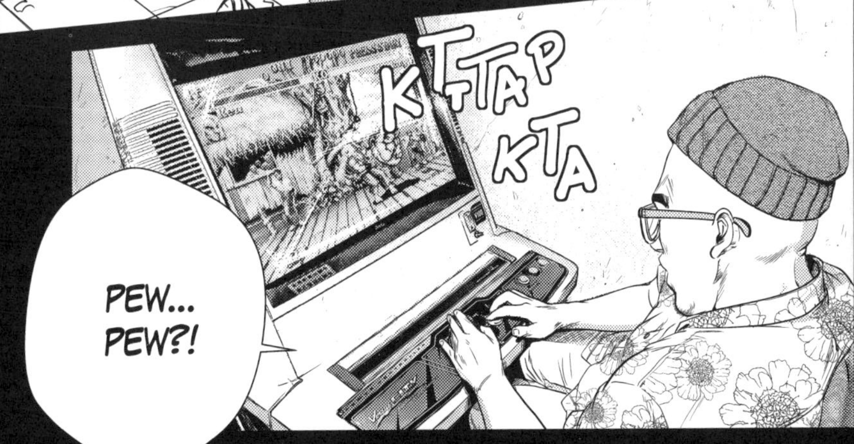
KTA
PEW... PEW?!

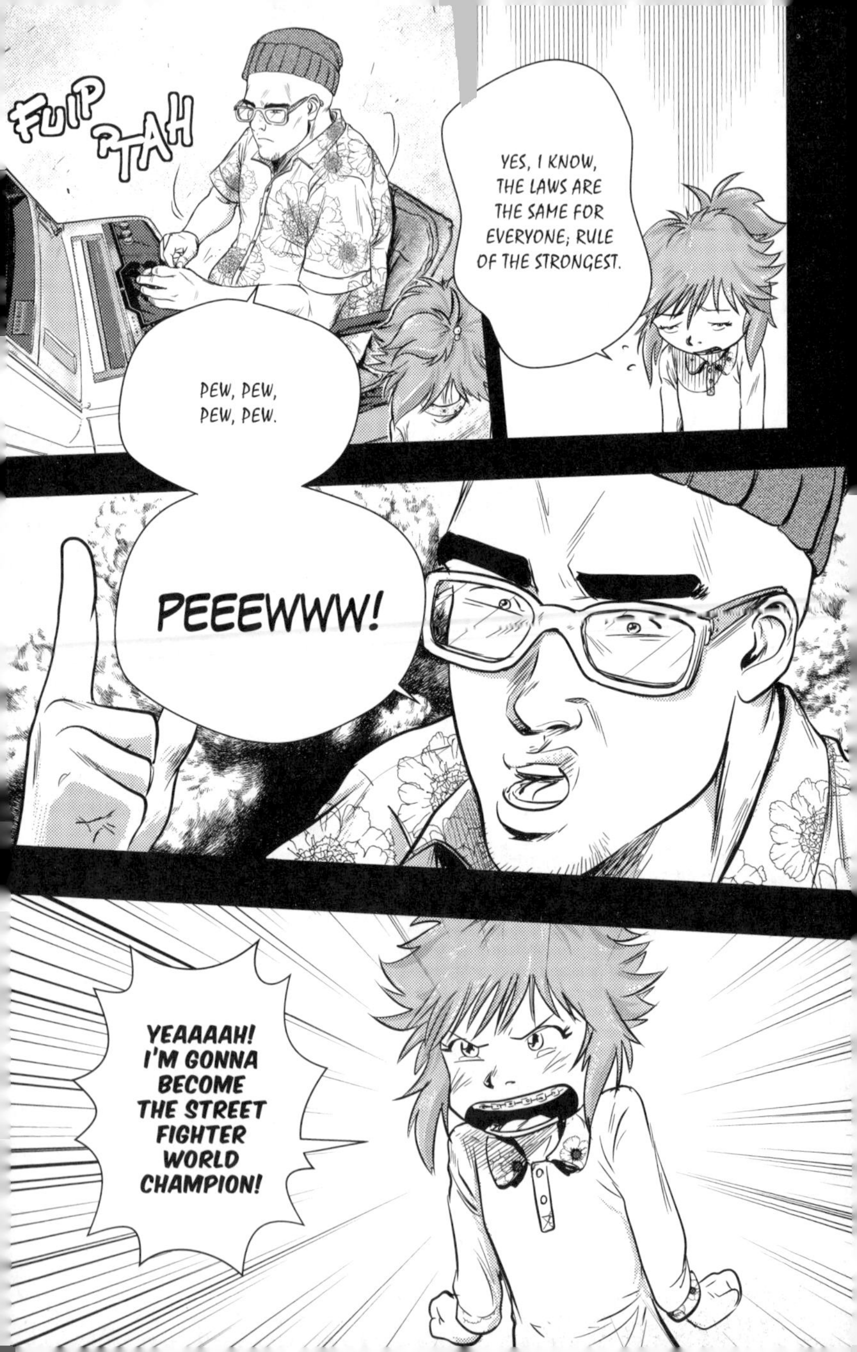
YES, I KNOW, THE LAWS ARE THE SAME FOR EVERYONE; RULE OF THE STRONGEST.
FLIP
TAH
PEW, PEW, PEW, PEW.
PEEEWWW!
YEAAAAH! I'M GONNA BECOME THE STREET FIGHTER WORLD CHAMPION!

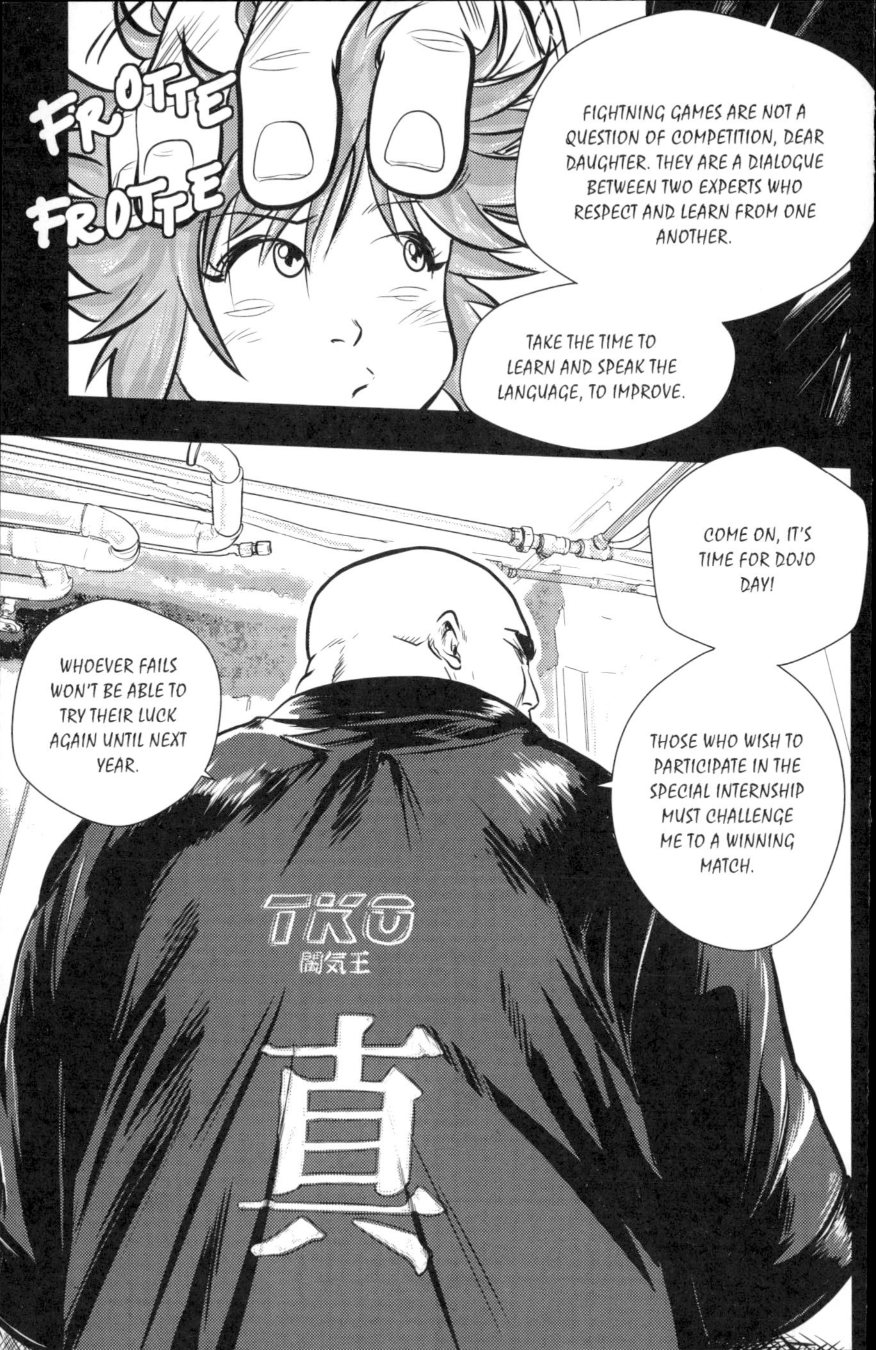
FROTTE FROTTE
FIGHTNING GAMES ARE NOT A QUESTION OF COMPETITION, DEAR DAUGHTER. THEY ARE A DIALOGUE BETWEEN TWO EXPERTS WHO RESPECT AND LEARN FROM ONE ANOTHER.
TAKE THE TIME TO LEARN AND SPEAK THE LANGUAGE, TO IMPROVE.
COME ON, IT'S TIME FOR DOJO DAY!
THOSE WHO WISH TO PARTICIPATE IN THE SPECIAL INTERNSHIP MUST CHALLENGE ME TO A WINNING MATCH.
WHOEVER FAILS WON'T BE ABLE TO TRY THEIR LUCK AGAIN UNTIL NEXT YEAR.
TKO
闘気王

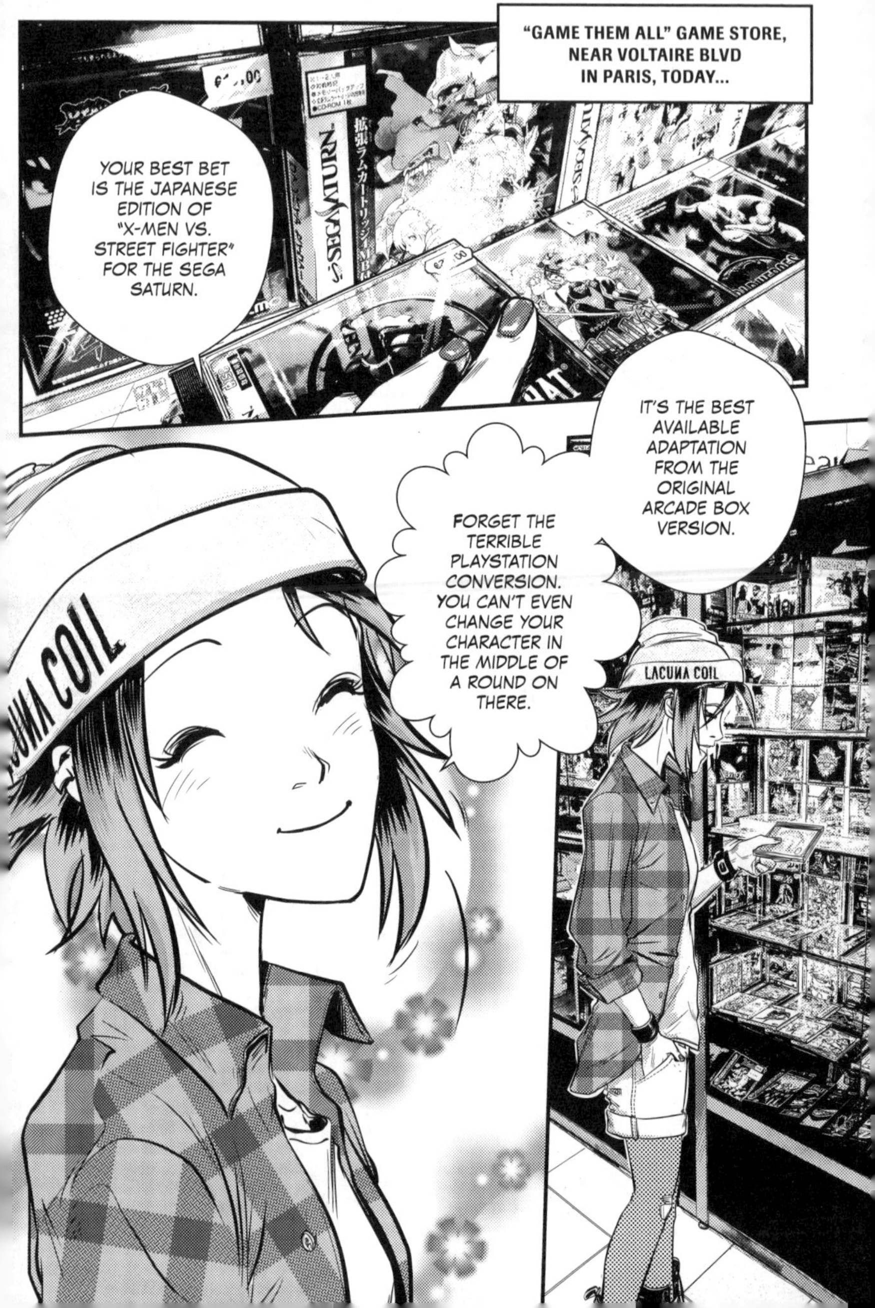
"GAME THEM ALL" GAME STORE, NEAR VOLTAIRE BLVD IN PARIS, TODAY...
YOUR BEST BET IS THE JAPANESE EDITION OF "X-MEN VS. STREET FIGHTER" FOR THE SEGA SATURN.
IT'S THE BEST AVAILABLE ADAPTATION FROM THE ORIGINAL ARCADE BOX VERSION.
FORGET THE TERRIBLE PLAYSTATION CONVERSION. YOU CAN'T EVEN CHANGE YOUR CHARACTER IN THE MIDDLE OF A ROUND ON THERE.
LACUNA COIL

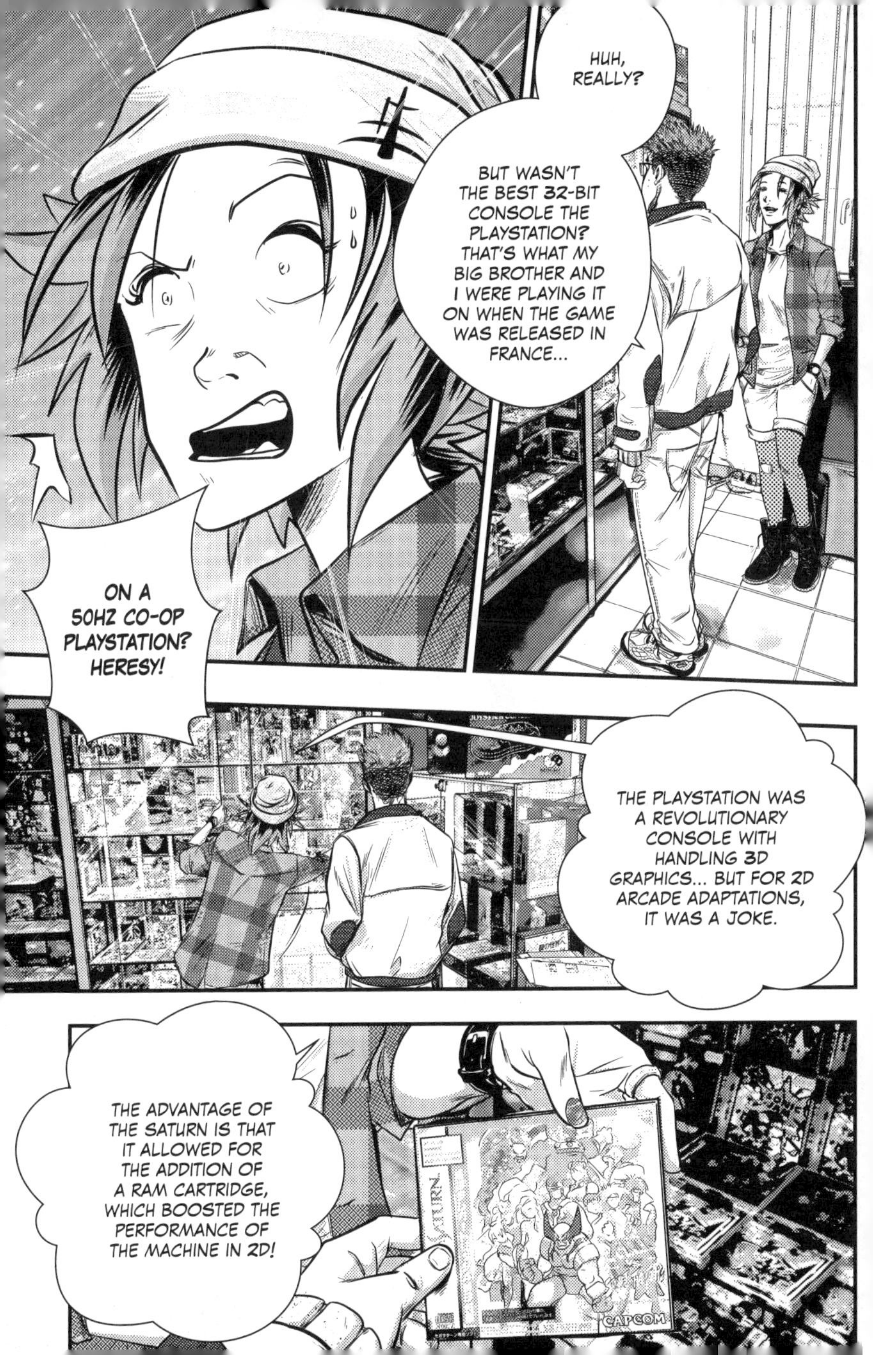
HUH, REALLY?
BUT WASN'T THE BEST 32-BIT CONSOLE THE PLAYSTATION? THAT'S WHAT MY BIG BROTHER AND I WERE PLAYING IT ON WHEN THE GAME WAS RELEASED IN FRANCE...
ON A 50HZ CO-OP PLAYSTATION? HERESY!
THE PLAYSTATION WAS A REVOLUTIONARY CONSOLE WITH HANDLING 3D GRAPHICS... BUT FOR 2D ARCADE ADAPTATIONS, IT WAS A JOKE.
THE ADVANTAGE OF THE SATURN IS THAT IT ALLOWED FOR THE ADDITION OF A RAM CARTRIDGE, WHICH BOOSTED THE PERFORMANCE OF THE MACHINE IN 2D!
SATURN
CAPCOM

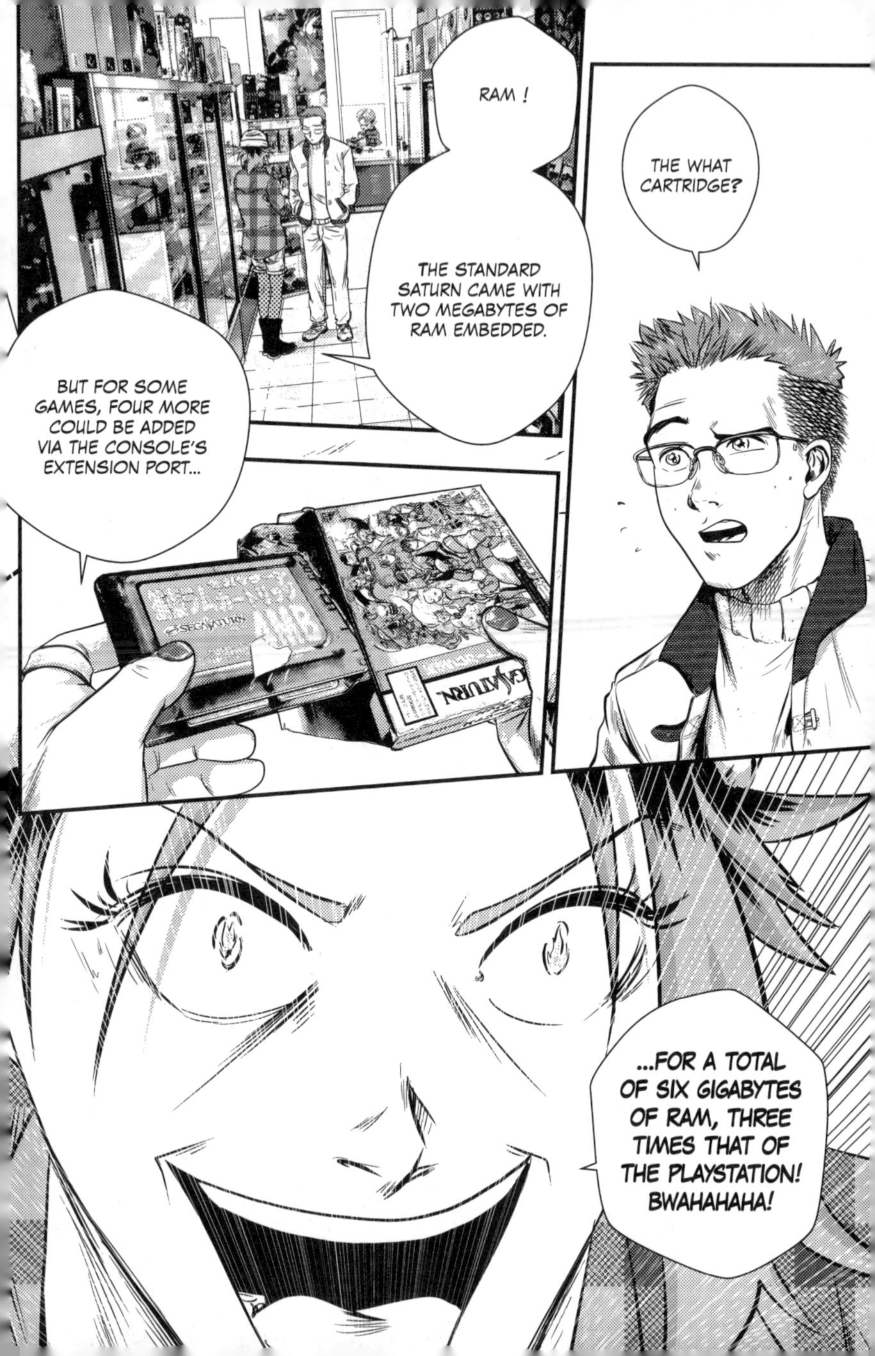
THE WHAT CARTRIDGE?
RAM !
THE STANDARD SATURN CAME WITH TWO MEGABYTES OF RAM EMBEDDED.
BUT FOR SOME GAMES, FOUR MORE COULD BE ADDED VIA THE CONSOLE'S EXTENSION PORT...
...FOR A TOTAL OF SIX GIGABYTES OF RAM, THREE TIMES THAT OF THE PLAYSTATION! BWAHAHAHA!

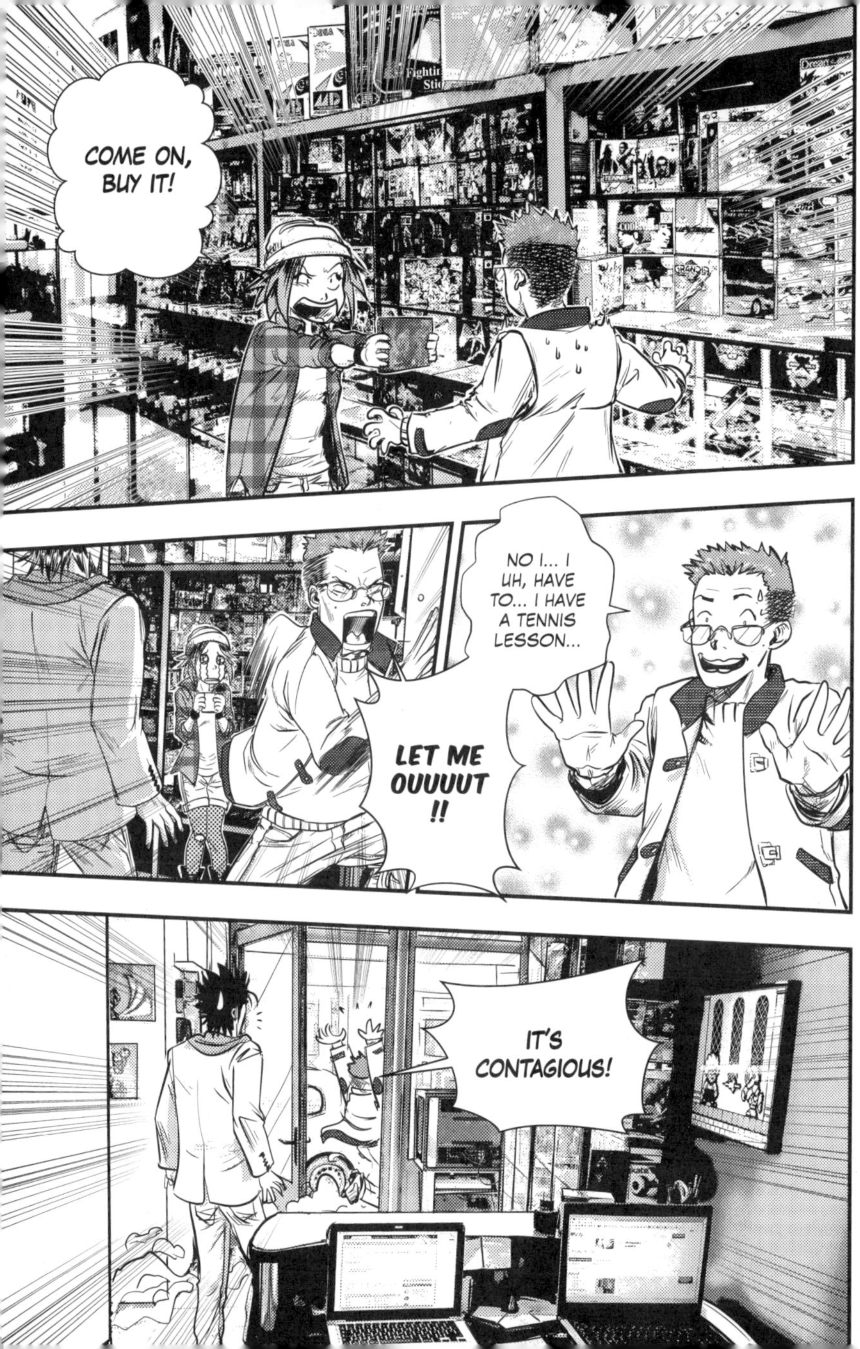
COME ON, BUY IT!
NO I... I UH, HAVE TO... I HAVE A TENNIS LESSON...
LET ME OUUUUT !!
IT'S CONTAGIOUS!

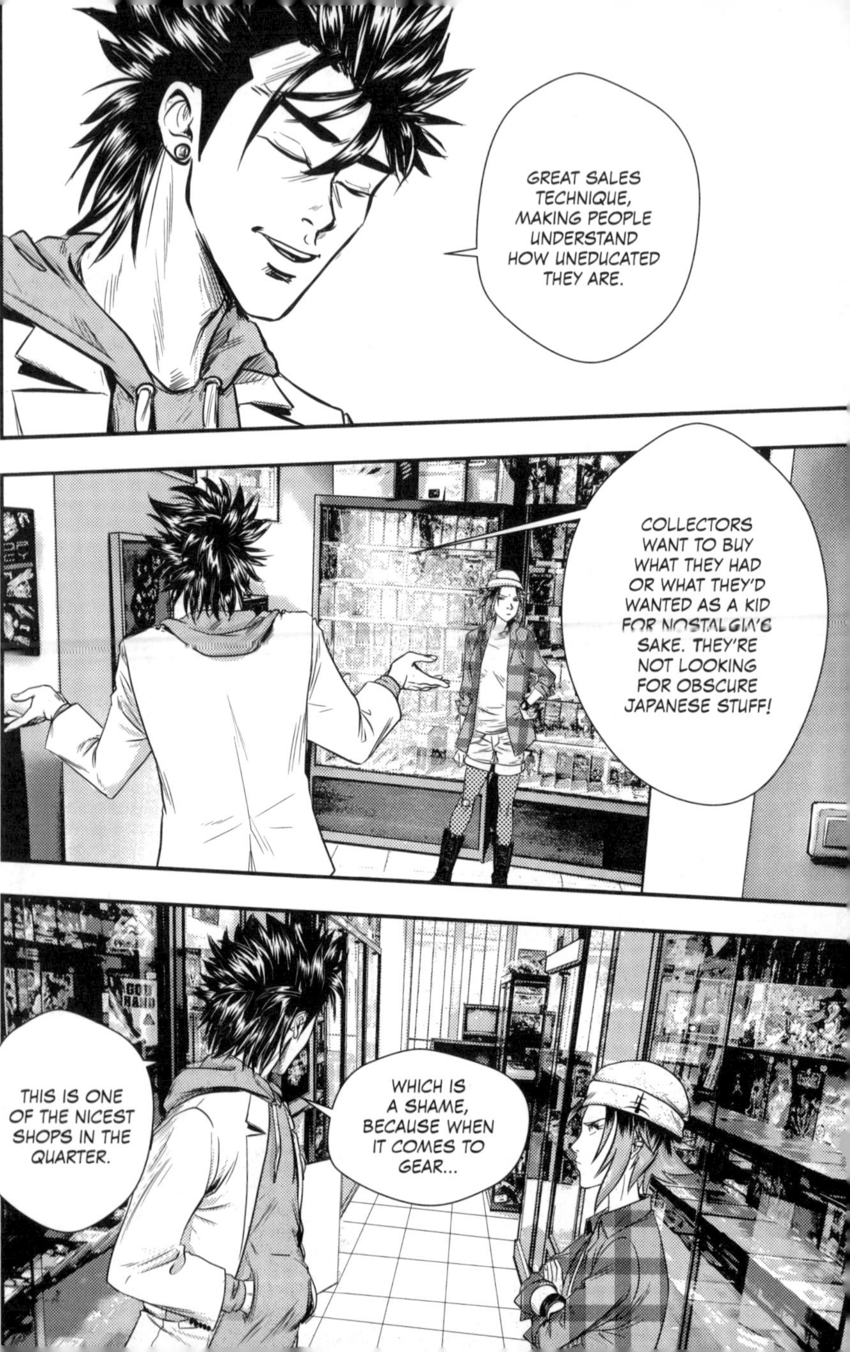
GREAT SALES TECHNIQUE, MAKING PEOPLE UNDERSTAND HOW UNEDUCATED THEY ARE.
COLLECTORS WANT TO BUY WHAT THEY HAD OR WHAT THEY'D WANTED AS A KID FOR NOSTALGIA'S SAKE. THEY'RE NOT LOOKING FOR OBSCURE JAPANESE STUFF!
THIS IS ONE OF THE NICEST SHOPS IN THE QUARTER.
WHICH IS A SHAME, BECAUSE WHEN IT COMES TO GEAR...

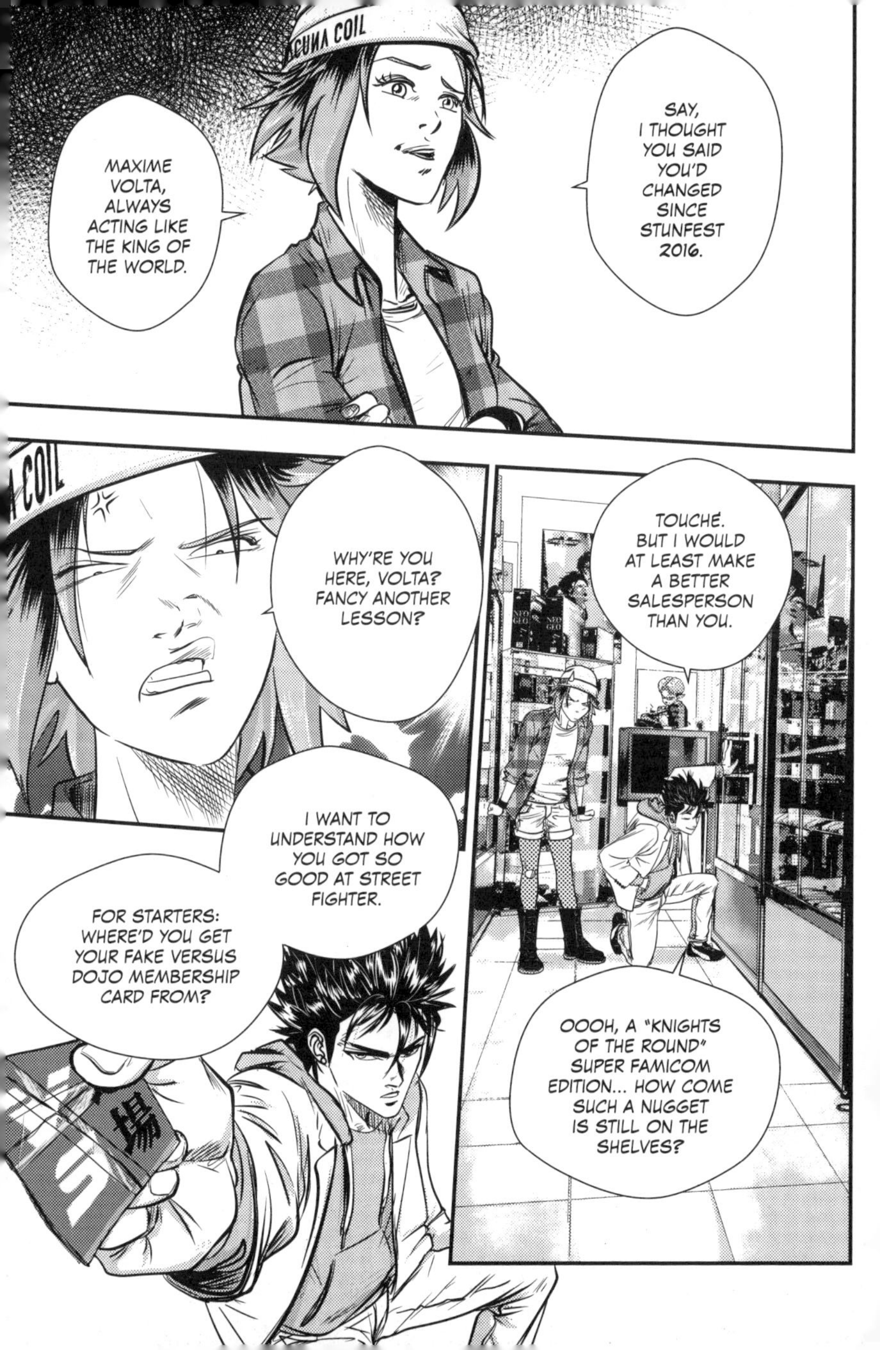
SAY, I THOUGHT YOU SAID YOU'D CHANGED SINCE STUNFEST 2016.
MAXIME VOLTA, ALWAYS ACTING LIKE THE KING OF THE WORLD.
TOUCHE. BUT I WOULD AT LEAST MAKE A BETTER SALESPERSON THAN YOU.
OOOH, A "KNIGHTS OF THE ROUND" SUPER FAMICOM EDITION... HOW COME SUCH A NUGGET IS STILL ON THE SHELVES?
WHY'RE YOU HERE, VOLTA? FANCY ANOTHER LESSON?
I WANT TO UNDERSTAND HOW YOU GOT SO GOOD AT STREET FIGHTER.
FOR STARTERS: WHERE'D YOU GET YOUR FAKE VERSUS DOJO MEMBERSHIP CARD FROM?

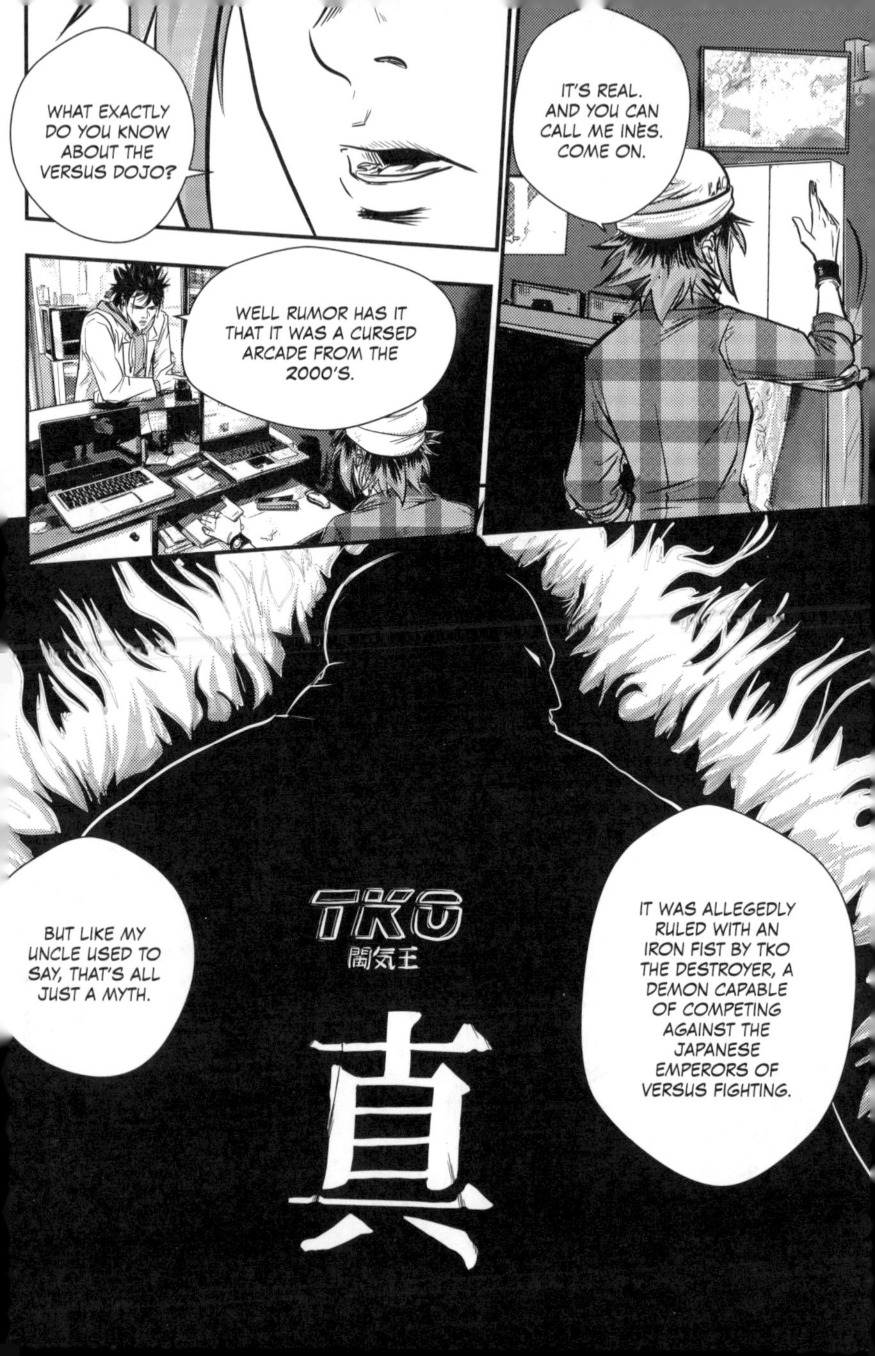
WHAT EXACTLY DO YOU KNOW ABOUT THE VERSUS DOJO?
WELL RUMOR HAS IT THAT IT WAS A CURSED ARCADE FROM THE 2000'S.
IT'S REAL. AND YOU CAN CALL ME INÈS. COME ON.
IT WAS ALLEGEDLY RULED WITH AN IRON FIST BY TKO THE DESTROYER, A DEMON CAPABLE OF COMPETING AGAINST THE JAPANESE EMPERORS OF VERSUS FIGHTING.
BUT LIKE MY UNCLE USED TO SAY, THAT'S ALL JUST A MYTH.
TKO
闇気王
真

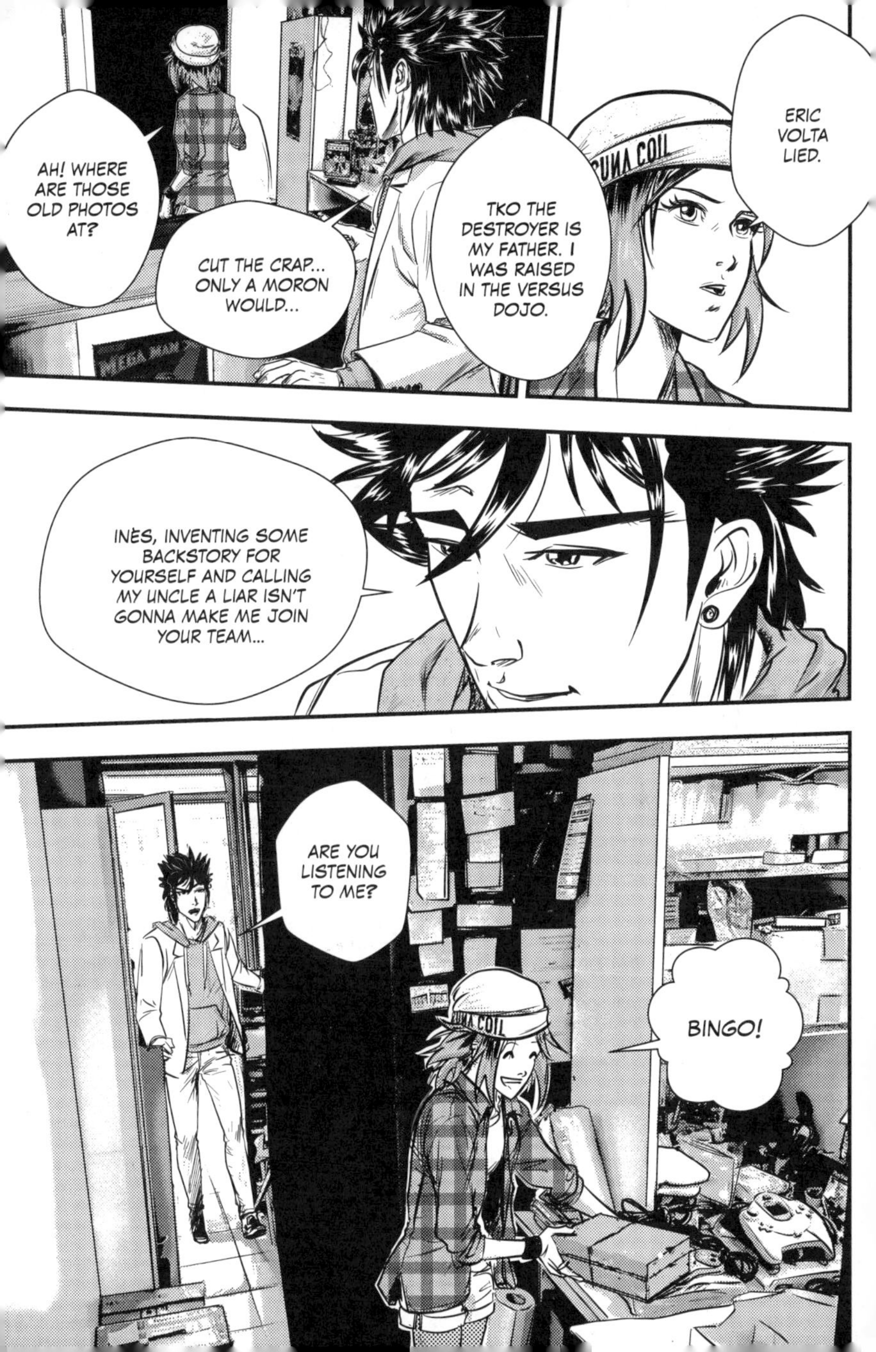
ERIC VOLTA LIED.
TKO THE DESTROYER IS MY FATHER. I WAS RAISED IN THE VERSUS DOJO.
CUT THE CRAP... ONLY A MORON WOULD...
AH! WHERE ARE THOSE OLD PHOTOS AT?
INÈS, INVENTING SOME BACKSTORY FOR YOURSELF AND CALLING MY UNCLE A LIAR ISN'T GONNA MAKE ME JOIN YOUR TEAM...
ARE YOU LISTENING TO ME?
BINGO!

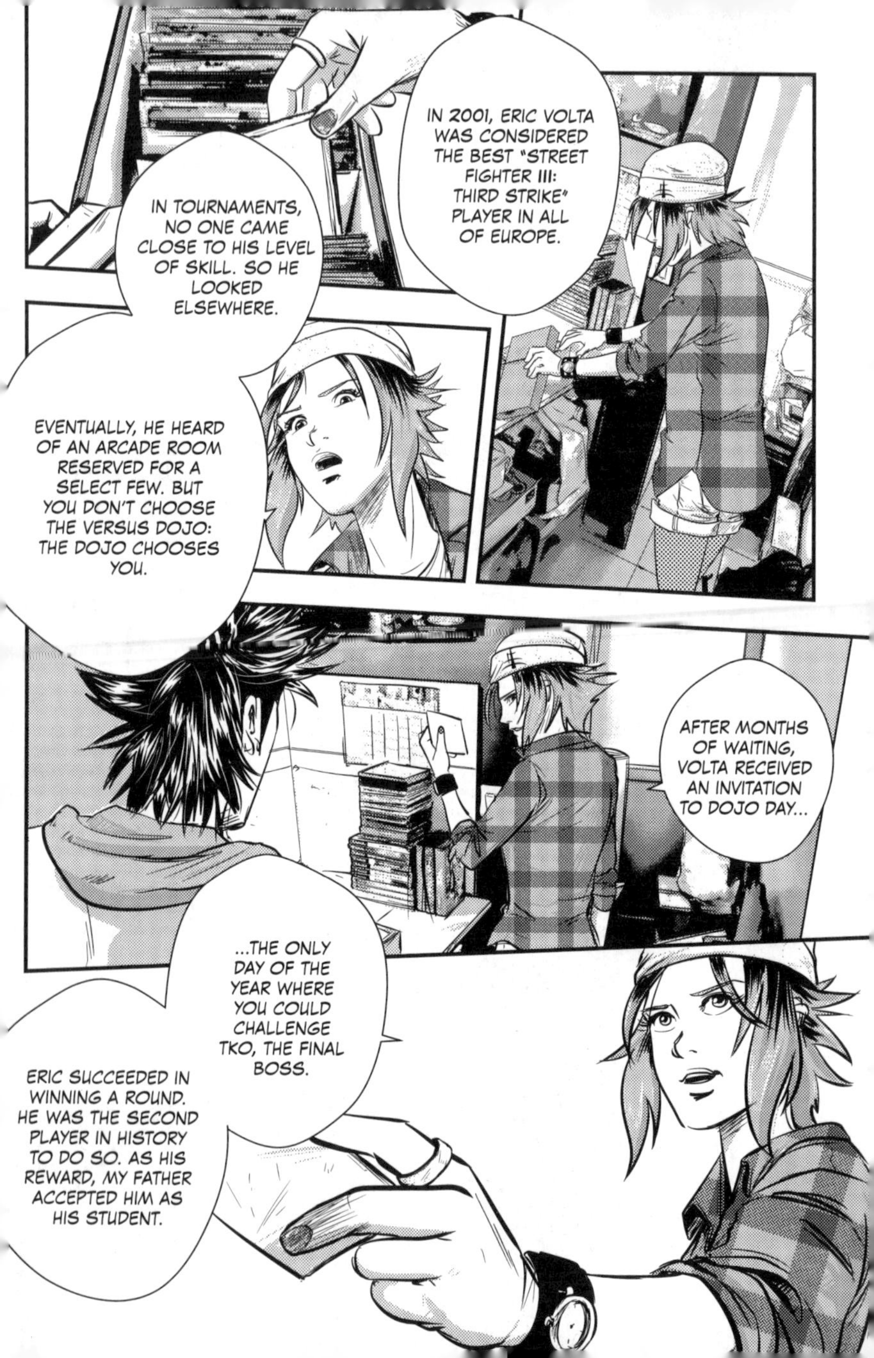
IN 2001, ERIC VOLTA WAS CONSIDERED THE BEST "STREET FIGHTER III: THIRD STRIKE" PLAYER IN ALL OF EUROPE.
IN TOURNAMENTS, NO ONE CAME CLOSE TO HIS LEVEL OF SKILL. SO HE LOOKED ELSEWHERE.
EVENTUALLY, HE HEARD OF AN ARCADE ROOM RESERVED FOR A SELECT FEW. BUT YOU DON'T CHOOSE THE VERSUS DOJO: THE DOJO CHOOSES YOU.
AFTER MONTHS OF WAITING, VOLTA RECEIVED AN INVITATION TO DOJO DAY...
...THE ONLY DAY OF THE YEAR WHERE YOU COULD CHALLENGE TKO, THE FINAL BOSS.
ERIC SUCCEEDED IN WINNING A ROUND. HE WAS THE SECOND PLAYER IN HISTORY TO DO SO. AS HIS REWARD, MY FATHER ACCEPTED HIM AS HIS STUDENT.

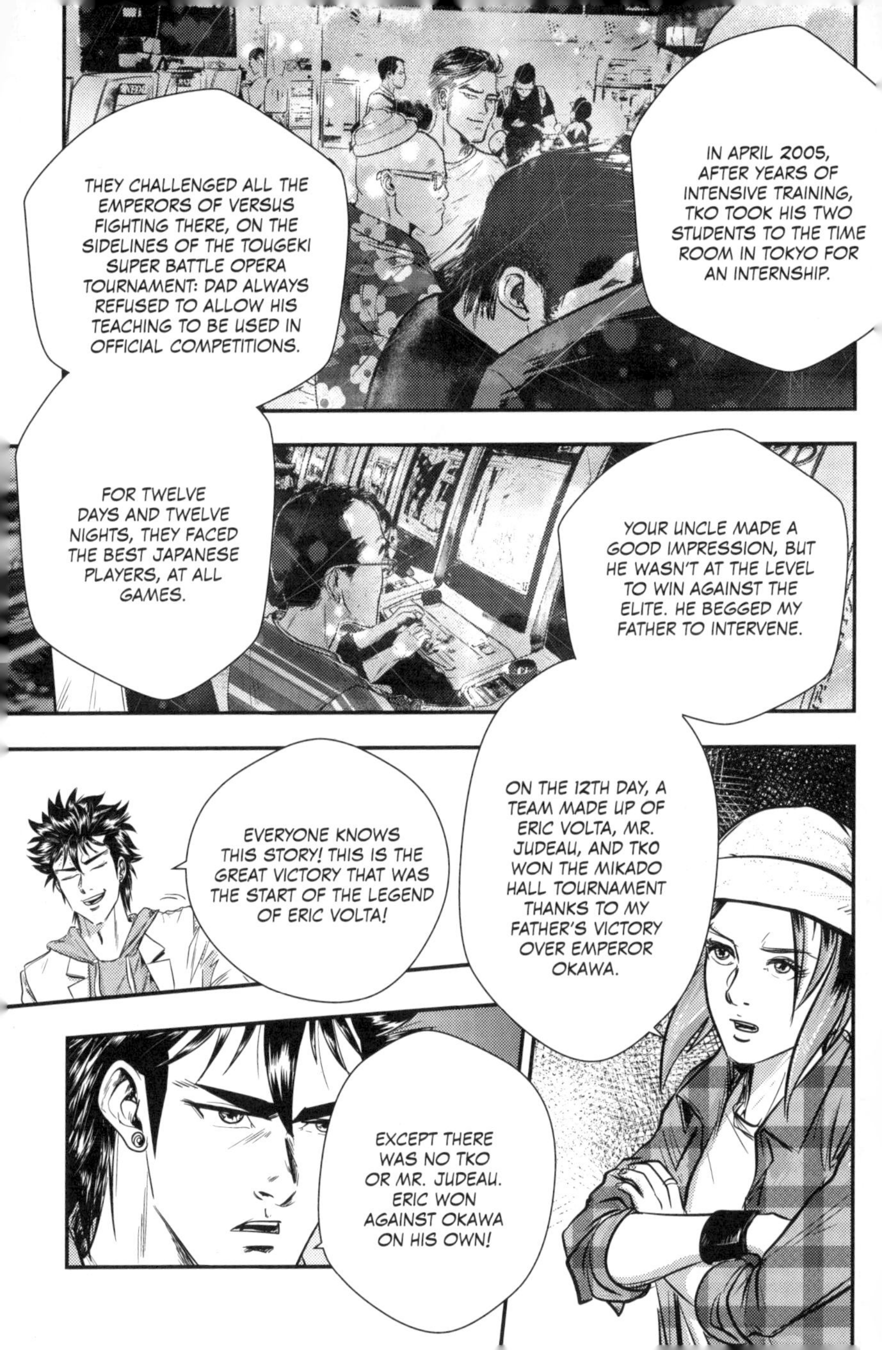
IN APRIL 2005, AFTER YEARS OF INTENSIVE TRAINING, TKO TOOK HIS TWO STUDENTS TO THE TIME ROOM IN TOKYO FOR AN INTERNSHIP.
THEY CHALLENGED ALL THE EMPERORS OF VERSUS FIGHTING THERE, ON THE SIDELINES OF THE TOUGEKI SUPER BATTLE OPERA TOURNAMENT: DAD ALWAYS REFUSED TO ALLOW HIS TEACHING TO BE USED IN OFFICIAL COMPETITIONS.
YOUR UNCLE MADE A GOOD IMPRESSION, BUT HE WASN'T AT THE LEVEL TO WIN AGAINST THE ELITE. HE BEGGED MY FATHER TO INTERVENE.
FOR TWELVE DAYS AND TWELVE NIGHTS, THEY FACED THE BEST JAPANESE PLAYERS, AT ALL GAMES.
ON THE 12TH DAY, A TEAM MADE UP OF ERIC VOLTA, MR. JUDEAU, AND TKO WON THE MIKADO HALL TOURNAMENT THANKS TO MY FATHER'S VICTORY OVER EMPEROR OKAWA.
EVERYONE KNOWS THIS STORY! THIS IS THE GREAT VICTORY THAT WAS THE START OF THE LEGEND OF ERIC VOLTA!
EXCEPT THERE WAS NO TKO OR MR. JUDEAU. ERIC WON AGAINST OKAWA ON HIS OWN!

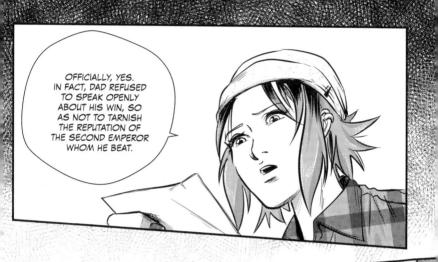

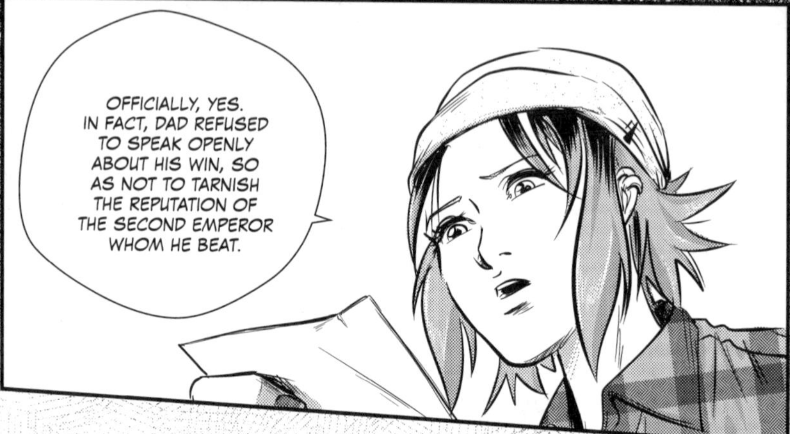
OFFICIALLY, YES. IN FACT, DAD REFUSED TO SPEAK OPENLY ABOUT HIS WIN, SO AS NOT TO TARNISH THE REPUTATION OF THE SECOND EMPEROR WHOM HE BEAT.

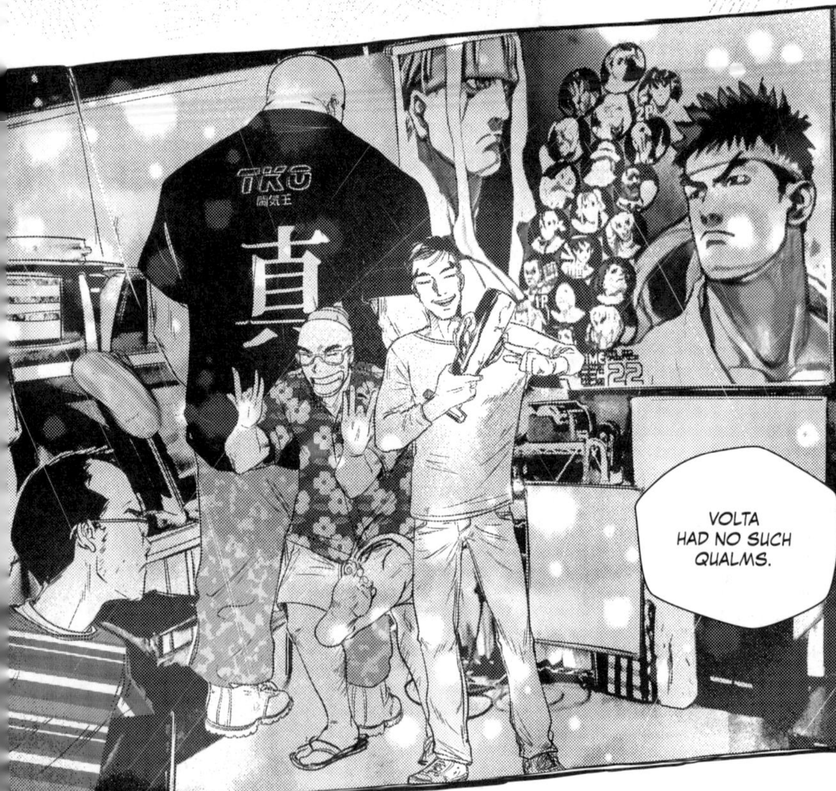
TKO
VOLTA HAD NO SUCH QUALMS.

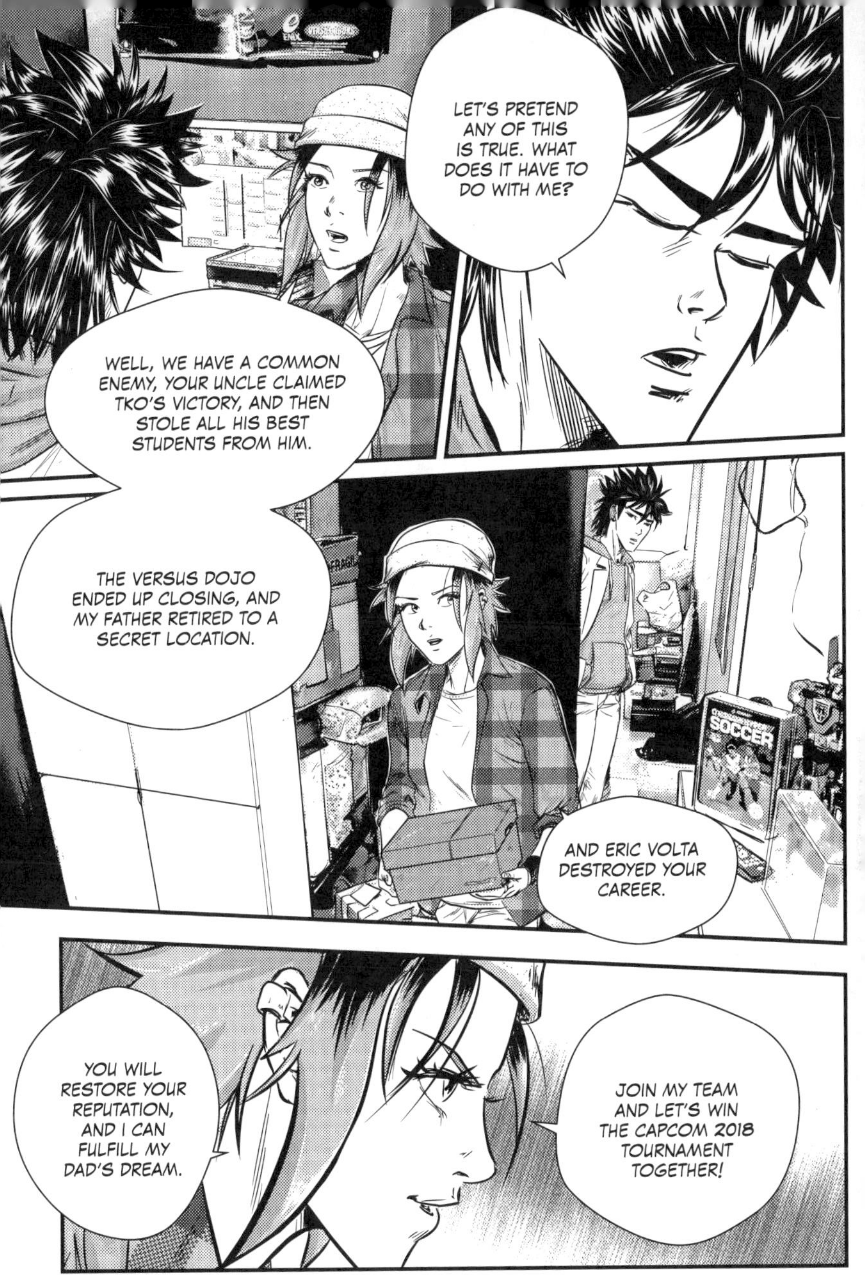
LET'S PRETEND ANY OF THIS IS TRUE. WHAT DOES IT HAVE TO DO WITH ME?
WELL, WE HAVE A COMMON ENEMY, YOUR UNCLE CLAIMED TKO'S VICTORY, AND THEN STOLE ALL HIS BEST STUDENTS FROM HIM.
THE VERSUS DOJO ENDED UP CLOSING, AND MY FATHER RETIRED TO A SECRET LOCATION.
AND ERIC VOLTA DESTROYED YOUR CAREER.
SOCCER
JOIN MY TEAM AND LET'S WIN THE CAPCOM 2018 TOURNAMENT TOGETHER!
YOU WILL RESTORE YOUR REPUTATION, AND I CAN FULFILL MY DAD'S DREAM.

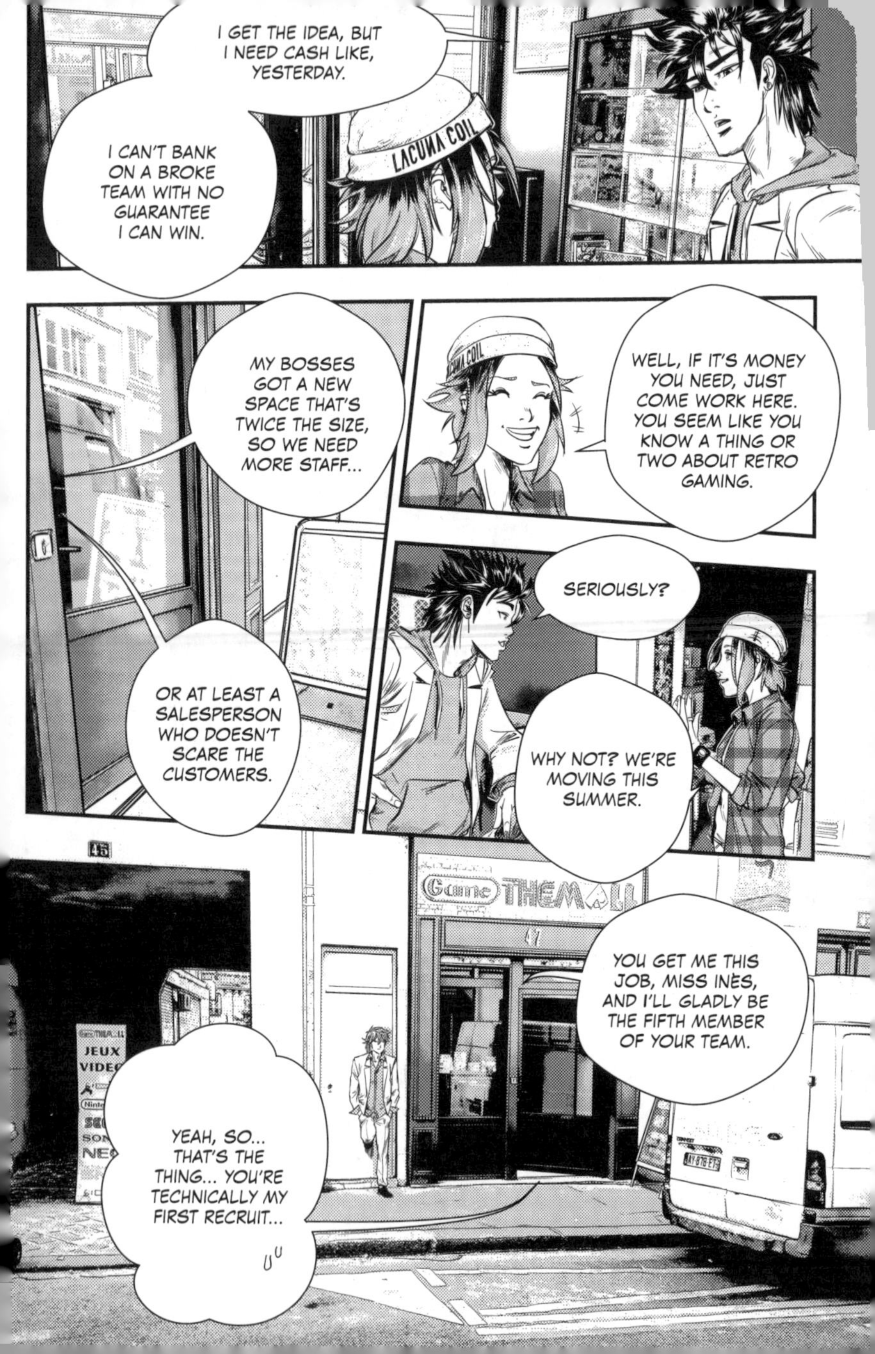
LACUNA COIL
I GET THE IDEA, BUT I NEED CASH LIKE, YESTERDAY.
I CAN'T BANK ON A BROKE TEAM WITH NO GUARANTEE I CAN WIN.
WELL, IF IT'S MONEY YOU NEED, JUST COME WORK HERE. YOU SEEM LIKE YOU KNOW A THING OR TWO ABOUT RETRO GAMING.
SERIOUSLY?
WHY NOT? WE'RE MOVING THIS SUMMER.
MY BOSSES GOT A NEW SPACE THAT'S TWICE THE SIZE, SO WE NEED MORE STAFF...
OR AT LEAST A SALESPERSON WHO DOESN'T SCARE THE CUSTOMERS.
45
47
JEUX
YOU GET ME THIS JOB, MISS INÈS, AND I'LL GLADLY BE THE FIFTH MEMBER OF YOUR TEAM.
YEAH, SO... THAT'S THE THING... YOU'RE TECHNICALLY MY FIRST RECRUIT...

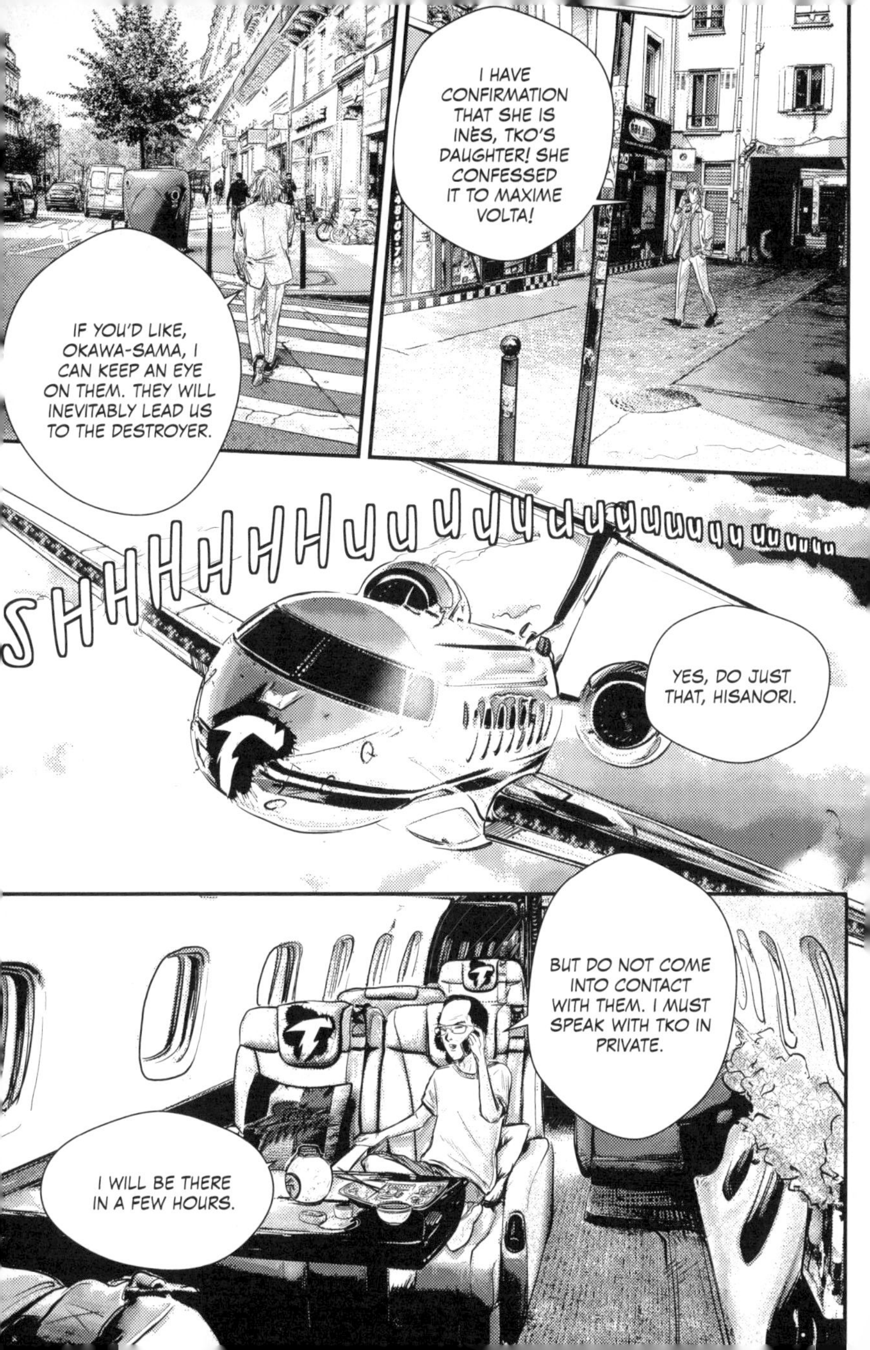
I HAVE CONFIRMATION THAT SHE IS INÈS, TKO'S DAUGHTER! SHE CONFESSED IT TO MAXIME VOLTA!
IF YOU'D LIKE, OKAWA-SAMA, I CAN KEEP AN EYE ON THEM. THEY WILL INEVITABLY LEAD US TO THE DESTROYER.
SHHHHHHuuuuuuuuuuuuuuuuuu
YES, DO JUST THAT, HISANORI.
BUT DO NOT COME INTO CONTACT WITH THEM. I MUST SPEAK WITH TKO IN PRIVATE.
I WILL BE THERE IN A FEW HOURS.

CHARACTER SELECT!

INÈS

THE COPYCAT

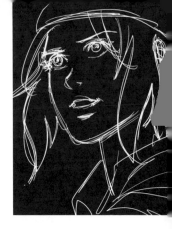

BACKGROUND

Inès grew up in the legendary arcade scene of French Versus Fighting, in the Versus Dojo. Surrounded by the best players in France, the young virtuoso has spent her days observing the techniques and styles of dozens of different players.

The daughter of TKO the Destroyer, one would wonder why she was never one of his students... a philosophical theory of the Unknowns may, perhaps, share some insight.

"To be or not to be, that is the sinusoidal question of the hypochondriac anchorite."

VERSUS FIGHTING STORY

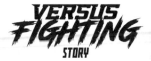

CHARACTER DESIGN

A little on the feminine grunge side, with her ever-present beanie (will we one day know why she wears it all the time? And does she wear it all the time?). Each of the hats bears the mark of a rock or metal band: it's up to you to list them all!

BY KALON

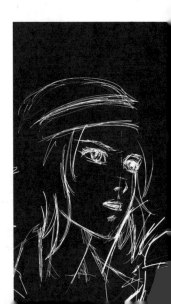

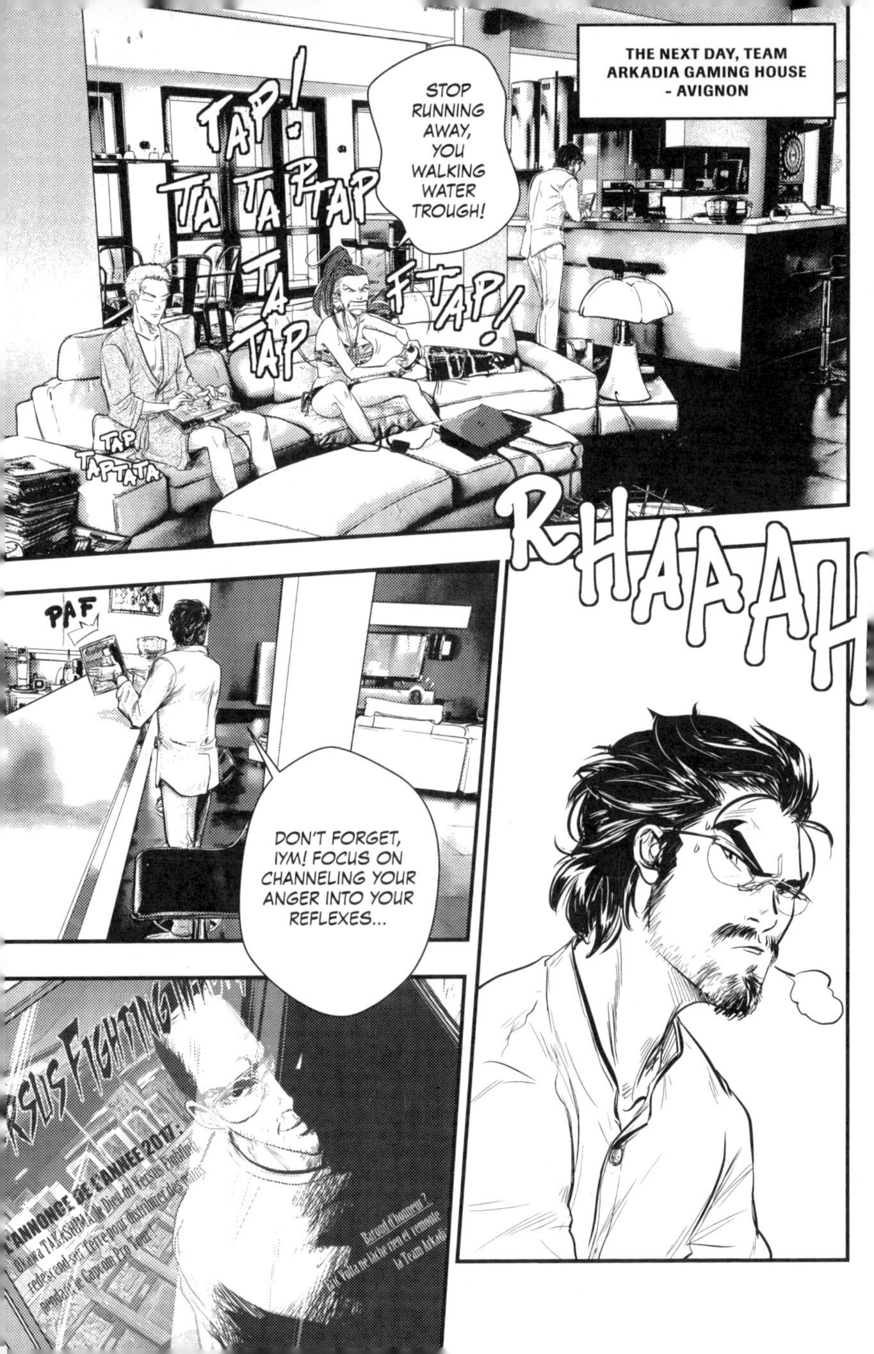
THE NEXT DAY, TEAM ARKADIA GAMING HOUSE - AVIGNON
TAP! TA TA TAP TAP TA TA TAP
STOP RUNNING AWAY, YOU WALKING WATER TROUGH!
FTAP!
TAP TAPTATA
PAF
DON'T FORGET, IYM! FOCUS ON CHANNELING YOUR ANGER INTO YOUR REFLEXES...
ANNONCE DE L'ANNEE 2017 :
RHAAAAH

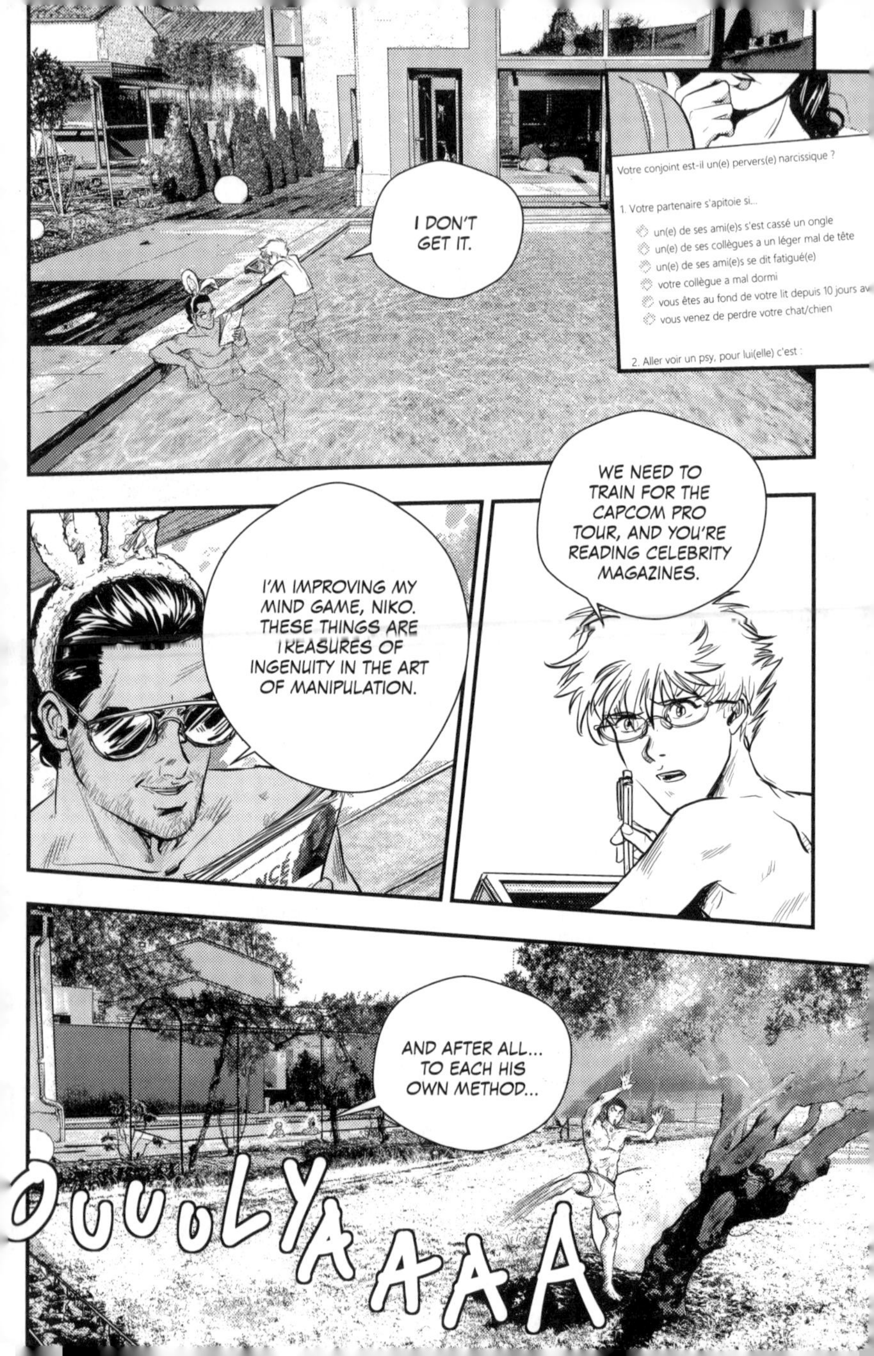
Votre conjoint est-il un(e) pervers(e) narcissique ?
1. Votre partenaire s'apitoie si...
un(e) de ses ami(e)s s'est cassé un ongle
un(e) de ses collègues a un léger mal de tête
un(e) de ses ami(e)s se dit fatigué(e)
votre collègue a mal dormi
vous êtes au fond de votre lit depuis 10 jours av
vous venez de perdre votre chat/chien
2. Aller voir un psy, pour lui(elle) c'est :
I DON'T GET IT.
WE NEED TO TRAIN FOR THE CAPCOM PRO TOUR, AND YOU'RE READING CELEBRITY MAGAZINES.
I'M IMPROVING MY MIND GAME, NIKO. THESE THINGS ARE TREASURES OF INGENUITY IN THE ART OF MANIPULATION.
AND AFTER ALL... TO EACH HIS OWN METHOD...
OUUULYAAAA

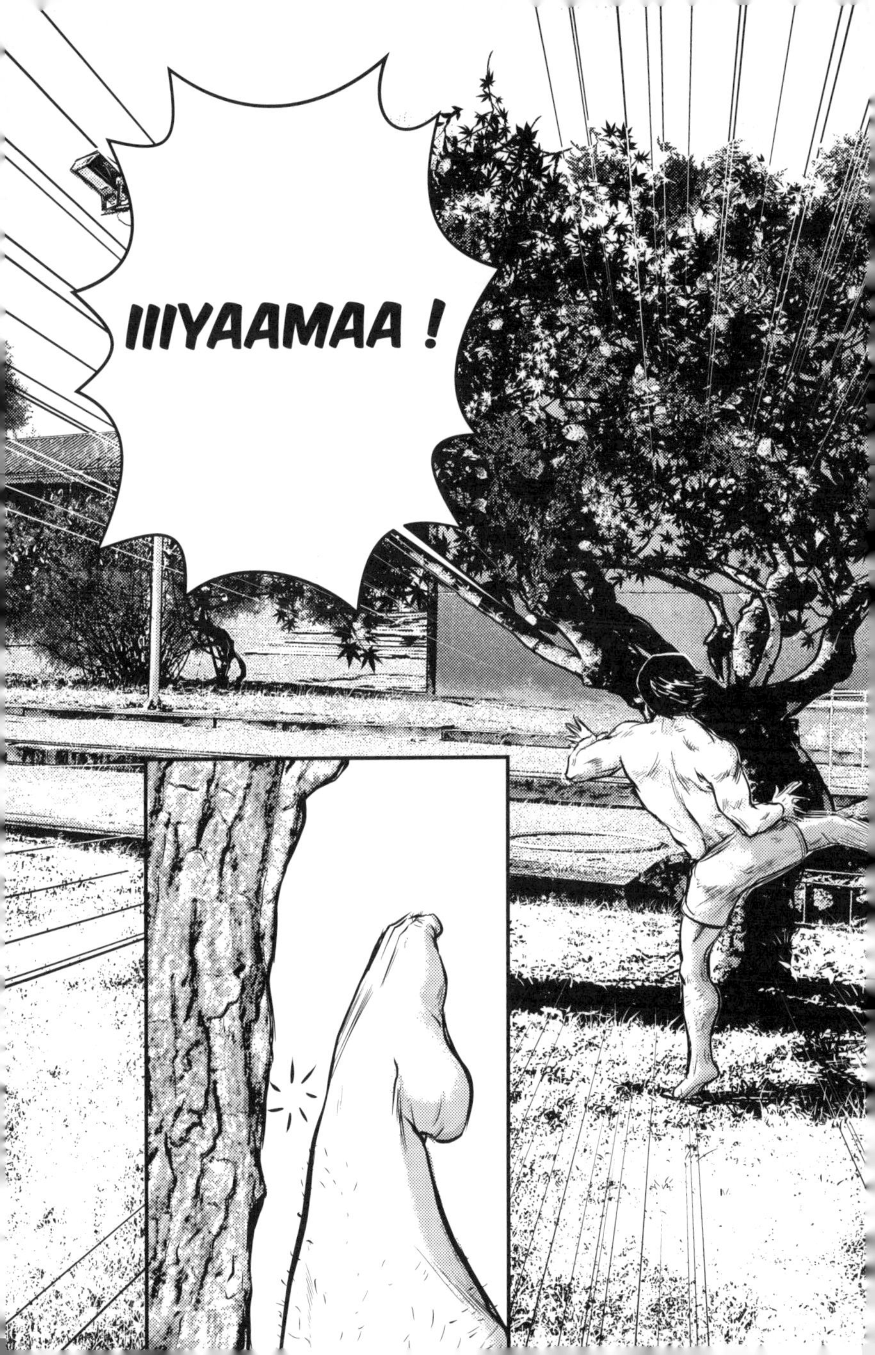
IIIYAAMAA !

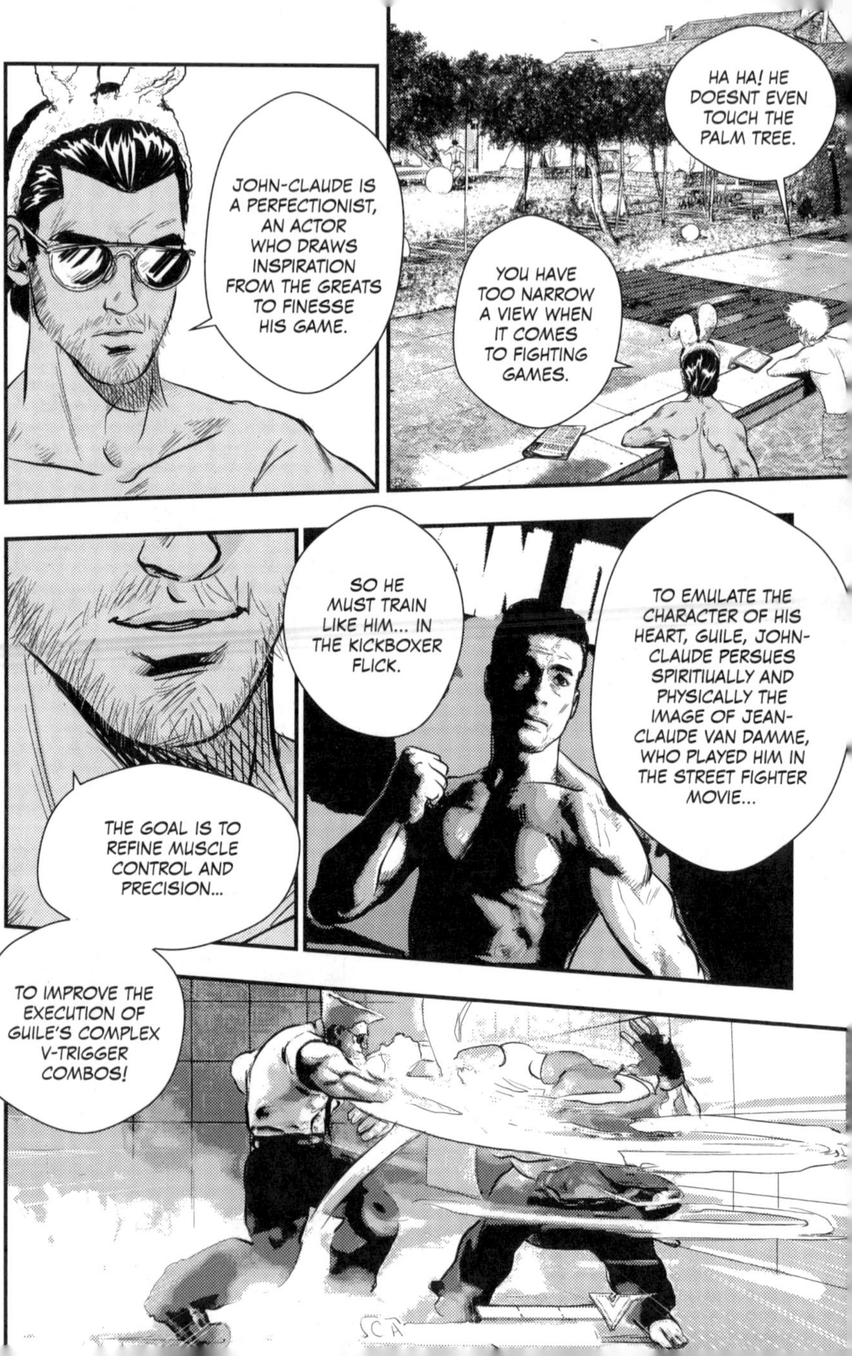
HA HA! HE DOESNT EVEN TOUCH THE PALM TREE.
YOU HAVE TOO NARROW A VIEW WHEN IT COMES TO FIGHTING GAMES.
JOHN-CLAUDE IS A PERFECTIONIST, AN ACTOR WHO DRAWS INSPIRATION FROM THE GREATS TO FINESSE HIS GAME.
TO EMULATE THE CHARACTER OF HIS HEART, GUILE, JOHN-CLAUDE PERSUES SPIRITIUALLY AND PHYSICALLY THE IMAGE OF JEAN-CLAUDE VAN DAMME, WHO PLAYED HIM IN THE STREET FIGHTER MOVIE...
SO HE MUST TRAIN LIKE HIM... IN THE KICKBOXER FLICK.
THE GOAL IS TO REFINE MUSCLE CONTROL AND PRECISION...
TO IMPROVE THE EXECUTION OF GUILE'S COMPLEX V-TRIGGER COMBOS!

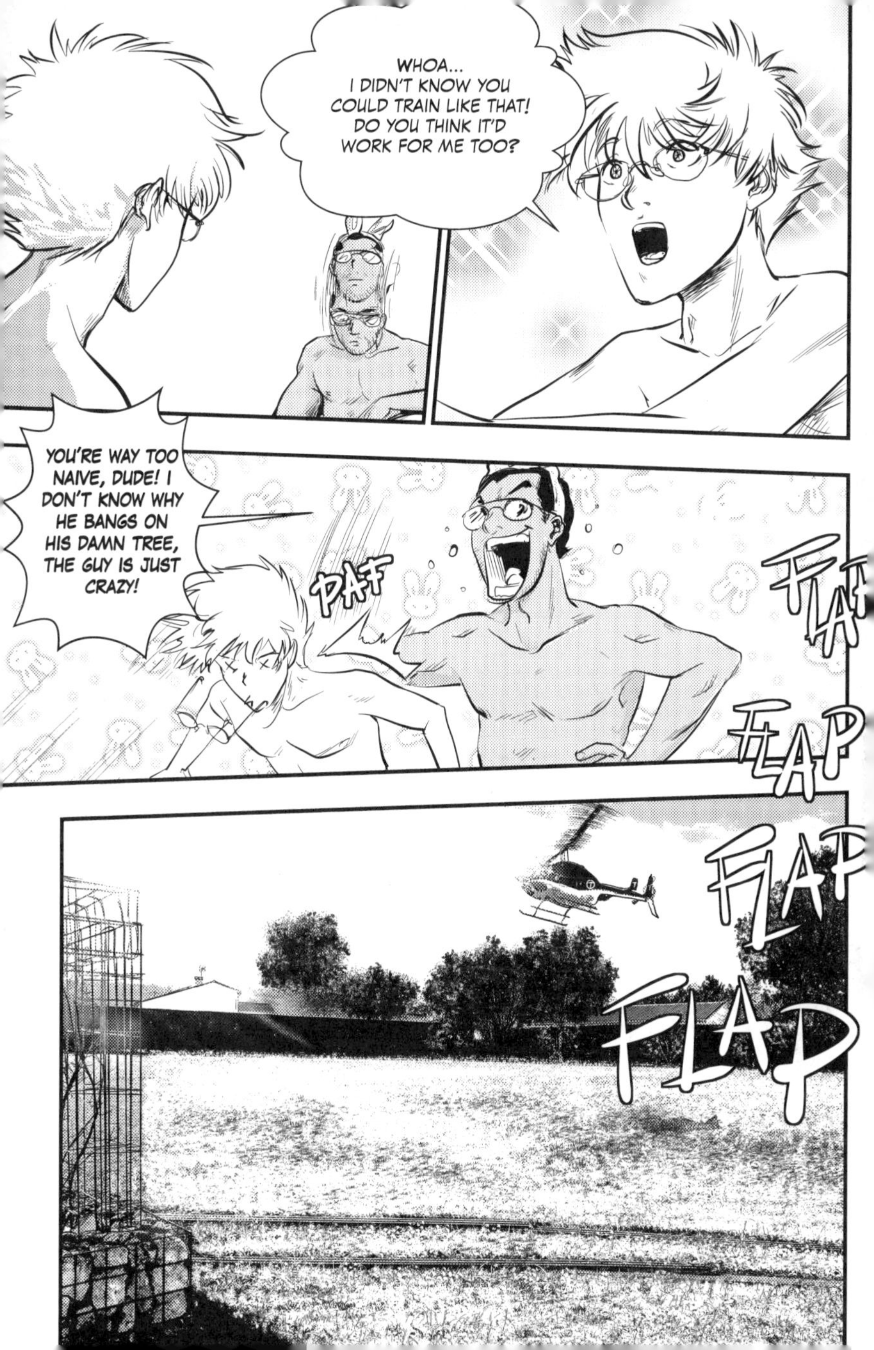
WHOA... I DIDN'T KNOW YOU COULD TRAIN LIKE THAT! DO YOU THINK IT'D WORK FOR ME TOO?
YOU'RE WAY TOO NAIVE, DUDE! I DON'T KNOW WHY HE BANGS ON HIS DAMN TREE, THE GUY IS JUST CRAZY!
PAF
FLAP
FLAP
FLAP
FLAP

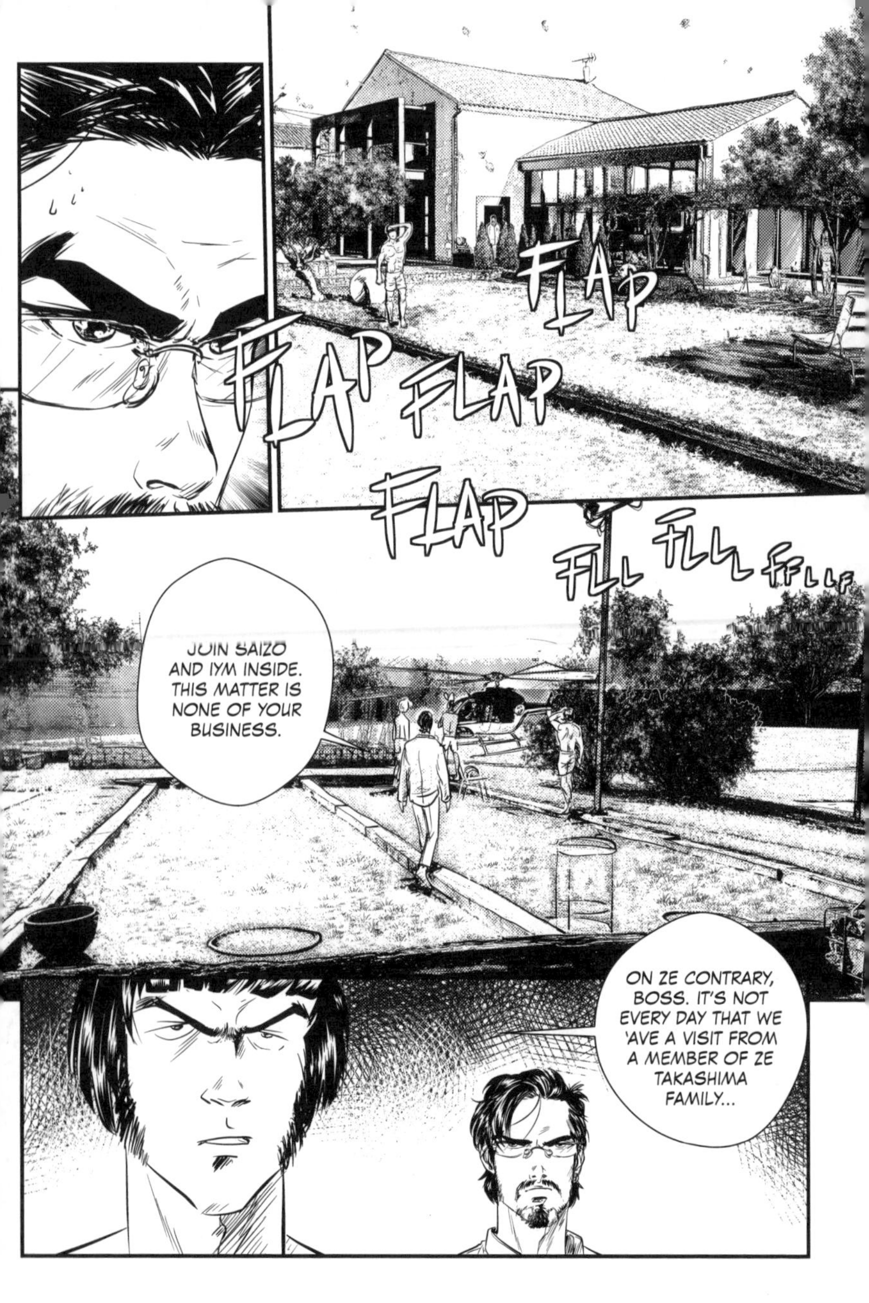
FLAP
FLAP
FLAP
FLAP
JOIN SAIZO AND IYM INSIDE. THIS MATTER IS NONE OF YOUR BUSINESS.
ON ZE CONTRARY, BOSS. IT'S NOT EVERY DAY THAT WE 'AVE A VISIT FROM A MEMBER OF ZE TAKASHIMA FAMILY...

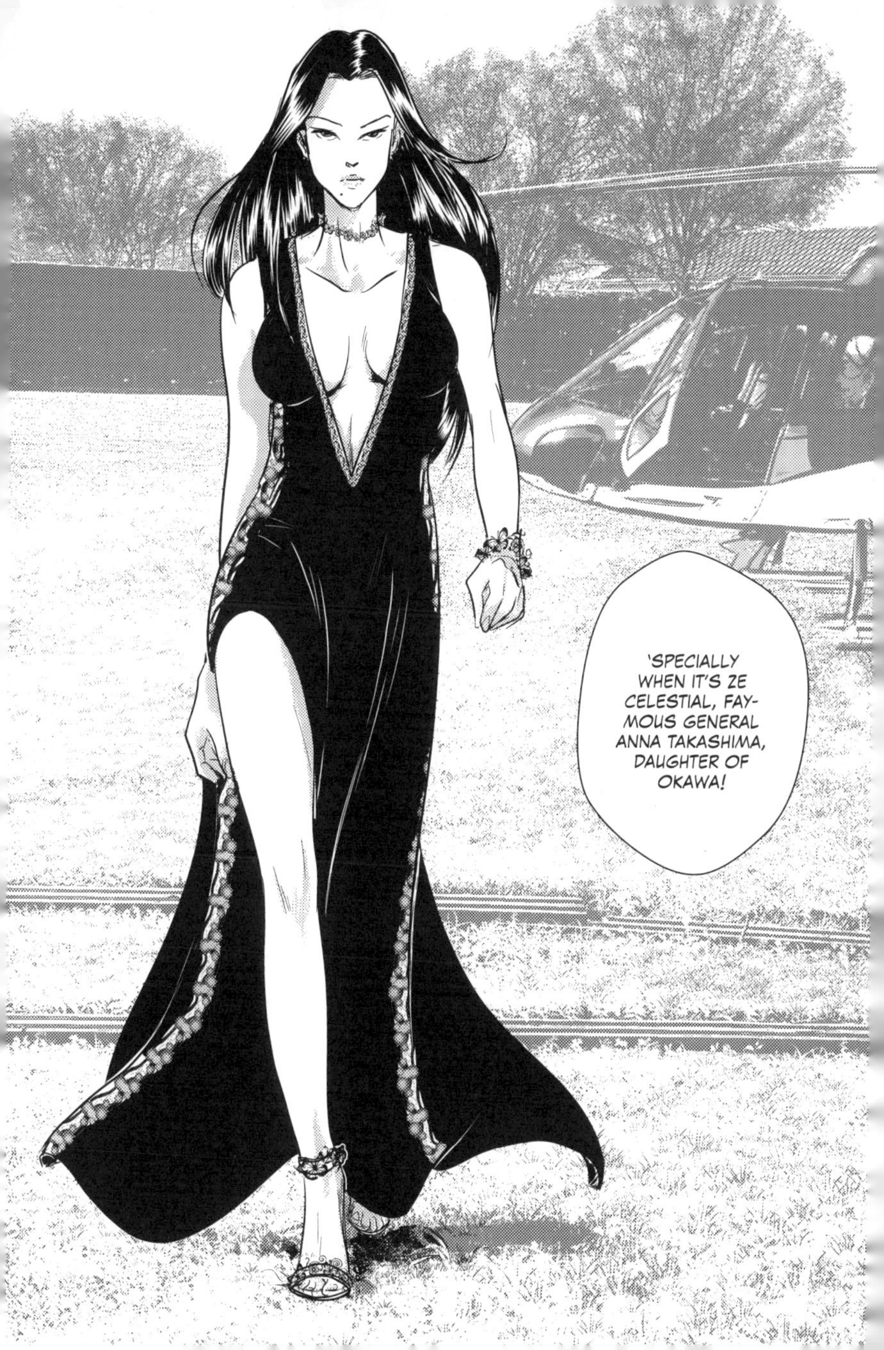
'SPECIALLY WHEN IT'S ZE CELESTIAL, FAY-MOUS GENERAL ANNA TAKASHIMA, DAUGHTER OF OKAWA!

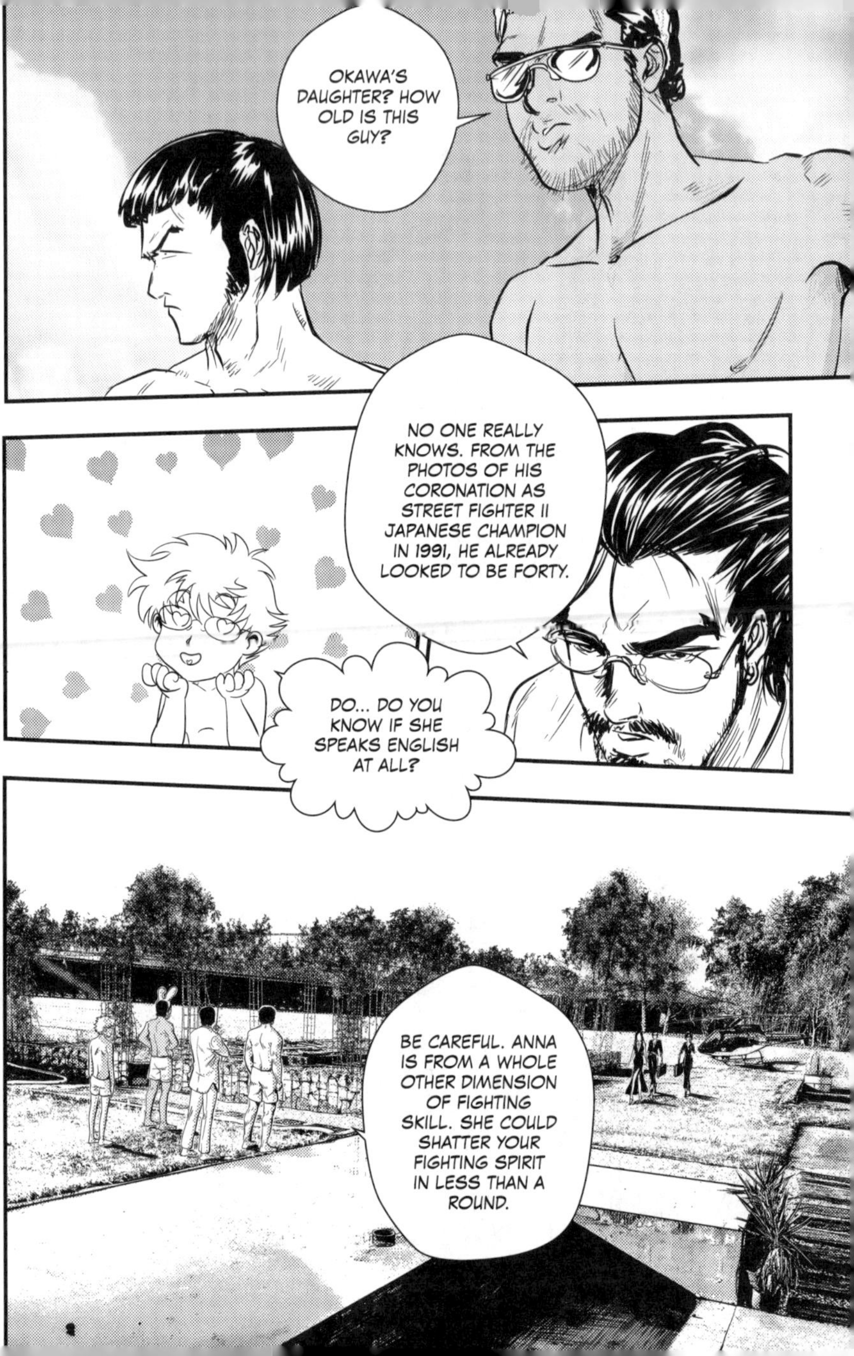
OKAWA'S DAUGHTER? HOW OLD IS THIS GUY?
NO ONE REALLY KNOWS. FROM THE PHOTOS OF HIS CORONATION AS STREET FIGHTER II JAPANESE CHAMPION IN 1991, HE ALREADY LOOKED TO BE FORTY.
DO... DO YOU KNOW IF SHE SPEAKS ENGLISH AT ALL?
BE CAREFUL. ANNA IS FROM A WHOLE OTHER DIMENSION OF FIGHTING SKILL. SHE COULD SHATTER YOUR FIGHTING SPIRIT IN LESS THAN A ROUND.

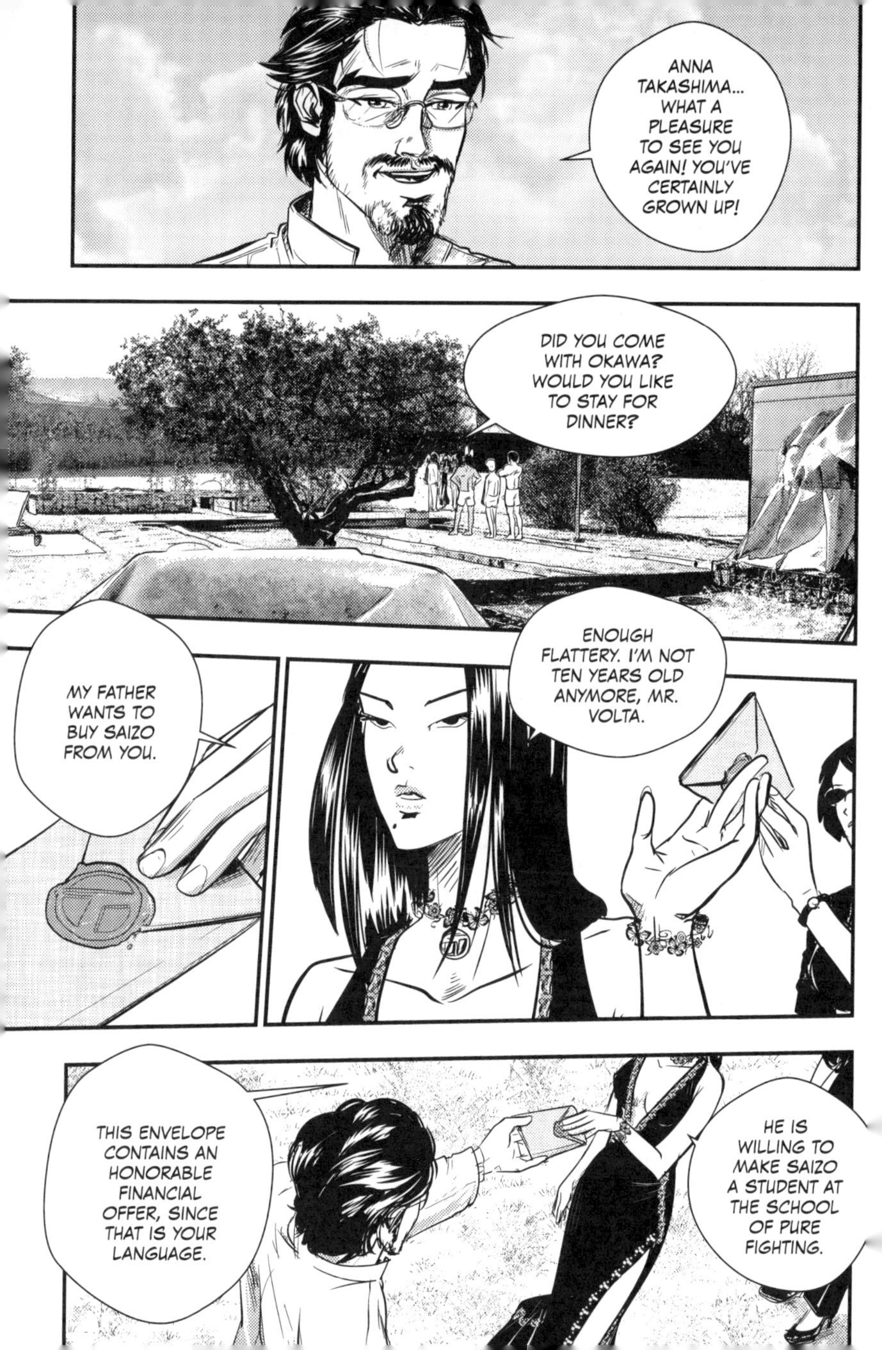
ANNA TAKASHIMA... WHAT A PLEASURE TO SEE YOU AGAIN! YOU'VE CERTAINLY GROWN UP!
DID YOU COME WITH OKAWA? WOULD YOU LIKE TO STAY FOR DINNER?
ENOUGH FLATTERY. I'M NOT TEN YEARS OLD ANYMORE, MR. VOLTA.
MY FATHER WANTS TO BUY SAIZO FROM YOU.
HE IS WILLING TO MAKE SAIZO A STUDENT AT THE SCHOOL OF PURE FIGHTING.
THIS ENVELOPE CONTAINS AN HONORABLE FINANCIAL OFFER, SINCE THAT IS YOUR LANGUAGE.

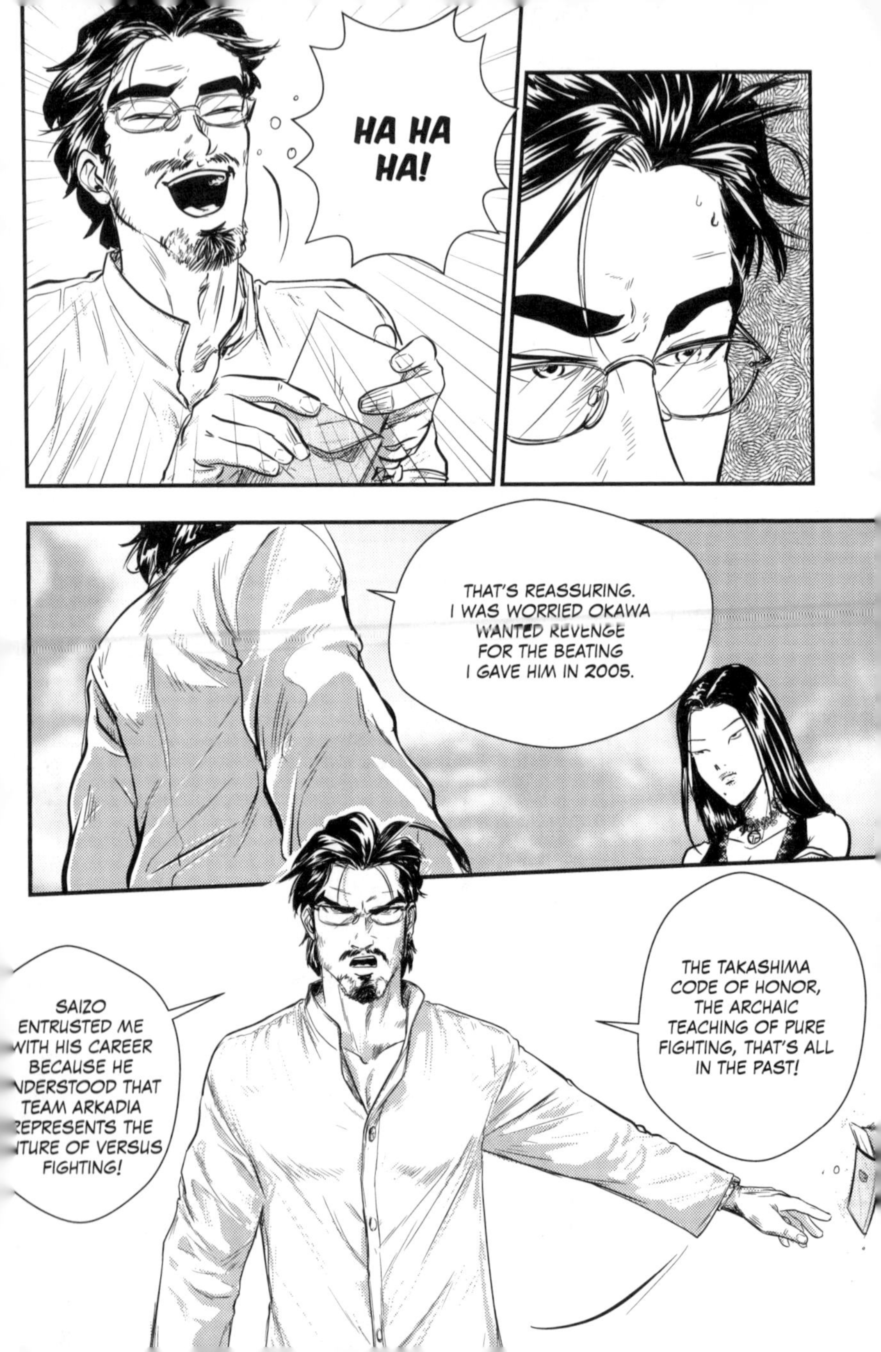
HA HA HA!
THAT'S REASSURING. I WAS WORRIED OKAWA WANTED REVENGE FOR THE BEATING I GAVE HIM IN 2005.
THE TAKASHIMA CODE OF HONOR, THE ARCHAIC TEACHING OF PURE FIGHTING, THAT'S ALL IN THE PAST!
SAIZO ENTRUSTED ME WITH HIS CAREER BECAUSE HE NDERSTOOD THAT TEAM ARKADIA EPRESENTS THE ITURE OF VERSUS FIGHTING!

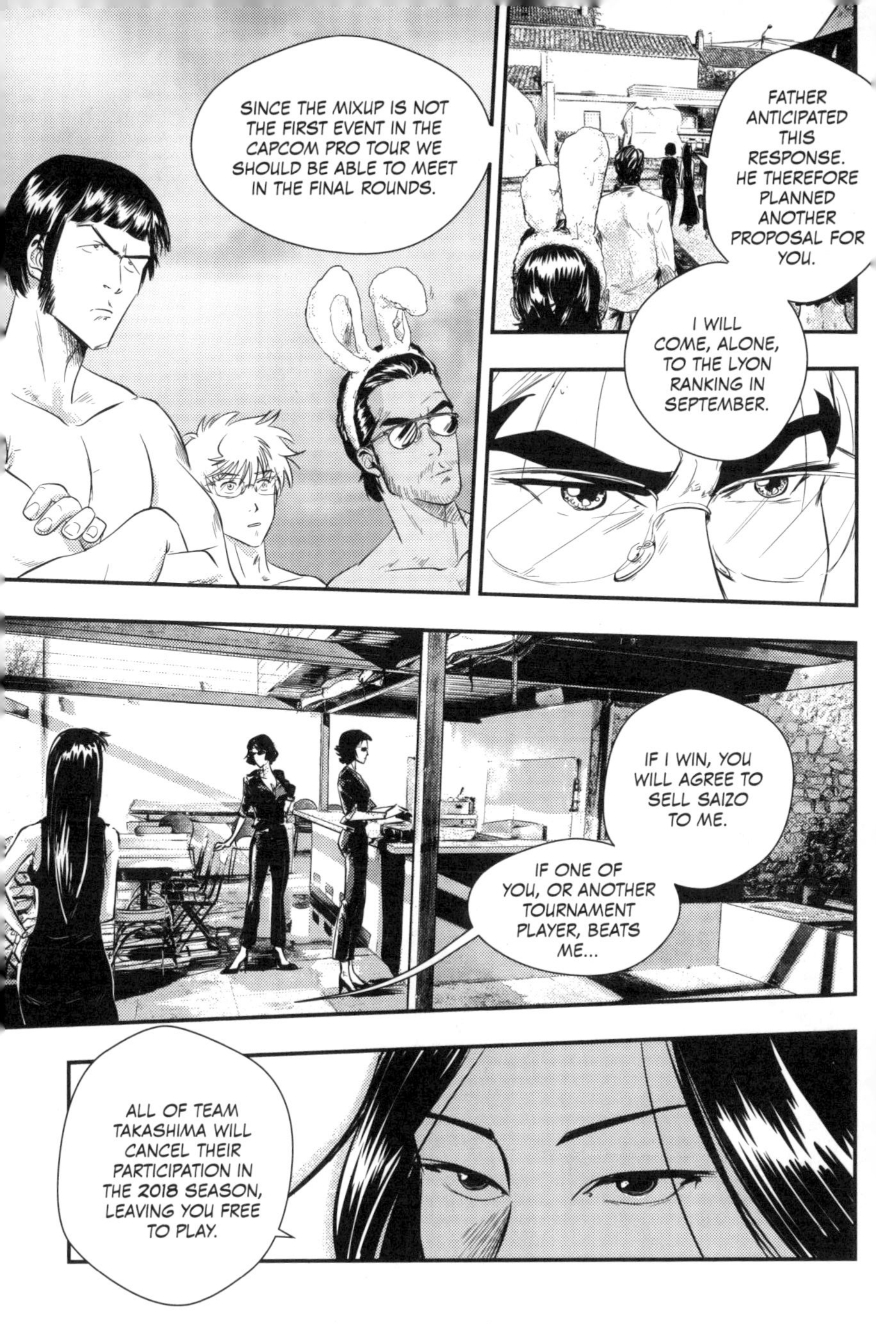
SINCE THE MIXUP IS NOT THE FIRST EVENT IN THE CAPCOM PRO TOUR WE SHOULD BE ABLE TO MEET IN THE FINAL ROUNDS.
FATHER ANTICIPATED THIS RESPONSE. HE THEREFORE PLANNED ANOTHER PROPOSAL FOR YOU.
I WILL COME, ALONE, TO THE LYON RANKING IN SEPTEMBER.
IF I WIN, YOU WILL AGREE TO SELL SAIZO TO ME.
IF ONE OF YOU, OR ANOTHER TOURNAMENT PLAYER, BEATS ME...
ALL OF TEAM TAKASHIMA WILL CANCEL THEIR PARTICIPATION IN THE 2018 SEASON, LEAVING YOU FREE TO PLAY.

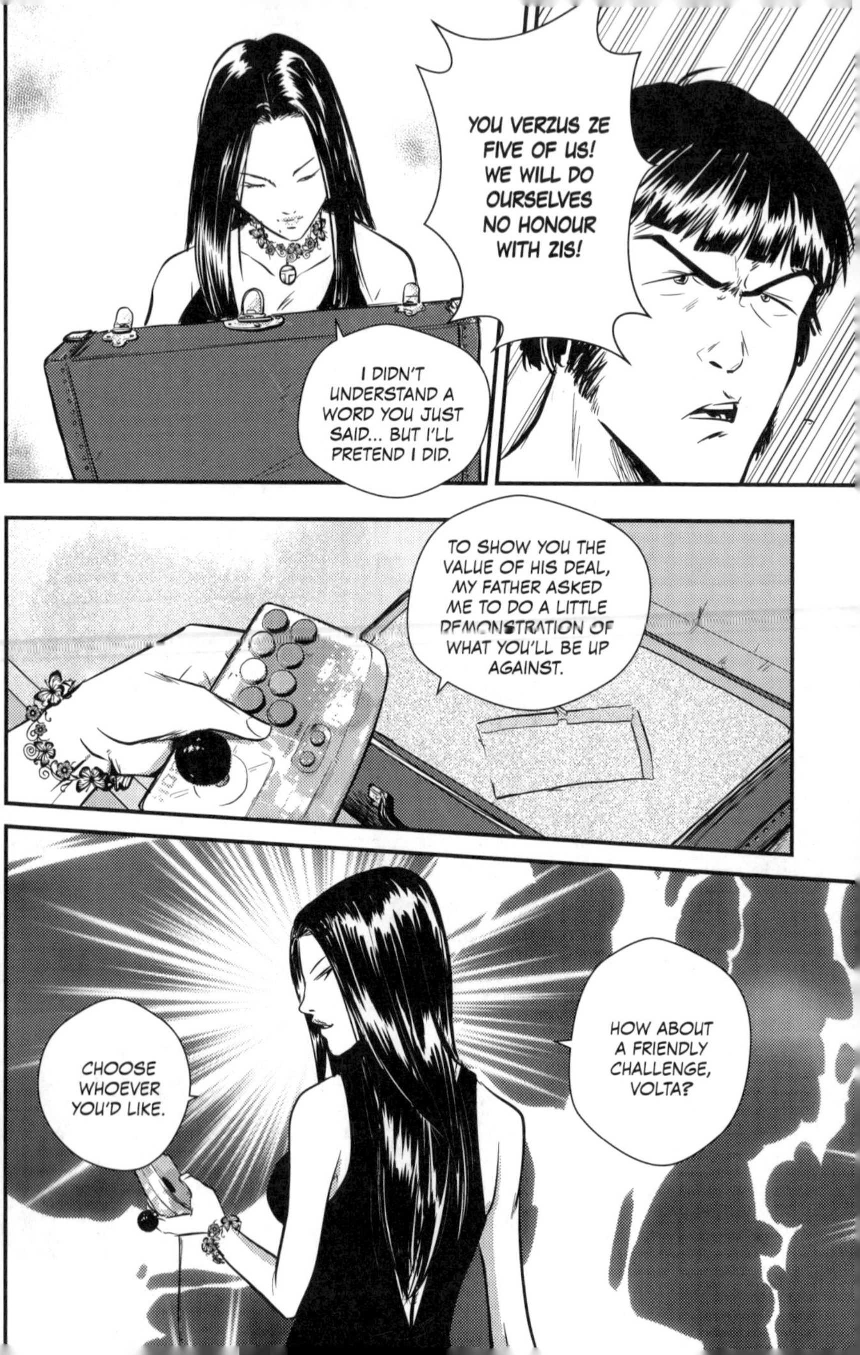
YOU VERZUS ZE FIVE OF US! WE WILL DO OURSELVES NO HONOUR WITH ZIS!
I DIDN'T UNDERSTAND A WORD YOU JUST SAID... BUT I'LL PRETEND I DID.
TO SHOW YOU THE VALUE OF HIS DEAL, MY FATHER ASKED ME TO DO A LITTLE DEMONSTRATION OF WHAT YOU'LL BE UP AGAINST.
HOW ABOUT A FRIENDLY CHALLENGE, VOLTA?
CHOOSE WHOEVER YOU'D LIKE.

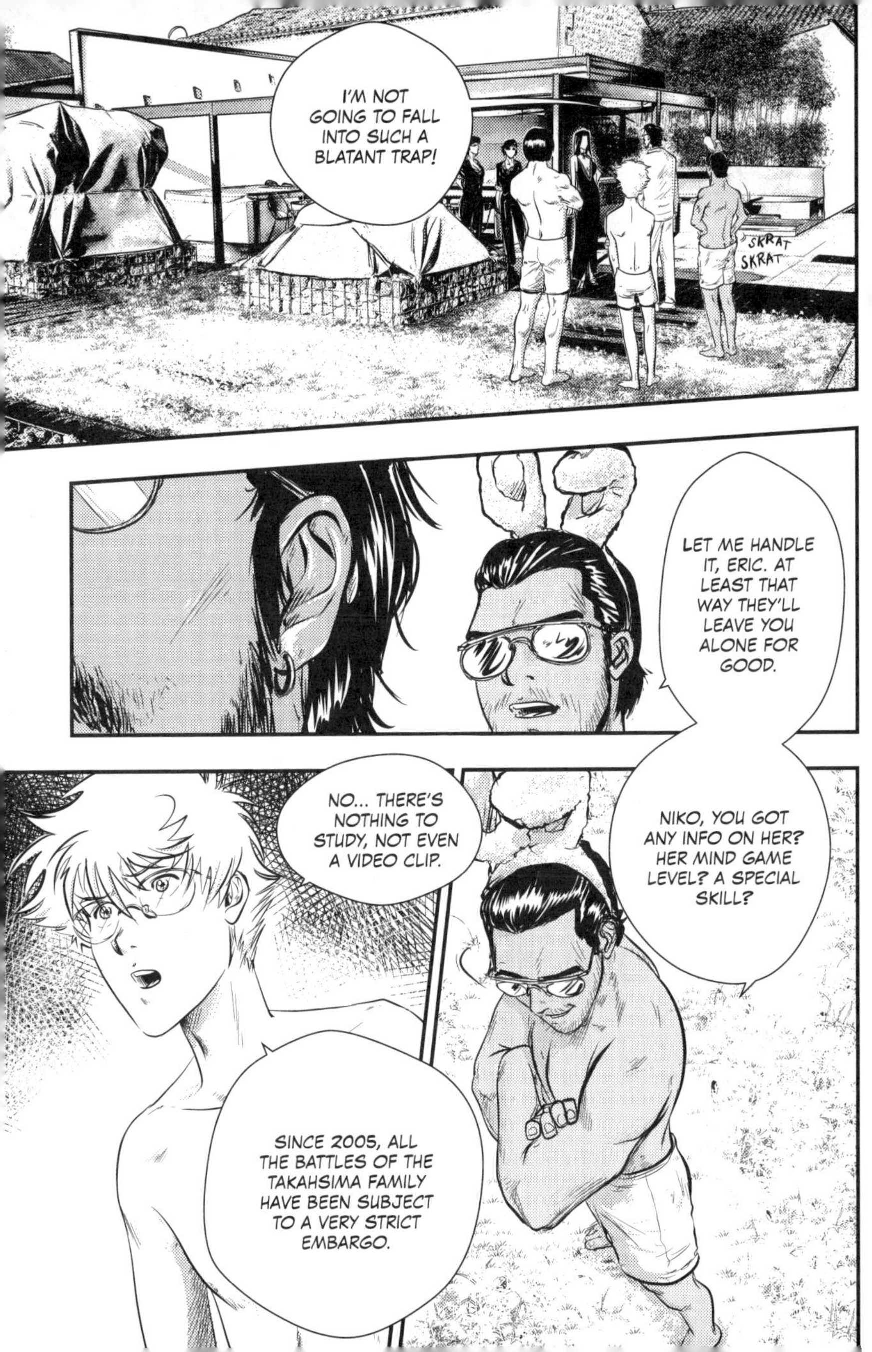
I'M NOT GOING TO FALL INTO SUCH A BLATANT TRAP!
SKRAT SKRAT
LET ME HANDLE IT, ERIC. AT LEAST THAT WAY THEY'LL LEAVE YOU ALONE FOR GOOD.
NIKO, YOU GOT ANY INFO ON HER? HER MIND GAME LEVEL? A SPECIAL SKILL?
NO... THERE'S NOTHING TO STUDY, NOT EVEN A VIDEO CLIP.
SINCE 2005, ALL THE BATTLES OF THE TAKAHSIMA FAMILY HAVE BEEN SUBJECT TO A VERY STRICT EMBARGO.

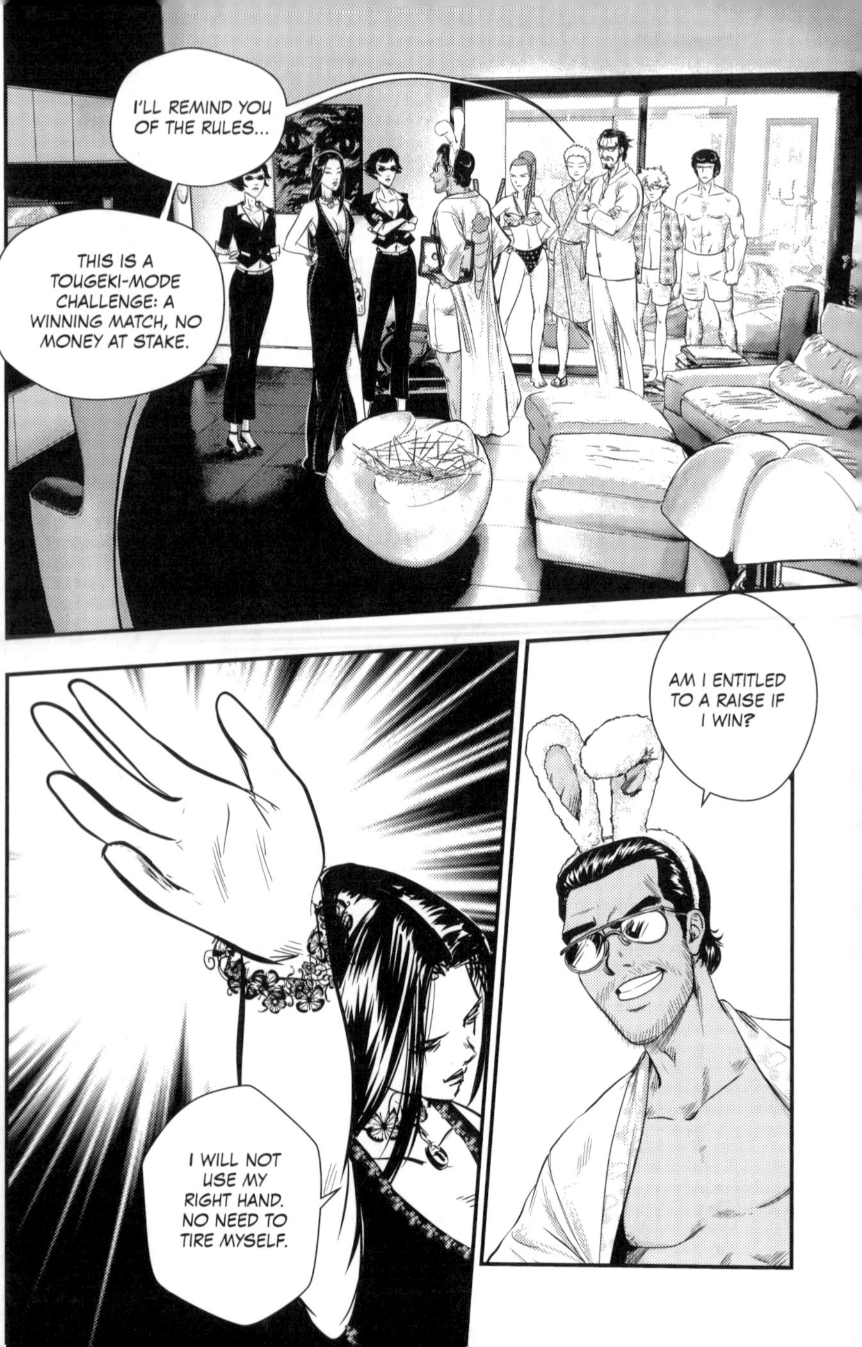
I'LL REMIND YOU OF THE RULES...
THIS IS A TOUGEKI-MODE CHALLENGE: A WINNING MATCH, NO MONEY AT STAKE.
AM I ENTITLED TO A RAISE IF I WIN?
I WILL NOT USE MY RIGHT HAND. NO NEED TO TIRE MYSELF.

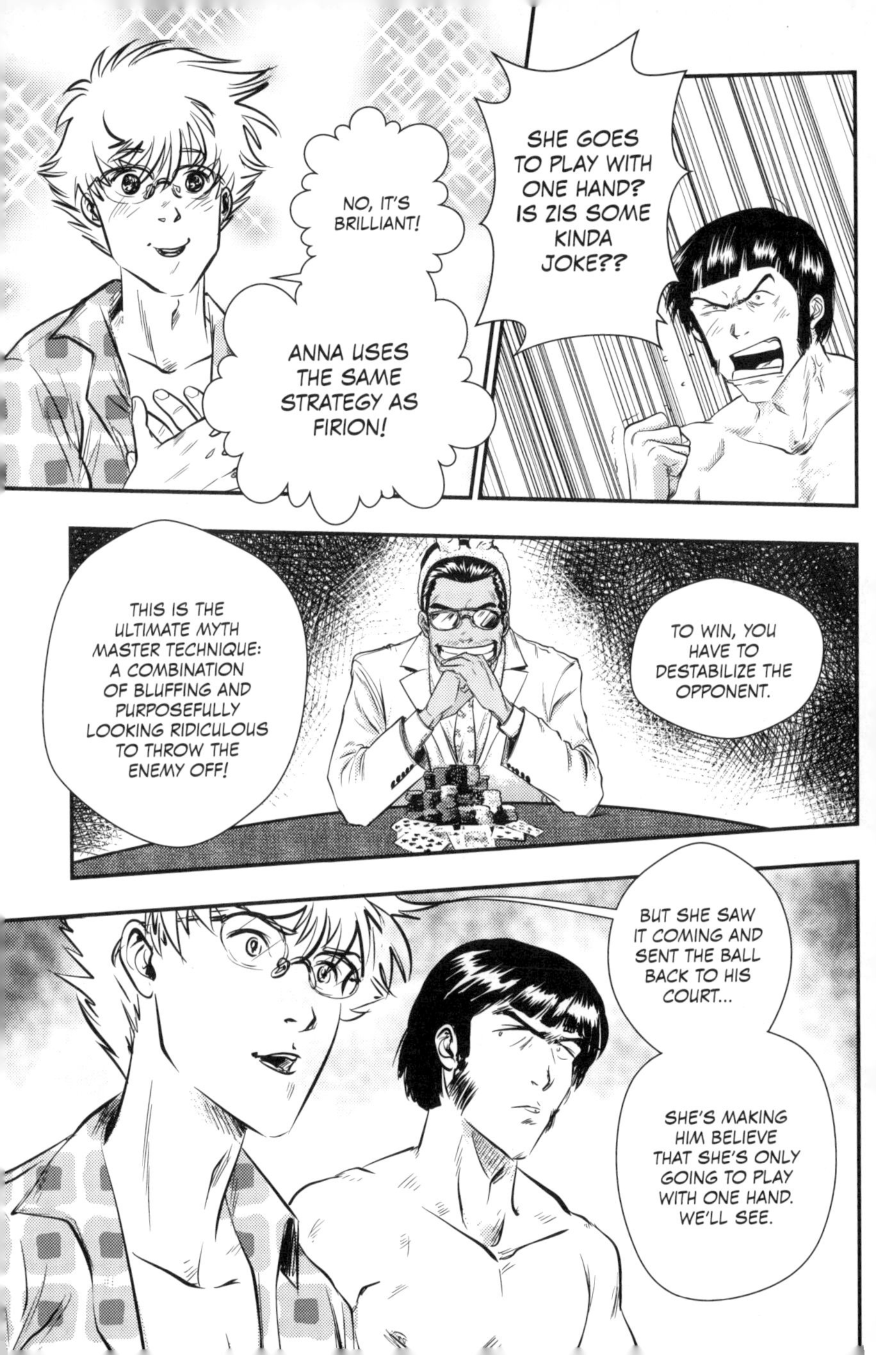
SHE GOES TO PLAY WITH ONE HAND? IS ZIS SOME KINDA JOKE??
NO, IT'S BRILLIANT!
ANNA USES THE SAME STRATEGY AS FIRION!
TO WIN, YOU HAVE TO DESTABILIZE THE OPPONENT.
THIS IS THE ULTIMATE MYTH MASTER TECHNIQUE: A COMBINATION OF BLUFFING AND PURPOSEFULLY LOOKING RIDICULOUS TO THROW THE ENEMY OFF!
BUT SHE SAW IT COMING AND SENT THE BALL BACK TO HIS COURT...
SHE'S MAKING HIM BELIEVE THAT SHE'S ONLY GOING TO PLAY WITH ONE HAND. WE'LL SEE.

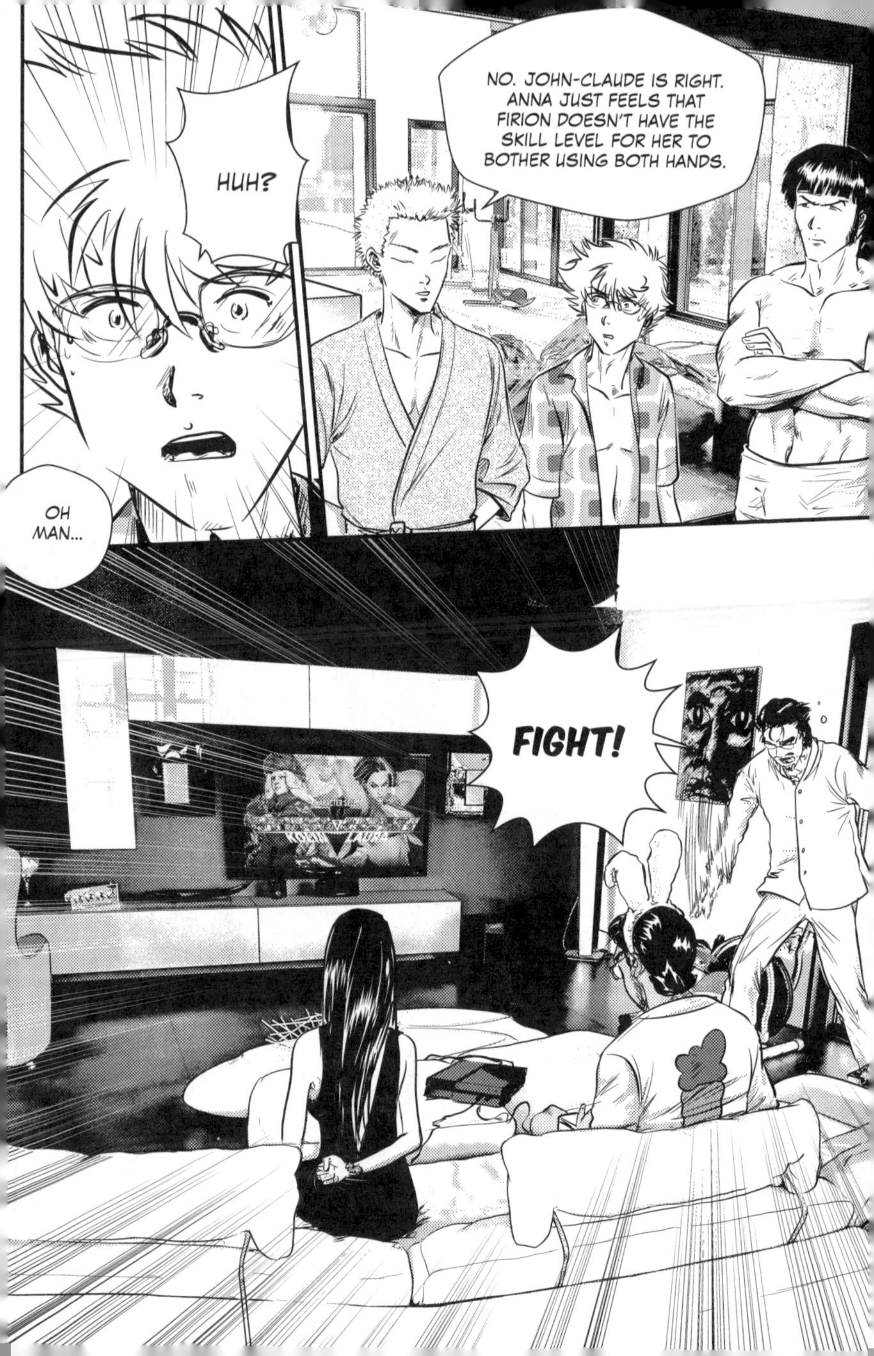
HUH?
NO. JOHN-CLAUDE IS RIGHT. ANNA JUST FEELS THAT FIRION DOESN'T HAVE THE SKILL LEVEL FOR HER TO BOTHER USING BOTH HANDS.
OH MAN...
FIGHT!

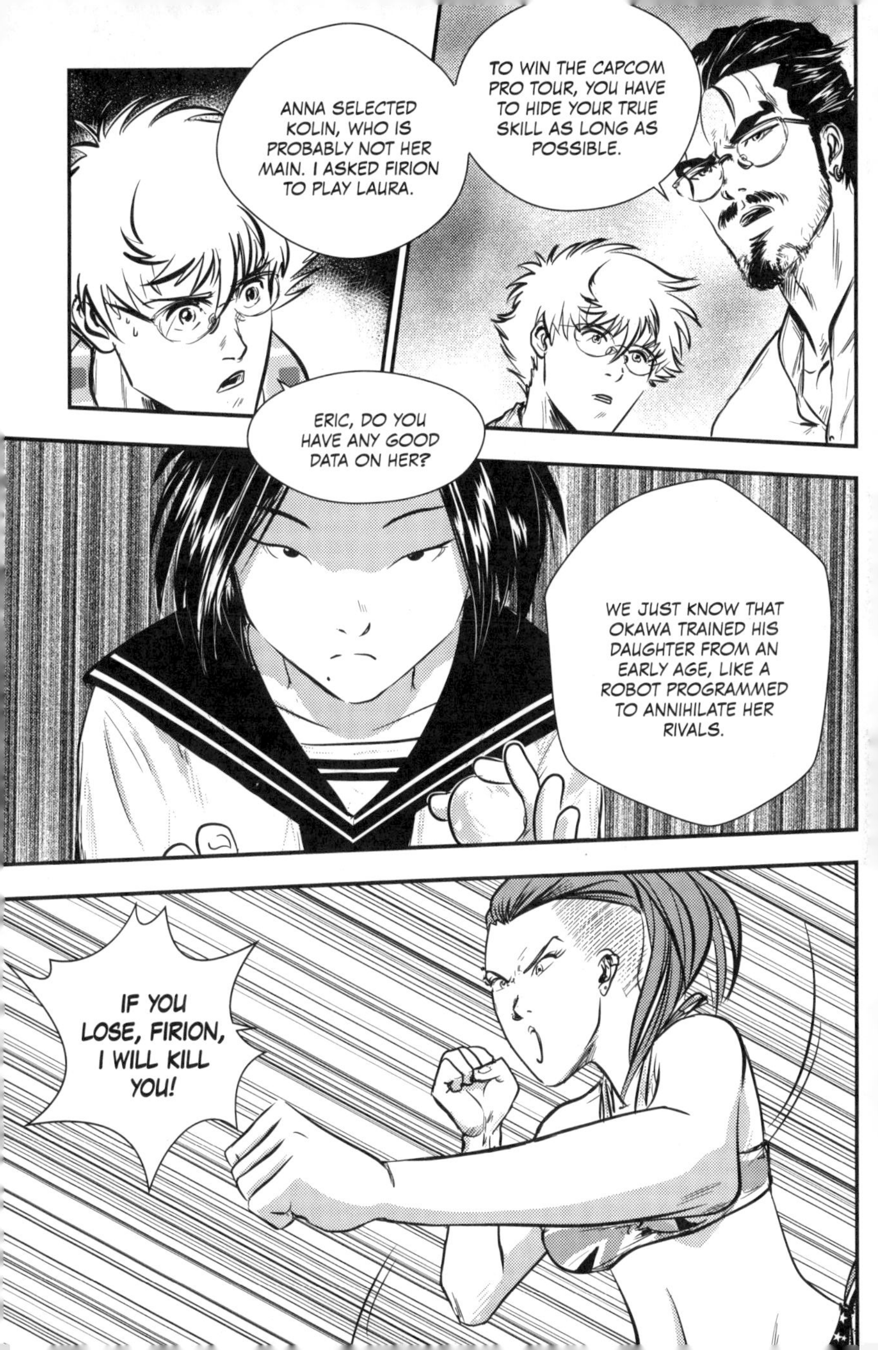
ANNA SELECTED KOLIN, WHO IS PROBABLY NOT HER MAIN. I ASKED FIRION TO PLAY LAURA.
TO WIN THE CAPCOM PRO TOUR, YOU HAVE TO HIDE YOUR TRUE SKILL AS LONG AS POSSIBLE.
ERIC, DO YOU HAVE ANY GOOD DATA ON HER?
WE JUST KNOW THAT OKAWA TRAINED HIS DAUGHTER FROM AN EARLY AGE, LIKE A ROBOT PROGRAMMED TO ANNIHILATE HER RIVALS.
IF YOU LOSE, FIRION, I WILL KILL YOU!

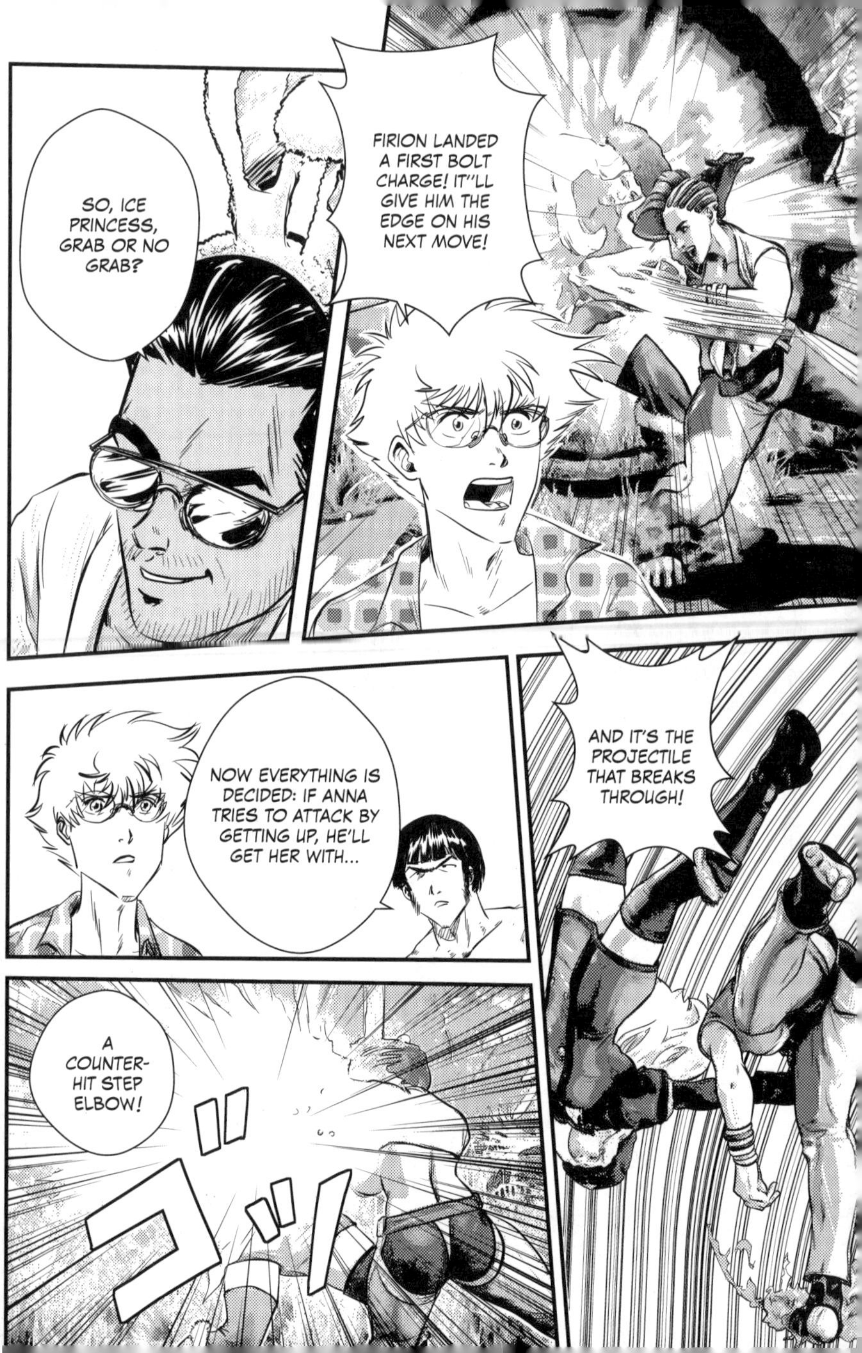
SO, ICE PRINCESS, GRAB OR NO GRAB?
FIRION LANDED A FIRST BOLT CHARGE! IT''LL GIVE HIM THE EDGE ON HIS NEXT MOVE!
NOW EVERYTHING IS DECIDED: IF ANNA TRIES TO ATTACK BY GETTING UP, HE'LL GET HER WITH...
A COUNTER-HIT STEP ELBOW!
AND IT'S THE PROJECTILE THAT BREAKS THROUGH!

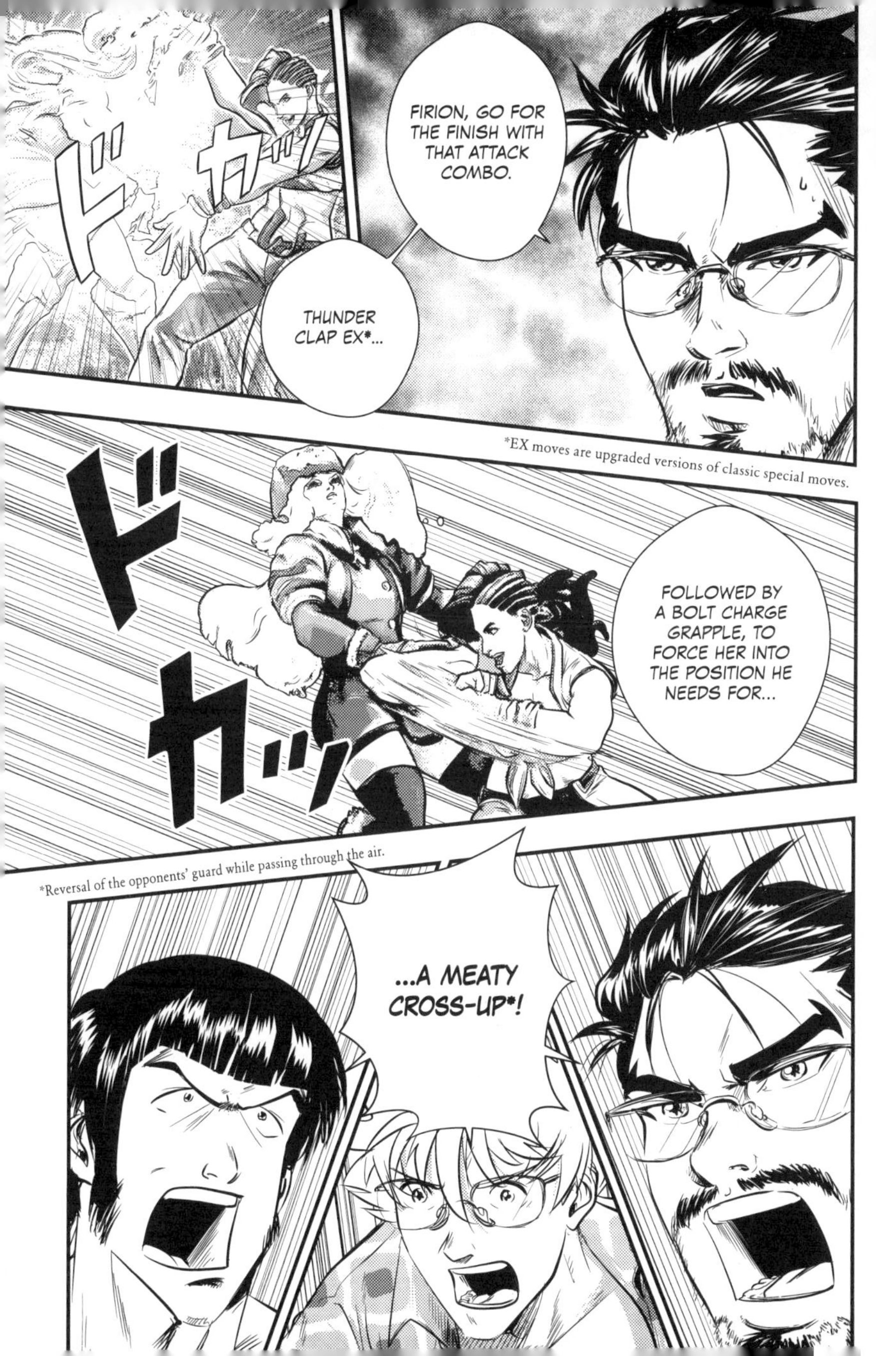
FIRION, GO FOR THE FINISH WITH THAT ATTACK COMBO.
THUNDER CLAP EX*...
ドガッ
FOLLOWED BY A BOLT CHARGE GRAPPLE, TO FORCE HER INTO THE POSITION HE NEEDS FOR...
ドガッ
...A MEATY CROSS-UP*!

*EX moves are upgraded versions of classic special moves.

*Reversal of the opponents' guard while passing through the air.

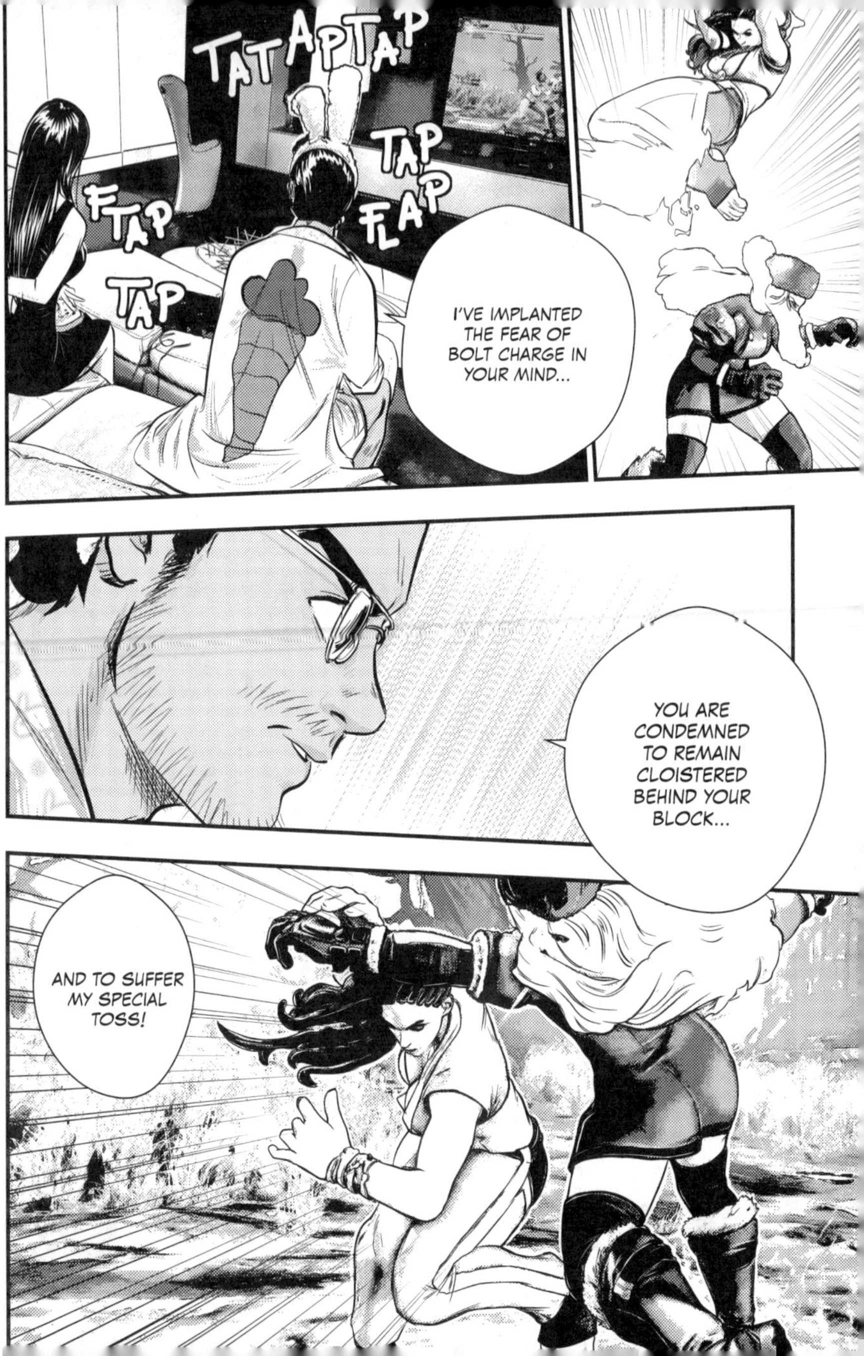
TATAPTAP
TAPTAP
FLAP
FTAP
TAP
I'VE IMPLANTED THE FEAR OF BOLT CHARGE IN YOUR MIND...
YOU ARE CONDEMNED TO REMAIN CLOISTERED BEHIND YOUR BLOCK...
AND TO SUFFER MY SPECIAL TOSS!

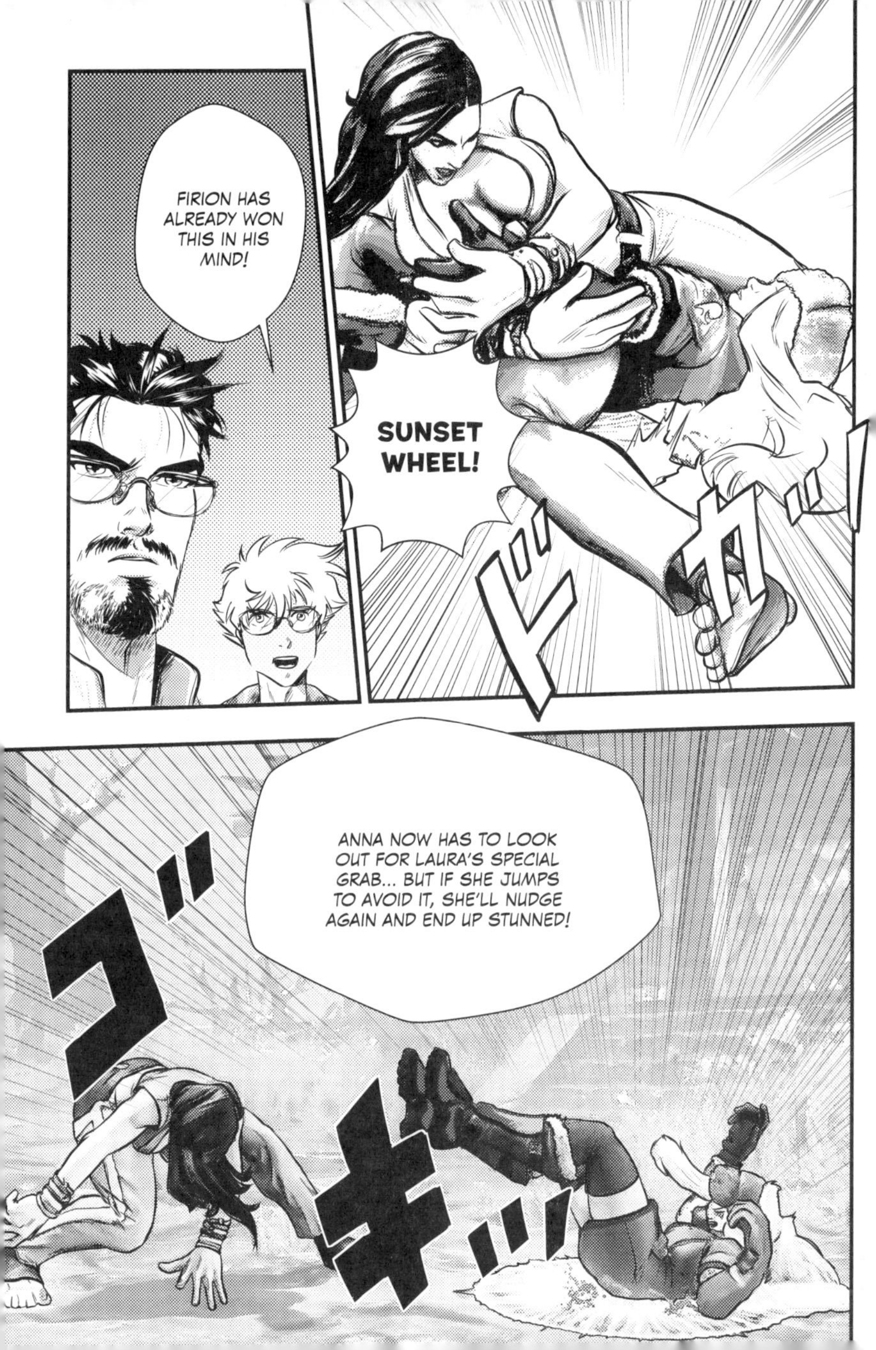
SUNSET WHEEL!
ドガッ!
FIRION HAS ALREADY WON THIS IN HIS MIND!
ANNA NOW HAS TO LOOK OUT FOR LAURA'S SPECIAL GRAB... BUT IF SHE JUMPS TO AVOID IT, SHE'LL NUDGE AGAIN AND END UP STUNNED!
ゴギッ

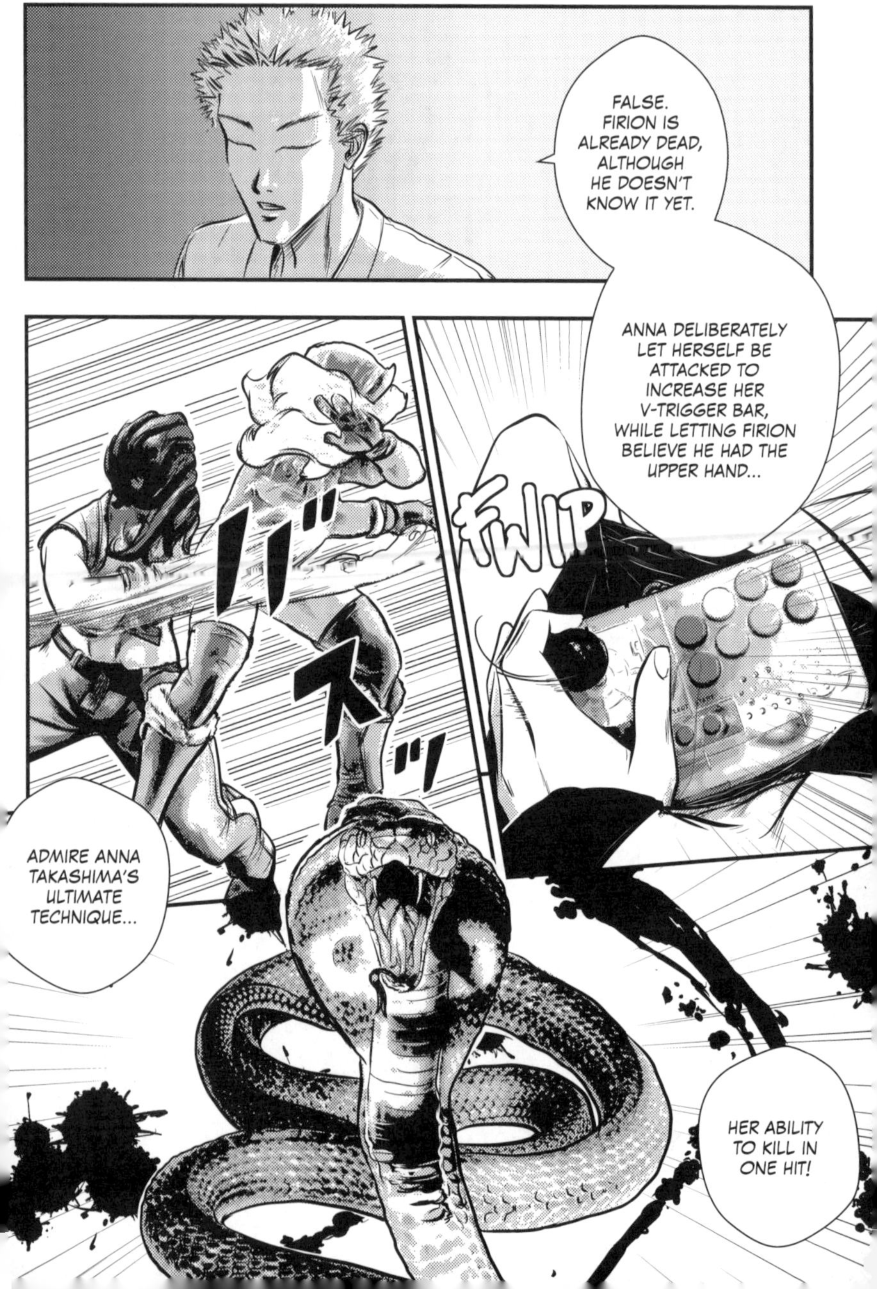
FALSE. FIRION IS ALREADY DEAD, ALTHOUGH HE DOESN'T KNOW IT YET.
ANNA DELIBERATELY LET HERSELF BE ATTACKED TO INCREASE HER V-TRIGGER BAR, WHILE LETTING FIRION BELIEVE HE HAD THE UPPER HAND...
FWIP
ADMIRE ANNA TAKASHIMA'S ULTIMATE TECHNIQUE...
HER ABILITY TO KILL IN ONE HIT!

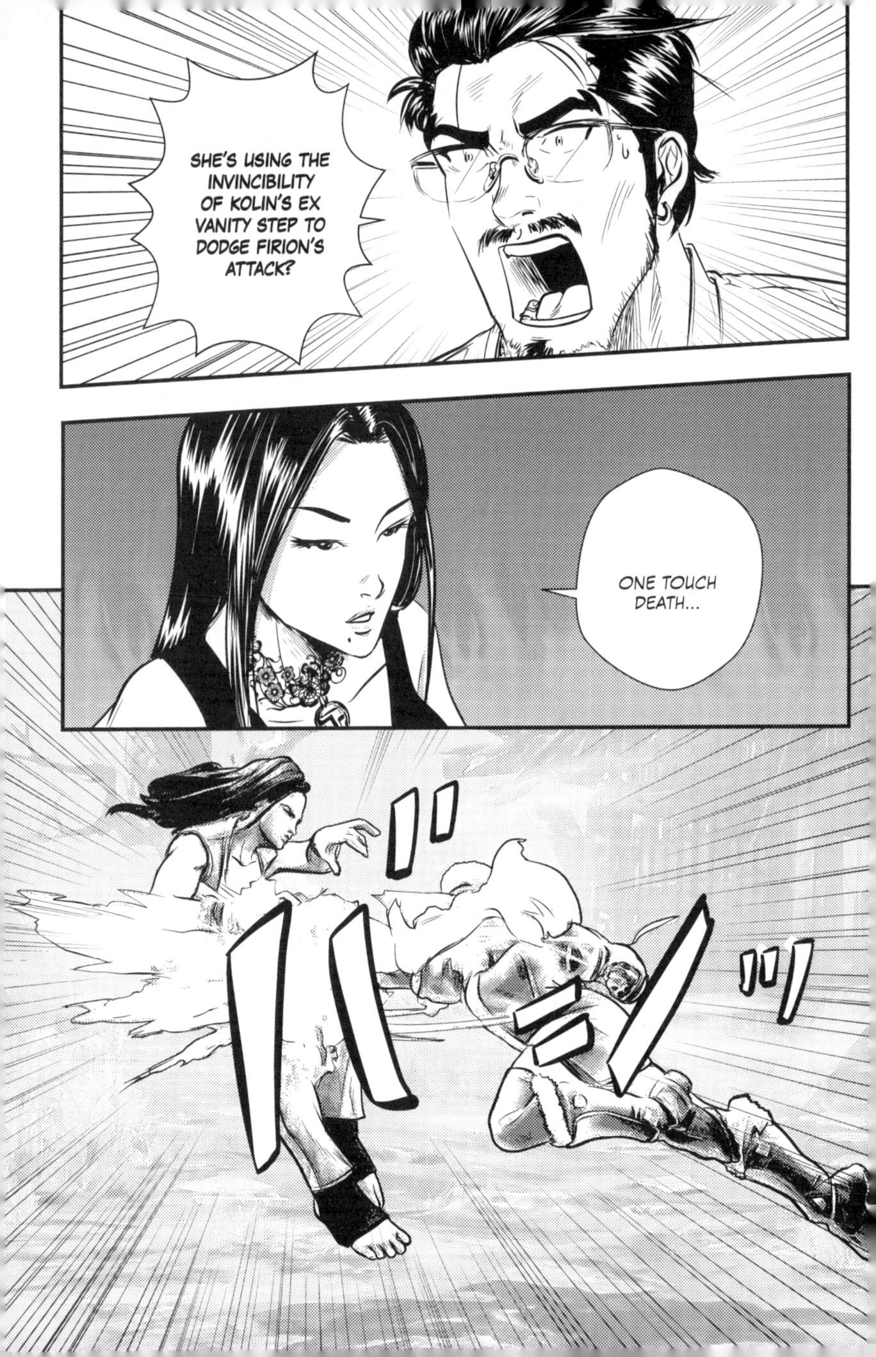
SHE'S USING THE INVINCIBILITY OF KOLIN'S EX VANITY STEP TO DODGE FIRION'S ATTACK?
ONE TOUCH DEATH...

CHARACTER SELECT!

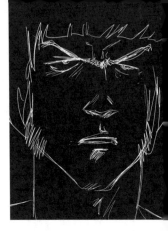

JOHN-CLAUDE LAFLEUR

THE COMBO GOD

BACKGROUND

A Belgian of Tunisian origin who speaks English with an French accent that he developed from speaking French with a Belgian accent in Southern Thailand, John-Claude is the Combo God.

Under his real name, Cheick Lasry (CCL), he learned fighting games at a school in Brussels where the challenges were paid for with a kebab. In 2015, his life changed completely when he discovered a documentary about the life of the champion Okawa, the Second Emperor of Versus Fighting, which taught him the importance for a player to merge (brain, hand, heart) with his character in Street Fighter. He then decided to take inspiration from his character's appearance as Colonel William F. Guile in the 1994 film Street Fighter: The Final Fight.

Thus, CCL became John-Claude Lafleur (JCL), one of the most powerful fighters in the Capcom Pro Tour, though no one really understands what he's saying...

VERSUS FIGHTING STORY

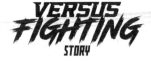

CHARACTER DESIGN

One of the many crossed out characters in the series. Unquantifiable. Unpredictable. Incomprehensible, above all. His mentor and role model is the same one who fascinated me when I was young. I hope he speaks to you just as much!

BY KALON

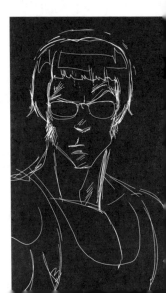

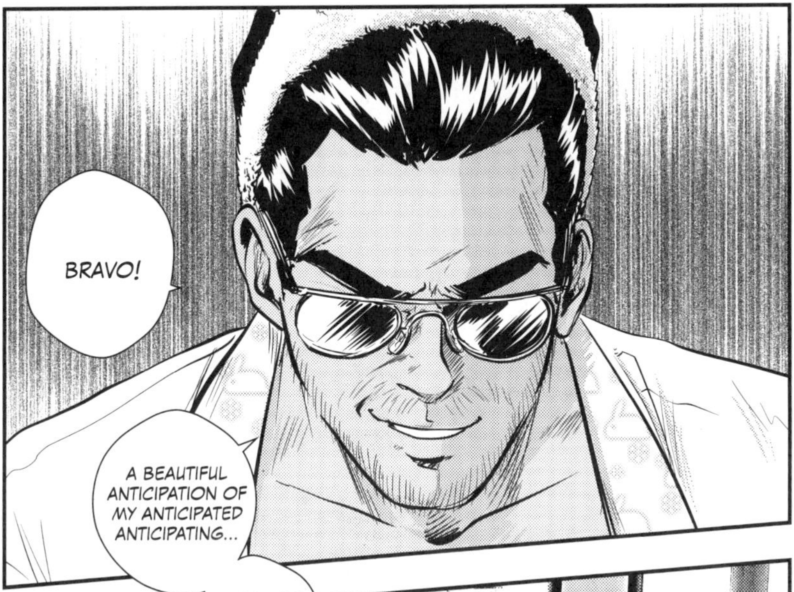
BRAVO!
A BEAUTIFUL ANTICIPATION OF MY ANTICIPATED ANTICIPATING...
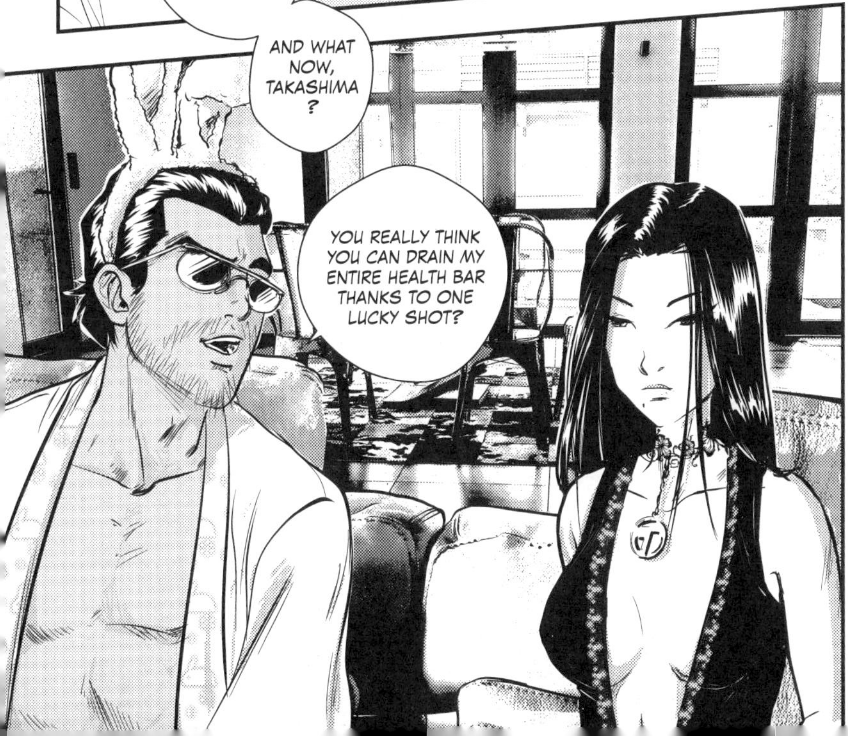
AND WHAT NOW, TAKASHIMA ?
YOU REALLY THINK YOU CAN DRAIN MY ENTIRE HEALTH BAR THANKS TO ONE LUCKY SHOT?

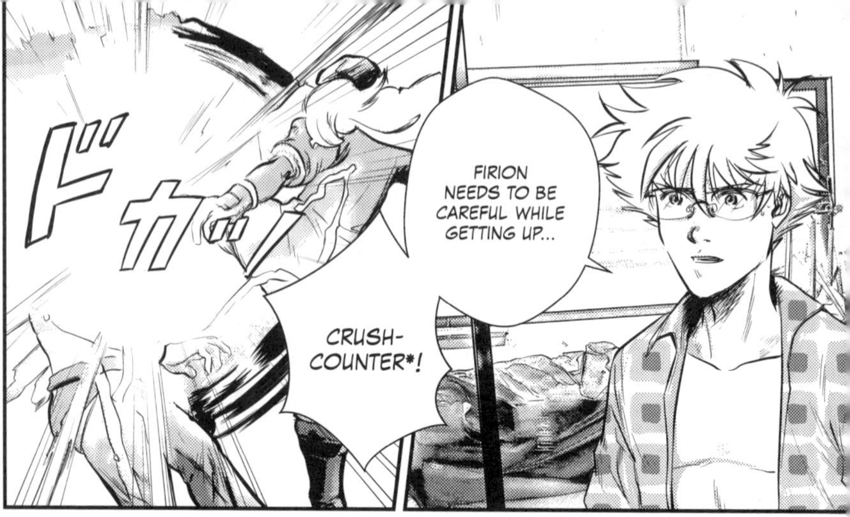
FIRION NEEDS TO BE CAREFUL WHILE GETTING UP...
ドガッ
CRUSH-COUNTER*!

*A destructive Counter-Hit with a specific hitbox.

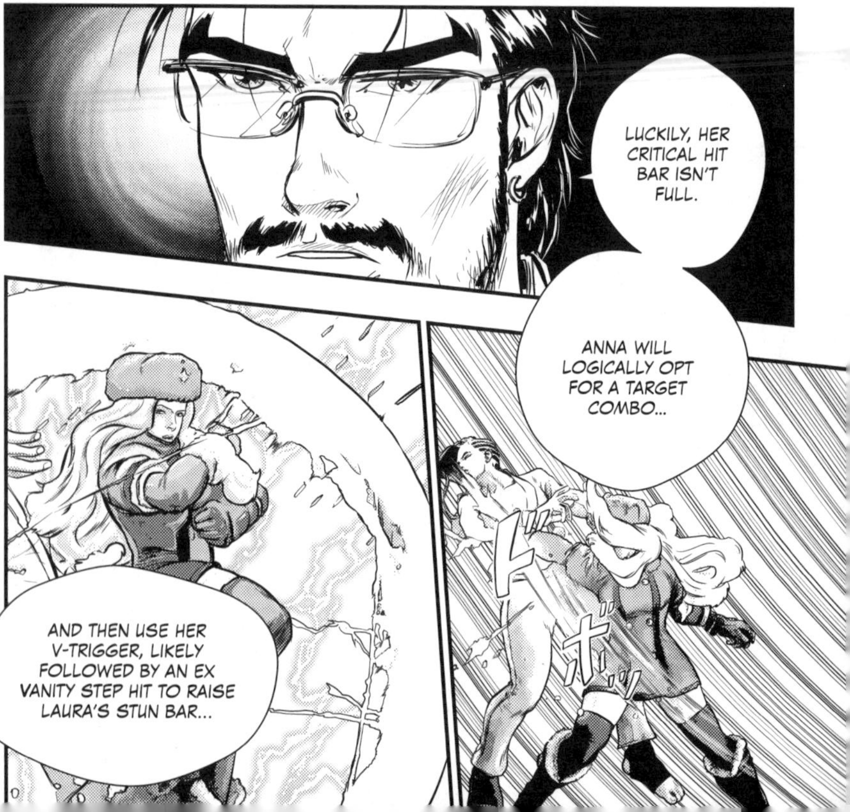
LUCKILY, HER CRITICAL HIT BAR ISN'T FULL.
ANNA WILL LOGICALLY OPT FOR A TARGET COMBO...
ドガッ
AND THEN USE HER V-TRIGGER, LIKELY FOLLOWED BY AN EX VANITY STEP HIT TO RAISE LAURA'S STUN BAR...

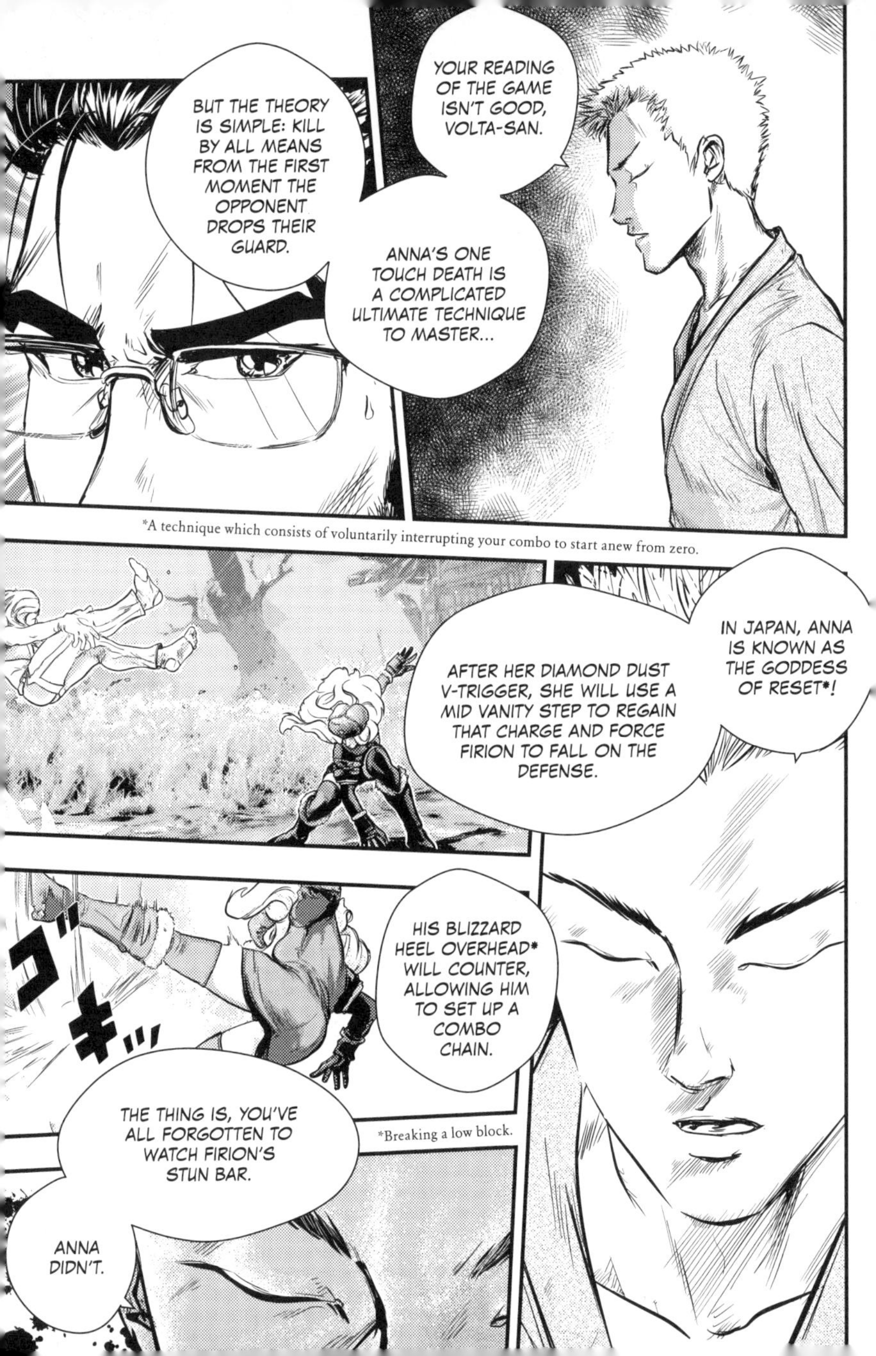
YOUR READING OF THE GAME ISN'T GOOD, VOLTA-SAN.
ANNA'S ONE TOUCH DEATH IS A COMPLICATED ULTIMATE TECHNIQUE TO MASTER...
BUT THE THEORY IS SIMPLE: KILL BY ALL MEANS FROM THE FIRST MOMENT THE OPPONENT DROPS THEIR GUARD.
IN JAPAN, ANNA IS KNOWN AS THE GODDESS OF RESET*!
AFTER HER DIAMOND DUST V-TRIGGER, SHE WILL USE A MID VANITY STEP TO REGAIN THAT CHARGE AND FORCE FIRION TO FALL ON THE DEFENSE.
HIS BLIZZARD HEEL OVERHEAD* WILL COUNTER, ALLOWING HIM TO SET UP A COMBO CHAIN.
ゴキッ
THE THING IS, YOU'VE ALL FORGOTTEN TO WATCH FIRION'S STUN BAR.
ANNA DIDN'T.

*A technique which consists of voluntarily interrupting your combo to start anew from zero.

*Breaking a low block.

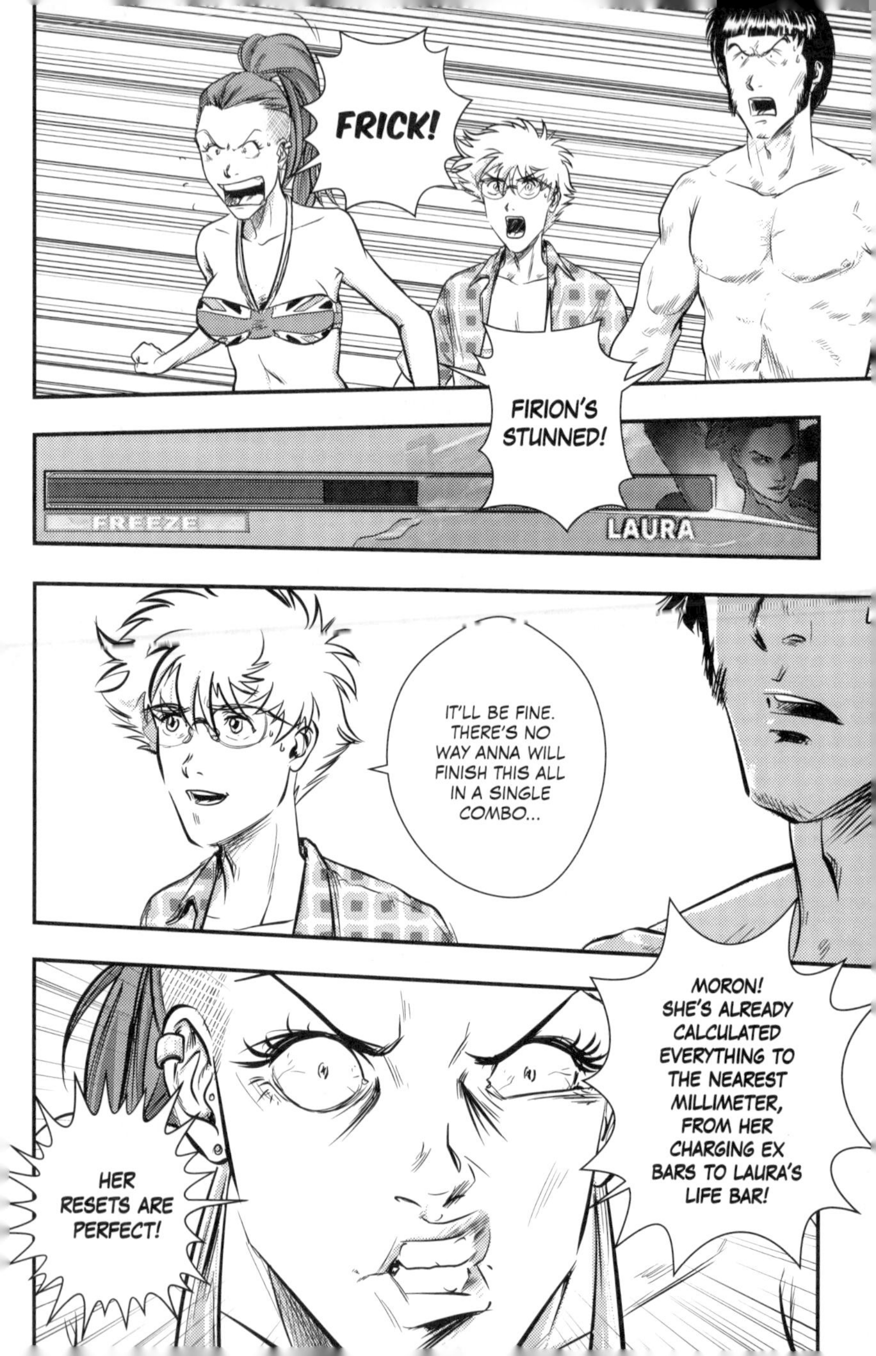
FIRION'S STUNNED!
FRICK!
LAURA
FREEZE
IT'LL BE FINE. THERE'S NO WAY ANNA WILL FINISH THIS ALL IN A SINGLE COMBO...
MORON! SHE'S ALREADY CALCULATED EVERYTHING TO THE NEAREST MILLIMETER, FROM HER CHARGING EX BARS TO LAURA'S LIFE BAR!
HER RESETS ARE PERFECT!

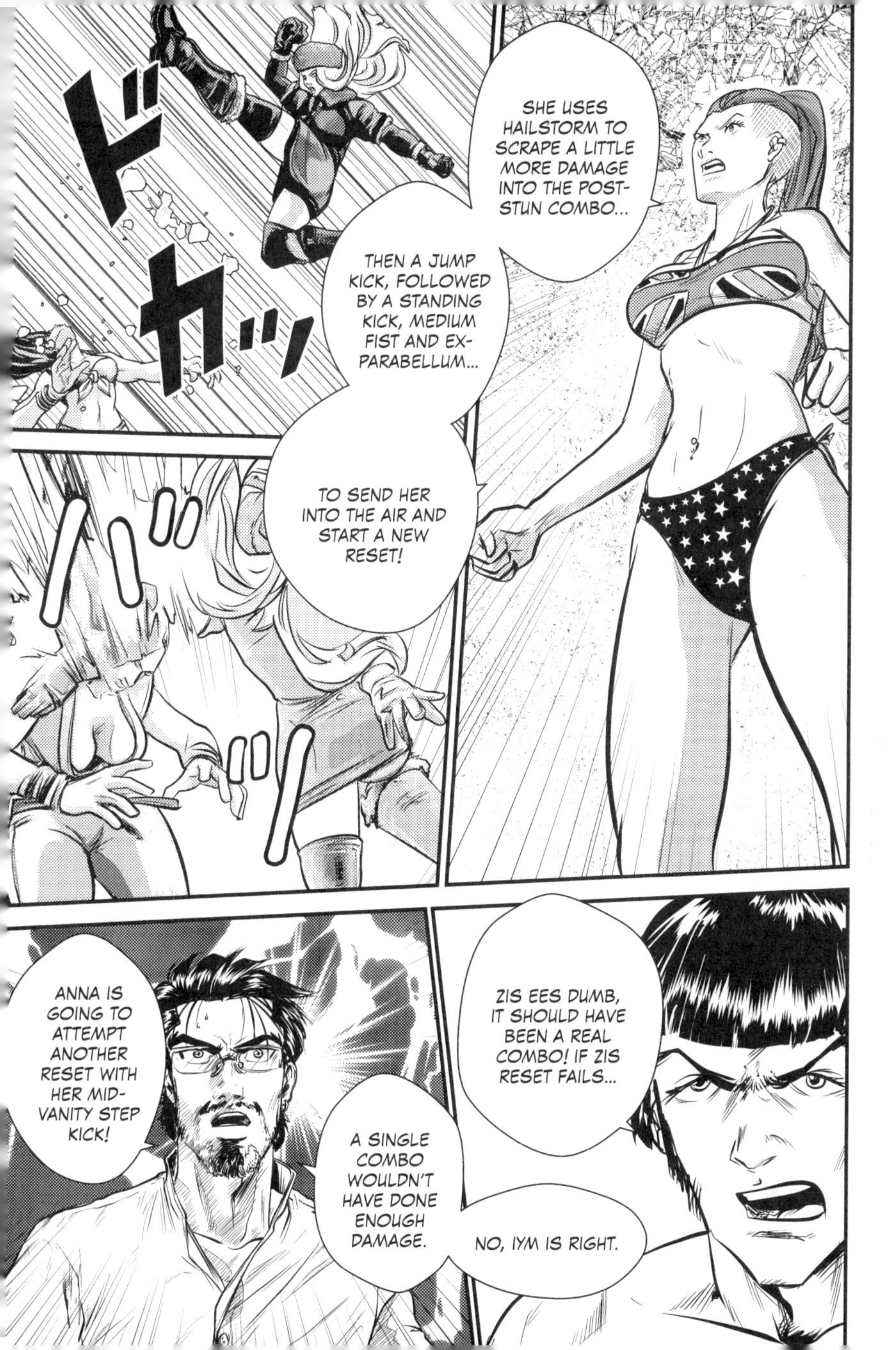
SHE USES HAILSTORM TO SCRAPE A LITTLE MORE DAMAGE INTO THE POST-STUN COMBO...
THEN A JUMP KICK, FOLLOWED BY A STANDING KICK, MEDIUM FIST AND EX-PARABELLUM...
TO SEND HER INTO THE AIR AND START A NEW RESET!
ZIS EES DUMB, IT SHOULD HAVE BEEN A REAL COMBO! IF ZIS RESET FAILS...
NO, IYM IS RIGHT.
A SINGLE COMBO WOULDN'T HAVE DONE ENOUGH DAMAGE.
ANNA IS GOING TO ATTEMPT ANOTHER RESET WITH HER MID-VANITY STEP KICK!

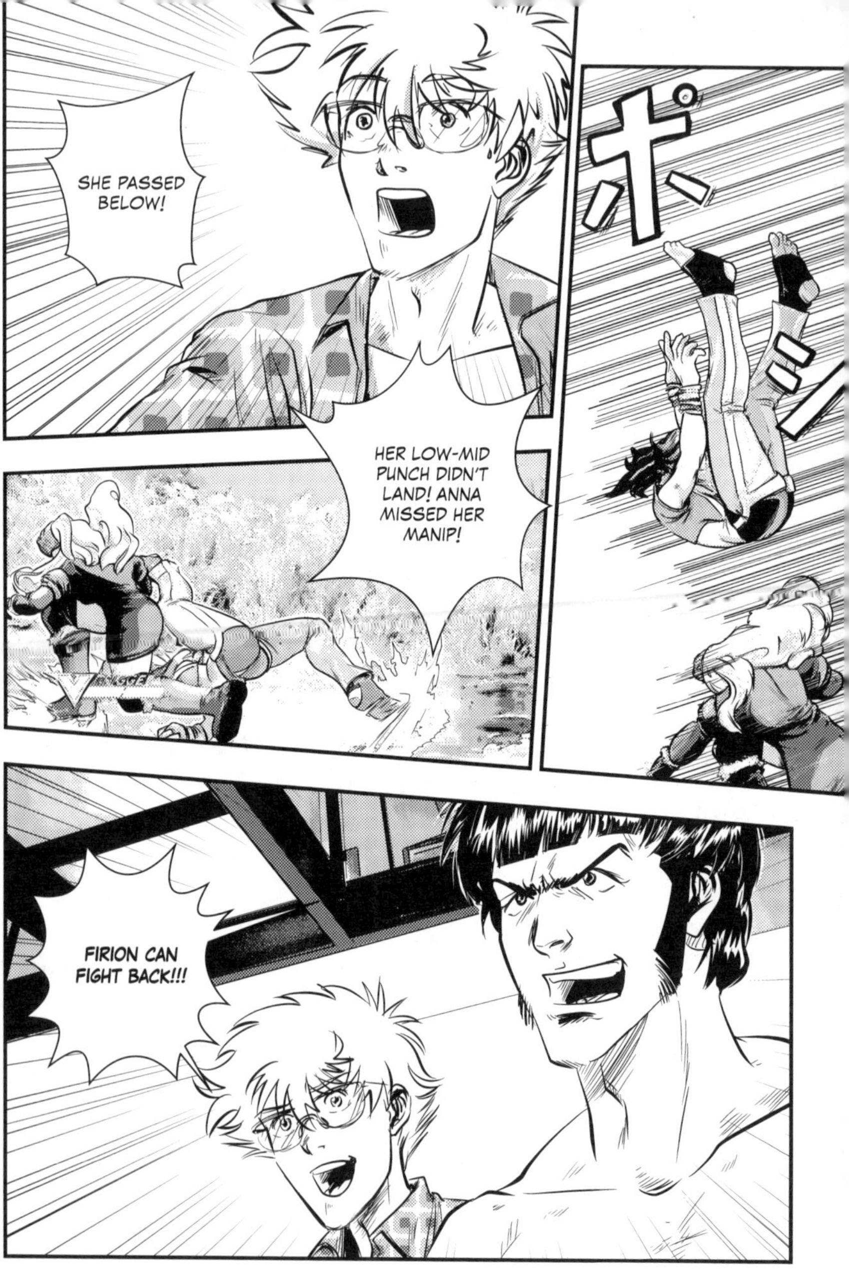
SHE PASSED BELOW!
HER LOW-MID PUNCH DIDN'T LAND! ANNA MISSED HER MANIP!
FIRION CAN FIGHT BACK!!!

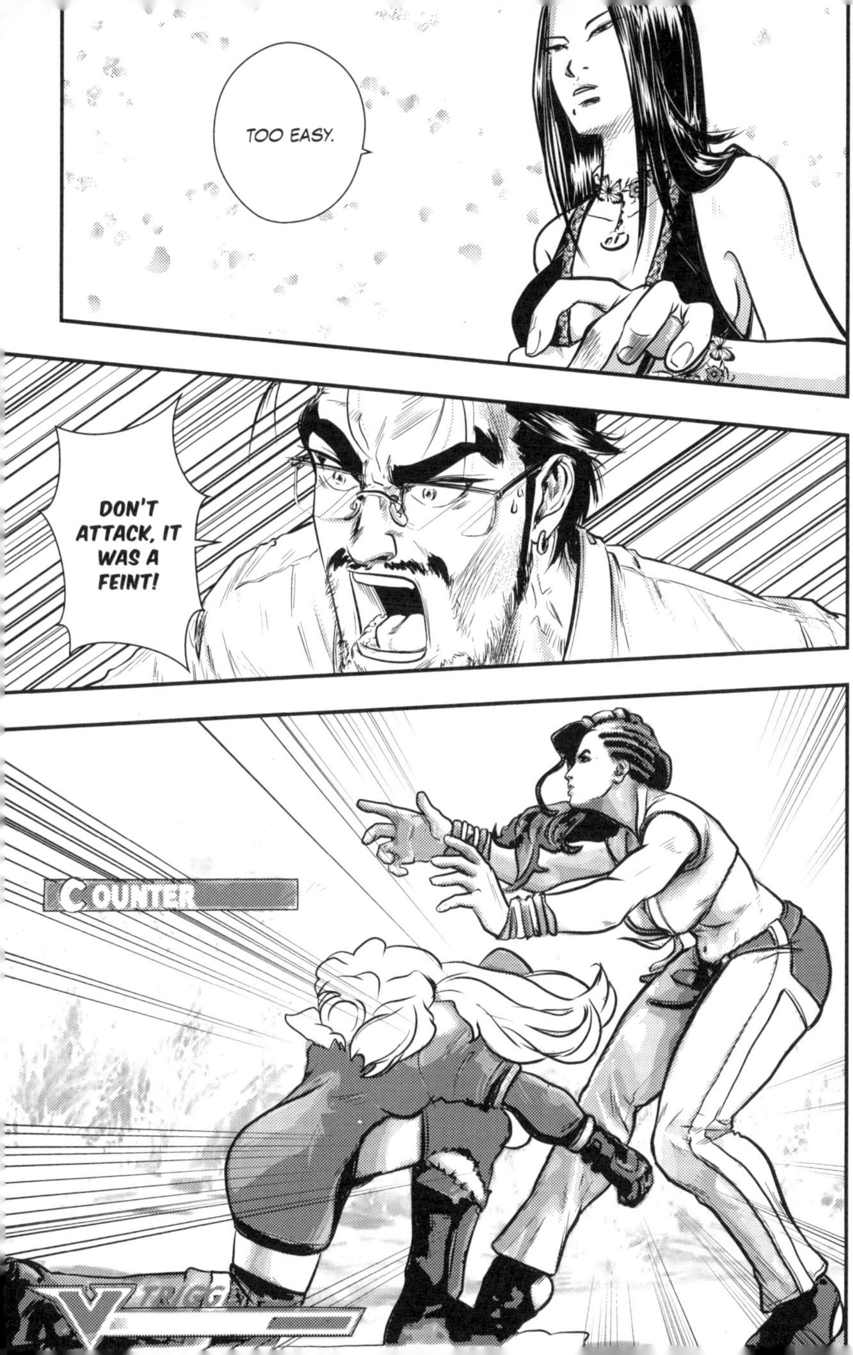
TOO EASY.
DON'T ATTACK, IT WAS A FEINT!
COUNTER

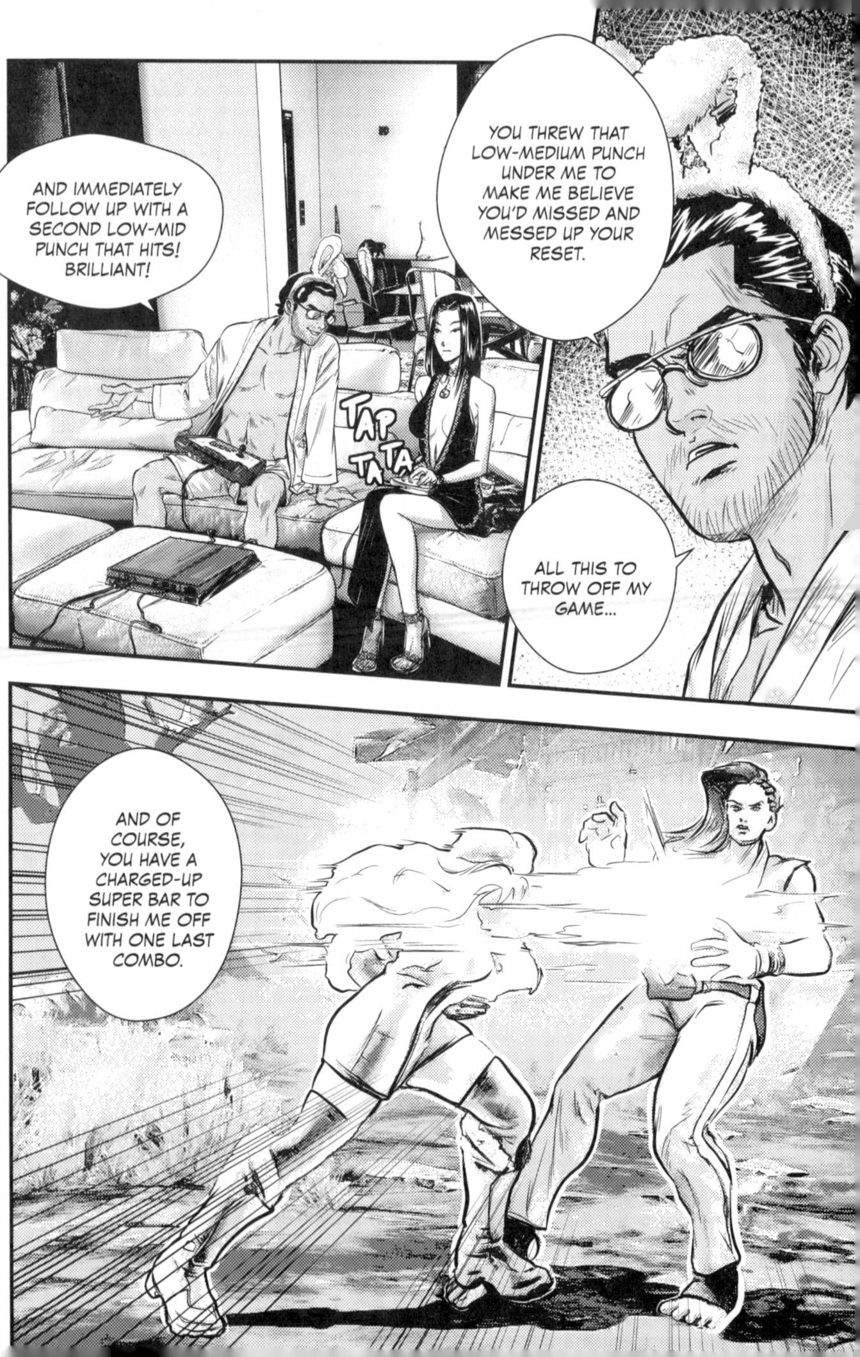
YOU THREW THAT LOW-MEDIUM PUNCH UNDER ME TO MAKE ME BELIEVE YOU'D MISSED AND MESSED UP YOUR RESET.
AND IMMEDIATELY FOLLOW UP WITH A SECOND LOW-MID PUNCH THAT HITS! BRILLIANT!
TAP TA TA
ALL THIS TO THROW OFF MY GAME...
AND OF COURSE, YOU HAVE A CHARGED-UP SUPER BAR TO FINISH ME OFF WITH ONE LAST COMBO.

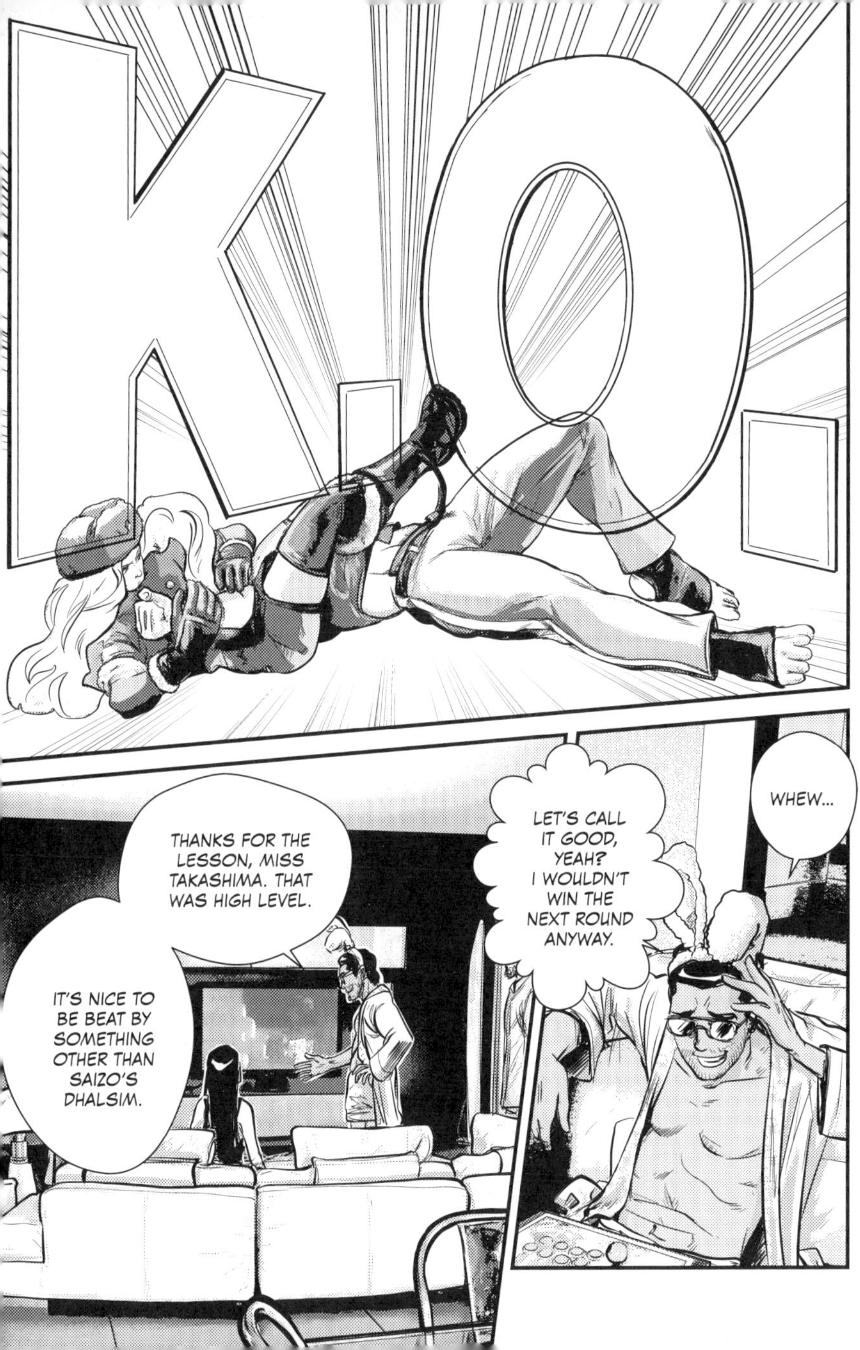
K.O.
WHEW...
LET'S CALL IT GOOD, YEAH? I WOULDN'T WIN THE NEXT ROUND ANYWAY.
THANKS FOR THE LESSON, MISS TAKASHIMA. THAT WAS HIGH LEVEL.
IT'S NICE TO BE BEAT BY SOMETHING OTHER THAN SAIZO'S DHALSIM.

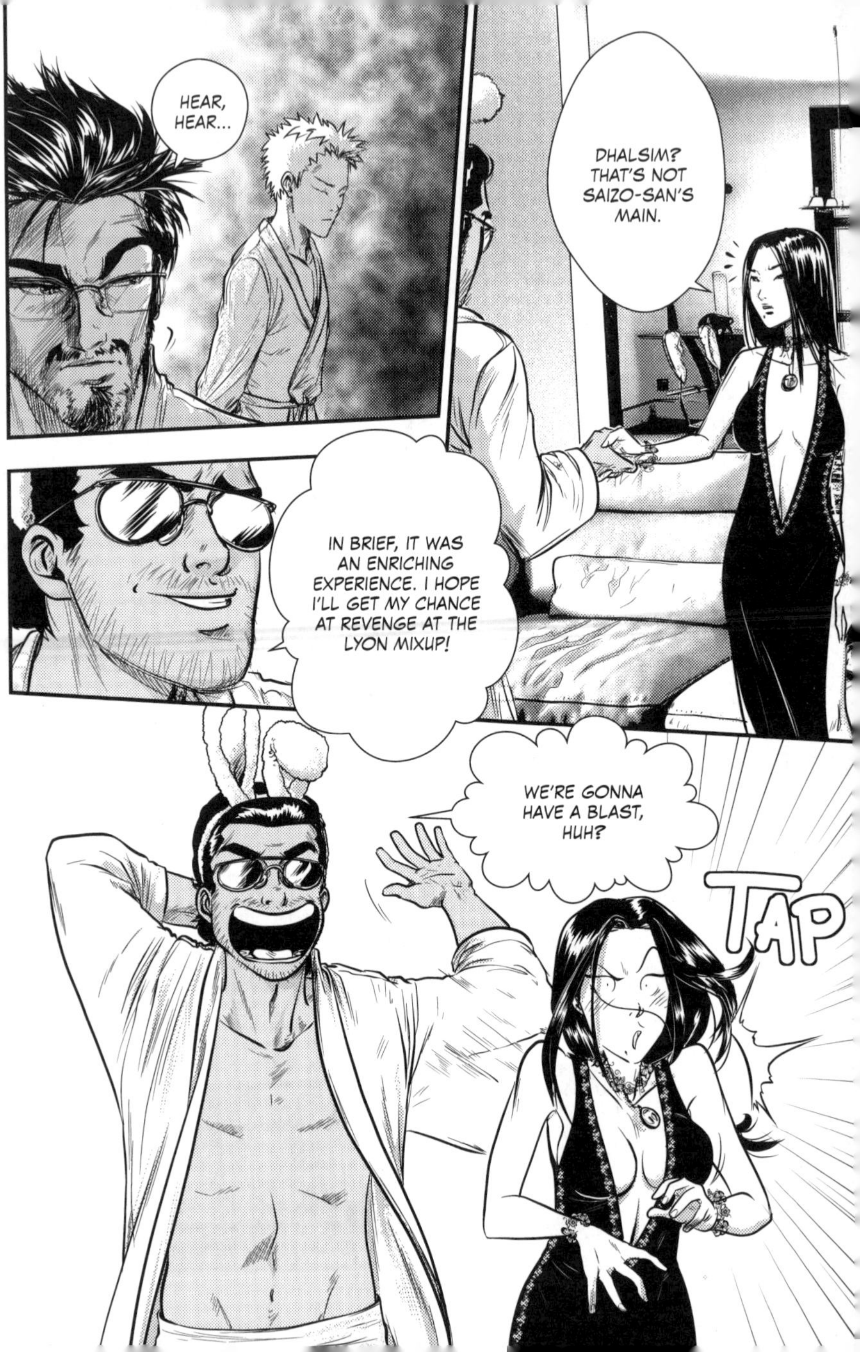
DHALSIM? THAT'S NOT SAIZO-SAN'S MAIN.
HEAR, HEAR...
IN BRIEF, IT WAS AN ENRICHING EXPERIENCE. I HOPE I'LL GET MY CHANCE AT REVENGE AT THE LYON MIXUP!
WE'RE GONNA HAVE A BLAST, HUH?
TAP

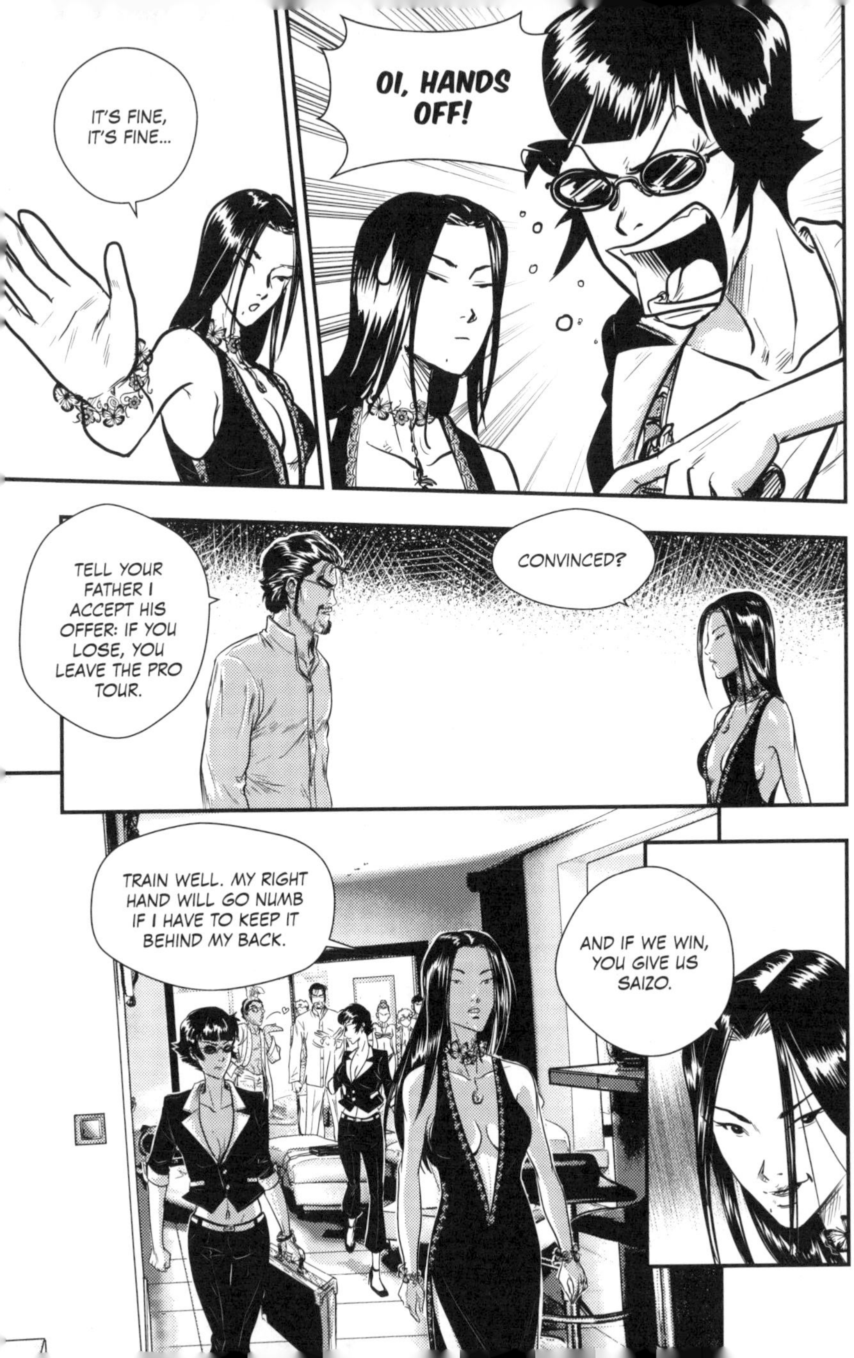
OI, HANDS OFF!
IT'S FINE, IT'S FINE...
CONVINCED?
TELL YOUR FATHER I ACCEPT HIS OFFER: IF YOU LOSE, YOU LEAVE THE PRO TOUR.
AND IF WE WIN, YOU GIVE US SAIZO.
TRAIN WELL. MY RIGHT HAND WILL GO NUMB IF I HAVE TO KEEP IT BEHIND MY BACK.

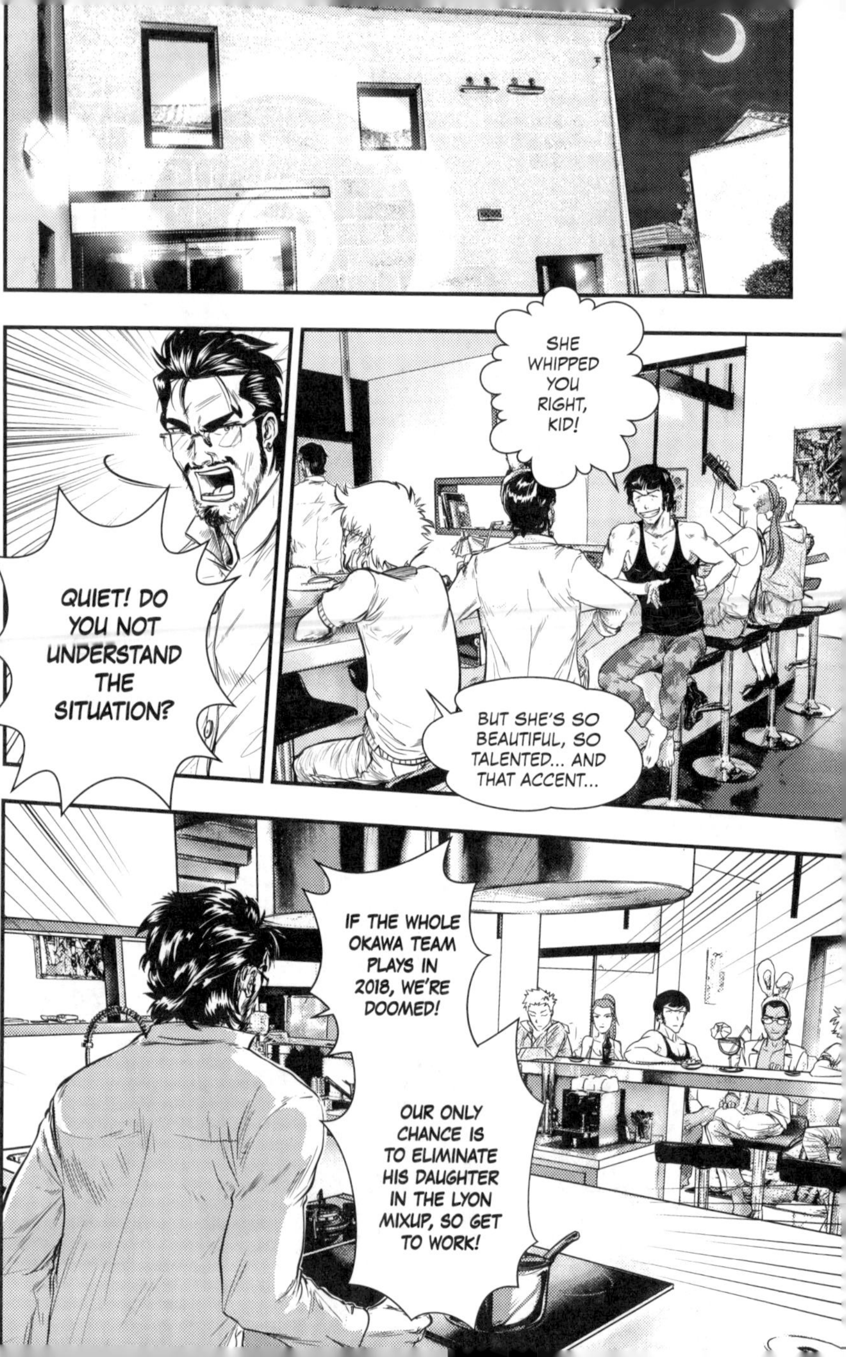
SHE WHIPPED YOU RIGHT, KID!
BUT SHE'S SO BEAUTIFUL, SO TALENTED... AND THAT ACCENT...
QUIET! DO YOU NOT UNDERSTAND THE SITUATION?
IF THE WHOLE OKAWA TEAM PLAYS IN 2018, WE'RE DOOMED!
OUR ONLY CHANCE IS TO ELIMINATE HIS DAUGHTER IN THE LYON MIXUP, SO GET TO WORK!

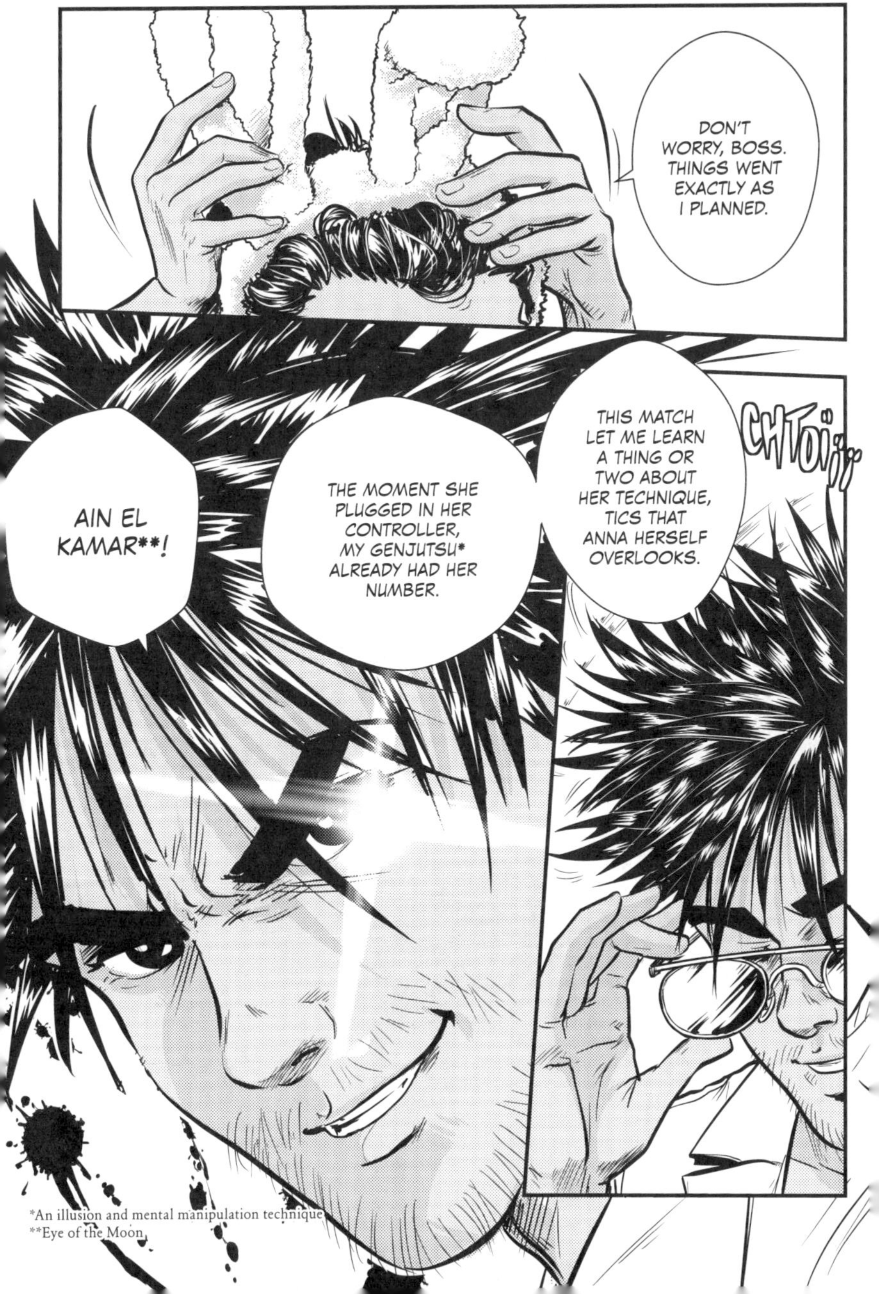
DON'T WORRY, BOSS. THINGS WENT EXACTLY AS I PLANNED.
CHTOI
THIS MATCH LET ME LEARN A THING OR TWO ABOUT HER TECHNIQUE, TICS THAT ANNA HERSELF OVERLOOKS.
THE MOMENT SHE PLUGGED IN HER CONTROLLER, MY GENJUTSU* ALREADY HAD HER NUMBER.
AIN EL KAMAR**!

*An illusion and mental manipulation technique
**Eye of the Moon

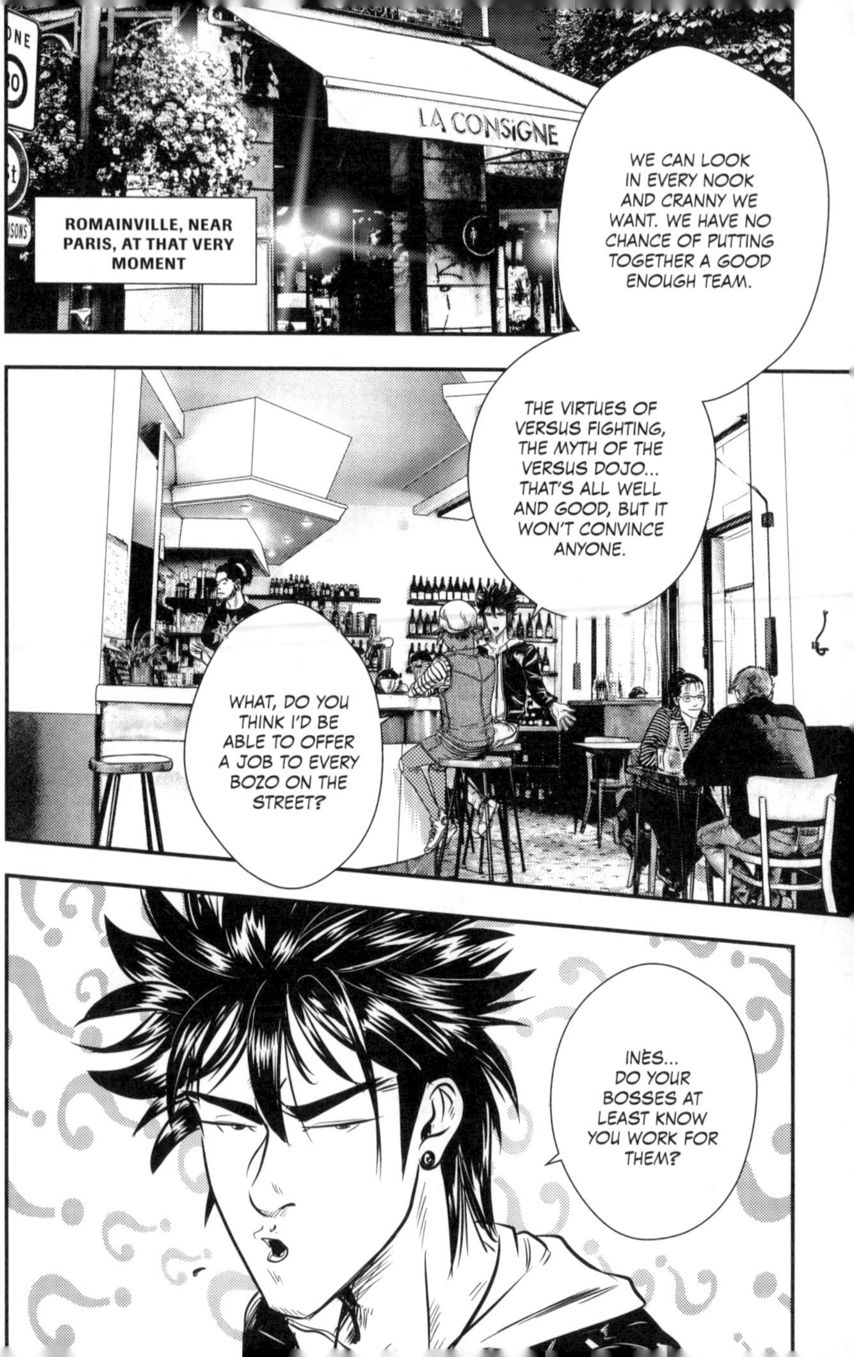
LA CONSIGNE
ROMAINVILLE, NEAR PARIS, AT THAT VERY MOMENT
WE CAN LOOK IN EVERY NOOK AND CRANNY WE WANT. WE HAVE NO CHANCE OF PUTTING TOGETHER A GOOD ENOUGH TEAM.
THE VIRTUES OF VERSUS FIGHTING, THE MYTH OF THE VERSUS DOJO... THAT'S ALL WELL AND GOOD, BUT IT WON'T CONVINCE ANYONE.
WHAT, DO YOU THINK I'D BE ABLE TO OFFER A JOB TO EVERY BOZO ON THE STREET?
INÈS... DO YOUR BOSSES AT LEAST KNOW YOU WORK FOR THEM?

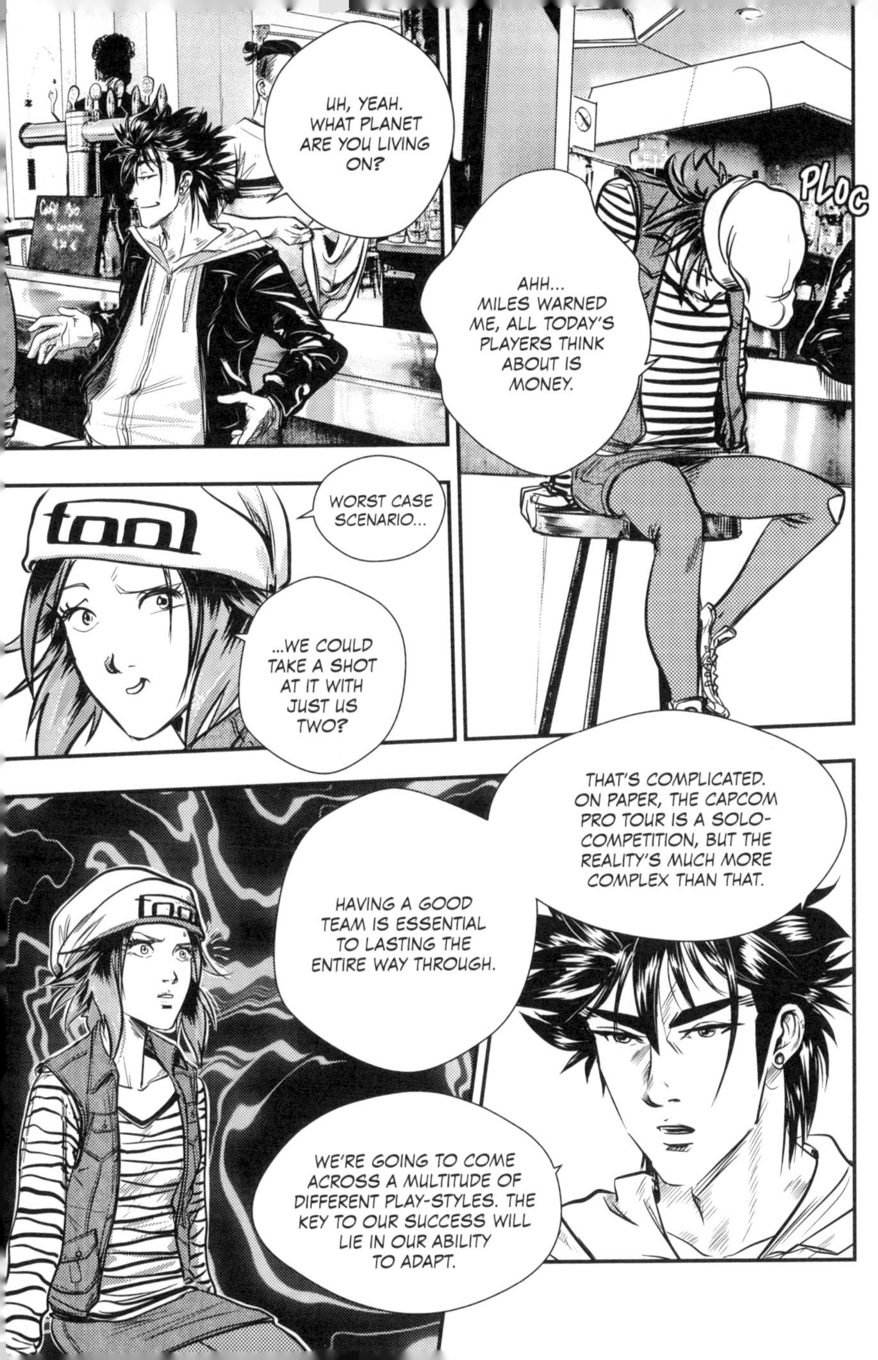
UH, YEAH. WHAT PLANET ARE YOU LIVING ON?
PLOC
AHH... MILES WARNED ME, ALL TODAY'S PLAYERS THINK ABOUT IS MONEY.
WORST CASE SCENARIO...
...WE COULD TAKE A SHOT AT IT WITH JUST US TWO?
THAT'S COMPLICATED. ON PAPER, THE CAPCOM PRO TOUR IS A SOLO-COMPETITION, BUT THE REALITY'S MUCH MORE COMPLEX THAN THAT.
HAVING A GOOD TEAM IS ESSENTIAL TO LASTING THE ENTIRE WAY THROUGH.
WE'RE GOING TO COME ACROSS A MULTITUDE OF DIFFERENT PLAY-STYLES. THE KEY TO OUR SUCCESS WILL LIE IN OUR ABILITY TO ADAPT.

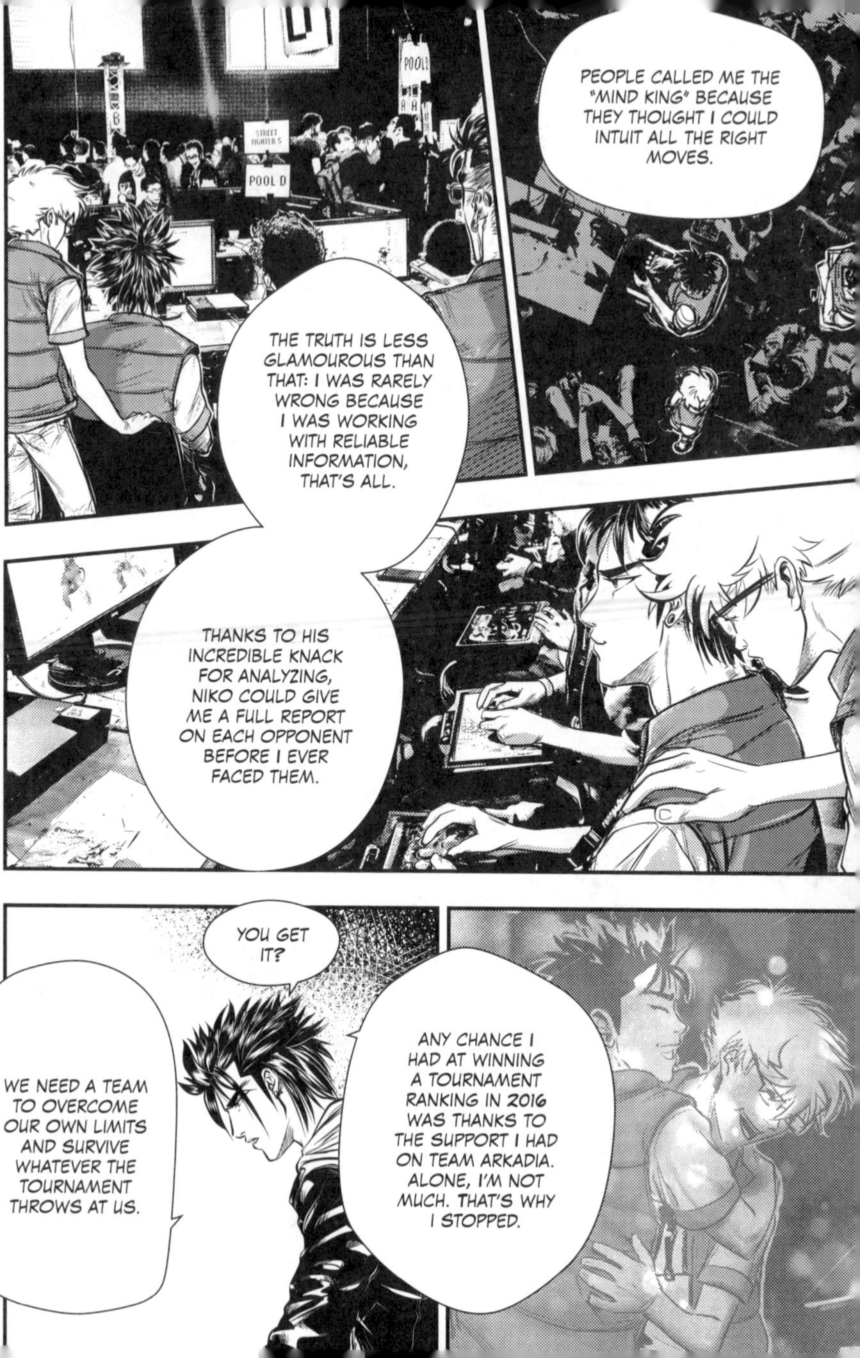
PEOPLE CALLED ME THE "MIND KING" BECAUSE THEY THOUGHT I COULD INTUIT ALL THE RIGHT MOVES.
STREET FIGHTER 5
POOL D
THE TRUTH IS LESS GLAMOUROUS THAN THAT: I WAS RARELY WRONG BECAUSE I WAS WORKING WITH RELIABLE INFORMATION, THAT'S ALL.
THANKS TO HIS INCREDIBLE KNACK FOR ANALYZING, NIKO COULD GIVE ME A FULL REPORT ON EACH OPPONENT BEFORE I EVER FACED THEM.
ANY CHANCE I HAD AT WINNING A TOURNAMENT RANKING IN 2016 WAS THANKS TO THE SUPPORT I HAD ON TEAM ARKADIA. ALONE, I'M NOT MUCH. THAT'S WHY I STOPPED.
YOU GET IT?
WE NEED A TEAM TO OVERCOME OUR OWN LIMITS AND SURVIVE WHATEVER THE TOURNAMENT THROWS AT US.

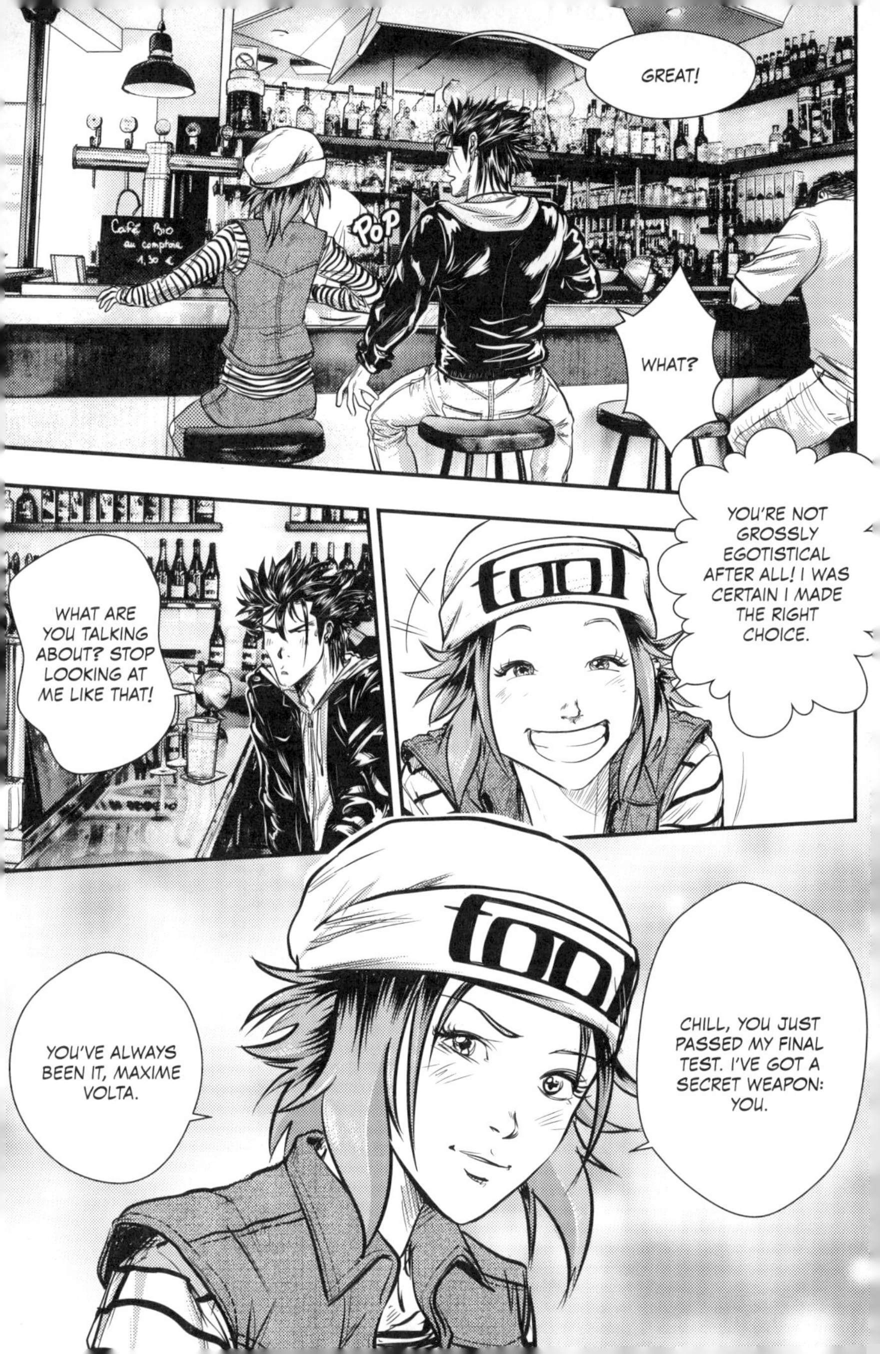
GREAT!
POP
WHAT?
Café Bio au comptoir 1,30 €
YOU'RE NOT GROSSLY EGOTISTICAL AFTER ALL! I WAS CERTAIN I MADE THE RIGHT CHOICE.
WHAT ARE YOU TALKING ABOUT? STOP LOOKING AT ME LIKE THAT!
CHILL, YOU JUST PASSED MY FINAL TEST. I'VE GOT A SECRET WEAPON: YOU.
YOU'VE ALWAYS BEEN IT, MAXIME VOLTA.

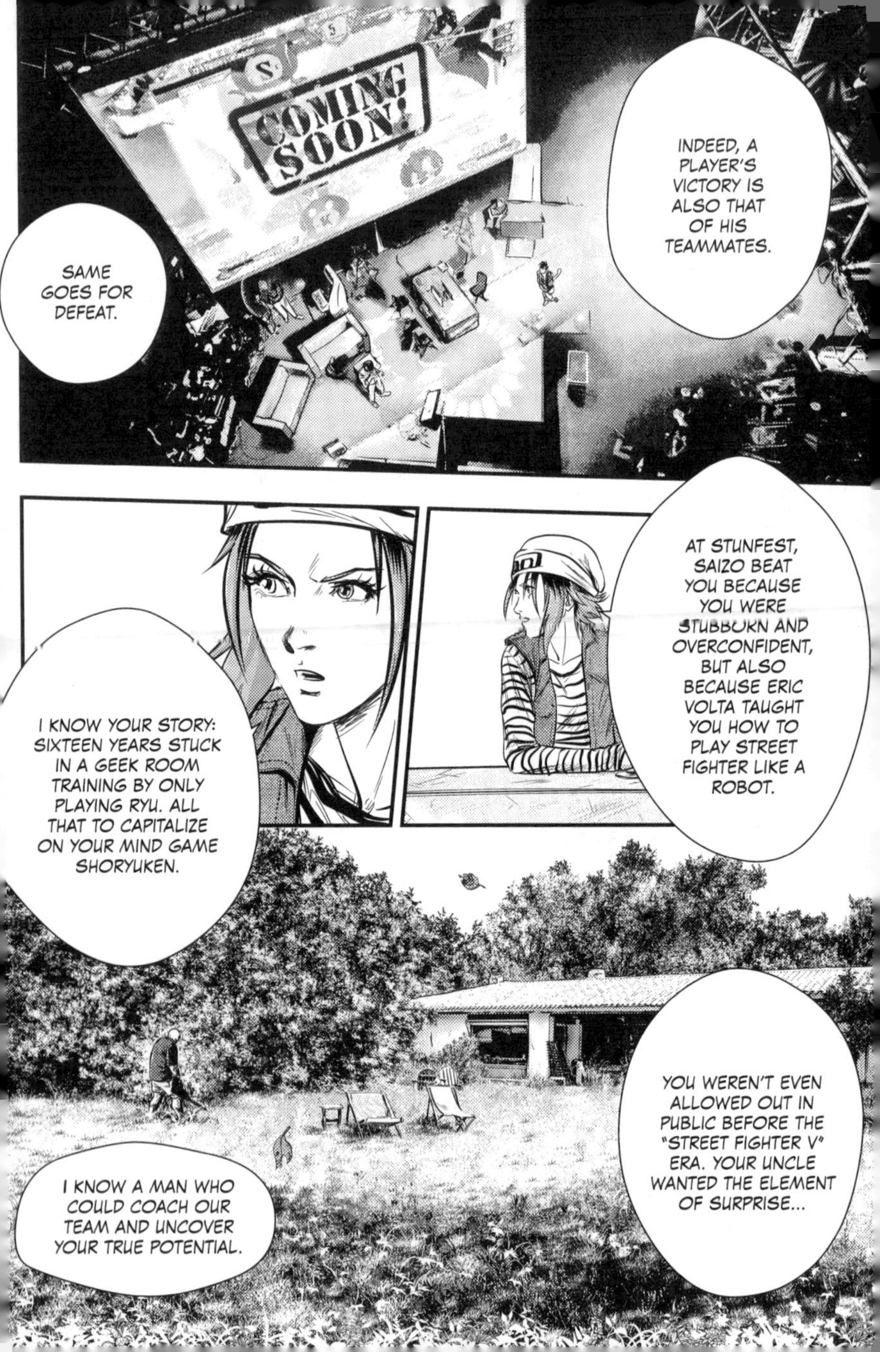

COMING SOON!
INDEED, A PLAYER'S VICTORY IS ALSO THAT OF HIS TEAMMATES.
SAME GOES FOR DEFEAT.
AT STUNFEST, SAIZO BEAT YOU BECAUSE YOU WERE STUBBORN AND OVERCONFIDENT, BUT ALSO BECAUSE ERIC VOLTA TAUGHT YOU HOW TO PLAY STREET FIGHTER LIKE A ROBOT.
I KNOW YOUR STORY: SIXTEEN YEARS STUCK IN A GEEK ROOM TRAINING BY ONLY PLAYING RYU. ALL THAT TO CAPITALIZE ON YOUR MIND GAME SHORYUKEN.
YOU WEREN'T EVEN ALLOWED OUT IN PUBLIC BEFORE THE "STREET FIGHTER V" ERA. YOUR UNCLE WANTED THE ELEMENT OF SURPRISE...
I KNOW A MAN WHO COULD COACH OUR TEAM AND UNCOVER YOUR TRUE POTENTIAL.

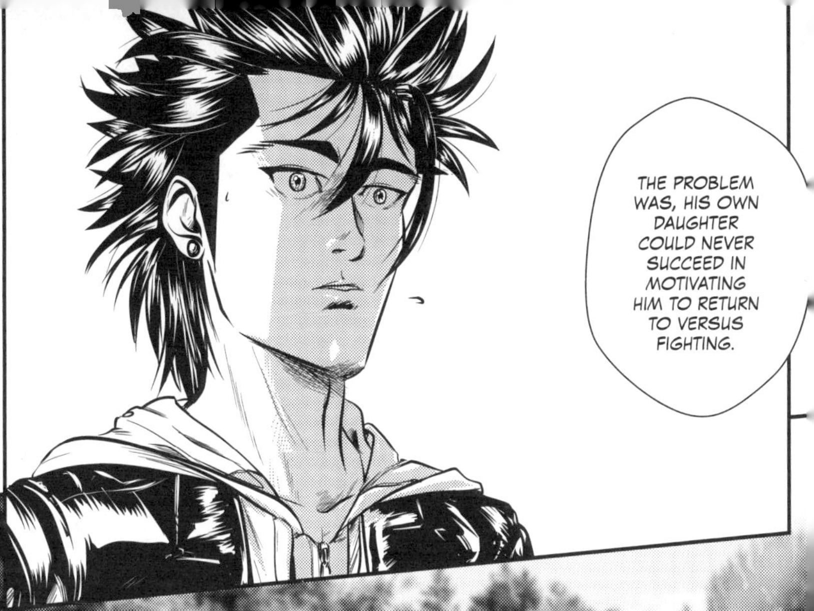
THE PROBLEM WAS, HIS OWN DAUGHTER COULD NEVER SUCCEED IN MOTIVATING HIM TO RETURN TO VERSUS FIGHTING.
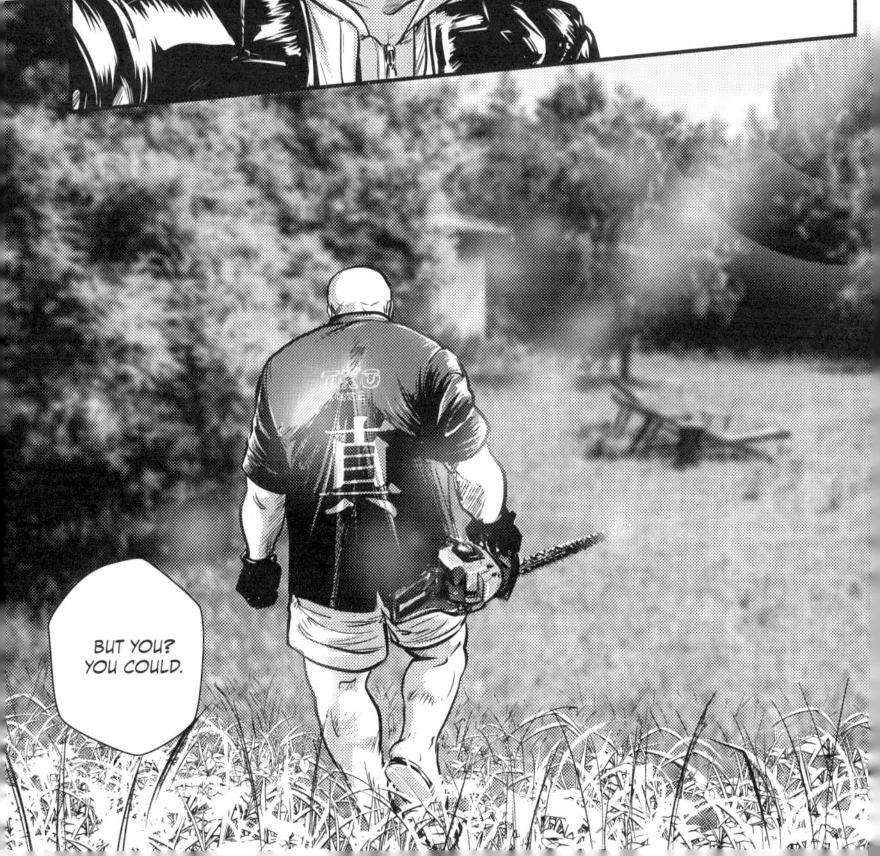
BUT YOU? YOU COULD.

CHARACTER SELECT!

FIRION

THE MYTH MASTER

BACKGROUND

Firion's technique is to confuse and cloud the minds of his opponents (and even his teammates) with a powerful pre-match spiel, to make them believe that they know that he knows that they know what he knows. Or so they think.

This Moroccan is one eof the most difficult players in "Versus Fighting Story" to predict because no one knows what his real hidden technique is... and he himself is aware of this. In short, he is a big deal.

Genius strategist or brilliant con artist? You'll learn which by reading the rest of this manga... or perhaps not, since his hypnosis is permanent anyhow.

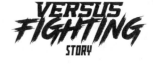

CHARACTER DESIGN

Modeled after a real-life genius, I had to try to not stick too much to reality (but hey, it caught up with me sometimes). I had a lot of fun designing a Firion without his bunny ears and glasses - let's hope we will see him again in Volume 2!

BY KALON

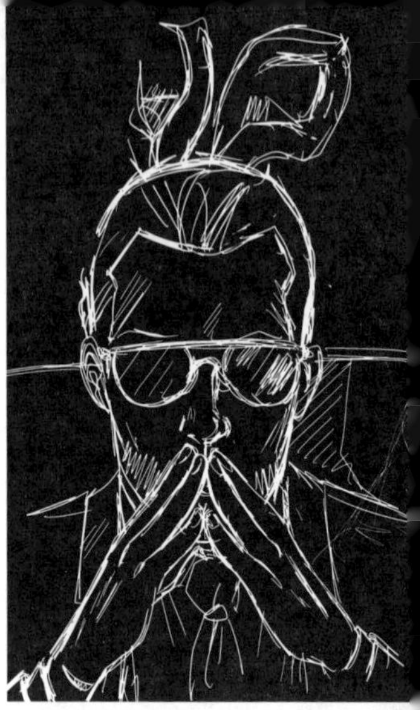

VERSUS FIGHTING STORY

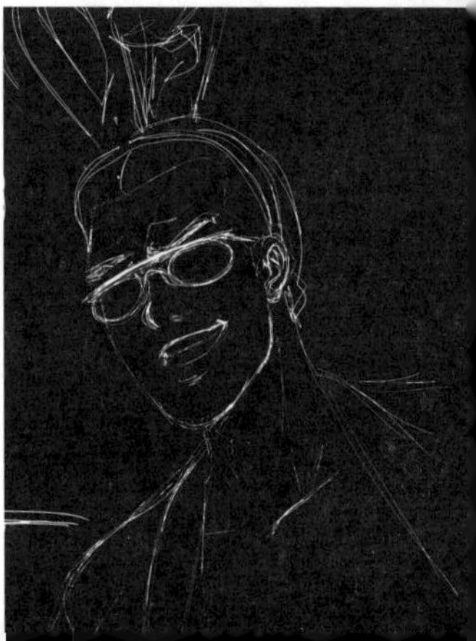

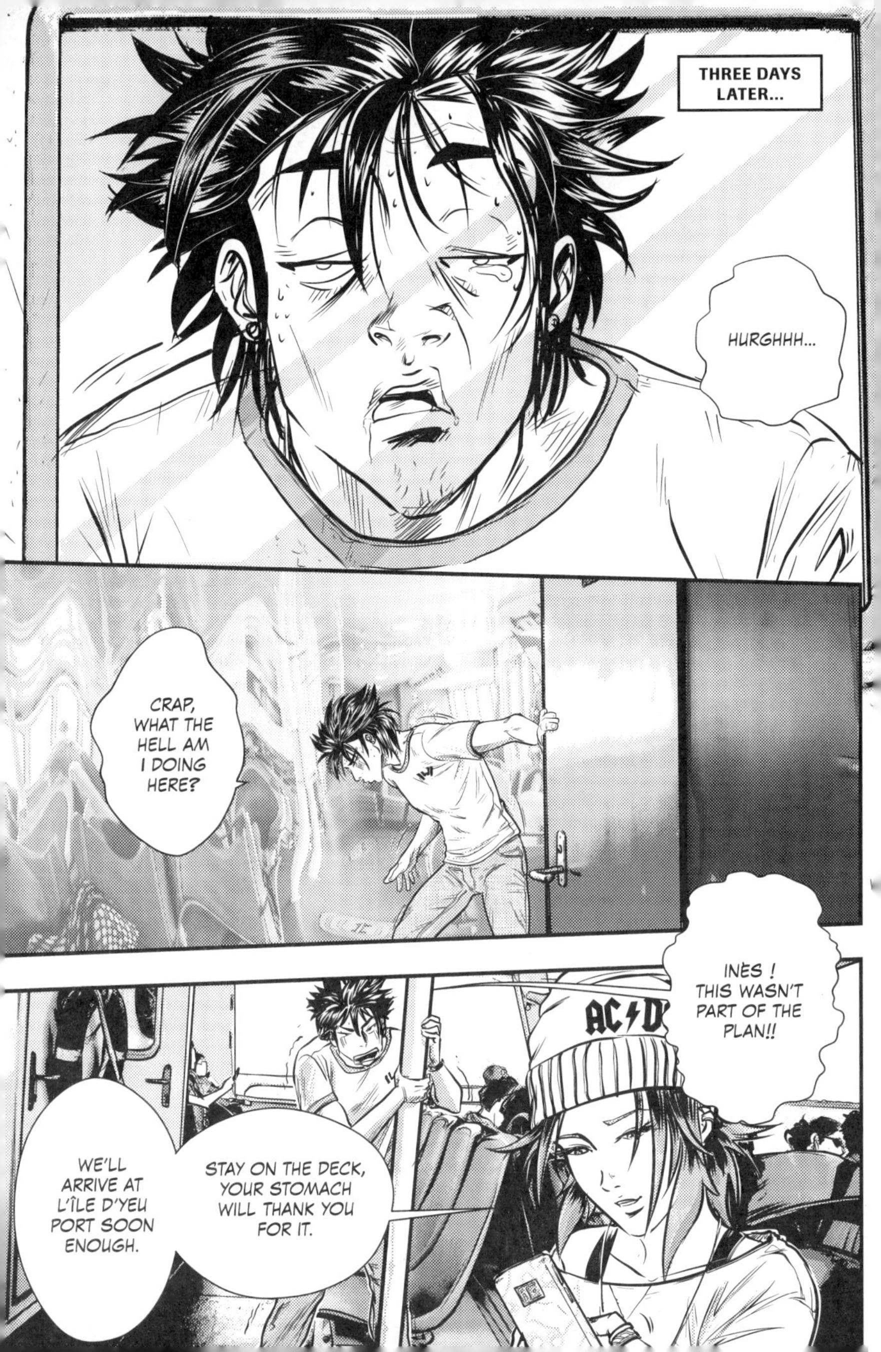
THREE DAYS LATER...
HURGHHH...
CRAP, WHAT THE HELL AM I DOING HERE?
INÈS ! THIS WASN'T PART OF THE PLAN!!
AC/DC
STAY ON THE DECK, YOUR STOMACH WILL THANK YOU FOR IT.
WE'LL ARRIVE AT L'ÎLE D'YEU PORT SOON ENOUGH.

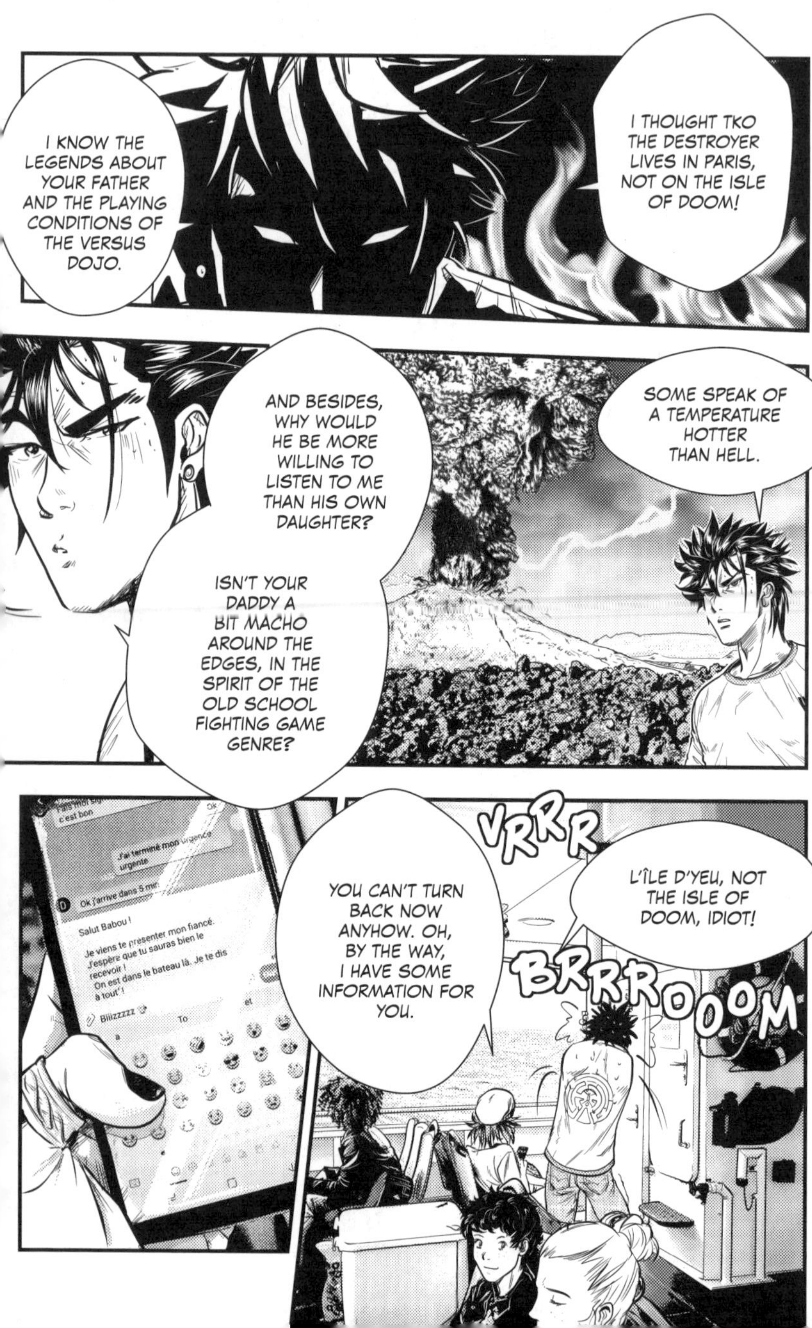
I THOUGHT TKO THE DESTROYER LIVES IN PARIS, NOT ON THE ISLE OF DOOM!
I KNOW THE LEGENDS ABOUT YOUR FATHER AND THE PLAYING CONDITIONS OF THE VERSUS DOJO.
SOME SPEAK OF A TEMPERATURE HOTTER THAN HELL.
AND BESIDES, WHY WOULD HE BE MORE WILLING TO LISTEN TO ME THAN HIS OWN DAUGHTER?
ISN'T YOUR DADDY A BIT MACHO AROUND THE EDGES, IN THE SPIRIT OF THE OLD SCHOOL FIGHTING GAME GENRE?
VRRR
L'ÎLE D'YEU, NOT THE ISLE OF DOOM, IDIOT!
BRRROOOM
YOU CAN'T TURN BACK NOW ANYHOW. OH, BY THE WAY, I HAVE SOME INFORMATION FOR YOU.
J'ai terminé mon urgence
Ok j'arrive dans 5 min
Salut Babou !
Je viens te présenter mon fiancé.
J'espère que tu sauras bien le recevoir !
On est dans le bateau là. Je te dis à tout' !
Biiizzzzz

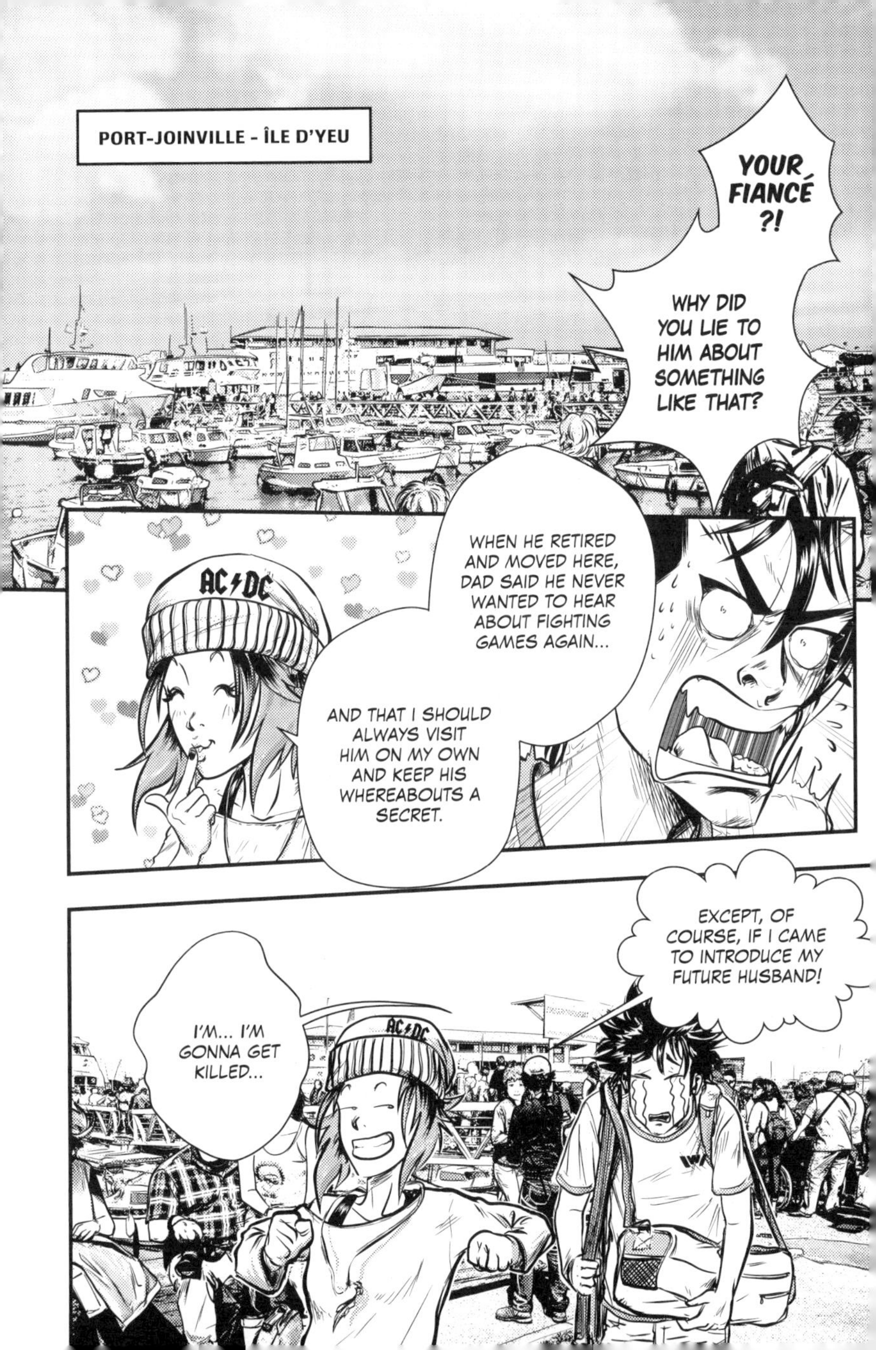
PORT-JOINVILLE - ÎLE D'YEU
YOUR FIANCÉ ?!
WHY DID YOU LIE TO HIM ABOUT SOMETHING LIKE THAT?
WHEN HE RETIRED AND MOVED HERE, DAD SAID HE NEVER WANTED TO HEAR ABOUT FIGHTING GAMES AGAIN...
AND THAT I SHOULD ALWAYS VISIT HIM ON MY OWN AND KEEP HIS WHEREABOUTS A SECRET.
EXCEPT, OF COURSE, IF I CAME TO INTRODUCE MY FUTURE HUSBAND!
I'M... I'M GONNA GET KILLED...

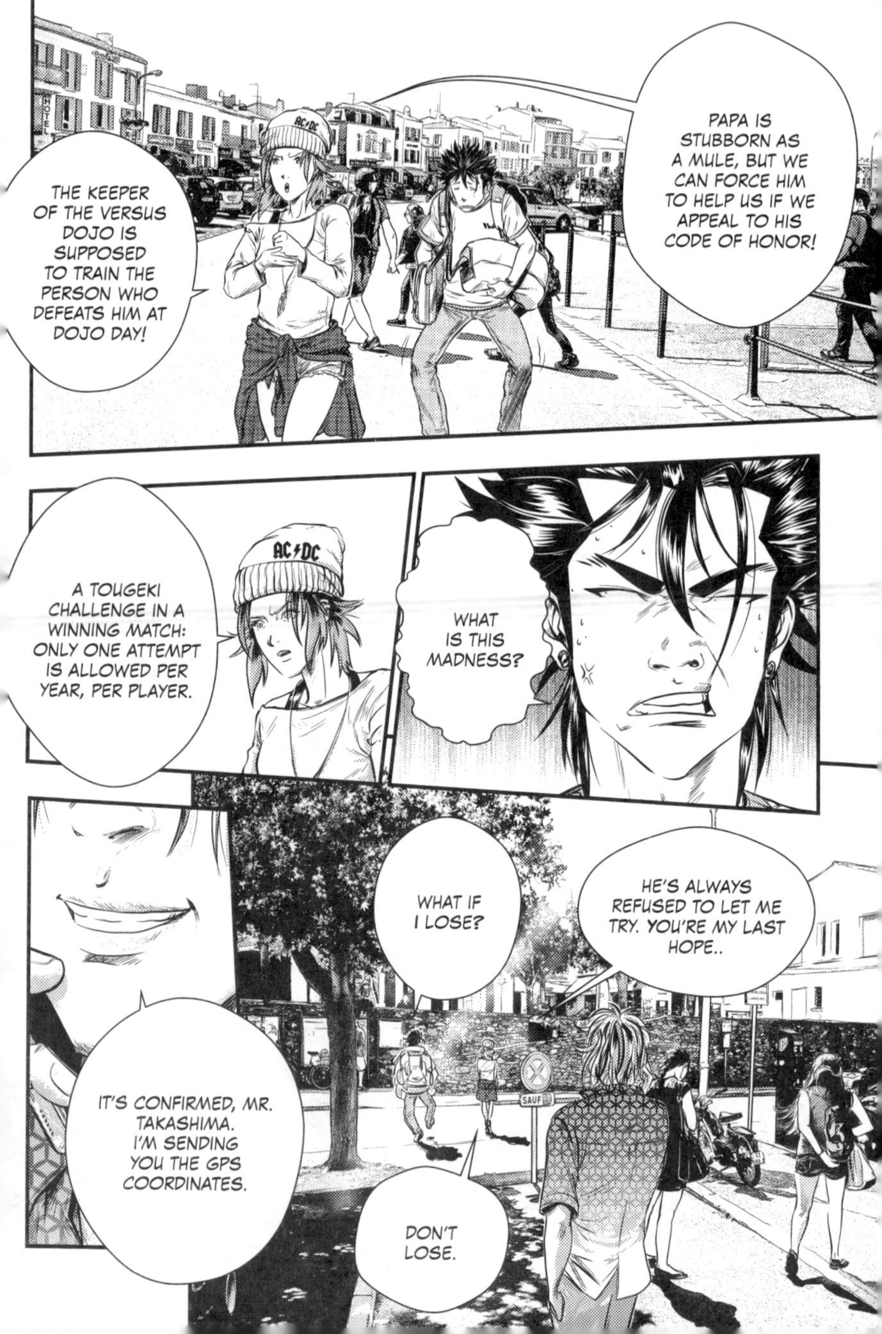
THE KEEPER OF THE VERSUS DOJO IS SUPPOSED TO TRAIN THE PERSON WHO DEFEATS HIM AT DOJO DAY!
PAPA IS STUBBORN AS A MULE, BUT WE CAN FORCE HIM TO HELP US IF WE APPEAL TO HIS CODE OF HONOR!
AC/DC
HOTEL
A TOUGEKI CHALLENGE IN A WINNING MATCH: ONLY ONE ATTEMPT IS ALLOWED PER YEAR, PER PLAYER.
AC/DC
WHAT IS THIS MADNESS?
IT'S CONFIRMED, MR. TAKASHIMA. I'M SENDING YOU THE GPS COORDINATES.
HE'S ALWAYS REFUSED TO LET ME TRY. YOU'RE MY LAST HOPE..
WHAT IF I LOSE?
SAUF
DON'T LOSE.

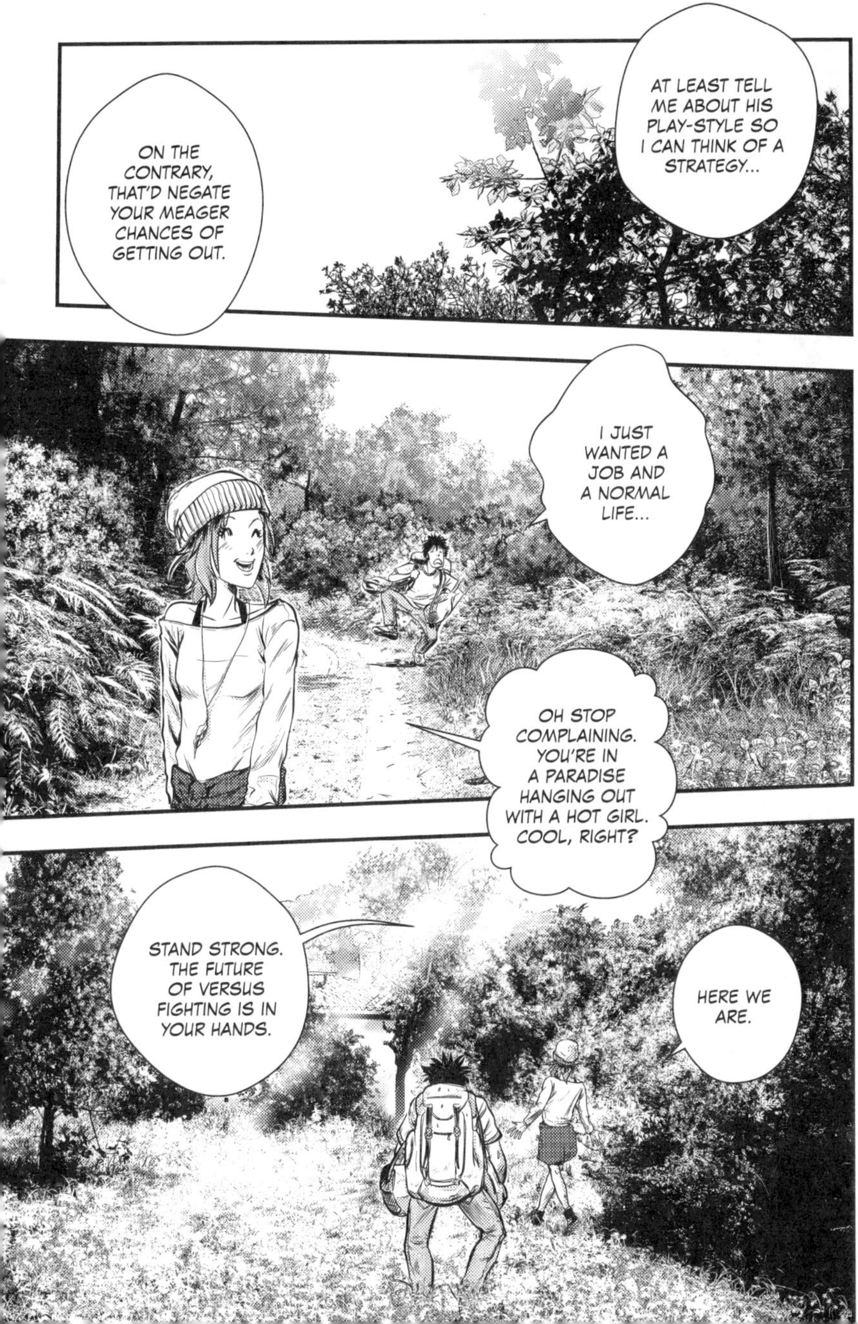
AT LEAST TELL ME ABOUT HIS PLAY-STYLE SO I CAN THINK OF A STRATEGY...
ON THE CONTRARY, THAT'D NEGATE YOUR MEAGER CHANCES OF GETTING OUT.
I JUST WANTED A JOB AND A NORMAL LIFE...
OH STOP COMPLAINING. YOU'RE IN A PARADISE HANGING OUT WITH A HOT GIRL. COOL, RIGHT?
STAND STRONG. THE FUTURE OF VERSUS FIGHTING IS IN YOUR HANDS.
HERE WE ARE.

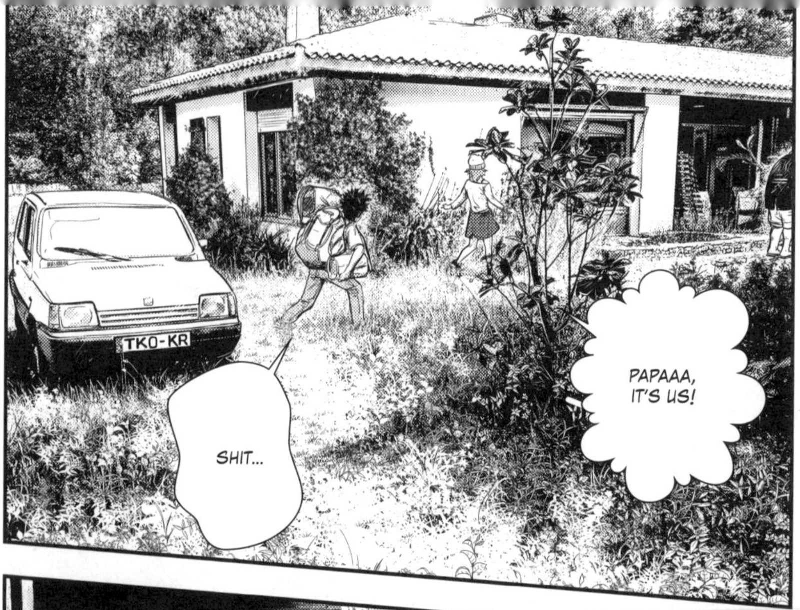
PAPAAA, IT'S US!
SHIT...
TKO-KR

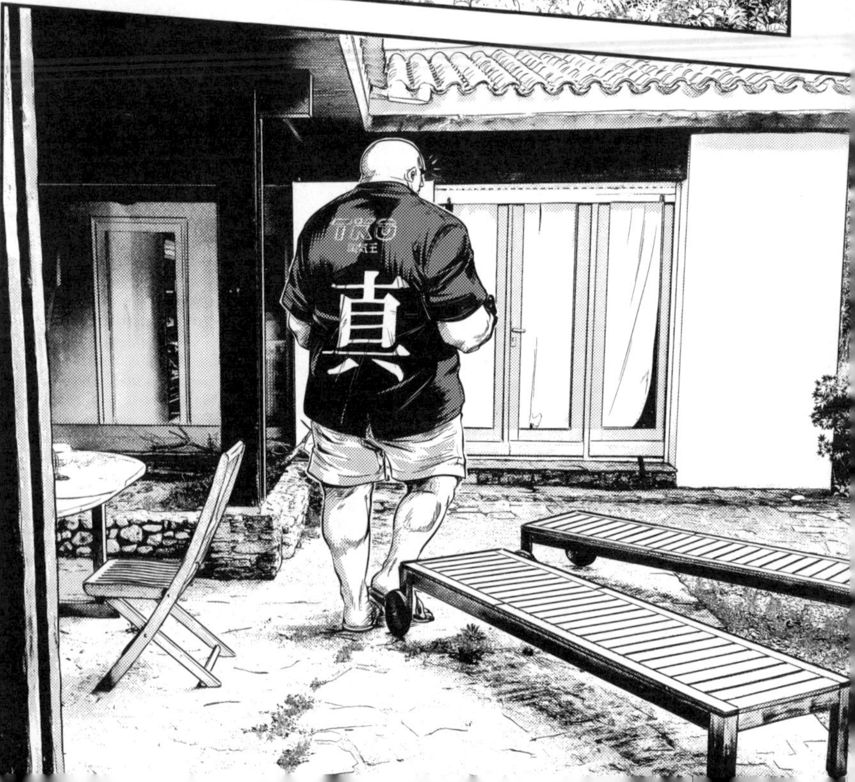
真

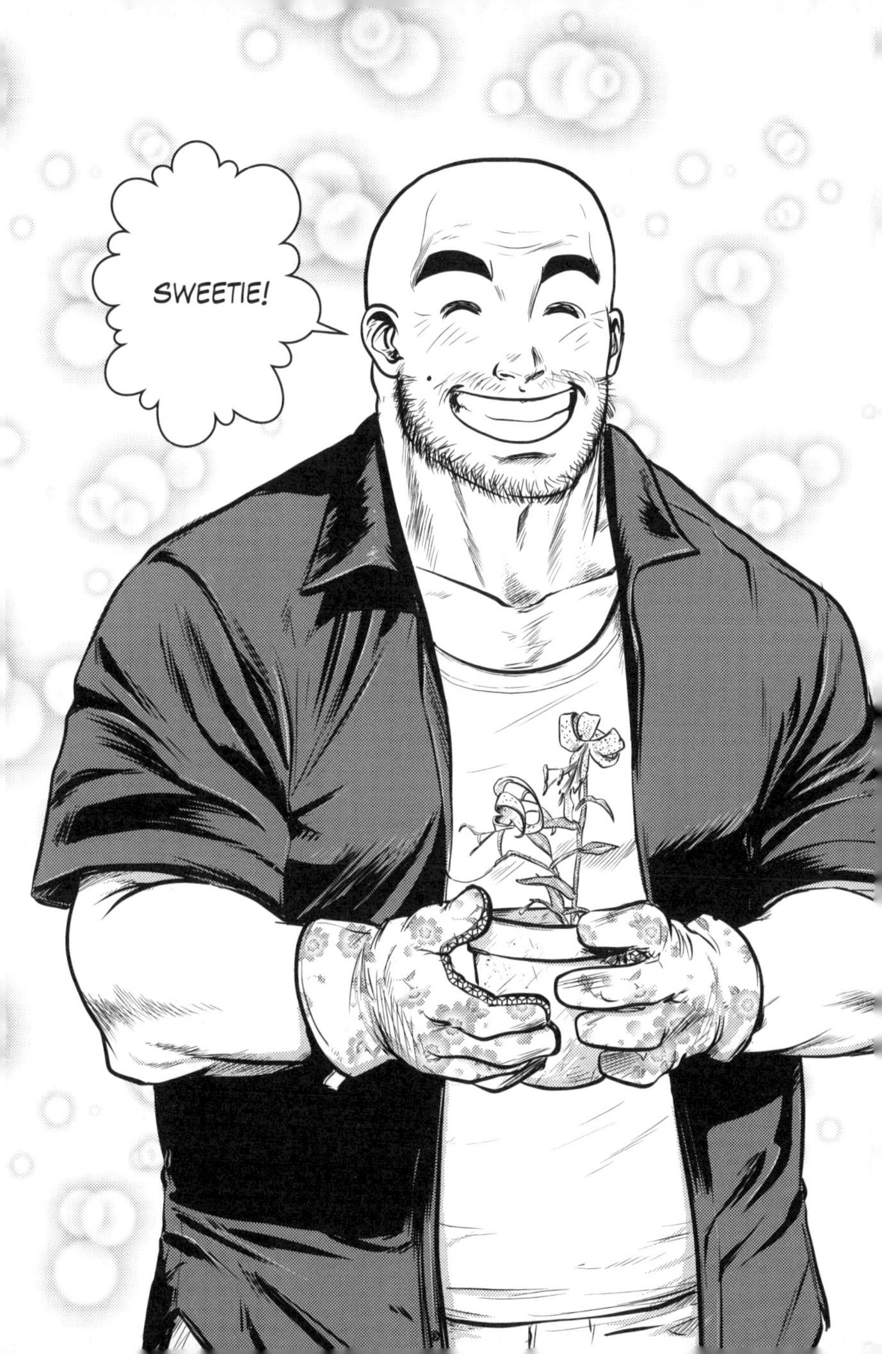
SWEETIE!

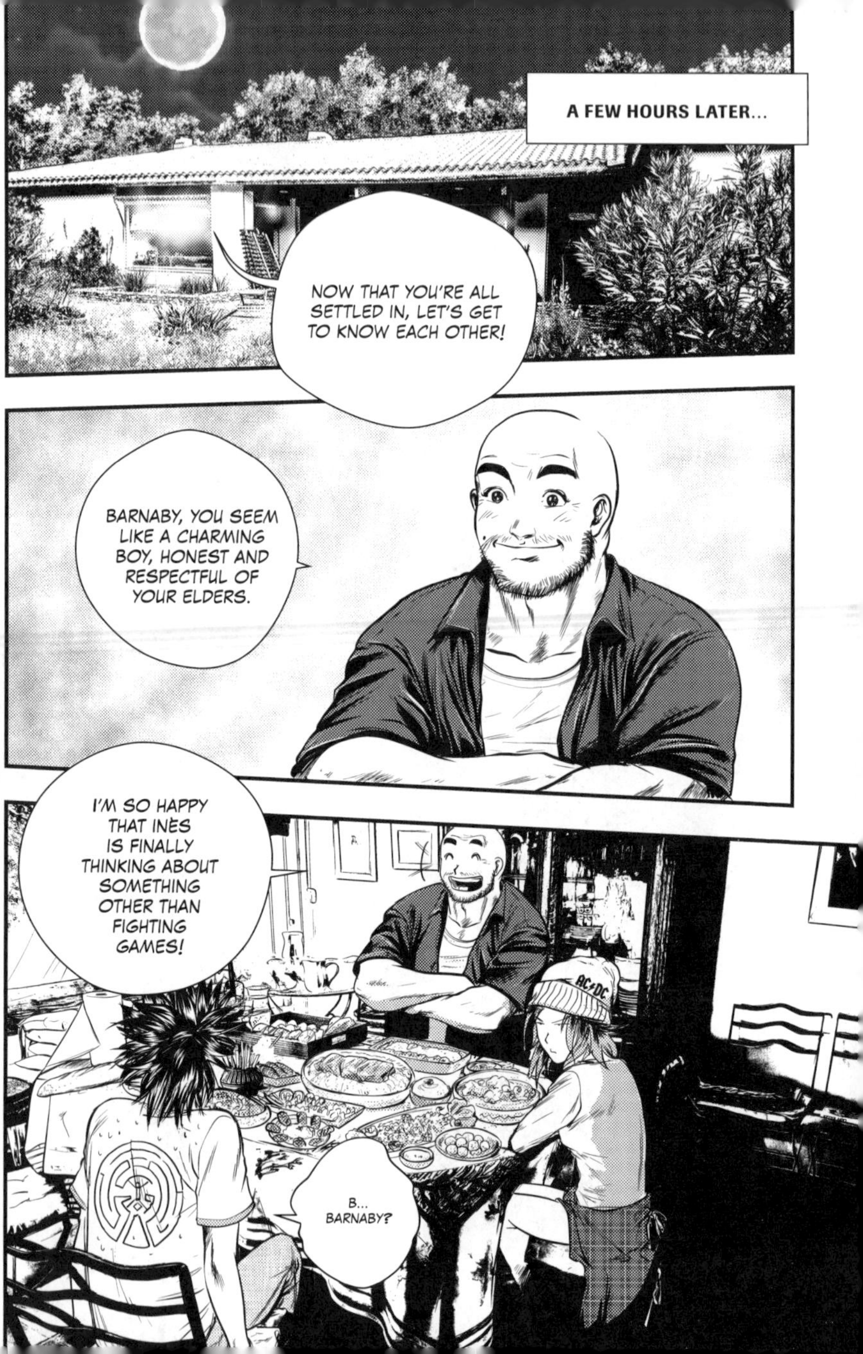
A FEW HOURS LATER...
NOW THAT YOU'RE ALL SETTLED IN, LET'S GET TO KNOW EACH OTHER!
BARNABY, YOU SEEM LIKE A CHARMING BOY, HONEST AND RESPECTFUL OF YOUR ELDERS.
I'M SO HAPPY THAT INÈS IS FINALLY THINKING ABOUT SOMETHING OTHER THAN FIGHTING GAMES!
B... BARNABY?

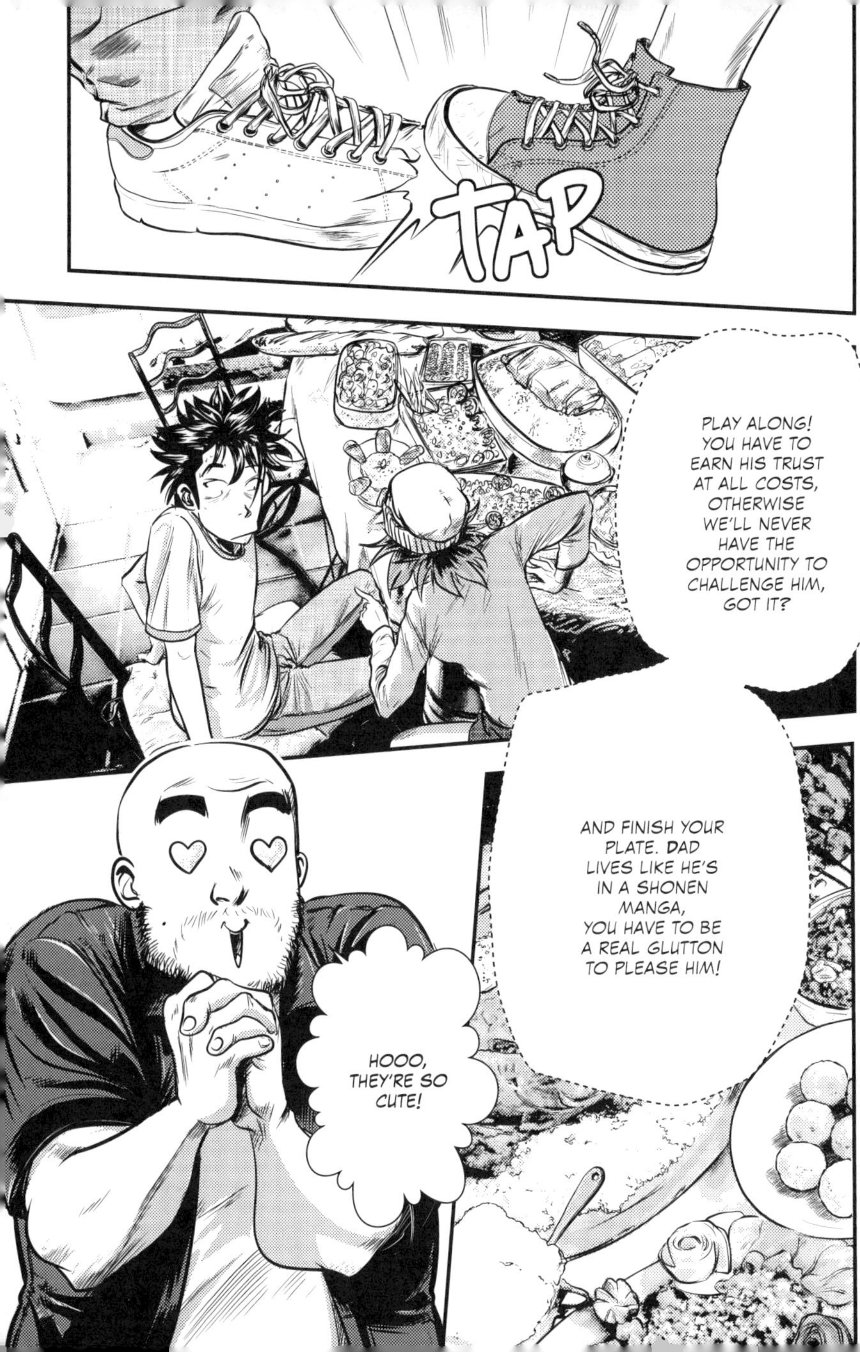
TAP
PLAY ALONG! YOU HAVE TO EARN HIS TRUST AT ALL COSTS, OTHERWISE WE'LL NEVER HAVE THE OPPORTUNITY TO CHALLENGE HIM, GOT IT?
AND FINISH YOUR PLATE. DAD LIVES LIKE HE'S IN A SHONEN MANGA, YOU HAVE TO BE A REAL GLUTTON TO PLEASE HIM!
HOOO, THEY'RE SO CUTE!

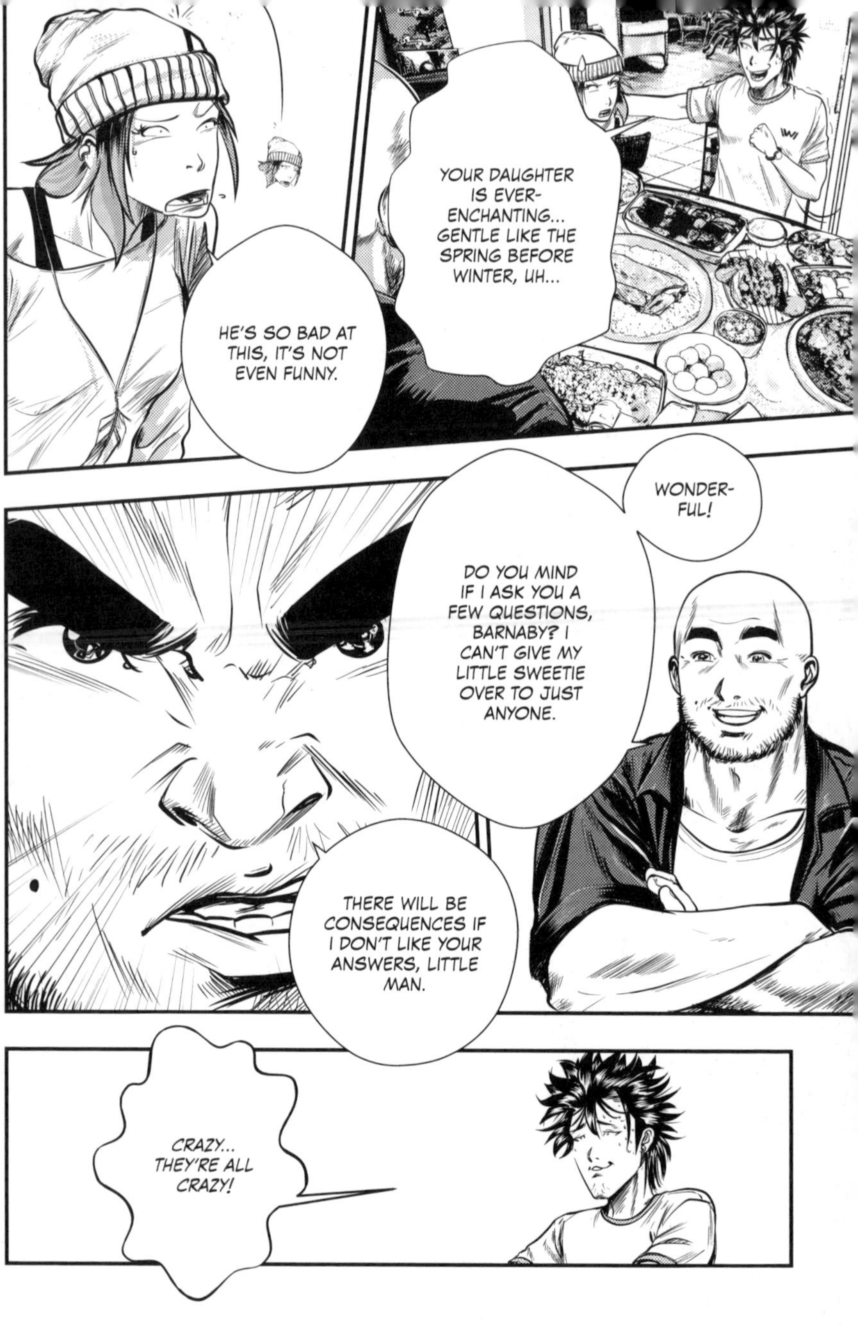
YOUR DAUGHTER IS EVER-ENCHANTING... GENTLE LIKE THE SPRING BEFORE WINTER, UH...
HE'S SO BAD AT THIS, IT'S NOT EVEN FUNNY.
WONDER-FUL!
DO YOU MIND IF I ASK YOU A FEW QUESTIONS, BARNABY? I CAN'T GIVE MY LITTLE SWEETIE OVER TO JUST ANYONE.
THERE WILL BE CONSEQUENCES IF I DON'T LIKE YOUR ANSWERS, LITTLE MAN.
CRAZY... THEY'RE ALL CRAZY!

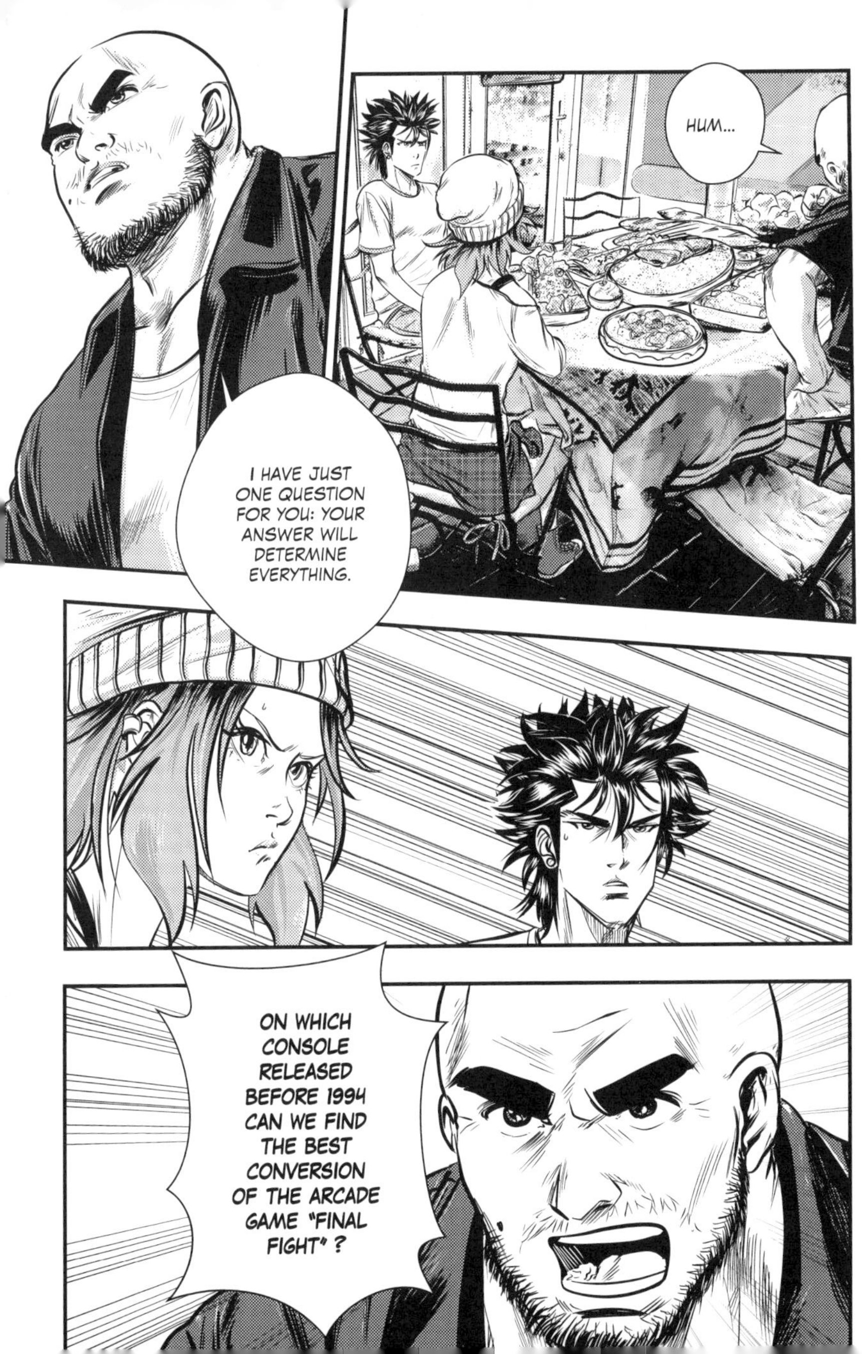
HUM...
I HAVE JUST ONE QUESTION FOR YOU: YOUR ANSWER WILL DETERMINE EVERYTHING.
ON WHICH CONSOLE RELEASED BEFORE 1994 CAN WE FIND THE BEST CONVERSION OF THE ARCADE GAME "FINAL FIGHT" ?

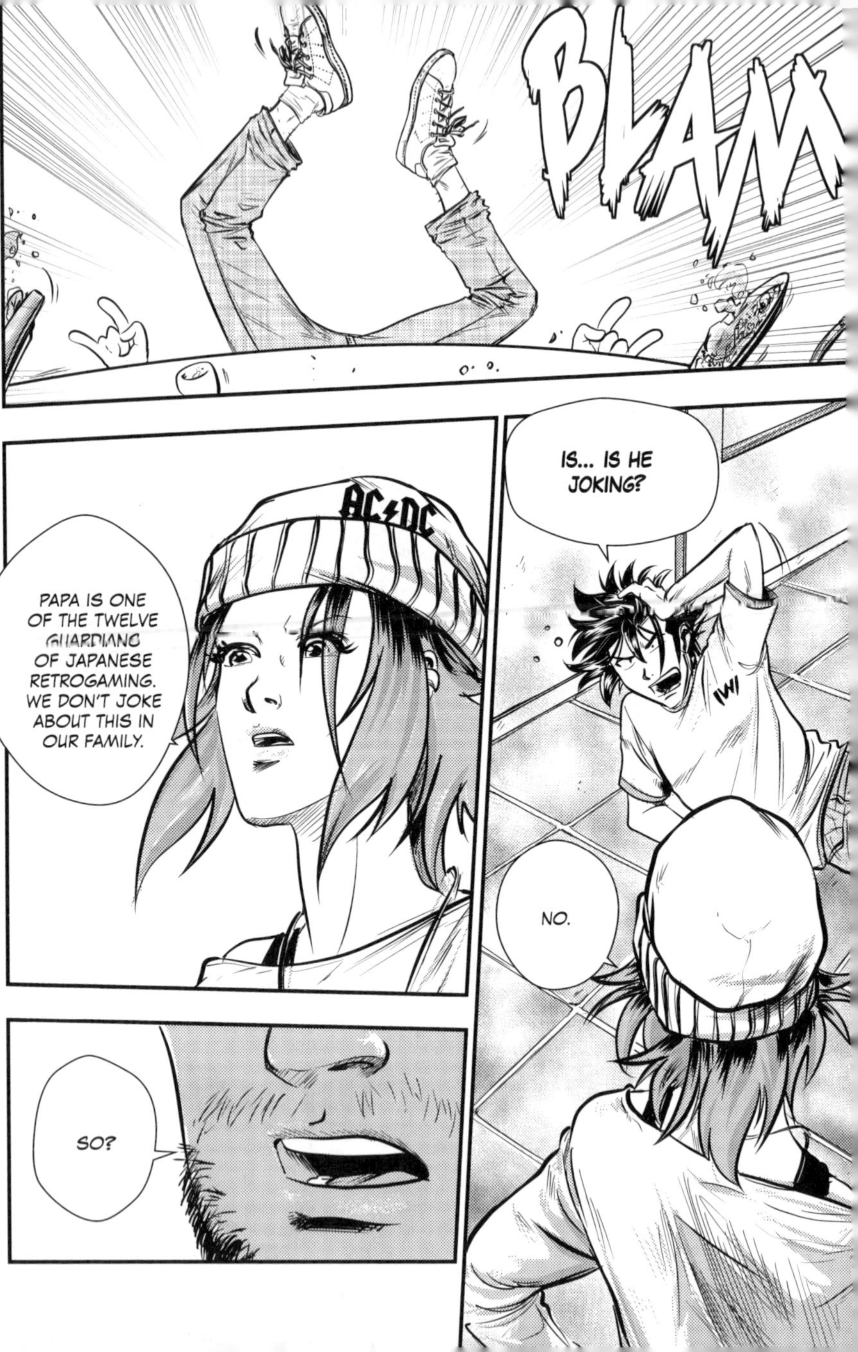
BLAM
IS... IS HE JOKING?
NO.
PAPA IS ONE OF THE TWELVE GUARDIANS OF JAPANESE RETROGAMING. WE DON'T JOKE ABOUT THIS IN OUR FAMILY.
SO?

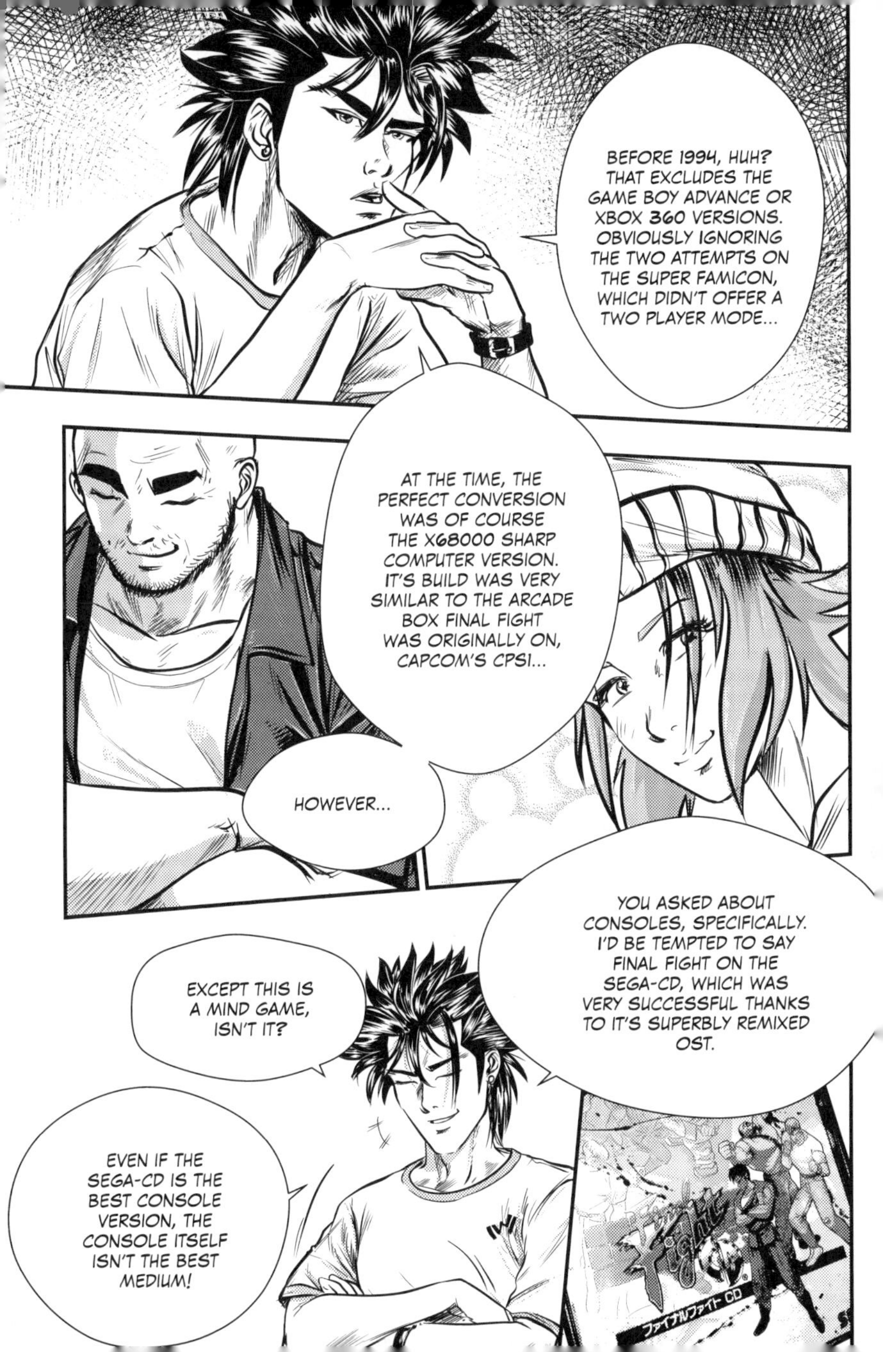
BEFORE 1994, HUH? THAT EXCLUDES THE GAME BOY ADVANCE OR XBOX 360 VERSIONS. OBVIOUSLY IGNORING THE TWO ATTEMPTS ON THE SUPER FAMICON, WHICH DIDN'T OFFER A TWO PLAYER MODE...
AT THE TIME, THE PERFECT CONVERSION WAS OF COURSE THE X68000 SHARP COMPUTER VERSION. IT'S BUILD WAS VERY SIMILAR TO THE ARCADE BOX FINAL FIGHT WAS ORIGINALLY ON, CAPCOM'S CPS1...
HOWEVER...
YOU ASKED ABOUT CONSOLES, SPECIFICALLY. I'D BE TEMPTED TO SAY FINAL FIGHT ON THE SEGA-CD, WHICH WAS VERY SUCCESSFUL THANKS TO IT'S SUPERBLY REMIXED OST.
EXCEPT THIS IS A MIND GAME, ISN'T IT?
EVEN IF THE SEGA-CD IS THE BEST CONSOLE VERSION, THE CONSOLE ITSELF ISN'T THE BEST MEDIUM!
ファイナルファイト CD

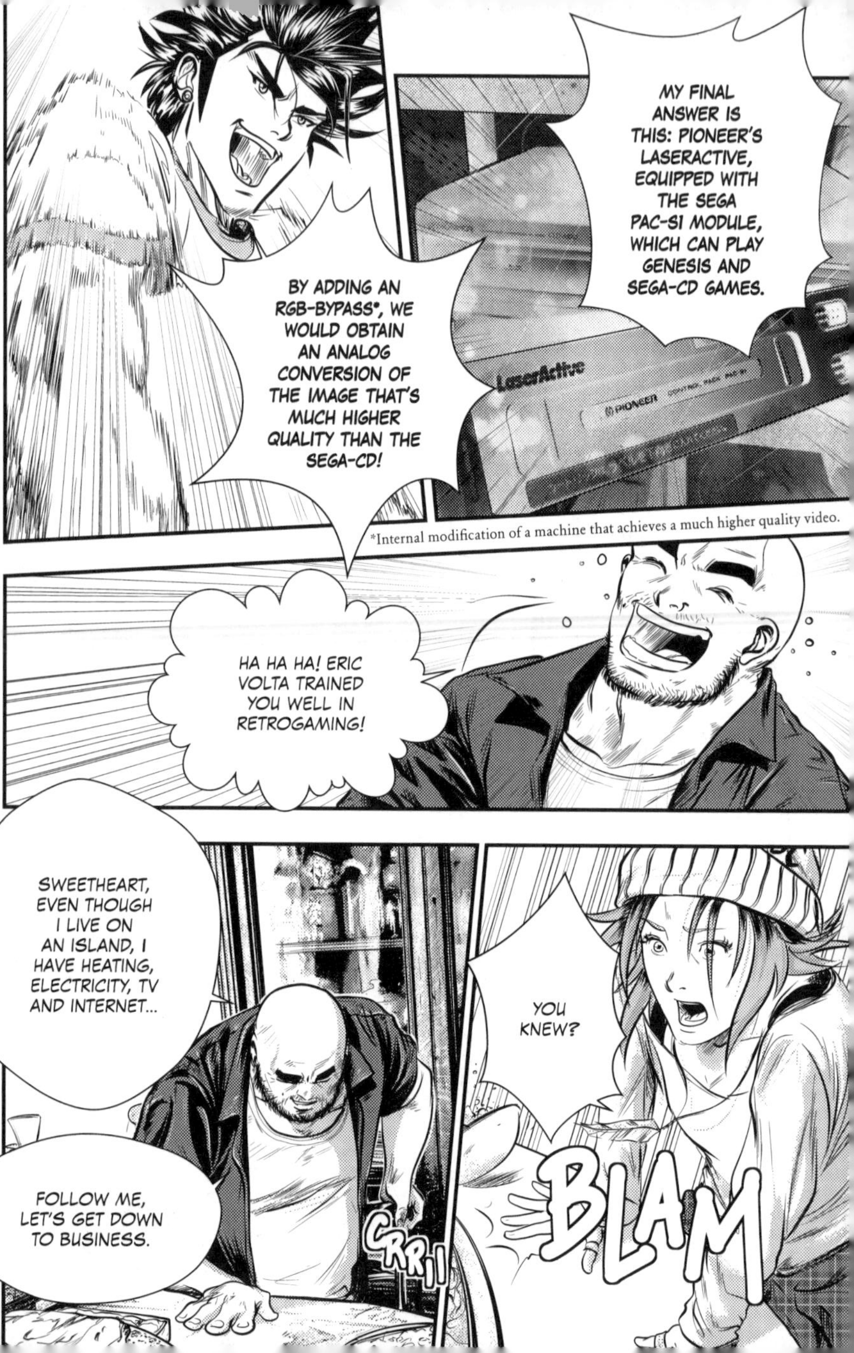
MY FINAL ANSWER IS THIS: PIONEER'S LASERACTIVE, EQUIPPED WITH THE SEGA PAC-S1 MODULE, WHICH CAN PLAY GENESIS AND SEGA-CD GAMES.
LaserActive
PIONEER
BY ADDING AN RGB-BYPASS*, WE WOULD OBTAIN AN ANALOG CONVERSION OF THE IMAGE THAT'S MUCH HIGHER QUALITY THAN THE SEGA-CD!
HA HA HA! ERIC VOLTA TRAINED YOU WELL IN RETROGAMING!
YOU KNEW?
BLAM
SWEETHEART, EVEN THOUGH I LIVE ON AN ISLAND, I HAVE HEATING, ELECTRICITY, TV AND INTERNET...
FOLLOW ME, LET'S GET DOWN TO BUSINESS.
CRRII

*Internal modification of a machine that achieves a much higher quality video.

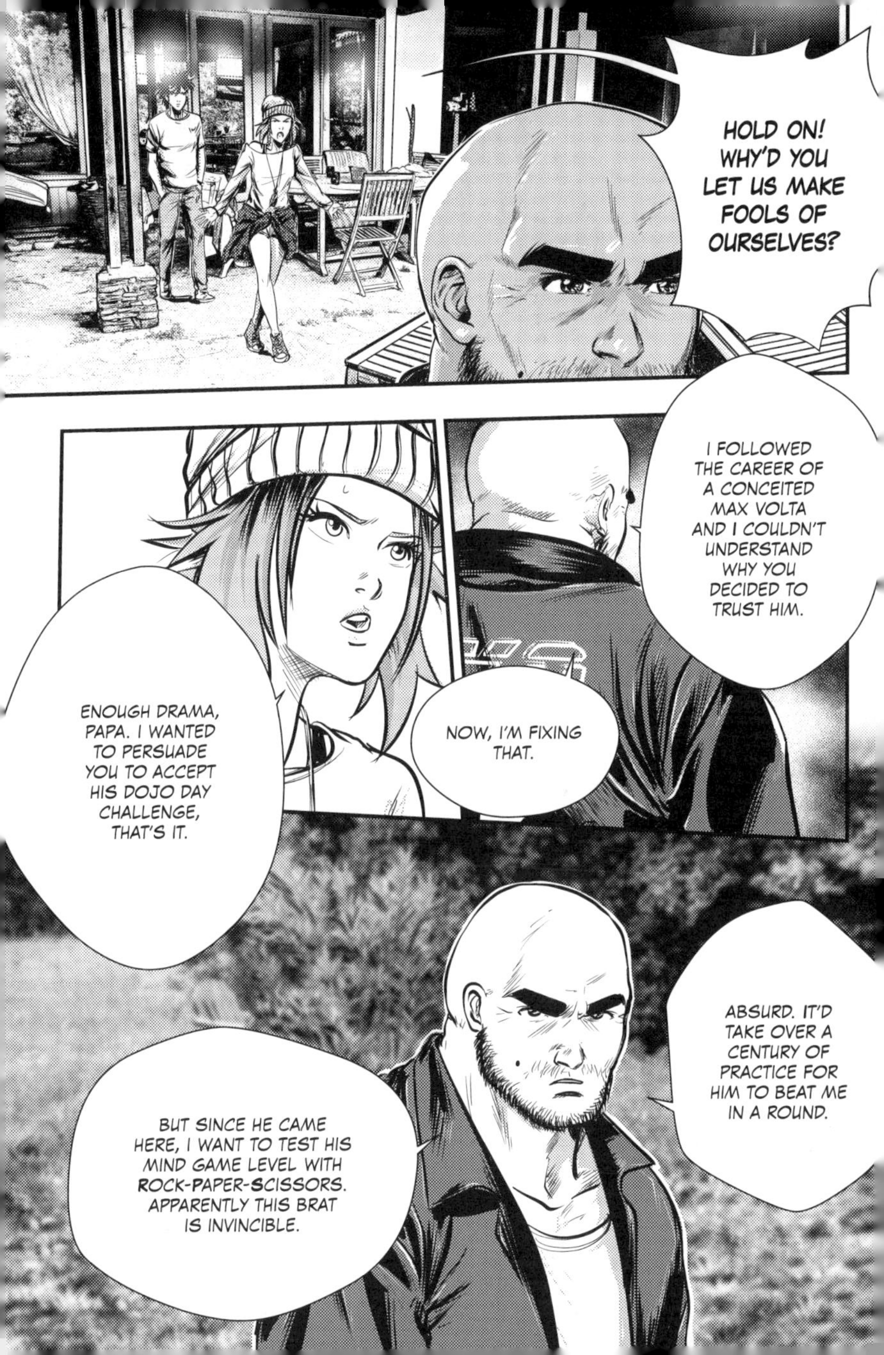
HOLD ON! WHY'D YOU LET US MAKE FOOLS OF OURSELVES?
I FOLLOWED THE CAREER OF A CONCEITED MAX VOLTA AND I COULDN'T UNDERSTAND WHY YOU DECIDED TO TRUST HIM.
NOW, I'M FIXING THAT.
ENOUGH DRAMA, PAPA. I WANTED TO PERSUADE YOU TO ACCEPT HIS DOJO DAY CHALLENGE, THAT'S IT.
ABSURD. IT'D TAKE OVER A CENTURY OF PRACTICE FOR HIM TO BEAT ME IN A ROUND.
BUT SINCE HE CAME HERE, I WANT TO TEST HIS MIND GAME LEVEL WITH ROCK-PAPER-SCISSORS. APPARENTLY THIS BRAT IS INVINCIBLE.

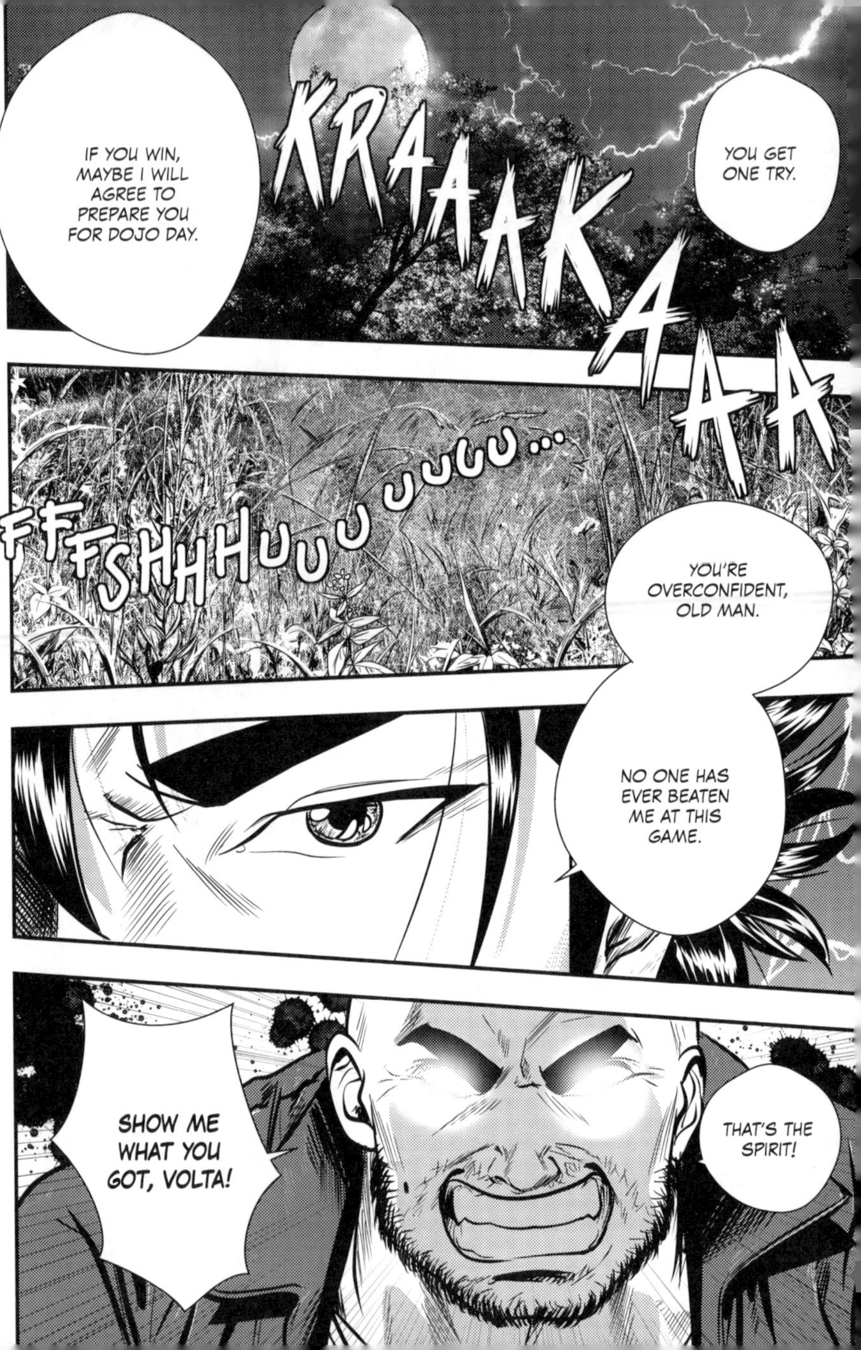
IF YOU WIN, MAYBE I WILL AGREE TO PREPARE YOU FOR DOJO DAY.
KRAAAKAAAA
YOU GET ONE TRY.
FFFSHHHUUUUUUU...
YOU'RE OVERCONFIDENT, OLD MAN.
NO ONE HAS EVER BEATEN ME AT THIS GAME.
SHOW ME WHAT YOU GOT, VOLTA!
THAT'S THE SPIRIT!

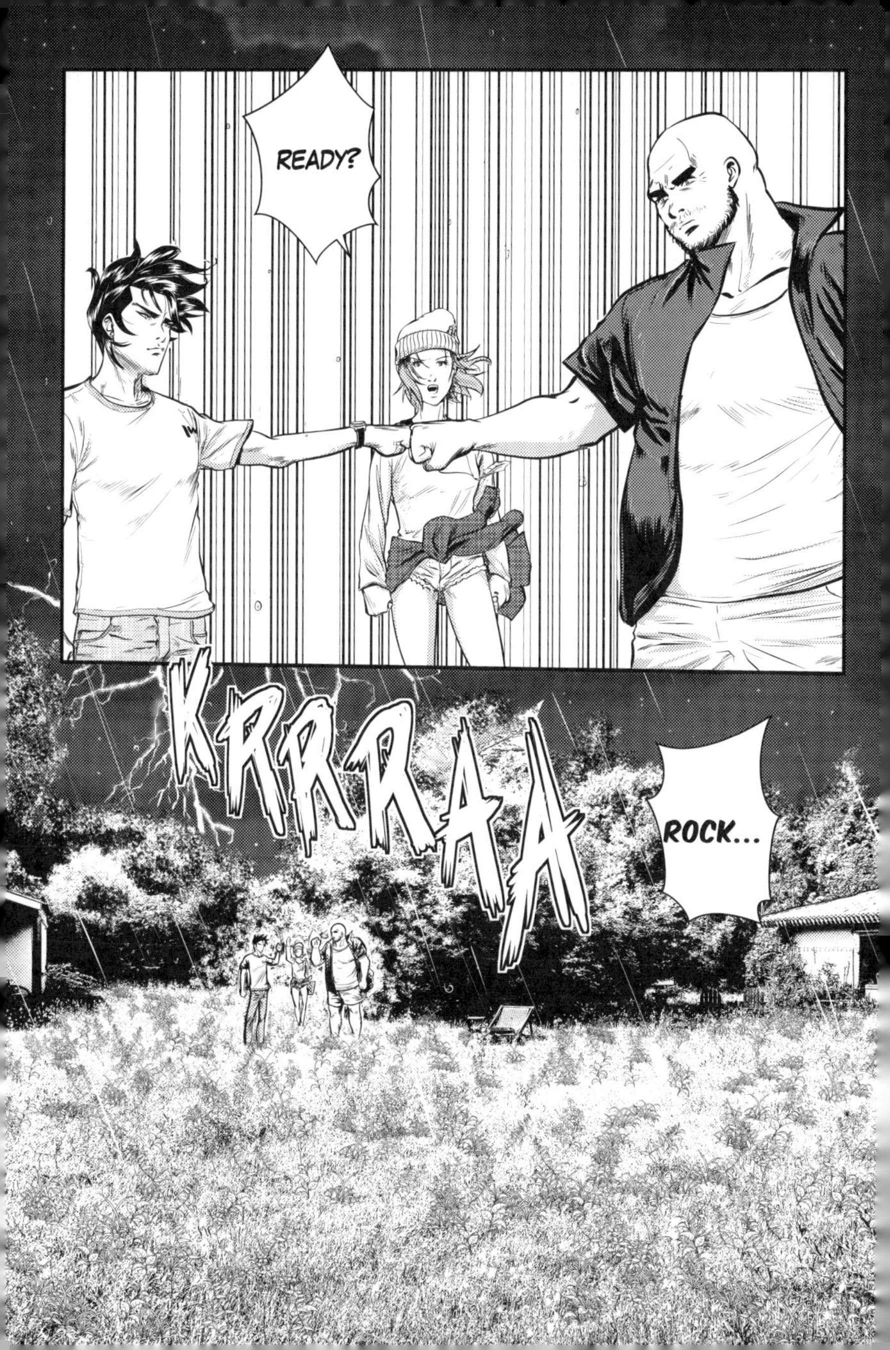
READY?
KRRRAA
ROCK...

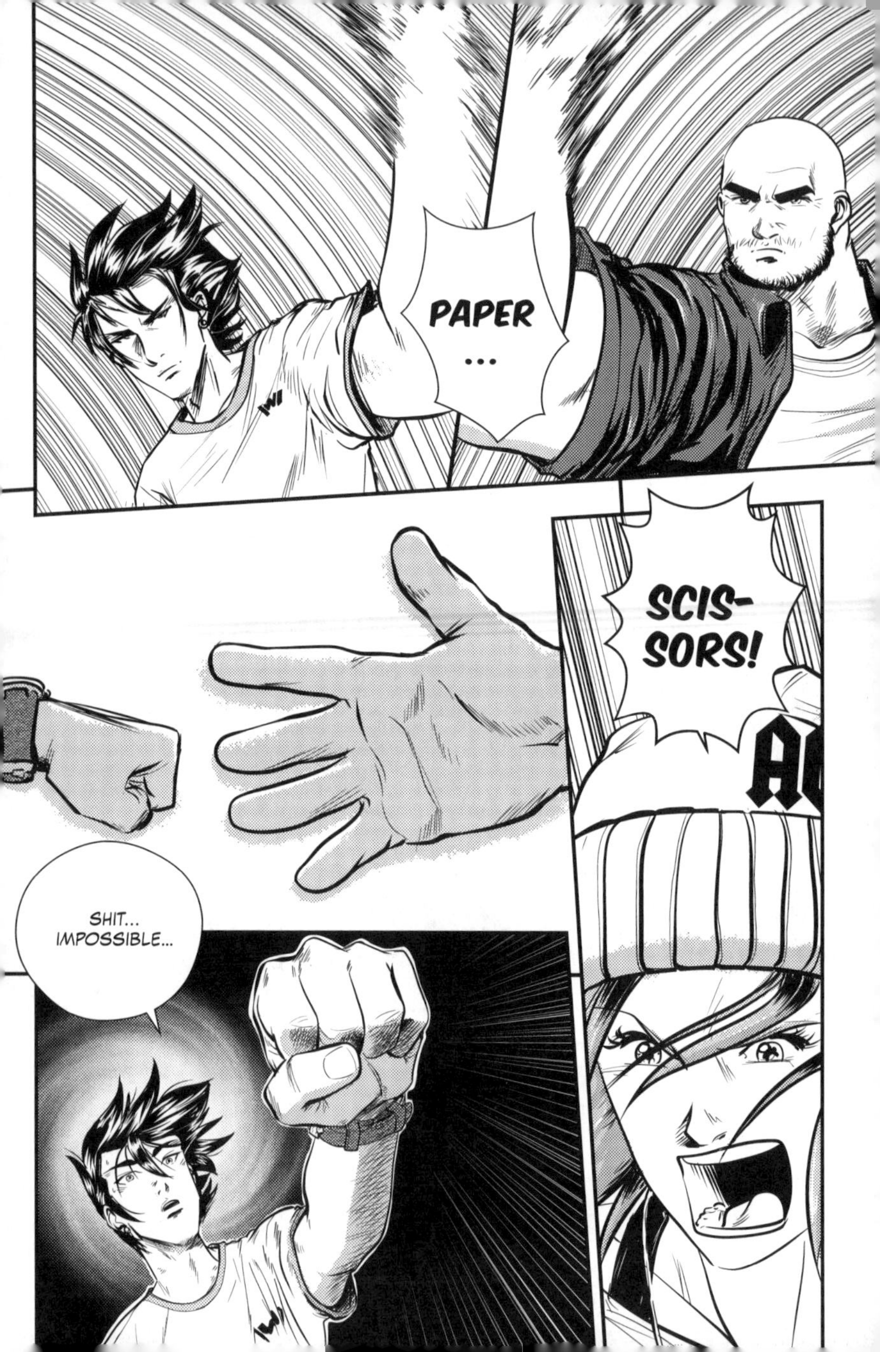
PAPER ...
SCIS-SORS!
SHIT... IMPOSSIBLE...

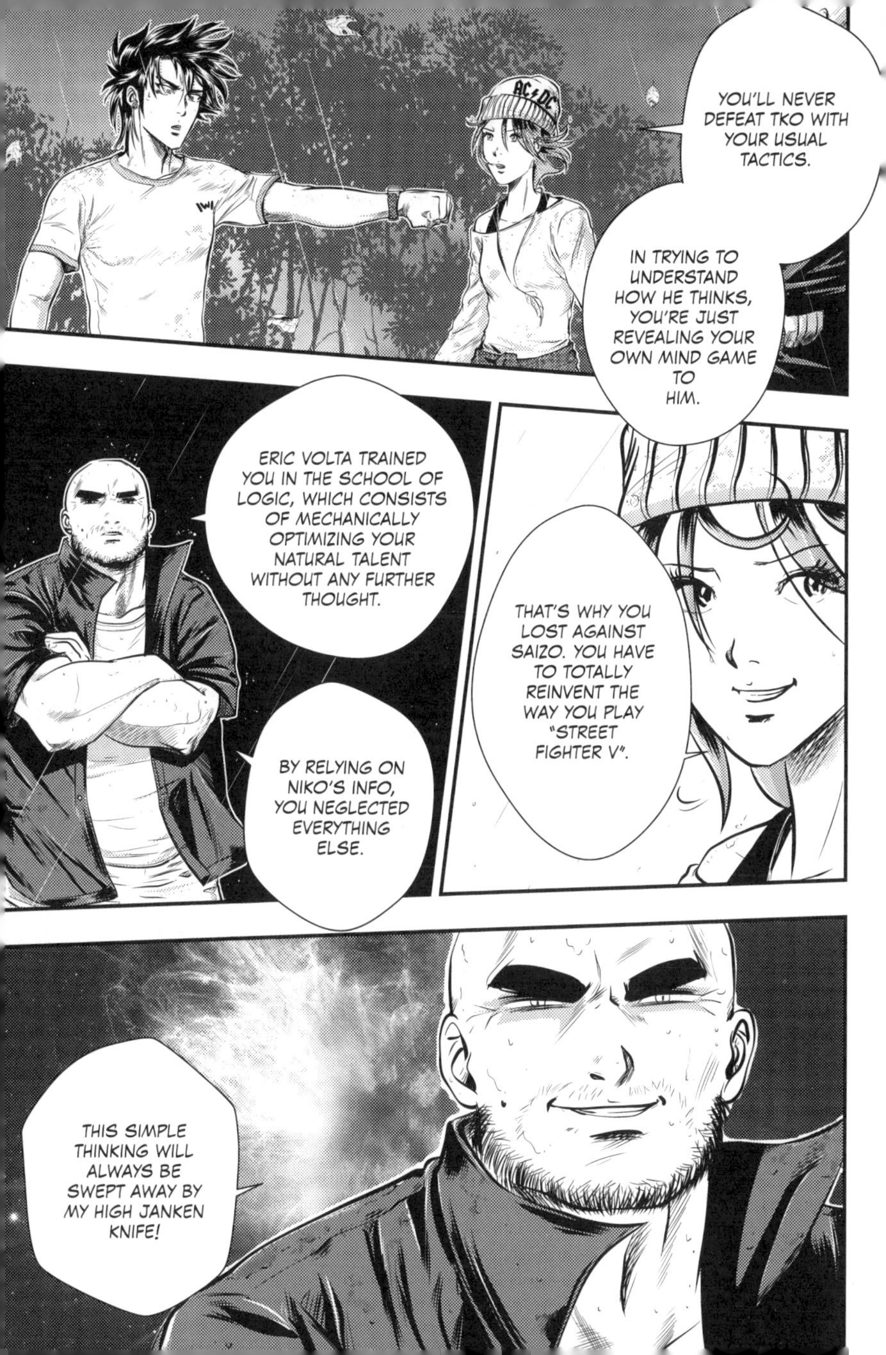
YOU'LL NEVER DEFEAT TKO WITH YOUR USUAL TACTICS.
IN TRYING TO UNDERSTAND HOW HE THINKS, YOU'RE JUST REVEALING YOUR OWN MIND GAME TO HIM.
ERIC VOLTA TRAINED YOU IN THE SCHOOL OF LOGIC, WHICH CONSISTS OF MECHANICALLY OPTIMIZING YOUR NATURAL TALENT WITHOUT ANY FURTHER THOUGHT.
BY RELYING ON NIKO'S INFO, YOU NEGLECTED EVERYTHING ELSE.
THAT'S WHY YOU LOST AGAINST SAIZO. YOU HAVE TO TOTALLY REINVENT THE WAY YOU PLAY "STREET FIGHTER V".
THIS SIMPLE THINKING WILL ALWAYS BE SWEPT AWAY BY MY HIGH JANKEN KNIFE!

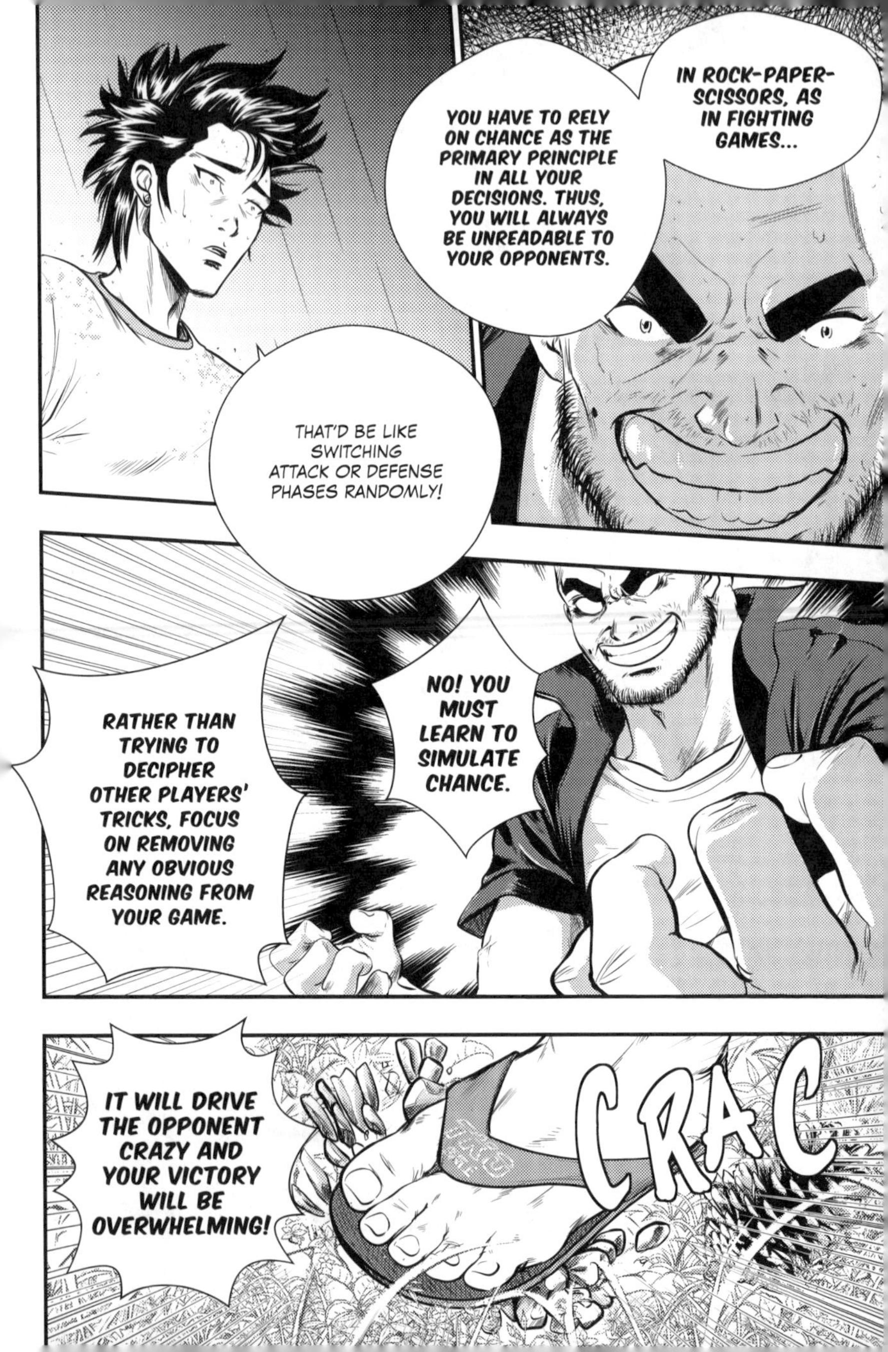
IN ROCK-PAPER-SCISSORS, AS IN FIGHTING GAMES...
YOU HAVE TO RELY ON CHANCE AS THE PRIMARY PRINCIPLE IN ALL YOUR DECISIONS. THUS, YOU WILL ALWAYS BE UNREADABLE TO YOUR OPPONENTS.
THAT'D BE LIKE SWITCHING ATTACK OR DEFENSE PHASES RANDOMLY!
NO! YOU MUST LEARN TO SIMULATE CHANCE.
RATHER THAN TRYING TO DECIPHER OTHER PLAYERS' TRICKS, FOCUS ON REMOVING ANY OBVIOUS REASONING FROM YOUR GAME.
CRAC
IT WILL DRIVE THE OPPONENT CRAZY AND YOUR VICTORY WILL BE OVERWHELMING!

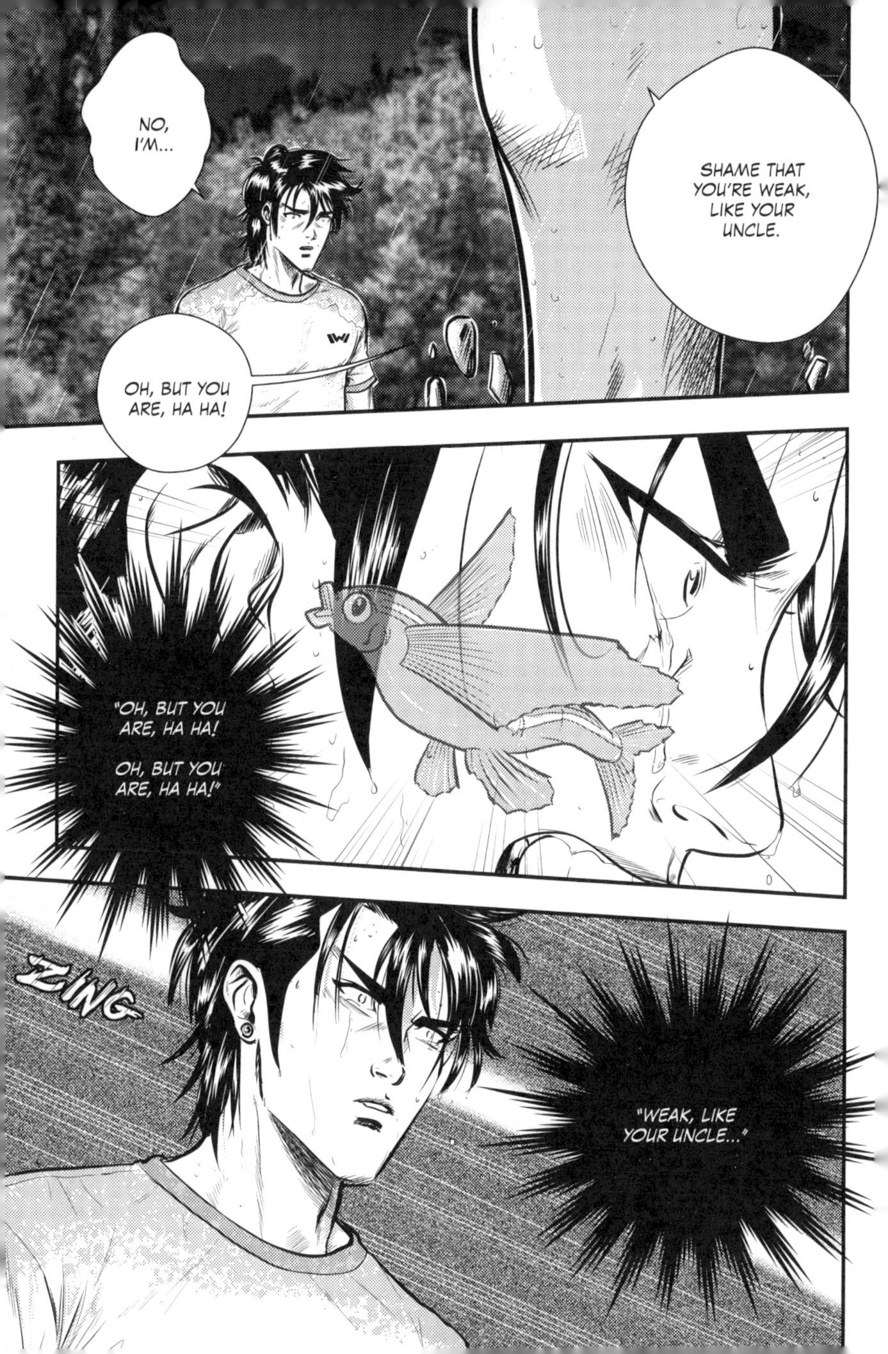
SHAME THAT YOU'RE WEAK, LIKE YOUR UNCLE.
NO, I'M...
OH, BUT YOU ARE, HA HA!
"OH, BUT YOU ARE, HA HA!
OH, BUT YOU ARE, HA HA!"
"WEAK, LIKE YOUR UNCLE..."
ZING

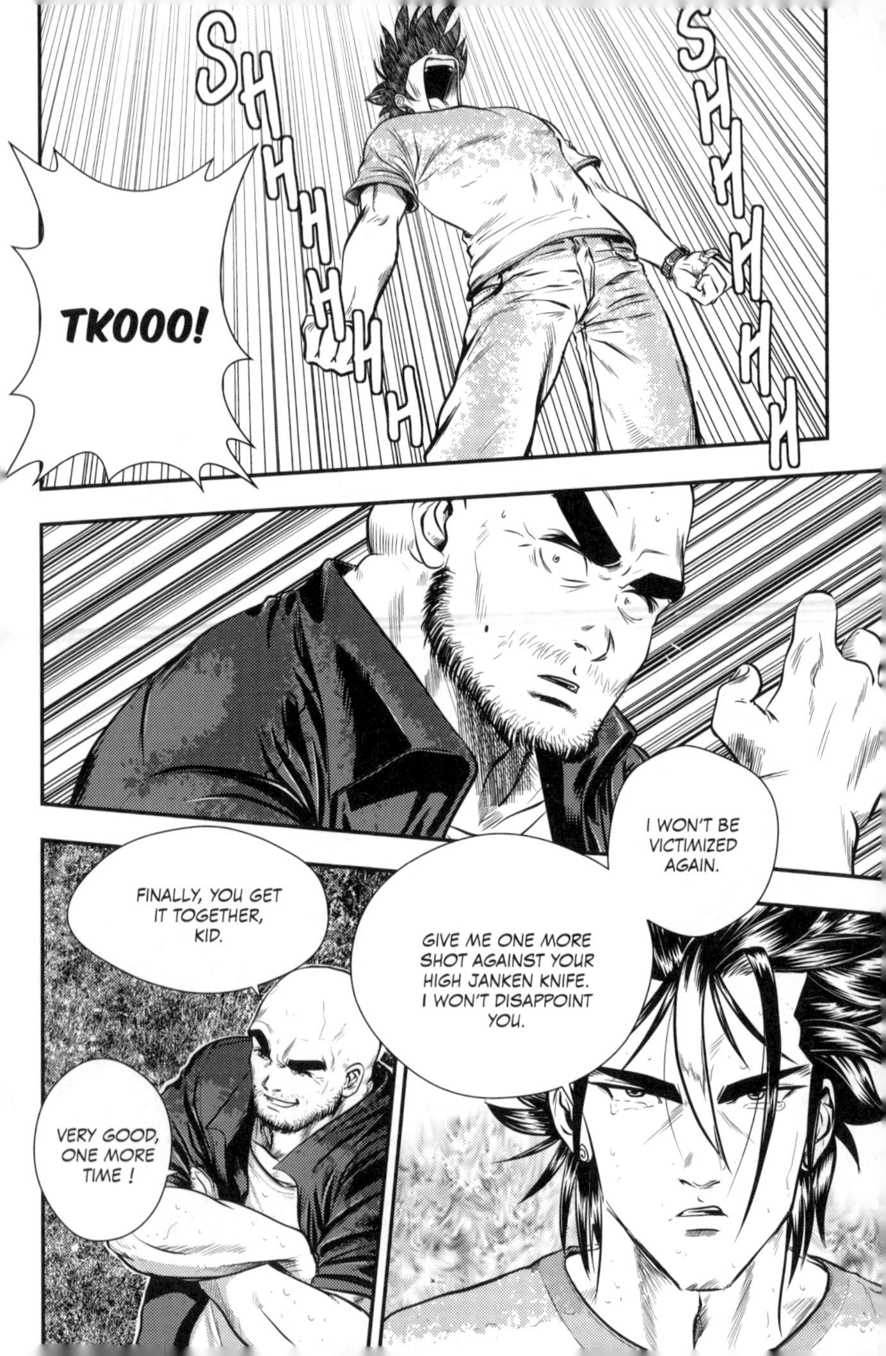
SHHHHHHHH
SHHHHHHHH
TKOOO!
I WON'T BE VICTIMIZED AGAIN.
GIVE ME ONE MORE SHOT AGAINST YOUR HIGH JANKEN KNIFE. I WON'T DISAPPOINT YOU.
FINALLY, YOU GET IT TOGETHER, KID.
VERY GOOD, ONE MORE TIME !

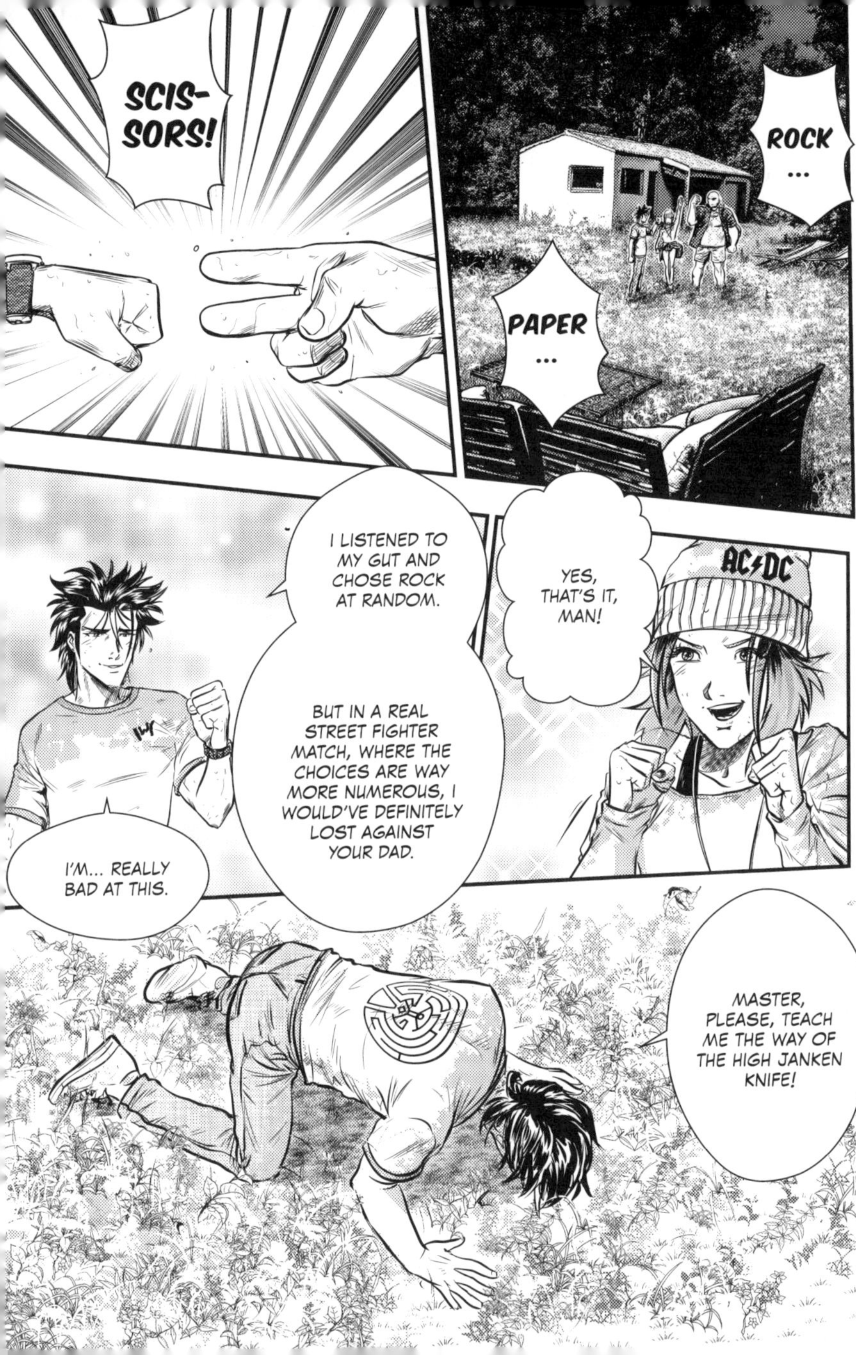
ROCK ...
PAPER ...
SCIS-SORS!
YES, THAT'S IT, MAN!
I LISTENED TO MY GUT AND CHOSE ROCK AT RANDOM.
BUT IN A REAL STREET FIGHTER MATCH, WHERE THE CHOICES ARE WAY MORE NUMEROUS, I WOULD'VE DEFINITELY LOST AGAINST YOUR DAD.
I'M... REALLY BAD AT THIS.
MASTER, PLEASE, TEACH ME THE WAY OF THE HIGH JANKEN KNIFE!

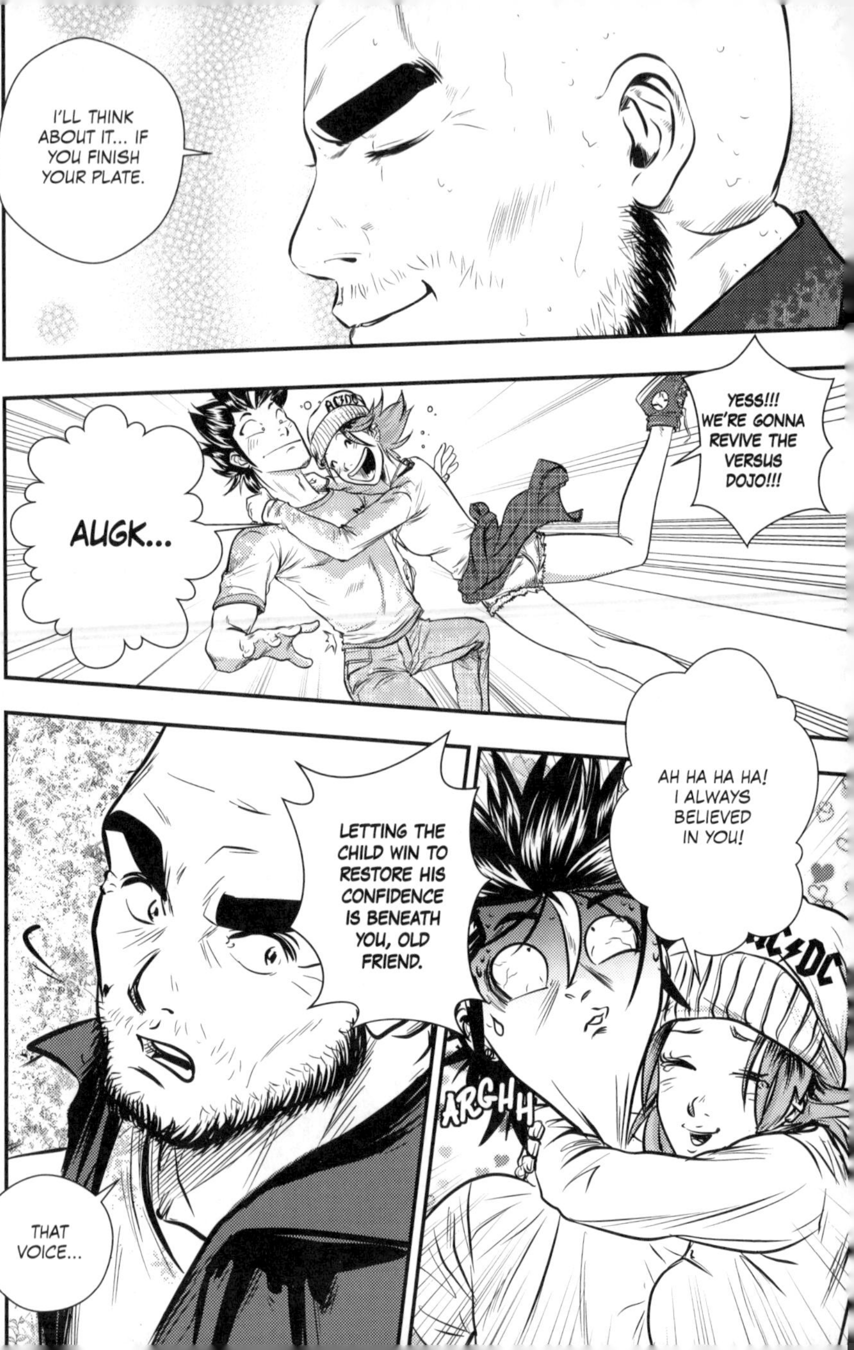
I'LL THINK ABOUT IT... IF YOU FINISH YOUR PLATE.
YESS!!! WE'RE GONNA REVIVE THE VERSUS DOJO!!!
AUGK...
AH HA HA HA! I ALWAYS BELIEVED IN YOU!
ARGHH
LETTING THE CHILD WIN TO RESTORE HIS CONFIDENCE IS BENEATH YOU, OLD FRIEND.
THAT VOICE...

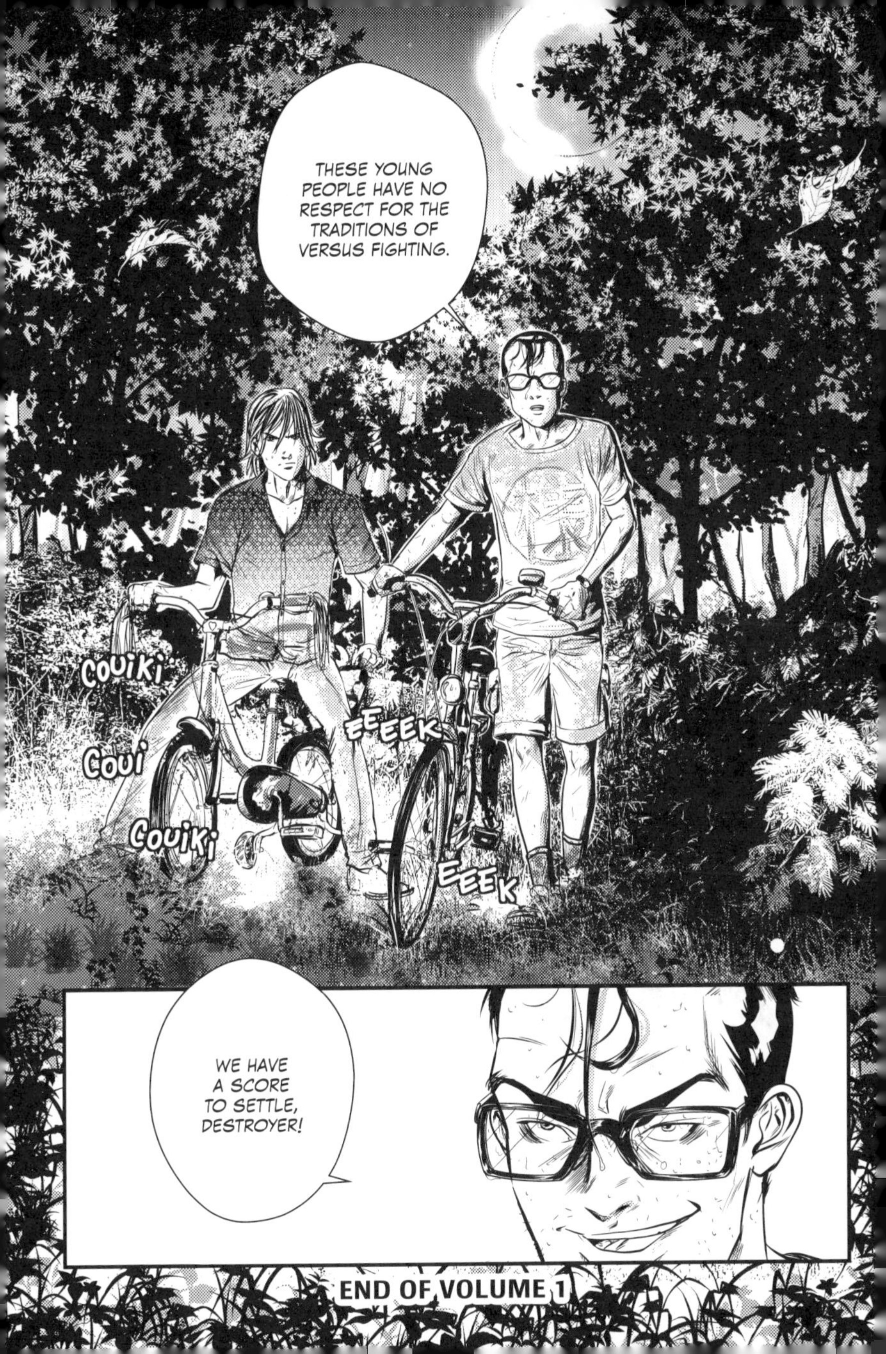
THESE YOUNG PEOPLE HAVE NO RESPECT FOR THE TRADITIONS OF VERSUS FIGHTING.
COUIKI
EEEEK
COUI
COUIKI
EEEK
WE HAVE A SCORE TO SETTLE, DESTROYER!
END OF VOLUME 1

VERSUS FIGHTING STORY

BONUS CONTENT

FEATURING

FIGHTING GAMES FOR DUMMIES

ADVANCED STRATEGY GUIDE: LAURA

TOP PLAYER INTERVIEW: LUFFY

THE POCKET-GUIDE TO *STREET FIGHTER V*

FIGHTING GAMES FOR DUMMIES
PART ONE

Since the March 1991 arcade release of *Street Fighter II*, Versus Fighting has evolved extensively, with each new interation bringing its own improvements or changes.

Within the franchise, the developers have kept refining their game: *Street Fighter V* dates back to 2016, with the Arcade Edition launching in January 2017. To help find your way around it and to better understand this manga, we've compiled a beginner's guide to *Street Fighter* that will span several volumes of the manga.

Our guide is invaluable to truly enjoying the experience that is the fighting game!

READING THE SCREEN

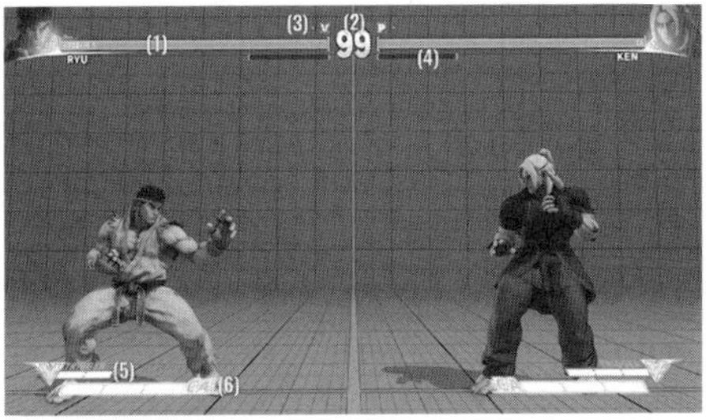
(3)
(2)
99
(1)
RYU
(4)
KEN
(5)
(6)

To get started, it's essential to have a good understanding of the game's screen displays. The most familiar are the long green gauges that represent the player's life points (1). If a player runs out of life, they concede the round, and their loss is marked by a victory icon (3).

The number counter between the life gauges is the Timer (2).

Beneath the life gauge is the stun gauge (4): as hits are taken, it fills up to its maximum and causes the character to be momentarily stunned. The stun gauge lowers on its own if no hits are taken or if a V-Reversal is used. However, be careful: the gauge remains full if the player continues to use a block.

Finally, there's the new feature introduced in *Street Fighter V*: the V-gauge (5). It's a set of slots to be filled (2 or 3 slots depending on the character), which unlock three essential game mechanics:

- The V-Skill, a completely new move that, when used, builds the V-gauge's charge
- The V-Reversal (requires 1 full slot to use)
- The V-Trigger, a powerful new ability (requires a full V-gauge to use)

All moves using the V-gauge are unique to each character in the game.

Finally, the Critical gauge (6) is divided into three levels. Each level you reach allows you to use an enhanced special move (EX moves). A super attack, or a Critical Art, is also unlocked if the gauge is full.

The use of the Critical gauge and the V-gauge is essential in your game strategy. In general, the dilemma is simple: should you use your EX hits from the start to have a better attack, or should you wait until your gauge is full and use the Critical Art? Should you use the V-Reversal to repel an overly aggressive player, at the risk of never being able to use your V-Trigger?

FIGHTING GAMES FOR DUMMIES
PART ONE

MOVE YOUR FIGHTER

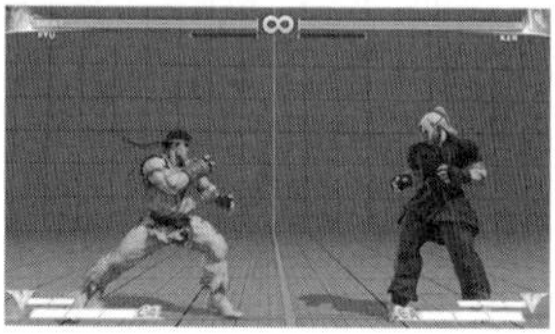

You have to move around unless you want to become some player's punching bag. There are a number of ways to get around, such as walking, dashing, and jumping. You have eight directions available, each with a specific utility:

Forward - To get closer to the opponent.
The forward jump - To attack from the air.
Vertical jump - Mainly to avoid projectiles.
The backwards jump - To escape!
Reverse - To move away from the opponent and / or activate their guard.
Low-reverse diagonal crouch - To activate the low guard.
Crouch - To avoid high hits.
Low-front diagonal crouch - To be used if you like danger.

One of the keys to victory is control of your direction. You have to be agile like a feline, without forgetting to protect yourself when necessary.

Like most fighting games, *Street Fighter V* offers a different movement speed in the dash. Its function is simple: dash forward to get closer to your opponent, or dash backward for defense. Dash execution is a cinch: just quickly double-tap in the desired direction.

GUARDING

Here's a key element of fighting games that is as old as the dinosaurs themselves. Just ask the pros! *Street Fighter V* offers two types of guard: high guard, and low guard. They automatically activate when an opponent's shot is thrown close enough while you're moving backward. To protect yourself from low attacks, just maintain the low-reverse diagonal crouch.

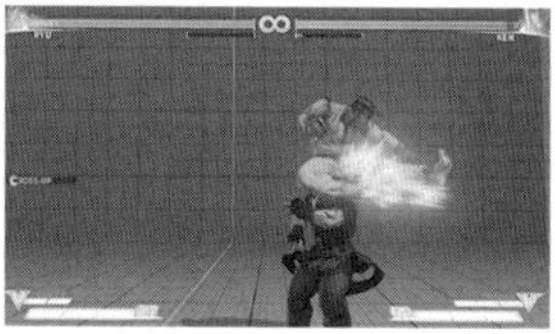

Some moves in the game, such as Cross-Up, allow you to break an opponent's guard by making them turn around, as if they're following a jump-shot that lands in their back.

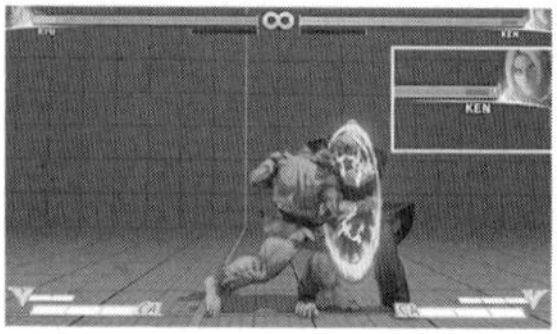

Finally, to aid offense, *Street Fighter V* has the distinction of including temporary damage if a normal hit is blocked by a guard. The attacked player takes "White Life" damage, which gradually disappears after a certain time, but can be transformed into real damage if an opening is found or if the guard can be broken through.

FIGHTING GAMES FOR DUMMIES
PART ONE

BASIC & SPECIAL MOVES

Like with all the games in the main *Street Fighter* franchise (first game excluded), *Street Fighter V* has a six-attack standard moveset: three different punches (light, medium, and heavy) and three kicks (light, medium, and heavy). Power, range, and speed are different for each character.
Likewise, your position (standing, crouching, or jumping) will give you access to a new variety of movements.

By combining these basic moves with different directions and particular joystick movements, you can perform special moves and Critical Arts.

Several types of direction movements exist in *Street Fighter V*: moving your joystick in a quarter-circle (Hadoken), in a half circle, or a "Z" (Shoryuken), and in a full-circle (360°), or holding one direction for a handful of seconds before releasing in the other (Charge Attack).

THROWING

Throwing (light punch + light kick), or a "grab", breaks through your opponent's defense, even when they have their guard up. However, they will still be able to counter your grab with their own light punch + light kick, which performs a drop.

At a certain level of play, the smartest will try to play with the reflexes of their opponent to get them to put up their guard. After a grab and throw has been executed, for example, there are a number of available choices. To find your way around, here is a very simple explanation at the core of each strategy:

Attacks trump grabs, grabs break guards, and guards protect you from attacks!

In *Versus Fighting Story* Volume 2, we'll get down to the business of exploring combos!

VERSUS FIGHTING STORY
ADVANCED STRATEGY GUIDE

LAURA

Did you understand all the confusing technical terms Niko spouted in the manga? Do you already spend your weekends watching the Capcom Pro Tour? Have you already mastered all the terms in our lexicon? Then this advanced game guide is for you. With every new Versus Fighting Story volume, we'll bring you some advanced technical tips for playing *Street Fighter V* characters! In this first volume, we're turning the limelight on Firion's fiesty main fighter: **Laura**.

THE GAME PLAN

Laura is a very effective melee character thanks to the limited options she imposes on your opponent in certain situations. If they misread your intentions, you'll be able to overwhelm them for the duration of the round. Logically, their Achilles heel, therefore, lies in their distance management...

ANTI-JUMPS

Laura's medium punch is effective. It has a 6 frame start-up and remains active for 5 frames. It can also be used to crowd the opponent into a corner, and is very practical with adding 3 frames to blockstun. Her heavy-punch Bolt Charge is likewise in your anti-jump toolkit, with a 7 frame start-up, a broad hitbox, and 8 frames of duration.

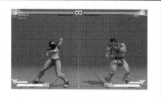

FRAME TRAPS

Considered one of her best moves, the middle punch doubles as a frame trap if you execute two moves in a row:

A standing heavy punch, then crouching medium kick: Stand HP > Crouch MK. In this specific case, the MK Stand Counter-Hit can be confirmed with a crouching medium punch, followed by a Bolt Charge.

Standing light kick, then crouching medium punch: Stand LK > Crouch MP.
Standing heavy punch, then EX Thunder Clap: Stand HP > EX Thunder Clap.

Be careful; the standing heavy punch is at a -2 frame disadvantage when blocked, which leaves an opening for both the special Shoryuken-style attacks that bypass throws, as well as 3-frame attacks.

VERSUS FIGHTING STORY ADVANCED STRATEGY GUIDE

COMBOS & MIX-UPS

After a standing heavy punch Crush Counter, cancel it with a heavy or medium Thunder Clap (depending on the opposing character), another heavy middle punch, and then use Thunder Clap a second time. At that precise moment, you have the choice of either ending up with a strong Bolt Charge if you chose to activate your V-Trigger, or you can use it for a deadly mix-up punch in the corner without activating V-Trigger.

Crush Counter Stand HP> Thunder Clap MP or HP (depending on the character)> Stand HP> Thunder Clap> Bolt Charge HP (in V-Trigger or in the corner without activating it).
HP booth > V-Skill> Mix-Up.
Stand HP > V-Skill > Mix-Up.

In case you opted for the heavy punch, cancel it by using your V-Skill. Depending on the timing, you will either end up in front of or behind your opponent. The offensive choices are then up to you.

Other variations of this combo exist. After the first EX Thunder Clap (in V-Trigger) either dash forward once and crouch medium punch followed by your V-Skill, or just replace the dash and punch with a medium kick on the spot. This allows you to surprise your opponent by suddenly switching sides.

Stand HP > EX Thunder Clap (V-Trigger) > Front Dash > Crouch MP > V-Skill > Mix-Up.
Stand HP > EX Thunder Clap (V-Trigger) > Stand MK > V-Skill > Mix-Up.

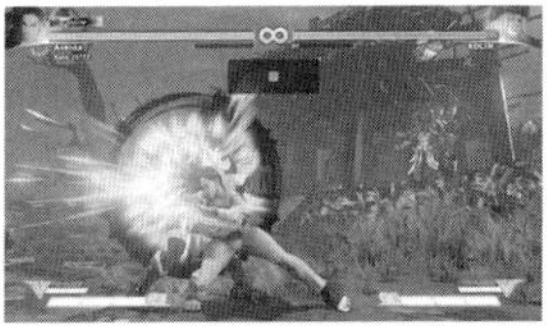

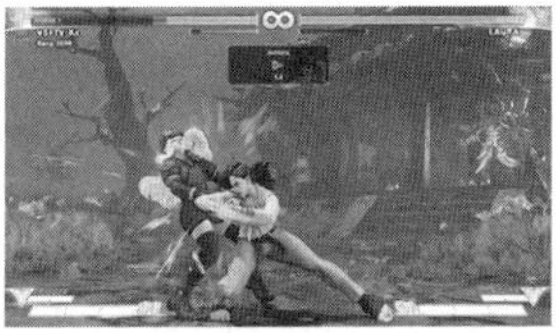

BONUS, NEUTRAL & MEATY

Her medium kick on the spot can be a deterrent! Even if she ends up with a -2 frame deficit on guarding, the recoil of each hit mostly prevents the cool-down from being taken advantage of. The 7 frame start lets players abuse it in many situations. Additionally, the activation of the V-trigger at the same time grants +5 frames on guarding, enough to maintain the pressure and impose another phase of the mix-up.

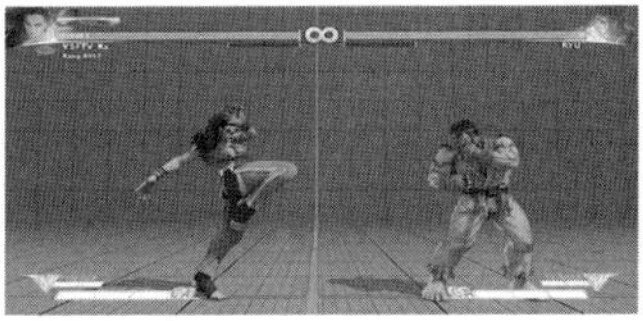

Stand MK: -2 frames on guard but good for recoil.

Stand MK with V-Trigger: +5 frames on guard.

Note: Laura also takes advantage of the Season 3 changes to the V-Skill (possible cancels) and its V-Trigger #1 (extended duration).

Laura also has footsie arguments. Her crouching medium kick leads to a light Bolt charge and therefore melee. Her heavy Crush Counter kick combined with a medium Bolt Charge makes for a takedown with a frame advantage when executed after a dash.

Finally, if her special throw is followed by a weak Bolt Charge, can be used as a meaty with only one negative frame on your guard. The EX Special Tankard, executed properly, can also be used as a meaty after a throw.

INTERVIEW

LUFFY

Olivier "Luffy" Hay is one of the greatest players in the history of Versus Fighting, and he's French! In 2014, he achieved the impossible by defeating the 12 houses of the Japanese Golden Knights (among others) to win the EVO on *Ultra Street Fighter IV* with Rose (EVO is considered the world's premiere tournament in regards to *Street Fighter*).

Luffy is the only European player to have achieved this feat in an arena once dominated by Japanese and Korean players. After a rocky start on *Street Fighter V* when the game was released, the French prodigy is back in force at Red Bull Tower of Pride (Tokyo) at the end of 2017; he finished second in this tournament of honor, in the heart of the bastion of the fighting game gods.

In December 2017, he was the only Frenchman to participate in the finals of the Capcom Pro Tour ...

Luffy, you've just returned from the Capcom Cup with a very 9th place finishing. However, we can sense your disappointment. Can you share your experience with us?

It was a great Capcom Cup, thoug I'm obviously disappointed with a very respectable 9th place, at the gates of the top 8. I had prepared myself well for this competition, with a training trip to Japan, and even more training when I returned to Paris as well. More than 16 hours a day on average. Regarding the tournament, the meetings went well, there were not too many expectations between games, we were well informed of the progress of the tournament. The spectators were there to bring the hype, and the best *Street Fighter V* players in the world were there... in short, it was cool!

You are one of the rare European players to have gone 100% professional with Versus Fighting. Was it difficult for you to give up your old job for E-sports?

Yes, the choice was very complicated to make. I had a permanent job, a good position in a globally recognized company. In addition, being a pro video game player is not necessarily well received by society.

Being a professional player is a very difficult job, because everyone has the same common goal: to become number 1. A career in E-sports can be fleeting because of this - other players can surpass us and become better. And in addition to all of that, the endowments and income in Versus Fighting are low compared to other disciplines of E-sports. But I was already semi-pro. I worked and competed at the same time for 7 years. I knew what I was headed for.

From afar, everyone imagines that becoming a pro video game player is living a lifelong dream. But what is the reality? Does playing video games as a job take away from the fun of it?

The reality is that it is the most difficult job I have ever had to date. Why? Because you are always asked to be the best. When you do a conventional job, you are asked to do your job, not to be the best in your field. As you say, there is no longer any form of pleasure, at least for me; especially when you make your passion your job. You absolutely no longer count the hours, the banal day of 8 hours of work can turn into a work day that ends at 3 AM, mainly before competitions. You can also add to this the fact that you never have a weekend because you are often in competition, you spend your life on planes, you are always tired from the different time differences, etc.

INTERVIEW

What is your typical training day?

I train with IRL or online players. I always play to improve, not for the fun of it. At the end of a game session, I must have learned something. It takes about 3 hours. Next, I analyze battle videos from international players, to see their game plans, strengths and weaknesses. It takes about 3 to 4 hours.

We can also add the moments when I simply think about the game, without necessarily having a controller in hand or a video in front of me.

The character of Max in *Versus Fighting Story* is somewhat inspired by your career with *Street Fighter V* - after a difficult start, he comes back in force to shine again.
Can you tell us about this period of your life? How did you find the strength to return to such a high level after this slump in early 2016?

The beginning of 2016 was indeed a rather difficult period with the release of *Street Fighter V*: new game, new gameplay, and my favorite character Rose was not one of the characters (Note: Luffy plays R. Mika now). It was also the first year I was at 100% pro. Even if my sponsor does not put any pressure on me, I am a perfectionist at heart, so I put the pressure on myself. I need to reach the top level on *Street Fighter V* as well.

After 1 month on the game, I realized that a defense-oriented style of play was not optimal on this new game, and I had to totally rethink my way of playing a fighting game, being a player of defensive type at the core. It was really hard, after 7 years at the highest level on *Street Fighter IV*, to question yourself.

It is by suffering many defeats, and especially by analyzing them, that I have been able to gradually correct and improve my game to return to the highest level. I think that's THE secret to being good at what you do, knowing how to learn from your mistakes.

Thank you for everything, Luffy, and good luck on the 2018 Capcom Pro Tour!

Follow Luffy's fighting career on Twitter @Louffy086

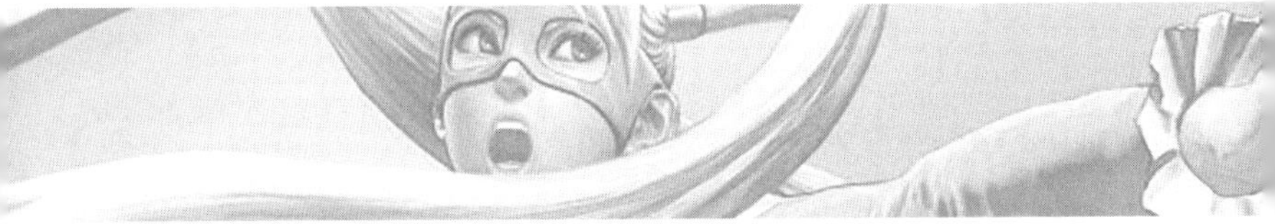

THE POCKET GUIDE TO
STREET FIGHTER V

- A -

Active Frames: These are stages of animation, more commonly known as "frames", during which an attack is able to hit.

Anti-air: This is a blow intended to interrupt air attacks, one of the fundamentals of the game!

- B -

Block Stun: When the opposing character lands a hit on your guard, it creates a more or less long stun depending on the blow struck. Everything is calculated in frames. We'll have to work on Frame Data!

Buffering: Depending on precise timing, you can input the controls for the next move while your character is sitll executing the current move. If successful, it is performed as soon as your character can. It can also be useful for Option-Select.

- C -

Camping: This is a strategy that can annoy your opponents, keep them at bay, and enjoy a better range of attack while limiting his movements.

Cancel: Consists of interrupting the animation one shot at a time in order to perform a combo. In this case, the shot is said to be "cancellable".

Charge characters: Guile and Balrog are examples of charge characters. They need to charge their special moves for a while to launch them.

Chip Damage: If you want your opponent's life to be reduced even on guard, then use a special move. If your opponent is close to being knocked out, then use a Critical Art. Either way, it will be Chip Damage (also called scratch damage).

Combo: A streak that cannot be interrupted for the opponent.

Corner, Corner, Ropes: As in boxing, this is the edge of a fighting arena.

Counter-Hit: If you stop an opposing action with one of your hits, there is a good chance that it will count as Counter Hit.

Counter Pick: So in difficulty after suffering a defeat, even the best can decide to change characters between two matches. This is called the Counter Pick.

Critical Art: Also called "Super", once the Critical Art gauge is fully loaded, it is possible to perform a super attack.

Cross-Under: Switching sides while the opponent is still in the air mid-attack.

Cross-Up: Always in the midst of an attacking situation, it is a matter of reversing the opponent's guard while in the air.

Crouch: By pressing the down key on your controller, your character goes into a crouched position.

Crouch-Tech: While crouching, you can counter your opponents' grab attempts.

Crush-Counter: If a specific hit enters a Counter Hit situation, it will do more damage and provide a larger opening window for a devastating combo.

- D -

Damage Reduce: The longer the combo, the more damage each hit decreases.

Dash: By quickly pressing twice in the same direction, your character will take a quick step forward.

Delay Moves: Consists of delaying your attack on the opponent's relief to give yourself an opening.

Dive Kick: An aerial shot with a diagonal downward angle of attack. Only certain fighters have it.

Double Jump: Perform a second jump after the first, by pressing the jump button a second time, or by special command.

Drop: Defeat your opponent's attempts to grab.

- E -

Empty jump: Jump without executing a single blow! Most players use it as a feint for the sole purpose of making it look like an aerial attack, only to strike down.

THE POCKET GUIDE TO
STREET FIGHTER V

- F -

Frame: This is an animation stage of the game. The pros use it to dissect and give an order of time to a particular sequence of play. For example *Street Fighter V* has an animation rate of 60 frames per second (60fps).

Frame Active: The amount of frames an attack animation spans.

Frame Data: The table that shows the number of frames of all the attacks of a character. Indispensable for pros.

Frame Trap: An attack that gives the opponent enough time to launch a counterattack but not enough time for the counterattack to hit its target before your next stroke. Very vicious, I must admit!

Footsies: A must for keeping your opponents at bay, managing space through movement.

- H -

Hit: An attack hitting its target.

Hit Advantage: This is the number of frames the player has to his advantage when one of his attacks land. Very useful for implementing combos.

Hitbox: You have to think of this as the zone of action of an attack in the form of an invisible rectangle. If an attack lands in this zone, it will hit the target.

Hitstun: When you take a hit, you find yourself in the middle of a hitstun. The recovery time before returning to its normal state is calculated in frames.

Hurtbox: Area where your character can be hit in the form of an invisible rectangle. A hit is considered valid if the opponent's hitbox comes into contact with your hurtbox.

- I -

Input Lag: This is the delay time in when certain animations are displayed compared to when the players inputted the command, often caused by the monitor. This value is important for the players but many complain about it, oddly only during a defeat ...

Instant Overhead: A blow intended to break the low guard with the help of the start of a jump.

- J -

Juggle: A condition that allows you to repeatedly hit an opponent who is suspended in the air.

Just Frame: If your attack activates in the smallest amount of time possible - that is, one frame - it is Just Frame.

- L -

Lag: Slowdown caused by bad internet connection. It also serves as an online excuse.

Launch: A move that sends an opponent flying high in the air, providing a juggle situation.

Link: One of the basics of the combo, the link between two hits.

Loop: Repetition of the same action, the same sequence, etc.

- M -

Match-up: It is the balance of power between two characters and according to their range of possibilities. It helps to define the advantage or the disadvantage in a face-to-face meeting. 2: 8 = Totally disadvantaged Match-Up. 5: 5 = Balanced match-up. 8: 2 = Fully matched advantage.

Meaty: A well-timed and early attack on a reliever will force the opponent to suffer the active frames of the blow.

Mind game: Max Volta's strong point! Reading and anticipating the opponent's game. Some smart people even created a verb: Minder.

Mix-up: Vary your attacks on the same offensive base to avoid predictability.

- O -

Okizeme: A term used in fighting games which refers to the choices in attacks you can use against the opponent while they are getting up after being knocked down. The pros like to call it "Oki".

THE POCKET GUIDE TO
STREET FIGHTER V

Option-Select: An action that covers multiple options and uses buffering. Performing a manipulation stealthily during another action and at precise timing will automatically cover several actions depending on those of the opponent.
On The Ground: Also called "OTG", it is a blow that can hit an opponent already on the ground.
Overhead: Many characters have it. It's a hit to the ground that absolutely requires the high guard to protect against it.

- P-
Pif, piffer: Launch a special attack often with invincible properties completely at random.
Poke: Harass the enemy with a few basic hits.
Pop off: Gesture of provocation performed by a player just after his victory.
Pressing: Chain of blows to the opponent's guard, without him being able to react.
Punishment: As Eric told Max as a kid, it's taking advantage of an opponent's mistake to inflict a devastating combo.

- R -
Recovery frames: This is the recovery time at the end of a shot that usually doesn't hit. The more of them, the more easily your opponent will be able to punish you.
Recovering: This is when the player gets up from a throw.
Reset: The reset is a phase where you voluntarily interrupt your combo to start another from the start. In theory, your opponent can interrupt you... if he reacts quickly enough.
Reversal: A perfect reversal move is performed on the first possible frame of action.

- S -
Bag: Derogatory term. Very mediocre player who is only good at taking punches like a punching bag.
Safe: An attack that has no risk of leaving room for any possible punishment.
Stance: The fighting stance specific to each character. Some have two, like Gen or Zeku.
Startup frames: The launch frames all at once. Try to know as much as possible as they go hand in hand with frame traps, punishments and combos.
Stun: Stun gauge shown below the health bar.
Super: Short for Super Attack, also called "Critical Art". Once the Critical Art gauge is fully charged, it is possible to perform a Super Attack.

- T -
Taunt: Gesture of provocation performed in the middle of a match by the character.
Tier list: Subject to endless debate. Ranking of characters in order of effectiveness in match-ups. Please note, each continent has its own tier list...

- V -
V-Skill: A unique attack for each character, used by pressing both the medium punch and the medium kick buttons simultaneously.
V-Trigger: A unique attack for each character that requires fully charged V-gauge. Operable by pressing the heavy punch and heavy kick buttons at the same time.
V-Reversal: An attack to push back the opponent or get out of one of his presses when his punches hit your guard. Requires at least one loaded V-gauge bearing. Performed by pressing both the forward direction and the three kick or punch buttons at once, depending on the character.

VERSUS FIGHTING STORY

Story: Izu
Art: Kalon
Layouts: Madd
Technical Advice & Bonus Content:
Anis " Kx" Hachemi

Thanks

There are far too many people to give thanks to for this project, which truly has been the culmination of my two greatest passions: manga and fighting games. After a first attempt with the talented Shaos in the video game magazine Game Fan in 2004, I was finally able to realize this concept of "shonen E-sports". This was only possible thanks to my friend Kalon, who's drawn my absurd stories since high school (yep!), MADD with his imperial sense of storytelling, my manager KX, all of the proofreaders (Frionel, Keldo, TKO, Chahid, El Chikito...) and of course to my editors at Glénat, who have always believed in this not-so-obvious project. Finally, thanks to Capcom for officially supporting this series and for creating the *Street Fighter* saga, which has had a huge influence on my life.

Izu

I want to thank Izu for his unwavering loyalty and unwavering faith in my work. Thanks to Madd for the inspiration he gives me. Thanks to John Shlouf for his "software" help. And above all else, thanks to B.K't who has allowed me to make all my dreams and passions come true by providing me with the necessary support since day 1.

Kalon

Documentation

PHOTO CREDITS

CHAPTER 1

All of the photos representing the Stunfest Festival in Rennes, organized by 3 Hit Combo, were taken during the 2016 edition. Stunfest Festival / @stunfest - 3 Hit Combo @3hitcombo / Information : www.stunfest.com
Panels 1 – 2 – 10 – 11 – 14 – 19 - 23
Richard Adenot / @richardadenot / www.richardadenot.com
Panels 12 – 15
Anis « Kx » Hachemi / @kahikusu / www.vsftv.com

CHAPTER 2

From the last two pages of the chapter, the Taito HEY room (Hirose Entertainment Yard), in the Akihabara district of Tokyo.

CHAPTER 4

The Arena, which is located at Webedia's headquarters in Levallois-Perret, served as the inspiration for Eric Volta's conference room.

CHAPTER 5

The photos that served as a reference for the visit to the Versus Dojo were actually taken in the legendary arcade! Same goes for the Game Them All store (https://www.gamethemall.com), which lent itself to the story by letting us "shoot" our manga in their pemises at 34 rue de Malte, in the 11th arrondissement of Paris.

CHAPTER 7

The bar "La Consigne" in Romainville.
All the photos representing the Stunfest Festival in Rennes, organized by 3 Hit Combo, were taken during the 2016 edition.

COPYRIGHTS

Story : Izu
Art : Kalon
Layouts : Madd
Technical Advisor: Anis Hachemi

Original Series Editor: Thomas Lameth
Bonus Layout: Catherine Bouvier